Betrayed

———◆———

Betrayed

A History of Presidential Failure to
Protect Black Lives

Earl Ofari Hutchinson

WestviewPress

A Division of HarperCollinsPublishers

Copyright © 1996 by Westview Press, Inc., A Division of HarperCollins Publishers, Inc.

Published in 1996 in the United States of America by Westview Press, Inc., 5500 Central Avenue, Boulder, Colorado 80301-2877, and in the United Kingdom by Westview Press, 12 Hid's Copse Road, Cumnor Hill, Oxford OX2 9JJ

Library of Congress Cataloging-in-Publication Data
Ofari, Earl.
   Betrayed : a history of presidential failure to protect Black
lives / Earl Ofari Hutchinson.
      p.   cm.
   Includes bibliographical references and index.
                            ISBN 0-8133-2466-1 (if published as pbk.)
   1. Discrimination in criminal justice administration—United
States—History—20th century.   2. Afro-Americans—Crimes against—
History—20th century.   3. Presidents—United States—History—20th
century.   I. Title.
HV9950.032   1966
364.973'089'96073—dc20   95-52170
                                                          CIP

The paper used in this publication meets the requirements of the American National Standard for Permanence of Paper for Printed Library Materials Z39.48-1984.

10   9   8   7   6   5   4   3   2   1

To the men and women of the NAACP
who fought a valiant fifty-year battle
to compel American presidents to protect black lives

Contents

Preface and Acknowledgments

———— •◆• ————

As a youngster I recall that whenever the subject of race was discussed my father would say that blacks could always depend on the "man in the White House" to protect them from violence. I later understood why he thought that. He grew up in Tennessee and Missouri during the era of rigid legal segregation. Many sheriffs in those states religiously lived by the creed that an African-American had no rights that a white man was bound to respect. To them terror and violence were acceptable weapons to humiliate and control blacks. My father had seen or heard about friends who had been beaten, killed, or run out of the state by the Klan or night riders. He knew that most local officials turned a blind eye and deaf ear to racially motivated violence.

My father was not alone in his almost schoolboy faith that federal power would protect blacks from violence. Over the years I heard many other blacks praise the federal government for protecting black lives. It was a myth. Civil rights activists in the South during the 1960s repeatedly told stories of how FBI agents would stand around and watch while black protesters were being beaten and jailed. Civil rights leaders demanded that FBI and Justice Department officials take action to prevent the violence. For the most part they didn't. FBI director J. Edgar Hoover served at the pleasure of the president. The attorneys general were presidential appointees. The FBI and Justice Department ultimately answered to the White House for their action or inaction.

Many historians, political analysts, and civil rights activists have debunked the myth that American presidents were the benevolent guardians of black rights. But I wanted to know why the men who occupied the White House, especially during this century marked by black protest, did so little to protect black lives from racially motivated violence.

In a four-year search, I examined Justice Department records and the public and private papers of the presidents since World War I. I interviewed and corresponded with former attorneys general and top officials of the Civil Rights Division of the Justice Department.

I received invaluable assistance in my search from Burke Marshall, Ramsey Clark, Jerris Leonard, Harland Braun, Kenneth O'Reilly, Garry Howard, Bikivu Hutchinson, Cathleen Smith, Barbara Bramwell, and Matt Blair. Their comments, criticisms, and suggestions helped clarify and shape my thinking and writing on many crucial points in this work. Dean Birkenkamp and Jill Rothenberg at Westview Press believed in the importance of my search and continued to encourage me.

I could not have succeeded in a project of this scope without the kind assistance of the staffs at the following libraries: The New York Public Library's Schomberg Research Center, Howard University's Moorland-Spingarn Collection, the Black Resource Center of the Los Angeles County Bilbrew library, UCLA's University Research Center, the University of Southern California's Von Kleinschmid Research Library, California State University at Long Beach's Special Collections Library, the Southern California Research Library, and the Library of Congress.

I thank all of them for helping me in my search for the answer. Any mistakes I made along the way are mine.

Earl Ofari Hutchinson

Introduction

Rodney King undoubtedly had more than a casual interest in the news that afternoon, for the Simi Valley jury deciding the fate of four white Los Angeles policemen accused of beating him had just reached a verdict. As he waited to hear the verdict, perhaps King relived the horror of the fateful night of March 2, 1991, when officers Stacey Koon, Laurence Powell, Timothy Wind, and Theodore Briseno beat him with nightsticks as he lay helplessly on the ground, his hand outstretched, and begged them to stop.

The beating, captured in all its raw fury on a videotape, touched off a wave of public revulsion and hurtled the issue of police violence, which had largely been hidden under deep official cover, to the center of a national debate. Now, with the verdict imminent, the world waited to see if America's legal system would punish white men who victimized a black.

King and nearly everyone else expected a conviction: The evidence on the videotape seemed overwhelming. But they were wrong. When Superior Court judge Stanley M. Weisberg asked the jury foreman if the jurors had reached a verdict, King heard the foreman say in a clear and loud voice that they had. Then King watched as Weisberg announced that the jurors had found Koon, Briseno, and Wind not guilty on all counts and had deadlocked on one count for Powell.

A perplexed King later told reporters, "I just can't believe that they would believe for one minute what they saw on the videotape didn't happen." The jury, which included no blacks, did not see it that way. One juror hinted why: "He was obviously, a dangerous person, massive size and threatening actions."[1]

By late that afternoon, Los Angeles had exploded in a frenzy of burning, looting, and killing. The verdict had touched off an even deeper national soul-searching over a justice system that was seemingly mocked and in disarray. There was, however, one last hope for justice—the federal government. Two federal statutes give the government the power to prosecute private citizens as well as public officials and law enforcement officers who, acting under color of law, commit or conspire with others to commit acts of racial violence.

Section 241 prohibits private citizens from conspiring to deny other citizens their rights. Violators are punished by fines of $5,000 and up to ten years of imprisonment. Section 242 prohibits law enforcement officers and public officials from willfully depriving citizens of "any rights, privileges or immunities secured or protected" by the Constitution and federal laws. Violators of this law face $1,000 fines and up to one year of imprisonment. (The two statutes were previously codified on the federal books as Sections 19 and 20 or, from the 1940s to 1968, as Sections 51 and 52.) In 1968, Congress added an additional statute that made the murder of a civil rights worker a federal crime. Sections 241 and 242 were based on the Fourteenth Amendment due process and equal protection clause. The statutes were expanded under the Civil Rights Act of 1866 and the Enforcement Act of 1870 to specifically punish racial attacks against blacks. However, federal officials rarely used them to prosecute racially motivated crimes against blacks.[2]

Although the attorney general must formally authorize a Justice Department probe, such decisions are almost always made at the White House in politically sensitive cases.[3] Now the question was whether the federal government would use the statutes in the King beating case to prosecute the four Los Angeles Police Department (LAPD) officers.

Following a crisis meeting with black leaders two days after the verdict, President Bush told a national TV audience that blacks "felt betrayed" by the decision. This was the signal that the federal government would prosecute the officers. The betrayal that blacks felt after the jury verdict in an obscure Simi Valley courtroom had deep roots.[4]

———— • ◆ • ————

After World War I, the fledgling National Association for the Advancement of Colored People (NAACP) lobbied President Warren G. Harding to press Congress to pass a federal antilynching law. No previous president had publicly promised a black organization to strengthen federal laws against racially motivated violence. Harding did. He became the first president to pledge to support an antilynching law. For many southern blacks, passage of the law was a matter of life and death. Between 1880 and 1920, more than three thousand blacks were burned, shot, and mutilated by lynch mobs. During those years, a succession of presidents and attorneys general repeatedly rebuffed black appeals to intervene. They claimed it was the job of the states to prosecute the murderers. However, less than 1 percent of the murderers were ever tried in state courts.[5]

For the next half century, black leaders waged an intense and relentless campaign to get the White House to support and Congress to pass an anti-lynching law and strengthen the two existing federal statutes. They never succeeded, and the White House largely escaped blame for the failure.

The popular view is that southern mobs beat, imprisoned, and murdered blacks and burned their churches and homes in order to maintain white supremacy. Southern sheriffs openly aided and abetted the lynch mobs. Local and state prosecutors refused to indict and bring the murderers to trial. Mayors and governors encouraged racial terrorism by ignoring state laws and statutes against racial violence. And southern business, civic, and church leaders, blinded by racism and political self-interest, refused to speak out against the violence.

According to this popular view, an enlightened and aroused federal government, prodded by the civil rights movement of the 1960s, finally enacted civil rights laws and aggressively enforced federal statutes to end racial terrorism against blacks. Since then, there have been few racially motivated killings. Today, state laws exist to prosecute police officials accused of committing racial violence. And should a state fail to act, the federal government will indict and prosecute those who have violated the civil rights statutes, as in the King case.

However, the popular view is only partially accurate. In law, segregation does not exist today and the federal government enforces the ban on discrimination through civil remedies. But this is completely different from the criminal prosecution of racially motivated violence. And though the three federal statutes give the White House the legal right and the Justice Department the legal weapons to prosecute racial terrorism, government officials have refused or have been reluctant to use them. The killing of two black students at Jackson State University in 1970 by Mississippi highway patrol officers, the beating death of black insurance executive Arthur McDuffie in 1980 by four white police officers, and the beating of King in 1991 exposed the weakness, flaws, and limitations of federal power in regard to prosecuting acts of racially motived violence.

The gnawing question still remains: Why did presidents and attorneys general fail to fully enforce federal laws against racial violence? Was it due to personality, racial outlook, limitations on executive authority, inadequate federal laws, or the conservative political mood of the nation?

Some presidents rationalized their hands-off policy by narrowly interpreting the federalist doctrine of state and national power. Some blamed their inaction on a Congress dominated by southern Democrats and northern Republican conservatives. They claimed that southern Democrats—by virtue of seniority, political manipulation, and ideological cohesion—controlled key congressional committees; if pressured to pass an antilynching law or strengthen criminal civil rights enforcement laws, they would bottle up or kill other vital legislation, paralyze the government, and politically embarrass the White House. Some presidents merely said the statutes were too weak and vague to permit sustained and successful prosecutions of racial terrorism.

The only arguable exceptions to the pattern of executive inaction were Lyndon Johnson and Harry Truman. Both made modest efforts to strengthen and enforce federal laws, but they did not act exclusively because of moral revelation or sudden racial enlightenment. Rather, they prosecuted selected, high-profile cases of white terrorism that provoked public outrage and triggered mass pressure by civil rights organizations.

The White House deliberately squandered countless opportunities to press for stronger criminal civil rights enforcement laws. Harding, Coolidge, Hoover, Roosevelt, and Truman had sufficient congressional votes and the executive muscle to pass or at least get a close vote on an antilynching law. They didn't. Eisenhower and Kennedy had the votes, political muscle, and a changing racial mood across the nation to help them push for tougher criminal civil rights statutes. They didn't.

Although federalist doctrine gives specific powers to the federal government and the states, presidents frequently ignored the distinctions or blurred the lines when it was politically expedient to do so. When the White House initiated and supported legislation that widened the jurisdiction and broadened the power of the Federal Bureau of Investigation (FBI) and the Justice Department to investigate and prosecute a multitude of crimes—including bank robbery, kidnapping, illegal weapons violations, and carjacking—there were no heated congressional debates, court challenges, or public protests that the White House had abrogated states' rights or infringed on the Constitution.

Even when racial issues were involved, specifically, the protection of black lives, federalism could not justifiably be used as a cover for do-nothingism. Blacks were American citizens and were entitled to full rights under the Fourteenth Amendment's equal protection clause. When state and local officials and law enforcement personnel blatantly refused to arrest and prosecute racist lawbreakers, the federal government was legally obligated to bring prosecutions. When presidents and federal officials pleaded legal impotence, they were disingenuous at best and hypocritical at worst.

The real reason they failed to act is more disturbing than bewildering. Put simply, presidents and their attorneys general have been trapped by a brutal history and legacy of slavery and segregation that has systematically devalued black lives.

The Constitution placed the value of a black man's life at three-fifths that of a white man's. Throughout the slave era, black inferiority was enshrined in law, custom, and practice. The dominance of the slavemaster was absolute. And the power that he wielded over his black chattel property was protected by a rigid system of legal, social, and political repression that legitimized violence and terror. To many whites, even the color black symbolized evil, villainy, and licentiousness. In *Huckleberry Finn*, Mark Twain brilliantly captured the popular perception of the utter worthlessness of black lives in Huck's exchange with his Aunt Sally. When Sally asked Huck why he was late arriving at her home, Huck lied and told her his boat had been delayed:

> Huck: "We blowed out a cylinder head."
> Aunt Sally: "Good gracious! Anybody hurt?"
> Huck: "No'm killed a nigger."
> Aunt Sally: "Well, it's lucky because sometimes people do get hurt."[6]

The message was clear: Blacks were not considered human, and they need not look to white law or society for protection from racial violence. In the Dred Scott decision in 1857, the Supreme Court made slavery a national institution, declaring that blacks had "no rights that a white man was bound to respect." This was yet another chilling reminder that much of white America regarded blacks as less than human. That sentiment became part of the political and cultural ethic that shaped law and public policy well into the twentieth century.[7]

Although the Civil War ended chattel slavery, it did not end systematic terror and violence against blacks. The few gains blacks made during Reconstruction were quickly wiped out as the former planters regained control of the state governments. Northern politicians and the public demanded national reconciliation and considered blacks expendable. Northern capitalists, in their drive to expand their control of industry and agriculture in the South, needed cheap, subservient black labor, and southern white power could guarantee it. The old slave codes quickly gave way to sweeping Jim Crow segregation laws, political disenfranchisement, and economic peonage. The Ku Klux Klan (KKK), White Knights, and other racist groups—under the guise of protecting property, white womanhood, and the southern way of life—unleashed wave after wave of violence against blacks.[8]

In the 1896 Plessy decision on racial discrimination in public transportation, the Supreme Court denied that blackness conferred a "badge of inferiority" on African-Americans. But both the spirit and intent of the ruling belied the Court's words. The Court made segregation the law of the land and in the process reaffirmed what much of white public opinion in the North and South already accepted as fact: Blacks were social inferiors.[9]

By the turn of this century, the carefully crafted image of blacks as lazy, ignorant, and crime-prone individuals had become an undisputed article of public faith. Sociologists, psychologists, and medical professionals even concocted elaborate biological and genetic theories to explain the alleged intellectual and moral failings of blacks.

In historian Rayford Logan's survey of the press from 1901 to 1912, respected and staid publications including the *New York Times*, *Chicago Tribune*, *Boston Evening Transcript*, *San Francisco Examiner*, *Harpers*, and *Atlantic Monthly* routinely referred to blacks as "brutes," "savages," "imbeciles," and "moral degenerates." Northern academics, businessmen, and public officials believed the myths and lies that were manufactured by the racialist propagandists.[10]

During the first half of the twentieth century, whites were accustomed to seeing blacks almost exclusively as shuffling, dim-witted buffoons with few intellectual impulses or moral scruples. The civil rights movement of the 1960s brought only slight improvement to the black image. The media and popular culture soon transformed the allegedly lazy, crime-prone clown of the past into the pimp, dope-dealer, and superstud of the present. The Reagan-Bush administration's slash-and-burn assaults on jobs, education, health and social programs, and civil rights touched off a fresh round of black bashing.

In the 1990s, America slyly resurrected the ancient racist stereotypes. Public discourse and policy rapidly degenerated into socially accepted name-calling and scapegoating of blacks. Politicians talked of sexually irresponsible blacks making babies and creating problems. Respected academicians called blacks genetically inferior. Many in the media made prominent black men the poster boys for sexual deviance. White males unleashed a full-scale conservative counterrevolt.

The shallow reservoir of white goodwill and tolerance generated by the civil rights movement of the 1960s had dried up. Nearly every region of the country saw a sharp rise in hate crimes. Blacks were still by far the biggest target. Crime and drug-related violence became rigidly associated in the minds of many whites with the black community.

Federal power expanded, and politicians and the public demanded and got more prisons and tougher laws. Police abuse of blacks became a flash point of the national crisis. When Ronald Reagan's drug czar, William J. Bennett, was asked why more blacks than whites were jailed for drug violations even though whites made up the bulk of the nation's drug abusers, he didn't hesitate in answering: "It's easier and less expensive to arrest black users and dealers than whites."[11]

It was a blunt and racially tinged comment. But like Huck's Aunt Sally a century earlier, Bennett honestly expressed the sentiment approved by much of white America and encoded in law and public policy. The past had never died. The hideous legacy of slavery and segregation continued to cast a long shadow across American society. Blacks were once more an expendable commodity.

The devaluation of black lives that led presidents and their attorneys general to shrink from fully using federal law to prevent racially motivated violence has had terrible consequences for American society. It has fortified political mean-spiritedness, deepened the crisis and turmoil in the nation's inner cities, polluted the political process, marred the criminal justice system, and widened the racial divide.

Throughout the twentieth century, there have been persistent warnings of racial crisis. At the turn of the century, black scholar and activist W.E.B. Du Bois prophetically declared that "the problem of the twentieth century is the problem of the color line." Following the Watts riots in 1965, the McCone Commission warned that the "racial breach if allowed to persist, could in time split our society irretrievably." The Kerner Commission, created by Lyndon Johnson in response to the dozens of riots that rocked northern cities in 1967, stripped away the political niceties and blamed ghetto violence on black poverty and oppression. It also named the culprit: "White institutions created it, white institutions maintain it, and white society condones it."[12]

The commission did not mean individual white prejudices but white institutional power, control, and domination. But Johnson disavowed the commission's witheringly precise indictment and ignored its far-reaching recommendations for change. He deluded himself that token reforms could bring permanent racial peace. This was one more lost opportunity.

The NAACP and other black organizations that battled an intransigent White House and Congress for an antilynching law and tougher criminal civil rights statutes had no such illusions. They did not expect presidents to recognize the moral correctness or legal justness of their appeals. They knew that black oppression and institutional racism were powerful and seemingly immutable forces that resisted change. They could only be destroyed by a massive social reformation of American society. The civil rights movement of the 1960s was a major start. The horrific spectacle of club-wielding sheriff's deputies, hoses, police armed with cattle prods and vicious dogs, Klan beatings, and the murders of blacks and civil rights activists exposed the cancerous sore of racial terror to the world. Public shock, revulsion, and shame at the violence, along with the trauma caused by the assassination of a young president in 1963, finally moved a hesitant White House and Congress to pass long-promised civil rights and voting rights legislation.

But this could not erase or reverse history. Every president who preceded Lyndon Johnson, including Truman, refused to draft or vigorously support a federal law to end lynching. And all the attorneys general who served between Harding and Johnson consistently refused to push for indictments against public officials or law enforcement officers complicit in racial murders.

FBI director J. Edgar Hoover successfully manipulated Presidents Roosevelt, Eisenhower, and Kennedy and kept the FBI out of the direct investigation of civil rights complaints. The Department of Justice (DOJ) seldom directed Hoover to conduct such investigations. Meanwhile, Congress refused to outlaw lynching or strengthen the two federal criminal statutes against racial violence.

When federal grand juries did return indictments against police or public officials who beat or killed blacks, the White House and the Justice Department often failed to vigorously exert strong political pressure and bring the full arsenal of legal weapons to bear to win convictions. On the rare occasions when they did, nearly all the white federal juries refused to convict the defendants. Or, as in the case of Rodney King, they rendered a mixed verdict.

Civil rights leaders gave Johnson and Kennedy high marks for federal civil rights enforcement, but their accomplishments in this area were more illusory than real. Almost exclusively, the Justice Department and the FBI investigated and prosecuted high-profile racial murder cases only when mass pressure forced them to do so. The killings of ordinary blacks and the bombing and burning of their homes and churches barely subsided in the South during the 1960s.

Today, despite the escalation in hate crimes and the increase in police shootings of young black males since the 1980s, the Justice Department still contends that it is the responsibility of local officials to prosecute. It will not intervene unless there is a "compelling federal interest"—a hazy term that neither the Justice Department nor the White House has ever fully defined.

In practice, the White House and Justice Department have always measured "compelling interest" by the yardstick of politics. In other words, the attorney general typically will not authorize investigations and prosecutions of police abuse cases or racist terrorists unless civil disturbances occur in major cities, such as Miami in 1980 and Los Angeles in 1992, or following mass national protests.

Given the White House's narrow view of what constitutes "compelling interest," Rodney King was fortunate. He, at least, received partial vindication from the federal government. Many other blacks, as we shall see, did not.

1

"At the Hands of Persons Unknown"

The Harding-Coolidge-Hoover Years

It was a brutally hot August day in 1920 when NAACP executive secretary James Weldon Johnson boarded an Ohio Central train at New York's Grand Central Station. Johnson, who had recently been selected to head the fledgling NAACP, was heading for Marion, Ohio, to meet with one of that state's senators. It was the first time that Johnson would meet face to face with Warren G. Harding, and he did not know what to expect. Harding had said next to nothing about race matters since receiving the Republican presidential nomination in July. The meeting was doubly significant for Johnson.[1]

For one thing, there was a good likelihood that Harding would be the next president. Americans were tired of the shortages and disruptions resulting from World War I and desperately wanted to return to peace and tranquillity. The Republican campaign slogan of Return to Normalcy was calculated to tap into America's mood. For blacks, the residue of the Reconstruction years still remained. During those years, the Republicans had championed civil rights and courted the black vote, and they were still the only major party that at least nominally supported political equality.

In addition, Johnson was keenly aware that this was the first time that a major presidential candidate had met with an NAACP official. This was his opportunity to find out where Harding stood on the vital issues of black political appointments, voting rights, and, most important, lynching. Johnson wanted Harding to endorse the antilynching bill introduced in Congress in May 1920 by Missouri Republican representative Leonidas Dyer. If passed, the bill would make lynching a federal crime punishable by five years of imprisonment and a $5,000 fine.[2]

Dyer had introduced the same bill in every session since 1918. Each time, it had been buried in the House Judiciary Committee, dominated by southern Democrats and conservative northern Republicans. These legislators played down the issue of race and hid their opposition behind the claim that passage of the bill would be an unconstitutional infringement on "states' rights" and a dangerous power grab by the federal government.[3]

Johnson knew that the bill would probably suffer the same fate again without Harding's support. But he was hopeful because in February, Harding had promised then NAACP executive secretary John Shillady that he would go along with the antilynching legislation if the Republican National Committee (RNC) endorsed it. Shortly before the Republican convention, Johnson had met with members of the platform committee in Chicago and persuaded them to insert a statement calling on Congress "to consider the most effective means to end lynching."[4]

Johnson had gotten his way partly because of the big upsurge in black voting strength. Between 1915 and 1920, nearly a half million blacks had fled the Deep South and moved to Chicago, New York, Detroit, Philadelphia, Cleveland, and dozens of other northern cities. Black scholar W.E.B. Du Bois, editor of the NAACP's *Crisis* magazine, immediately saw the political possibilities: "We can vote in the North, we can hold office in the North." For the first time, blacks held the political balance of power in more and more districts, and they were now in a position to wring some concessions from the Republicans.[5]

When Johnson arrived for the scheduled meeting, Harding greeted him cordially, seeming genuinely pleased at the chance to speak with Johnson. After a few moments of small talk, Johnson asked Harding to endorse the Dyer bill. Harding agreed. But whatever excitement Johnson may have felt initially soon passed. When he asked Harding to issue a public statement denouncing the Klan, Harding brushed him off. He claimed that he wasn't making any public statements at that time.

Johnson later expressed bitter disappointment that a presidential candidate in the midst of a political campaign for the nation's highest office would refuse to take a public position on a vital policy issue. Johnson left Marion that evening convinced that Harding knew almost nothing about racial problems and was listening too closely to what his southern advisers told him about blacks. Despite his misgivings, however, Johnson still believed that Harding was a man with whom the NAACP could work.[6]

———•◆•———

The month after Harding was elected president, Johnson tried to get a meeting with him to discuss the Dyer bill. Harding put Johnson off but assured him that he would always welcome his views on racial problems. Although Johnson was disappointed, he chose to take this as a sign that Harding had not closed the door on the NAACP. But Johnson was still racing the clock and was desperate to meet with Harding before the presidential inaugural address in April 1921.

Johnson hoped that Harding's denouncement of lynching in his speech would shore up support among congressional Republicans for the Dyer bill. The week before his address, Harding agreed to see Johnson for five minutes. Johnson was determined to make every second count. He reminded the incoming president of his promise to back the antilynching bill. To Johnson's relief, Harding had not forgotten.[7] In his inaugural address, Harding told Congress to "wipe the stain of barbaric lynching from the banners of a free and orderly, representative democracy." Harding had verbally challenged Congress to take action against lynching.[8]

NAACP officials were ecstatic. With a newfound ally in the White House, they prepared to throw all their energies and resources into the tough and painful job of congressional lobbying. They had good reason to be hopeful. There were many Republicans in Congress, some of whom were elected with black support and represented districts with substantial black populations. Missouri Republican Dyer was perhaps the best example. Between 1910 and 1920, there was a 33 percent increase in the number of blacks in St. Louis, and most of the newcomers had settled into four wards in the Twelfth Congressional District that Dyer represented. Now, he was one of the 299 Republican representatives and 59 senators in Washington who gave the Republican Party a lopsided majority in Congress.[9]

NAACP officials began a furious national campaign to drum up support for Dyer's bill. They took out newspaper ads and secured the endorsements of mayors, governors, and prominent business, civic, and religious leaders. They appealed to their growing body of members and flooded Capitol Hill with letters to congressmen.

Southern opponents, as expected, pounded away on the issue of the constitutionality of the bill. They insisted that lynching was murder and could only be punished by state courts. Johnson came to the hearings on the bill well prepared, for he had secured the testimony of legal scholars as well as former high-ranking state and national government officials.

He zeroed in on the issue of state enforcement and exploded the myth that lynchings were merely private acts. He cited dozens of examples in which sheriffs, local prosecutors, local and state officials, and prominent businessmen either actively conspired with lynch mobs or tacitly encouraged them. The NAACP and other investigators had long since established that lynchings had very little to do with punishing crimes of rape or murder allegedly committed by blacks, in fact, rape was not even mentioned as the cause of the lynching in the majority of cases. Rather, they contended, lynching was a system of state-supported terror designed to maintain white supremacy and black economic and political subserviency.[10]

Moorfield Storrey, prominent constitutional attorney and NAACP board member, backed Johnson. In a letter to skeptical Attorney General George Wickersham in January 1921, Moorfield noted: "The governor of the state, the prosecuting officers, the grand juries, the sheriffs, and all the instrumentalities of the law refuse to operate so as to protect Negroes against lynching."[11]

Johnson's hard work and solid preparation paid off. In September, after a month of grueling testimony, the House Judiciary Committee approved the Dyer bill for floor debate. But though Johnson was fairly confident the House would pass the bill, he knew the Senate was another matter. Southern Democrats, by virtue of seniority, held a tight grip on key committees there, including the Senate Judiciary Committee. The instant the Dyer bill was introduced in the Senate, southern senators loudly threatened to filibuster it "to death." Under Senate rules, they had a huge advantage, for a handful of senators could tie up any piece of legislation indefinitely by filibustering. And the only way a filibuster could be broken was through cloture, which meant that two-thirds of those members present and voting would have to vote to cut off debate. The Senate had rarely invoked this measure.[12]

———•◆•———

The looming Senate battle was only one of Johnson's worries. During the fall of 1921, the Ku Klux Klan enjoyed a massive resurgence. Hundreds of chapters sprang up nationally, and with thousands of new recruits and a huge campaign chest, the Klan quickly became a dominant force in local and state politics in the South and Midwest. Johnson repeatedly implored Harding to denounce the secret organization but the president refused. The Klan threat, however, was too big for federal officials to totally ignore.

The new attorney general, Harry Daugherty, mostly because of NAACP pressure, momentarily seemed to contemplate a Justice Department probe of the KKK. He asked the Bureau of Investigation (BOI) director, William Burns, to find out if there was evidence that the Klan had broken any federal laws. Daugherty quickly decided that the legal issues were too "complex" to nail Klan leaders for any crimes, but a few congressmen thought it was at least worth the effort to investigate.[13]

In late September, the House Rules Committee subpoenaed Klan grand dragon William Simmons to testify. Simmons was in top theatrical form. The self-appointed "colonel," who wore an oversized vest and displayed a penchant for imitation gold jewelry, was described decades later by *Atlanta Constitution* publisher Ralph McGill as a "salesman or confidence man." He was every bit the latter. Limping into the conference room to testify, he gave the appearance of being a frail, benign, grandfatherly type.[14]

Simmons played the committee like a fine-tuned instrument. He swore that the Klan was a "moral teaching fraternity" that merely wanted to convert Americans to the Christian path of righteousness. Not one committee member challenged anything he said. Several southern members fawned over him and praised him for his testimony, and one member even accused Burns, who was in the room, of spying on the committee. When Simmons finished, the committee members took all of ten minutes to permanently close the hearings. Their indifference to Klan violence was a strong signal that an antilynching bill would be a tough sell in Congress—but perhaps not an impossible sell if Harding would go all out for it.[15]

Three days after Congress finished its charade with the Klan, Harding traveled to Birmingham, Alabama, to do a little political fence-mending with the South. In an open-air speech, with the whites filling the main street and blacks clustered on the sidewalks in the back, Harding told the crowd of several thousand that blacks should be "full participants in the benefits" of American society.

This was an enlightened statement considering the time and place, but Harding didn't forget the audience he was addressing. He quickly added that there were "fundamental, eternal and inescapable differences" between the two races. Harding played directly to the segregationist sentiments of the whites and lectured blacks, telling them they "should not aspire to be like a white man."

Did the president mean that blacks were inferior—or just different? Harding didn't leave much doubt. He called social equality an "inconceivably dangerous and undemocratic demand." The speech touched off a firestorm of protest from blacks. *Crisis* branded the speech an "appeal to the Frankenstein of racial exclusiveness." Black editors expressed shock that a president had openly tossed his hat into the ring with segregationists.[16]

Privately, NAACP officials still tried to get assurances from Harding that he would not back away from his support of the Dyer legislation. Although Harding told Johnson that he expected Congress to pass the Dyer bill, Johnson was not satisfied. With the president's Birmingham speech fresh in his mind, he was suspicious that Harding was searching for a way to break his promise to actively work for the bill. Johnson put the president to the test and asked him to firmly endorse the bill in his second congressional speech in December. Harding refused.[17]

Fortunately, as Johnson expected, things were going fairly well in the House. The Dyer bill was moving toward a favorable vote. Johnson continued to mobilize support, leaving nothing to chance. The day before the final vote, hundreds of blacks packed the upper galleries of the House chamber, applauding and cheering the remarks of any congressman who spoke for the bill.

Southern Democrats could barely contain themselves at the sight of these "uppity" blacks. After one outburst from the gallery, a number of Democrats jumped to their feet, shook their fists at the gallery, and shouted, "Sit down, niggers." This time, the blacks were not intimidated. They shouted back, "We are not niggers, you liars." The House over-whelmingly passed the Dyer bill that afternoon.[18]

NAACP officials issued a cautious statement thanking the House for "taking a step to end fifty years of shame" but warned that "the fight's not yet over." With a huge battle shaping up in the Senate, it was crucial that Harding help push Dyer. The first job was to get the bill out of the Senate Judiciary Committee. There was some hope since nine of the six-teen senators on the committee were Republicans.[19]

———————•◆•———————

NAACP officials stepped up their attack. They took out full-page ads in the *New York Times* and seven other newspapers to explain "the facts about lynching." *Crisis* urged its readers to flood the Senate with letters and telegrams supporting passage of the bill. NAACP officials again se-cured endorsements and support statements from hundreds of religious and business leaders and from major newspapers, as well as mayors and several state governors.[20]

During testimony before the Senate Judiciary Committee, Johnson once more countered southern charges that the bill was unconstitutional and would "usurp" state laws. He pointed out that lynching was not a private act but mob violence and that state officials, by refusing to prosecute lynchers, deprived the victims of their constitutional rights to equal pro-tection and due process. Johnson reminded the senators that the Consti-tution, not state law, was the supreme law of the land. Former Attorney General Wade H. Ellis supported Johnson, and the NAACP got a major boost from the American Bar Association, which also endorsed the Dyer bill. After weeks of arduous testimony, the committee passed the bill by a scant margin and sent it on to the full Senate.[21]

The joy that NAACP officials may have felt was only momentary, for the southern Democrats quickly issued an ultimatum: Drop the Dyer bill, or face a prolonged filibuster that would bring congressional business to a halt. Johnson immediately turned to the White House for support. Senate Republicans outnumbered Democrats nearly two to one, and if Harding would do a little political arm-twisting with the fence-sitting Republican senators, the bill might have a chance. It was now or never.

In June, Johnson asked Harding to lobby the Senate on behalf of the bill. Harding was cordial. He assured Johnson again that he supported Dyer, but he also said that he had doubts about the constitutionality of the bill.[22] At that point, Johnson probably suspected that the president had bought the argument of the conservatives. If so, Dyer was in big trouble. Harding had evidently calculated the risks and concluded that Dyer was probably dead, so why would he risk alienating the southerners and Republican conservatives whose support was vital to passage of his "must" legislation? Johnson had no choice but to continue to press Harding.

When Johnson learned that the president would be meeting Senate leaders in September to discuss that "must" legislation, he sent him a telegram and begged him to "use [his] power and influence" to secure passage of Dyer. Johnson got a clue about Harding's intention when the president told a delegation from the National Council of Negro Women that tariff and bonus bills had to be passed before Dyer. Harding didn't mention the Dyer bill when he finally met with the Senate leaders.[23]

In November, Harding sent another signal that he regarded racial problems as a nuisance to be avoided at all costs. At that time, state officials in Louisiana were alarmed that the Klan had launched a wave of terror and intimidation and paralyzed local government in several parishes. Louisiana governor John M. Parker met with Harding and Daugherty for one and a half hours at the White House. Parker walked a tightrope. He made it clear to the two men that he was not asking for federal intervention in the state, which would have been political suicide for him; what he wanted, he said, was for the Justice Department to determine whether the Klan leaders had gone into Louisiana from other states to incite violence.

Daugherty, after conferring privately with Harding, told Parker that there was "nothing at this time the federal government could do." Meanwhile, New York senator David I. Walsh, who was thoroughly disgusted with Harding's appeasement of the Klan, demanded that the president both issue a national proclamation ordering the KKK to disband and direct Daugherty to bring federal conspiracy charges against its leaders. However, Daugherty told Walsh that he could find no evidence that the Klan had broken any federal laws.[24]

———— • ◆ • ————

It was increasingly apparent to a frustrated Johnson that Harding wouldn't lift a finger to help the Dyer bill. But the NAACP had spent too much money and invested too much time—and he had personally driven himself far too hard—to give up the fight. Again, Johnson doggedly appealed to Harding to ask Congress to pass the bill in his annual congressional address in December. This time, Harding skipped the usual pleasantries and bluntly told Johnson that he couldn't mention every bill in his speech and that he intended to speak "exclusively" on the subject of the merchant marine. Johnson probably knew better.

Like every other president, Harding would use the annual congressional speech to discuss numerous domestic and foreign policy issues and to tout the accomplishments of his administration. In his wide-ranging talk, he discussed debt, transportation, the tariff, railroad construction, and emigration.[25]

The *New York Times* accurately sensed the political drift in the White House and Congress. The paper noted that many Republicans would "not shed tears" if Dyer was withdrawn because if it were, they could avoid a painful, nasty battle that would have forced them to choose sides.[26]

As it turned out, Congress never had to take a vote. When Dyer came up for a possible vote, Democratic leaders in the Senate punctuated their remarks about states' rights and federal intrusion with a few "darky jokes," to the great amusement of many of their colleagues. Finally, Alabama senator Oscar Underwood issued the ultimatum: Withdraw Dyer, or the Democrats would permanently bury Harding's multimillion-dollar ship subsidy bill, as well as all other appropriations bills and appointments.[27]

On December 1, Republican leaders hastily called an evening caucus and agreed to drop the bill. If Harding had forcefully intervened at that point with Republican leaders, he may have been able to force Congress to vote on the bill. But he chose not to do so.

Du Bois, as editor of *Crisis,* had worked as hard as Johnson to rally support for the Dyer bill, and he was furious. He was convinced that the whole matter was a farce from the start. The Republicans, he charged, "never intended the Dyer bill to pass." It certainly appeared that Harding and Republican leaders had played a smoke-and-mirrors game with blacks, suggesting that they really cared about black rights—as long as they didn't have to fight for them at least.[28]

It was difficult to tell from his public statements whether Harding was happy or sad at the demise of Dyer. He claimed he was sad, but his words seemed less than convincing. Moreover, he spent most of his time telling reporters he was relieved that the ship subsidy bill would pass.[29] Johnson wasn't convinced of the president's sincerity regarding Dyer's fate. When Johnson expressed disappointment about Harding's silence at the critical hour, the president reacted defensivly. He disputed the charge that the Republicans had not fought for the bill and blamed the defeat on the Democrats. The president pleaded that he had been powerless to stop the filibuster that would work to the detriment of the country.

Anticipating that Johnson would try again to get Congress to pass the bill and ask for his support, Harding was determined not to be drawn into another congressional fight. He warned Johnson that the future appeared unpromising and that no one should deceive himself that an antilynching bill could be passed. This time, it was Johnson who skipped the pleasantries, angrily telling Harding that there was deep chagrin and even resentment among blacks at the Republican betrayal. Johnson was now ready to believe Du Bois: He strongly implied that the Republicans were never serious about passing Dyer.[30]

Senator Henry Cabot Lodge, whom Johnson had considered a Republican friend, tried to smooth things over. He expressed regrets to Johnson about the bill's failure and reiterated that a drawn-out battle over Dyer would have jeopardized the passage of the ship subsidy bill, the extension of credit to farmers, and several pending confirmations. Lodge may have been well intentioned, but it is difficult to believe that he really thought he could convince Johnson that saving ship subsidies was more important than saving black lives.[31]

Even if there was no truth to the charge that the Republicans and Harding had deliberately deceived NAACP leaders, the fact was that the president and his party had deserted blacks at a critical moment. As a result, the NAACP learned a hard reality: A president and Congress could easily sacrifice black rights for the sake of political expediency.[32]

NAACP officials were bitter about the Republican betrayal for reasons that white men like Lodge and Harding could never understand. After all, whites could afford to be cavalier about antilynching legislation since *their* lives weren't in danger every day. Even as the House debated the Dyer bill in May, for example, twelve blacks were lynched.[33]

May also brought a shocking report from Jasper County, Georgia, that the bodies of eleven blacks had been found in shallow graves on the farm of John Williams, a well-to-do white planter. The blacks, who had been held in virtual slave-labor conditions in violation of federal peonage laws, were murdered by Williams when they tried to escape from the farm. Despite eyewitness testimony and an exhaustive FBI investigation, the Justice Department declined to prosecute Williams.

Furthermore, during the very week that Lodge and Harding had tried to explain to Johnson why the Dyer bill was withdrawn, four blacks were lynched. And by year's end, a total of fifty-seven lynchings had occurred in the United States in 1922—a five-year high.[34]

———— • ◆ • ————

The sudden death of Harding on August 2, 1923, meant that the NAACP had to start its campaign over again. And by all accounts, the new president was a cold, private man who revealed little of his personality or thoughts to anyone and who seemed determined to avoid rocking any political boats. It was hardly surprising, then, that Calvin Coolidge played it close to the vest politically, especially on racial matters. NAACP officials therefore tried a different approach to get the new president's ear.[35]

Three weeks after Harding's death, Johnson dispatched his assistant, Walter White, to meet with one of the few black Bureau of Investigation agents in New York. Since he had joined the NAACP in 1918, White had worked almost exclusively on antilynching matters. The blond, fair-skinned, blue-eyed White was the son of a prominent black Atlanta family and could easily pass for white. His reputation had grown to near legendary proportions among blacks because of his daring forays to the sites of lynchings to collect statements and take pictures. His book *Rope and Faggot,* which detailed his gruesome findings, had been wildly popular and further enhanced his celebrity status among blacks.

At the meeting with the BOI agent, White and NAACP president Arthur Spingarn insisted that blacks were law-abiding citizens and that in nine out of ten lynchings cases, no crimes had been committed. White also deliberately painted a nightmarish vision of black retaliation against whites if the White House did not take action to prosecute lynchers. He was trying a shock tactic, undoubtedly hoping that he could play on latent fears of black violence. But White and Spingarn also quickly assured the agent that they would do "all in their power to prevent the spread of radicalism among Negroes." The men expected that their words would be duly reported to BOI Director Burns, who, in turn, would relay them on to the DOJ and the White House.[36]

If their veiled threat had any impact, Coolidge certainly gave no indication of it. In his first message to Congress in December 1923, he made only brief reference to the "hideous crime" of lynching, then promptly shifted into a defense of states' rights, insisting that racial "difficulties" were "local problems" that could not be resolved with "outside interference." In fact, the only time that Coolidge seemed to recognize that blacks even existed during his first few months in office was when he sent a pro forma message of congratulations to the NAACP annual conference in August.[37]

Johnson had to work doubly hard to find a way to get a response from the man whom the press quickly dubbed "Silent Cal." In February 1924, Johnson reported to the NAACP board that Coolidge would meet with congressional leaders in March to discuss strategy for passing his "must" legislation. When Johnson asked Coolidge if the discussion would include antilynching legislation (Dyer had reintroduced his bill), Coolidge claimed that he had discussed the Dyer bill during a meeting with the congressmen and urged them to consider it after his appropriations bills were passed. The president then passed the buck and advised Johnson to take up the matter with Republican congressional leaders.[38]

As much as he would probably have preferred to avoid racial issues altogether, the president nonetheless had a minimal obligation to occasionally meet with the black Republicans who still loyally delivered votes to the party. Many of them were deeply troubled about Coolidge. A delegation of black Republican officials politely told him that blacks had the impression he was opposed to antilynching legislation. Coolidge brushed their criticism aside and said that he had supported the Dyer bill in 1922 and still did. The question the men didn't ask—but should have—was, What about now?[39]

Silent Cal's taciturn personality may have puzzled many, but there was little mystery about his racial views. Coolidge was very much a man of his times. America during the mid-1920s was a rigidly segregated society, and most whites believed that blacks were intellectually inferior and unfit to be their social equals. In a candid moment, Coolidge essentially said as much after White challenged him to spell out his racial views. He suggested that White read the speech he delivered in June 1924 at the commencement ceremony at Howard University. In that address, Coolidge had called blacks the "great resources of industrial capacity." Although he had noted that slavery was unfortunate, he had also stated that it helped save blacks from "the tragic fate" of "many aboriginal people" who collapsed before the "more advanced communities."

Coolidge had given the students and White a textbook example of the white man's perceived burden, with a vengeance: Not only did he view slavery as a blessing, he also thought blacks were best suited to be manual laborers. His bigotry might have been overlooked if Coolidge was a private citizen. But he was the president of the United States, and his private views inevitably translated into public policy, as would soon became evident.[40]

In July, following the party conventions (the Progressive Party, a short-lived third party, held a convention and ran Wisconsin senator Robert La Follette for president), Coolidge had the dubious distinction of being the only presidential candidate who refused to publicly denounce the Klan. If blacks could have found a political home anywhere else, they would have immediately waved good-bye to the Republican Party. But the Democrats were still a thoroughly segregationist party, and the Progressives had too little money and insufficient voter support to be a credible alternative. Consequently, Johnson trudged ahead and tried to keep open the NAACP's tenuous lines to the White House.[41]

In March 1925, when a black was burned at the stake in Rocky Ford, North Carolina, Johnson sent Coolidge a clipping and a letter about the murder. Johnson evidently hoped that the extreme barbarity of this particular lynching might prick Coolidge's conscience enough to get him to think more favorably about antilynching legislation. But Johnson probably also realized that clippings and letters weren't likely to prod a president who eschewed any controversy and had little sensitivity to racial issues. Perhaps the only thing the president would understood was mass action and public pressure—and that would require an issue or an act so heinous that even the White House could not ignore it.[42]

———— • ◆ • ————

It began in a small county courthouse in Aiken, South Carolina, on a warm day in October 1926. For a brief moment, it looked like a miracle was about to befall the three young blacks on trial. A year earlier, Damon Lowman, his sister Bertha, and their cousin Clarence had been arrested at their farmhouse on the outskirts of town. Sheriff Henry Howard and his deputies had gone to the farmhouse to serve a warrant on Damon and Bertha's father for suspected moonshining.

The elder Lowman wasn't there. But according to the story the deputies later told, the sheriff was hit by gunfire as he approached the house to serve the warrant. In the ensuing gun battle, Damon and Bertha's mother was shot dead and Sheriff Howard was killed. The Lowmans claimed that the deputies had killed their mother without provocation; they contended they had not fired any shots and suggested Howard may have been killed by one of his own men.

The Lowmans were immediately arrested and charged with Howard's murder. In the hypercharged racial climate of the town, the young blacks were in serious danger: Howard was not only the town sheriff, he was also a Klan official. For several days, his body lay in state at the town's funeral home while hundreds of Klansmen in full regalia marched past. More than a thousand people attended the burial service. (On the first anniversary of the killing, the Klan would burn a cross on the courthouse lawn in commemoration.) The Klansmen praised Howard and openly vowed revenge.

For the moment, cooler heads prevailed, and the Klan leaders seemed to be willing to let justice take its course, certain that the Lowmans would be convicted and quickly executed. They were partly right. The Lowmans were, as expected, convicted in local court. Clarence and Damon were sentenced to death and Bertha to life imprisonment. But amazingly, after reviewing the evidence, the state supreme court decided that there was enough doubt about the testimony and trial procedures to reverse the convictions and order a new trial.

It seemed that the Lowmans' luck might hold. At the second trial, a local judge found Damon not guilty and leaned toward freeing Bertha and Clarence. But observers noted that as the proceedings continued, more and more Klansmen filled the courtroom. They sat solemnly, some with their guns openly displayed, and glared at the defendants. There would be no victory celebration for the Lowmans.

On the evening of October 8, 150 armed men cut off electricity and water at the jail and tore down the front door. Sheriff Nollie Robinson later claimed that three men pinned him on the floor while others stole his keys. The Lowmans were then ordered out of their cells at gunpoint. When Bertha tried to resist, the men punched and kicked her; witnesses said they could hear her screams throughout the jail. The Lowmans were then shoved into two autos. As the cars started from town, Clarence also tried to fight his captors. He was shot in the chest, dumped out of the car, and tied to the rear bumper with a rope. The path that the kidnappers took could later be traced by the blood-streaked trail on the road that Clarence's body had left. Two miles from town, the kidnappers dragged the trio out, shotgunned them in the face and chest, and set Bertha's clothes on fire.

The local prosecutor expressed outrage when the crimes were discovered and promised a thorough investigation. But the county coroner had a different idea. It took him less than twenty-four hours to pronounce that the Lowmans had died at the "hands of persons unknown."

In a telegram to Coolidge, Johnson poured out his frustrations about the incident. He had not forgiven the Republicans for their betrayal on the Dyer bill, and now he angrily reminded Coolidge that even before the Aiken murders, twenty-three blacks had been lynched in 1926—five more than in the previous year. He blamed the Aiken murders and the other lynchings on the Republicans. Johnson demanded that Coolidge make amends by issuing "a forcible pronouncement" to the nation against mob violence.[43]

He knew there was little chance that Coolidge would order the Justice Department to investigate the Aiken murders unless he could somehow prove that Robinson and other local officials had been complicit with the lynchers. That was the angle that White worked. Posing as a reporter for the black weekly *New York World*, White scoured Aiken looking for anyone who had information about the murders and was willing to talk.

His search paid off. With the help of an informant and a local attorney, he was able to get sworn affidavits from Lucy Mooney and Charles Lee, two prisoners who were in the jail the night the Lowmans were abducted. Mooney claimed that she saw Robinson drag Bertha from her cell and shove her into the car. When the *World* broke the story of Robinson's involvement, the black press at large quickly picked up on it. Robinson hotly denied the story and blamed it on political enemies he claimed were out to get him.

Meanwhile, White, with the help of a private detective hired by the NAACP, pieced together the details of the story. In addition to Robinson and a deputy, White identified by name, address, and profession more than a dozen conspirators. They included local and state officials, deputies, police officers (one of whom was in full uniform at the time of the crime), a prominent local attorney, and four of the county's leading businessmen. White promptly sent his report and the prisoners' affidavits to South Carolina governor Thomas McLeod.

A few days later, McLeod told White that he had talked with Robinson by phone and that the sheriff had protested his innocence and promised the governor he would aid in any state investigation. The governor seemed satisfied and assured White that he would conduct a full investigation. White was, to say the least, skeptical: In his report, he had also mentioned that three of McLeod's cousins had watched the massacre.[44]

White had even more reason to be skeptical of how much cooperation he could expect from state officials. A week after McLeod received White's report, South Carolina senator Cole Blease got into the act. Blease had a national reputation as a rabid racist and had once publicly bragged that the "lynching of a man for the unmentionable crime [rape] is a protection to our civilization." Indignant that the Lowman family had retained an attorney and planned to sue the county for indemnity, he announced that he would donate his legal services to fight the suit.[45]

Despite the senator's bluster, White did not intend to let state officials off the hook. He reminded McLeod of his promise to reveal the names of the attackers to the media. But McLeod suddenly developed a case of amnesia and claimed that he had made no such promise and could not identify anyone.[46]

It was apparent that South Carolina officials intended to stonewall the murder. But White's and Johnson's efforts in the case hadn't gone unnoticed at the White House. In December, Coolidge told Congress that the federal government was "charged with the obligation" to protect blacks from lynching. Perhaps mindful of Johnson's rebuke, the president also claimed that lynchings had declined during his administration. Whether he was simply misinformed or deliberately twisting the facts, the truth was that lynchings had not decreased but had nearly doubled over the year before.[47]

Even as Coolidge spoke, White's informer accused McLeod of having Klan ties and warned White that state officials were going to whitewash the case. He was right. McLeod, who had only a few weeks left before his term expired, pressed the grand jury to delay its findings until he was out of office in January. The governor almost certainly knew or suspected that the grand jury would not return any indictments. (White noted in a follow-up report to McLeod that one and possibly two members of the grand jury were part of the lynch mob.) When the jury's decision was announced, McLeod's successor would catch the flak. More important, McLeod was angling for a position on the Federal Trade Commission. White was furious when he found out that Coolidge was considering appointing the governor to that post. He called the appointment a "mark of approval" for a governor who was "derelict in his duty." NAACP officials vowed to do everything they could to stop it. In the end, McLeod didn't get the job, but the fact that Coolidge had even considered giving it to him indicated to the NAACP just how lightly the president took the events in Aiken.[48]

The Aiken fiasco made White even more determined to keep the pressure on Coolidge. In February, the NAACP and the National Equal Rights League (NERL)—a direct activist group led by the fiery editor of the *Boston Guardian*, William Monroe Trotter—launched a national drive to collect signatures on a petition urging Coolidge to send a special message to Congress by backing immediate passage of the Dyer bill. When the sponsors turned up at the White House with petitions bearing more than 20,000 names, the president wasn't impressed. He coolly told the group that southern Democrats would kill the Dyer measure. He may have been right, but he also made it clear that he would make no effort to push the bill.[49]

During his remaining years in the White House, apart from offering a few perfunctory words praising the NAACP when it convened its annual conferences in 1926 and 1927, Silent Cal more than lived up to his nickname when it came to racial problems. When he departed, more than ninety-six blacks had been lynched over his term as president. And not a single federal prosecution had been launched.[50]

———•◆•———

Coolidge's successor seemed to be cut from a different political cloth. There were good reasons for calling Herbert Hoover "the Great Humanitarian." He often boasted of his Quaker stock. He also took pride in his record as the coordinator of food and disaster relief during World War I and was credited with saving thousands from starvation in Europe.

In an era when rugged individualism and capitalist laissez-faire economic policies toward the poor were the norm, Hoover was generally considered a liberal or even progressive thinker on social and economic issues and a man who was especially sensitive to the economic "plight of the little man." In his acceptance speech at the Republican convention in August 1928, he urged compassion for the poor and downtrodden. Hoover seemed like a president who might be willing to consider and act on racial problems.[51]

But NAACP officials were disturbed because Hoover seemed to be listening closely to his southern advisers. Following his election triumph, he spent several weeks vacationing in Florida. Between sunning and fishing, Hoover wined and dined a parade of southern Republican officials and businessmen. In addition to seeking appointments, jockeying for political advantage, and procuring government contracts, the officials were trying to sell Hoover on the idea that the way to make the Republican Party competitive with the Democrats in the South was to oust the few blacks (and their white moderate supporters) from party positions, committees, and appointive posts.

The "lily white regulars," as the press labeled these southern Republicans, were careful not to make their views seem to be a matter of race. They claimed that the party's blacks were engaged in widespread corruption and were undermining the GOP's reputation and strength. Indeed, a few black Republicans had been prosecuted on corruption charges, but the "lily whites" wanted the blacks out not because of any concern for good government but because of racism.

Hoover seemed to buy their argument. When he returned to Washington, he told the press that he wanted to build up a sound Republican organization in the South "in a permanent form." Hoover promised to personally scrutinize all future appointments to make sure the appointees had "standing and character in the community." The president might have been motivated by ideals of clean government and not racism, but as the *New York Times* concluded, the consequence of his purge would "clearly foreshadow a Republican Party almost purely a white man's party."[52]

Black leaders would have to fight a two-front battle with Hoover to preserve the few political gains they had managed to squeeze out of past Republican administrations and to keep the drive for an antilynching law alive. During the first year of Hoover's tenure, White, Johnson, and *Guardian* editor William Monroe Trotter continued to press Hoover for a meeting to discuss lynching. The president didn't seem interested, but another man named Hoover did.[53]

J. Edgar Hoover, who had replaced the fired Burns as director of the BOI, was, in fact, very interested in White's and Johnson's plans. He had instructed his special agent in New York to compile a dossier on the NAACP and its officers, and he repeatedly stressed the importance of keeping an eye on the organization's attempts to gather support for antilynching legislation. Actually, he didn't care about the antilynching activities per se because he didn't intend to take any action against lynchers or support antilynching legislation. But he *was* on the alert for any sign of black discontent. He regarded the NAACP as just another radical group "out to stir up the Negroes."[54]

Meanwhile, Johnson and White continued to use whatever political influence they had with the Republicans to try to force a White House meeting. In September 1930, President Hoover, almost certainly with an eye on reelection in 1932, realized that he needed to retain some minimal black support in order to win. He therefore issued a terse three-and-a-half-line message calling lynching an "evil" that was "undermining the very essence of justice and democracy" in America. White and Johnson were not willing to accept more empty platitudes or moral pieties from the White House about lynching; they wanted specific action.[55]

White fired off a memo to President Hoover detailing the twenty-three lynchings that occurred during 1930. He asked him to call a conference of southern governors to coordinate a state and national strategy to combat lynching. Hoover refused to call a conference but agreed to meet with black leaders. He listened politely to their pleas for federal action but was evasive when White brought up the idea of a conference.[56]

With an election year approaching, Hoover could not afford to completely ignore black voters, so in December 1931, he agreed to meet with a delegation from the National Equal Rights League led by contentious newspaperman William Monroe Trotter. Trotter pleaded with Hoover to propose antilynching legislation. This time, the president had two ploys for pacifying the NERL and the NAACP. First, he suggested that the delegation talk to congressional leaders. Hoover must have known that no antilynching bills had been proposed in Congress since 1927 and that none were planned.[57] The tactic he chose to pacify White was even more farfetched. Hoover told him that he had discussed with Attorney General William D. Mitchell the feasibility of using troops to arrest lynchers.

White couldn't possibly believe that a president who had waited nearly two years before uttering a word about lynching (and then doing so only in the most general terms) would really employ federal troops in the South. Mitchell told the president his idea wouldn't work; Congress would not approve the funds or pass any legislation authorizing such a scheme. Mitchell also pointed out that even if troops were used and arrests were made, local juries weren't going to convict anyone. Hoover quickly dropped the idea.[58]

During his final year in office, Hoover emulated Coolidge in regard to racial matters. Aside from sending a brief congratulatory message to the NAACP annual conference in May 1932, he did not say another word about lynching during the remainder of his term. The GOP also quietly deleted the antilynching plank from its 1932 platform. Hoover continued to believe that the Republicans could win a national election by inducing enough white southern voters to defect from the Democratic Party.[59]

In another time, this strategy might have worked. But as the Great Depression deepened, the breadlines lengthened, and the relief rolls swelled, Hoover and the Republicans stubbornly clung to their laissez-faire economic palliatives. This only typed the president in the minds of many voters as a man who simply didn't care. In any case, Hoover did not have a political prayer in the South. The Roosevelt landslide in the 1932 elections swallowed up Republicans—including Hoover—across the nation.

Hoover got less than half as many votes in the South as he had received in 1928. Worse, the Republican vote total fell to a twenty-year low, and the Republican percentage was the lowest since 1912. The South remained as solidly Democratic as ever. Ultimately, the 1932 election stood as a towering monument to Republican economic failure. And in the end, the Great Humanitarian had done little to stem the tide of lynching. During his term in the White House, fifty-two blacks had been lynched, and no federal prosecutions had been pursued.[60]

Overall, NAACP officials could be proud of their efforts. White and Johnson had waged a brilliant, even heroic, struggle against great odds. During a decade in which segregation and racial violence were commonplace and in an era when many whites barely saw blacks as human beings, the NAACP leaders pricked the conscience of many Americans and finally forced them to face the brutal truth that lynching was a savage act that defied the rule of law and Christian morality. They had also challenged three reluctant Republican presidents and a divided Congress to pass a law to make lynching a federal crime—and they had nearly succeeded.

The NAACP gained valuable experience in political lobbying, won many supporters in the press, and got hundreds of state and local officials, business and church leaders, and prominent organizations to endorse its campaign. Moreover, the antilynching campaign probably saved hundreds of black lives. After 1922, southern law enforcement and state officials, partly fearing the threat of a federal law, increased their efforts to protect blacks, and in a few cases, lynchers were actually prosecuted and convicted. Over the next few years, more than twenty states, including seven southern states, would put antilynching laws on the books.[61]

But the nation was now economically prostrate, and millions of Americans were desperately searching for ways to survive the hard times. Lynching might have receded entirely from the political agenda of the White House and Congress if not for the dogged effort of one man. Walter White was determined not to let the nation forget that blacks were still dying at the hands of mobs. After taking over as the NAACP's executive director in 1930 following the retirement of James Weldon Johnson, White continued to believe that the only way to stop lynching was for the leaders of the federal government to act. He therefore prepared to challenge the newly elected president to do just that.

2

No New Deal on Racial Violence

The Roosevelt Years

Harvard University professor George Elliot Baker had a well-deserved reputation among his students as a tough taskmaster. Every two weeks, each student in his English 18 class had to write a speech or an essay on an assigned topic. Baker was especially impressed with one essay written by a seventeen-year-old freshman in 1903.

Young Franklin Roosevelt, the author of this essay, was adamant that southerners should attend Harvard. How else, Roosevelt argued, could northerners "know and sympathize with our brothers of the South?" For those who had doubts about this, Roosevelt had a ready example: "Harvard has done honor to perhaps a half dozen Negroes—men all of them who have given their lives for their race. Yes, Harvard has sought to make a man out of a semi-beast."

These words were not simply the unpolished crudity of an immature freshman. In 1903, many northerners were enthralled with the white southern way of life, and they thought little about using derogatory terms to describe blacks. Roosevelt was no different. And even in later years, when writing to his wife, Eleanor, and close friends, he routinely referred to blacks as "darkies" and "niggers."[1]

In public, Roosevelt was usually careful to observe proper political etiquette and not offend anyone's racial sensitivities. As governor of New York, he did nothing special to promote civil rights or speak out against lynching, but Roosevelt nonetheless had a good reputation as a mild reformer on economic and labor issues.

NAACP executive secretary Walter White was not too concerned about what FDR said or did in private or about his political decisions as a state governor. But he knew that as president, FDR, with the backing of the Democratic Party, could do a great deal to change the lives of millions of Americans.

With his landslide presidential victory in 1932, Roosevelt became the first Democrat to occupy the White House in more than a decade. This worried White, for Roosevelt was now the standard-bearer for a party dominated by southern segregationists. Yet there was something about the new president that captivated black Americans. Roosevelt offered a new vision for the United States, and he actually seemed to care for the poor and the workers. Now the crucial test was whether Roosevelt would expand his humanitarian sentiments to include blacks.[2]

————— ◆ · —————

For millions of blacks trapped in the cycle of poverty and racial terror in the South, this was a life-and-death matter. By the end of Roosevelt's first year in office in 1933, twenty-eight blacks had been lynched by white mobs, three times as many as in 1932. NAACP officials, along with liberal church groups and civic organizations, were outraged that the federal government had done nothing in response.[3]

The NAACP was under intense pressure from blacks to revive the campaign it had begun in the 1920s to get a federal antilynching law passed. In the summer of 1933, White outlined a proposed congressional antilynching bill and consulted with the American Civil Liberties Union (ACLU) and other social reform groups to gain their support.[4]

White wanted to avoid the mistakes that NAACP officials had made a decade earlier in fighting for an antilynching law. They had spent thousands of dollars and for months had patiently lobbied House members to pass an antilynching bill introduced by Missouri Republican Leonidas Dyer in 1922. But they saw their hard work go down the drain when a handful of southern Democrats and northern Republican conservatives scuttled the bill in the Senate. This time, White got Senator Robert Wagner of New York and Senator Edward Costigan of Colorado, two of the Senate's most respected and savvy leaders, to sponsor the proposed new bill.

The Wagner-Costigan antilynching bill was almost a carbon copy of the Dyer bill. Under the new measure, public officials and law enforcement officers who failed to protect prisoners could be prosecuted under conspiracy statutes, fined $5,000, and given prison sentences of from five years to life. It was important that the bill targeted southern sheriffs: In the majority of lynchings, blacks were seized by mobs from jails or other custody, often with the connivance of police and public officials. The bill also contained a clause that made counties liable to pay damages of up to $10,000 to the families of lynching victims. NAACP officials believed that if lynching was made expensive for taxpayers, local officials would be more diligent in enforcing the law.[5]

White anticipated that the same coalition of southern Democrats and northern conservatives would again try to kill the bill by arguing that it was unconstitutional and usurped the authority of the states to punish crimes. He also knew it would be almost impossible to beat them without Roosevelt's support. Therefore, he banked on FDR using his popularity, position, and influence to prod fence-sitting Democrats to vote for the new bill. The question was whether Roosevelt would take vigorous action.

During the presidential campaign, FDR had said nothing about lynching or racial issues. The Democratic platform contained not a word about civil rights. And furthermore, Roosevelt was a consummate political animal who closely counted votes. Southerners held key Democratic Party posts and sat on the strategic congressional committees.

White was at a disadvantage in another way, as well: He didn't have the political numbers. Although there were strong signs during the 1928 and 1932 elections that more and more blacks were defecting from the Republicans, especially in northern big cities, the majority of blacks still voted Republican. In essence, then, White was going to Roosevelt as a political pauper with hat in hand, asking the president to do something that might be morally correct but politically costly.[6]

———— • ◆ • ————

White was committed to working through traditional legal and political channels. The Communist Party was not. As the depression worsened and increasing numbers of Americans faced poverty, the Communist Party accelerated its direct-action campaign against segregation, racial violence, and economic destitution. Party leaders shrewdly realized that lynching and racial terrorism would continue to be major issues among blacks.

For a brief time in 1931, the International Labor Defense (ILD), set up by the Communists during the 1920s to defend labor radicals and party activists, even worked with NAACP attorneys on the legal defense of the "Scottsboro boys"—eight young black men falsely accused of raping two white women in Alabama. But it was a partnership that couldn't last. The ILD and the NAACP quickly parted company, with each side accusing the other of political opportunism. Since then, the ILD had branched out to defend black sharecroppers, farmers, and workers who were charged with murdering or assaulting whites and faced the death penalty. On several occasions, ILD attorneys narrowly escaped from white mobs in the South who were angered by the sight of white and black "Commie" attorneys defending poor blacks.

In August 1933, three "Red" attorneys once more found themselves in a dangerous spot in a case that almost cost them their lives and that challenged the Roosevelt administration for the first time to confront the lynching issue head on.[7]

On August 1, 1933, Frank B. Irvin, Irving Schwaub, and Allen Taub traveled to Tuscaloosa, Alabama, to defend Dan Pippen Jr., and A. T. Harden. The two young black men were scheduled to stand trial for the murder of a white woman. The attorneys had been retained by Pippen's mother. The mood in Tuscaloosa was ugly, volatile, and tense, and the city might have exploded into violence at any time.

When word spread that the three attorneys would defend the young men, more than 1,000 angry mob members marched to the local courthouse. Authorities quickly hustled the attorneys from the building and shoved them onto a train to Birmingham, disguised in old coats and slouch hats. National Guard troops, armed with bayonets and automatic weapons, were stationed at various spots along the route to keep the mob from attacking the train.

The next day, a trembling Lucindy Pippen took the stand in court. After being badgered by the judge and stared down by armed whites in the courtroom, she vehemently denied that she had authorized the attorneys to defend her son. Local officials assured the terrified mother that her son was in no danger and that Tuscaloosa sheriff R. L. Shamblin could handle any trouble. As a good-faith gesture, Shamblin said that he would take the young men to Birmingham for safekeeping. They never arrived. In the early morning hours of August 13, Shamblin claimed, he and the two black men were ambushed by two carloads of armed men on a side road twelve miles outside Tuscaloosa.

The kidnappers abducted the two handcuffed prisoners. Several hours later, a search party found their bullet-riddled bodies in a ditch. Shamblin never explained why he decided to take a side road or transfer the prisoners so quickly. Judge Henry B. Foster said that he hadn't authorized Shamblin to remove the young men.

The murders, coming close on the heels of the Scottsboro case, angered the nation. Even Alabama governor B. M. Miller denounced the murders, and Judge Foster promised that a grand jury would "leave no stone unturned" in finding the killers. But Communist leaders and NAACP officials had heard that kind of talk before from southern politicians, and each time in the past, the politicians had done nothing to catch or prosecute the murderers of blacks.[8]

The Communists and NAACP officials suspected that Shamblin's story was phony and that he and his deputies had actually helped the lynchers. NAACP investigators also claimed that Shamblin had supplied information on the route he would take to the lynchers. If these allegations proved true, White knew they were grounds for possible prosecution under the federal statutes that punished law officers and public officials for civil rights violations. The NAACP's chief legal counsel, Charles

Houston, thought there was a good chance that if he could talk to Roosevelt directly, he could convince the president to act.

Houston and George Murphy, publisher of the *Baltimore Afro-American*, trooped to the White House, apparently believing that a meeting had been arranged with Roosevelt. When they arrived, however, they were told that Roosevelt was too busy to see them and to come back the next day. They returned promptly the next morning and for more than an hour sat fuming in an outer lobby. When they finally approached a secretary to ask about the meeting, the secretary rudely asked, "What do you boys want?" Houston and Murphy got the message and stormed out of the building. Houston now turned his attention to the Justice Department.[9]

The Communists did, too. After being ousted from Tuscaloosa, the ILD had launched a national campaign to bring the lynchers to justice. The Communists and the NAACP demanded that FDR's new attorney general, Homer Cummings, immediately open a federal investigation of the lynching. At the end of August, the ILD and NAACP sent a joint delegation to meet with Cummings.

The attorney general bluntly told the delegates that he couldn't "interfere very well with the Alabama judicial system." Houston was not satisfied. When he continued to press, Cummings countered by demanding that Houston draw up a brief and specify what federal laws he thought had been broken. Houston probably wondered why he had to prove to the nation's top law enforcement official that federal statutes had been violated, but he accepted the challenge.[10]

In Tuscaloosa, local officials continued to drag their feet while Walter White and the Communists attacked the governor for delaying the investigation. A month later, State Attorney General Thomas E. Knight finally convened the grand jury. But the jurors ignored both testimony from an eyewitness that directly linked Shamblin to the lynchers and a surprisingly spirited effort by Knight to get the witnesses to identify mob members. Eventually, they ruled that Pippen and Harden had died "at the hands of persons unknown."[11]

White and Houston were hardly surprised by the decision. They knew from bitter experience that the real battle to get the Justice Department to take action began after a state grand jury refused to return indictments. By October, Houston had prepared the detailed brief Cummings claimed he needed to justify federal action. Carefully reviewing the facts in the case, he reminded Cummings that the evidence linking Shamblin and local officials to the lynchers provided a clear basis for federal prosecution under Section 20 of the conspiracy statute.

Houston had called the attorney general's bluff and made a compelling case for prosecution. Yet Cummings sat on Houston's report for two months without giving any indication of what, if any, action he would take. By December, NAACP officials were tired of waiting. White sent a copy of Houston's brief to every U.S. senator and state governor and to President Roosevelt. Months later, he found out that Cummings had ultimately decided not to prosecute. The attorney general never bothered to tell him why.[12]

————————— • ◆ • —————————

Four months after the Tuscaloosa lynching, Roosevelt finally broke his silence. He told the Federal Council of Churches in December 1933 that he could not excuse those who condoned the lynch law. But he was not specifically talking about the lynching of black men like Pippen and Harden. Rather, Roosevelt was angry at California's Republican governor, James Rolph, who stupidly congratulated members of a mob "for making a good job of it" after they had lynched two white men. But even though the victims there were white and even though FDR might have been cynically using the issue to rebuke a political foe, the president had finally spoken out about lynching. The local district attorney immediately announced that he would file charges against members of the lynch mob.[13] The *New York Times* praised FDR for speaking out and stated that his pronouncement would make lynchers "more ashamed of themselves."

Evidently, however, there was not much shame in Beaumont, Texas, or Saint Joseph, Missouri. The day after Roosevelt spoke, Daniel Gregory, a young black man, was lynched in Beaumont, and two days later, Lloyd Warner, a black teenager in Saint Joseph, was accused of rape and dragged from his jail cell and lynched (the victim later recanted). Though eleven persons were later arrested for the Warner lynching, all except one were released. It is interesting that Roosevelt did not rebuke the governors of Texas or Missouri, both of whom were Democrats, nor did he condemn the mobs that lynched Gregory and Warner.[14]

Despite Roosevelt's ambiguity on lynching, black leaders were somewhat encouraged that he had at least addressed the subject. It was a small opening, and the *Defender's* outspoken publisher, Robert Abbott, immediately tried to pry it wider. Abbot, who unabashedly styled himself a "race man," had for years repeatedly called on the government to prosecute lynchers. Though he was skeptical about Roosevelt, he was willing to give the president a chance.

Before FDR's scheduled congressional address in January 1934, Abbot claimed he had exchanged telegrams with him and that the president had promised to push an antilynching bill. In truth, however, Roosevelt had made no such pledge. In his speech, he did not mention lynching, but he did make a guarded call to use the "strong arm of the government" to suppress those who commit "violations of the law." Black leaders, accustomed to receiving so little from the White House, gladly interpreted this as Roosevelt's signal to Congress to act.[15]

In February 1934, White and NAACP president Arthur Spingarn appeared before the Senate Judiciary Committee to testify for the Wagner-Costigan bill. Under ferocious questioning from the southerners, both men calmly tried to assure the committee members that the bill was constitutional and did not violate state sovereignty.

Spingarn repeatedly insisted that law enforcement personnel and local officials still weren't doing their jobs. He cited the staggering death toll: Between 1900 and 1930, there were 3,500 documented lynchings. Yet only 12 persons had been convicted. The few antilynching laws on the southern books were more for show than anything else, he noted, since they were almost never enforced.

White went beyond the numbers and tried to make the senators feel the personal devastation and loss suffered by the families of lynching victims. He also wanted them to understand the terror that blacks in general felt, knowing that at any time they could be brutally murdered on the flimsiest of evidence while hundreds gleefully watched. White and Spingarn got their message across. In April, the committee recommended the bill to the full Senate.[16]

There was no time to celebrate, for White knew that the greatest danger lay ahead: In open debate in the Senate, anything—especially something negative—could happen. He was right. Southern Democrats again had worked themselves up into political apoplexy. They shook the chambers with their shouts, protesting that the bill violated states' rights and was a naked power grab by the federal government to take over state courts. South Carolina's geriatric senator "Cotton" Ed Smith even trotted out the tired and thoroughly discredited myth that lynching was a punishment for black rapists. "Certain acts committed are beyond the reach of a court or jury," he said.[17]

No matter how bigoted and irrational their attacks, members of the southern bloc posed a formidable obstacle for the NAACP. White needed Roosevelt. "If the president puts the Costigan-Wagner bill on his 'must' program of legislation," said White, "it will almost surely pass." Meanwhile, Roosevelt seemed to be warming up to White; in April, he told White that he was "much interested" in the bill. But Roosevelt didn't elaborate. Was he for it, against it, or merely curious? Now more than ever, White wanted to meet with the president to find out.[18]

But Roosevelt refused to commit himself to a meeting. A frustrated White turned to the only person who might help—Eleanor Roosevelt, the first lady. She and White had been corresponding for months and had developed something of a mutual friendship. By then, it was well known that the first lady was sympathetic to the plight of blacks. She ignored the taunts of racists who called her a "nigger lover." Her husband's two close advisers, Press Secretary Steven Early and Appointments Adviser Marvin McIntyre, were southerners who barely concealed their animosity toward her. They also took every opportunity to slander White and block him from seeing the president. Eleanor ignored them, too, and continued to stay in contact with White.

When White asked her to press Roosevelt for a meeting, Eleanor complied. But she also knew her husband's sentiments. She warned White that he wouldn't like or agree with everything the president thought. But she agreed that White had to meet FDR personally and present his case. Consequently, she continued to badger her husband until he finally gave in.[19]

On May 14, 1934, White sat quietly in an anteroom at the White House waiting for Roosevelt to return from a yachting excursion on the Potomac River. When FDR entered, he greeted White with a huge smile. Since it was a warm day, the president suggested that they move to the veranda that overlooked the White House garden. The men traded small talk for a few moments as Roosevelt's mother, Sara, sat quietly with them. Then they got down to business. When White mustered his best arguments to persuade the president to join his fight, Roosevelt parried with him. He told White that he had been informed the bill was unconstitutional. White was not intimidated. He opened his valise and pulled out a sheaf of documents that contained the opinions of legal scholars that the bill was not unconstitutional. Roosevelt tried another tack. He protested that if he supported the bill, southerners who controlled the vital congressional committees would bottle up his New Deal program; he also said that he might not be able to withstand a long filibuster.

White assured Roosevelt that the majority of southerners held the president in great esteem and that his support of the bill would probably not diminish his standing with them. White also noted that the South was the nation's poorest region and heavily dependent on federal relief programs. He tallied up the numbers for Roosevelt, calculating that 47 Senate Democrats and 222 congressional Democrats favored passage. Another 11 Republicans, Progressives, and Farmer-Labor senators backed the bill. It was inconceivable, White argued, that these men would oppose FDR's New Deal legislation.

White's political logic escaped the president. And when the ninety-minute meeting ended, Roosevelt still had not given White his word that he would actively support the bill. White was particularly troubled that Roosevelt continued to doubt the constitutionality of the Wagner-Costigan measure; it sounded to him like FDR had been listening a little too closely to the bill's Southern opponents.[20]

Two weeks later, White sent FDR a brief by the prominent legal scholar Charles H. Tuttle that detailed the constitutional merits of the bill. But White was bucking a strong tide, and FDR still would not budge. When a reporter asked him to comment on the Wagner-Costigan bill, Roosevelt claimed, "It is a terribly difficult subject."[21]

Roosevelt shrewdly played both ends against the middle. He kept White at bay since he did not want to totally alienate the black electorate, which had been getting stronger and which, in northern urban areas, was voting in bigger numbers for the Democrats. In a special message to the NAACP annual conference in June, FDR said that he felt "hope and inspiration" in black progress.

White wasn't satisfied with a few platitudes from the president: If Roosevelt really wanted to see more black progress, he should push Wagner-Costigan. White reminded Roosevelt that since the bill was put on hold in June, there had been more than one lynching a week. He asked FDR again to make Wagner-Costigan a "must" item on his legislative agenda.[22]

Roosevelt *did* have his "must" legislation—the Social Security Act, the National Labor Relations Act, the Banking Act, the Public Utilities Holding Company Act, and several other bills. He knew that a tough battle loomed ahead if he was to get these bills through Congress and that he would need all the allies he could get. And as long as racial matters were not an issue, his best Senate allies came from south of the Mason-Dixon line.

Roosevelt believed that southern Democrats would threaten to tie up his real "must" legislation if he made any kind of effort on the Wagner-Costigan measure—and he was not about to risk that for a bill that he didn't think could pass. If it did pass and if he went to the wall with it, the fight would leave political scars on senators who would neither forget them nor forgive him.[23]

When the number of lynchings jumped sharply in May and June, White sent FDR a frantic telegram reminding him that this was the best "proof that the states will not stop lynching." His warning fell on deaf ears; Roosevelt did not reply. With the Senate at an impasse, the Wagner-Costigan bill was temporarily withdrawn.[24] With the bill on the congressional shelf, White searched desperately for a way to keep images of the horror of lynching before Congress and the public. It didn't take him to long to find an appropriate issue.

———— •◆• ————

In June 1932, reacting to the national outrage provoked by the kidnap and murder of famed aviator Charles Lindbergh's infant son, Congress had proposed to make it a federal offense to transport a kidnapping victim across state lines. Herbert Hoover's attorney general, William Mitchell, had some reservations about the constitutionality of the Lindbergh bill, and a few congressmen balked at the idea of supporting it. They weakly raised the argument that it would infringe on the authority of the states to prosecute crimes. But unlike lynching, kidnapping at the time had no racial overtones. So the bill easily passed Congress, and Hoover quickly signed it.

Under the new law, if the victim's body was not found in three days, the FBI would automatically assume that the kidnappers had crossed state lines. A few months later, at Cummings's request, Congress inserted an amendment that made kidnapping a federal crime whether or not a ransom demand was made. When the amended legislation became law in June 1934, virtually every kidnapping case was made a federal offense.

The NAACP saw a glimmer of hope in the new law. Most lynching victims were abducted from jails or forcibly removed from police custody (perhaps with the help of officials) and often transported by the lynch mob to other locations, where they were murdered. Their bodies sometimes were not recovered for days or even weeks.[25]

The NAACP quickly had its first case under the Lindbergh Act. On October 4, 1934, Curtis James, a young black farmworker, was abducted from his home by a mob in Darien, Georgia. After eleven days had passed and James's body had not been found, the NAACP asked the Justice Department to investigate. Cummings refused, claiming that the NAACP had not supplied any evidence that James had been kidnapped or transported across state lines.[26]

A few days later, the NAACP had a more compelling case. Claude Neal, another black farmworker, accused of murdering a white woman, was kidnapped from a jail in Brewton, Alabama, by a white mob and driven across the state line to Florida. There, he was tortured, blowtorched, and castrated. Several days later, his mutilated body was found hanging from a tree near the town square in Marianna, Florida. This case met all the requirements for a Justice Department investigation. White quickly pieced together the brutal facts from informant statements and eyewitness testimony. He named three of the mob members and traced the path the kidnappers had taken from Alabama to Florida. In November, he forwarded a 5,000-word report to Cummings and FDR.

White thought it was an airtight case and asked Roosevelt to instruct Cummings to "apprehend and punish" the lynchers. When Roosevelt didn't answer, White complained to Eleanor that blacks had become cynical toward the president. White thought that if he told Eleanor, she would tell FDR and he might react. But neither Roosevelt nor Cummings was impressed. Cummings, apparently forgetting his own amendment to the Lindbergh Act, issued a statement saying that the FBI would not investigate since no ransom demand had been made.[27]

White's executive assistant, Roy Wilkins, exploded. In a sarcastic editorial in *Crisis* magazine, he said it was ironic that the government could "muster troops, machine guns, airplanes, brains, and money to hunt down a bank robber" but couldn't "muster a good yawn" to prevent mob action against blacks.[28]

Although Cummings had grave doubts that lynching qualified as a federal crime, he had no qualms about expanding federal enforcement for "real" crimes. When he spoke of "real" crimes, he meant the robberies, burglaries, and shoot-outs with lawmen staged by John Dillinger, Ma Barker, Pretty Boy Floyd, Machine Gun Kelley, and other depression-era desperadoes.

In 1933, Cummings submitted a laundry list of new statutes he wanted Congress to give to the Justice Department. Congress quickly obliged and made any illicit activity a federal offense if it involved the mails, interstate commerce, racketeering, extortion, stolen money, stolen property, bank robbery, or illegal firearms.[29]

With no hint that he was aware of any contradiction in his position, Cummings proudly declared that the new statutes were intended not to "supplant" but to "supplement" state authority when local officials didn't have the ability or resources to control crime. It was difficult to fathom Cummings's reasoning. NAACP officials had argued for years that a federal antilynching law would supplement state law when local officials didn't have the ability, resources, or will to arrest and prosecute lynchers. Apparently, Cummings thought a stolen car was one thing and a black life was another. An angry White didn't pull any punches with FDR. He called Cummings's position "legalistic fiddlesticks."[30]

NAACP officials decided to confront Cummings on the crime issue. The attorney general announced with great media fanfare that the Justice Department would sponsor a national crime conference in December 1934. He saw the conference as a way to promote better coordination between law enforcement agencies in battling crime. The NAACP saw it differently. When they asked him if lynching could be placed on the conference agenda, Cummings replied that "it was not probable that the subject of lynching [would] be given a place on the program."

The NAACP bombarded him with letters and telegrams, but he wouldn't give in. On the opening day of the conference, NAACP members staged a noisy demonstration on the sidewalk outside the Justice Department building, which resulted in a confrontation with capital police and the arrest of several demonstrators. An embarrassed Cummings finally agreed to let two NAACP representatives sit in on the workshops as "unofficial delegates." White also managed to get a small concession from FDR. He asked for "a word from him" on lynching in his speech to the convention. And that's exactly what he got: In his address, FDR referred to lynchings as "horrifying" and then moved on.[31]

Although it was a token gesture, White was happy to get even that because during the week before Roosevelt spoke at the conference, White
told Eleanor he heard rumors that FDR was preparing to openly oppose
the Wagner-Costigan bill. White said that though he didn't believe the rumors, he wanted another meeting to get a sense of where FDR stood. He
never got his meeting and he had to settle instead for Eleanor's assurance
that FDR "hoped very much" to get Wagner-Costigan passed.[32]

With the bill scheduled to come up again for debate in the Senate in
1935, White sent Roosevelt a petition signed by dozens of governors,
mayors, church and business leaders, and prominent editors, writers, and
artists. The petition urged FDR to back Wagner-Costigan. Roosevelt did-
n't even bother to respond. When a reporter asked him to comment on
the antilynching bill, Roosevelt's answer was a terse "no."

Although FDR insisted that he still had doubts about the constitution-
ality of the measure, he conceded that it was useful to try and get a vote.
To the NAACP, this sounded like more Roosevelt double-talk, and
Wilkins again criticized the silence of the president.[33]

Wilkins also tried to play on Roosevelt's fierce patriotism and his increasing concern about America's international image. He told FDR that
lynching was embarrassing America abroad. In the meantime, NAACP
officials dropped a few hints that it might be time for blacks to "resort to
physical force" to protect themselves, but their words were sheer hyperbole. The NAACP would never endorse retaliatory violence against
whites. In fact, that would go against the grain of every principle—nonviolent protest, political lobbying, and legal appeals—that the NAACP had
stood for since its founding. But the remarks were also a sign of the
group's desperation. The president, however, wasn't moved. Congress
adjourned, and the bill went back on the shelf again.[34]

NAACP officials were, to put it mildly, deeply disappointed with
Roosevelt. Wilkins flatly blamed him for the failure of Wagner-Costigan
and said that FDR had "placed his stamp of approval on lynching." A
total of sixty-three men and women had died at the hands of lynch mobs
during Roosevelt's first term. All but six were black, and there were few,
if any, recorded convictions.[35]

In November 1936, Roosevelt was reelected in a landslide. And this time,
he did it with nearly unanimous black support. In one of the greatest political shifts since Reconstruction, blacks had deserted the Republicans in
droves to vote for Roosevelt. They did so out of pure self-interest. Actually,

many New Deal relief and farm programs blatantly discriminated against blacks, who were the most destitute and impoverished of Americans during the depression. But the few dollars that they did receive from government programs often meant the difference between having shelter and bread on the table or starvation and life in the streets. Wilkins hoped that the president would now feel secure enough politically to back antilynching legislation: "Roosevelt can afford to be independent of the reactionary Negrophobic wing of the Southern democrats."[36]

The problem was that Roosevelt, still facing a stiff battle in Congress to get the remainder of his New Deal programs passed, continued to believe that he needed his southern allies. Also, since Roosevelt had locked up the votes of most blacks because New Deal programs benefited them, he didn't really have to do anything special to keep their allegiance. Blacks, like most of the poor and the workers, regarded Republican economic policies as bankrupt; the Democrats offered them their only hope.

Beyond that, Roosevelt was also very much bound by the racial thinking of his times. By the mid-1930s, many whites had shed some of their racial blinders and come to realize that blacks weren't stereotyped mammies, "coons," and "pickaninnies," as whites had been taught from birth. Nonetheless, most whites still accepted segregation as the natural order of things. This was true of many New Dealers, liberals, and even some radicals. For instance, the Socialist Party, which had actively opposed segregation as late as 1932, still refused to endorse social equality. And the Communist Party, which loudly proclaimed a doctrine of black-versus-white struggle, still had to wage fierce internal fights (not always successfully) against the racism of many comrades.

In that era, it was impossible for Roosevelt to be immune from racial bigotry. Yet he did manage to hide his racial feelings well. He was careful not to make any remarks publicly that could be construed as racist, but it was clear from his letters and private comments that he believed and accepted many of the common stereotypes about blacks. In any case, whatever Roosevelt's thoughts were about racial matters, the grim fact that Walter White and his colleagues had to deal with was that the president still refused to extend any active help to the antilynching cause.[37]

However, the NAACP had some chips to play. Times were changing. The depression had heightened public awareness of social and labor issues and made more people aware of and sensitive to the plight of the needy. The NAACP's antilynching campaign had also made more Americans think about racial problems. A poll by the American Institute in 1936 found that 70 percent of white Americans favored an antilynching law—and amazingly, 65 percent of white southerners did, too![38]

Dozens of governors, local officials, and labor organizations, as well as nearly every major religious group, had endorsed the Wagner-Costigan bill. Major newspapers, including many in the South, wrote editorials supporting it. White personally saw that every member of the House and the Senate got a copy of a *Crisis* article entitled "A Texas Lynching," which detailed the social and economic causes of lynching. Missouri senator Harry Truman was impressed enough to thank White for the article and assure him that he would look favorably upon the bill.

In December 1936, more than 251 congressmen signed an NAACP pledge to support the Wagner-Costigan measure. Roosevelt's smashing victory had decisively tipped the balance in Congress. Northern and western Democrats now outnumbered southerners by a margin of nearly two to one.[39] White, however, was realistic. He knew that the battle for the bill would be won or lost in the Senate. Though the ranks of southern and northern conservatives had thinned, their strength could not be measured by numbers alone. They were a shrewd bunch with years of political experience and influence, and they still wielded power over the important Senate committees. Roosevelt's support would be critical in breaking a southern filibuster. Everything still depended, said White, "on the attitude of the President."[40]

In April 1937, the House overwhelmingly passed the bill. But the Senate immediately pushed it aside to debate the president's farm bill. When Wagner-Costigan came up again in July, southerners brought out their loudest windbags and began filibustering against the bill.

They were in no particular hurry. They knew chances were remote that Senate supporters could get the two-thirds vote needed to invoke Rule 22 (cloture) and cut off a filibuster debate. Since the rule was passed in 1917, senators had used cloture only a handful of times, partly due to traditions of Senate courtesy and partly due to fear of political reprisal.[41]

The days rolled on, and the senators talked around the clock. They recited poetry, read letters, or just blathered on. South Carolina senator Jimmy Byrnes even killed some time at the expense of White. Pointing straight at White, who was seated in the gallery, Byrnes shook his fist and angrily shouted, "One Negro has ordered this bill to pass." Byrnes's backhanded compliment neither flattered White nor did anything to relieve the mounting anxiety felt by Roosevelt and Senate leaders.[42]

As the southerners' filibuster reached its forty-seventh day, FDR and the Senate leaders neared their breaking point. They were desperate to get Roosevelt's $250 million emergency relief bill passed. When a reporter asked the president to comment on the bill, he snapped, "There [is] enough discussion going on in the Senate." But despite FDR's anxiety, the southerners were not about to relent. One reporter asked Texas senator Tom Connally, the leader of the southern bloc, whether he could talk until Christmas; the Texan huffed, "Why not?"

Nebraska senator Olin Norris, who opposed the bill, warned that "psychological differences" stemming from the debate could have serious longer-term repercussions. This was a clear message to Roosevelt to either stay out of the fray or risk having his future "must" bills defeated. Since FDR had neither sufficient political will nor enough confidence in the Wagner-Costigan bill to call his opponents' bluff, the only solution was for Senate supporters to find a way to step aside gracefully. In March, when Roosevelt's housing and crop control legislation came up, the Senate simply set aside the bill. FDR did not object and did not intervene.[43]

———— •◆• ————

During the remainder of 1938, Roosevelt was spared the need to publicly deal with the lynching issue. But he couldn't afford to completely ignore racial violence. As war clouds gathered over Europe, FDR began to worry more about the fascist threat posed by Hitler and Mussolini. He knew that America would soon be drawn into a European war and that race conflict could damage home-front morale and disrupt mobilization efforts.

Attorney General Frank Murphy created a separate Civil Liberties Unit in the Justice Department's Criminal Division (later renamed the Civil Rights Section [CRS]) in February 1939. Murphy instructed the unit "to direct, supervise and conduct prosecution of violations of the Constitution or Acts of Congress guaranteeing civil rights to individuals." This was a step forward, particularly given the Justice Department's pitiful record on civil rights prosecutions.

Assistant Attorney General Frank Coleman, who worked with the CRS unit during those days, was appalled to discover that before the CRS was formed, the Justice Department had brought only two criminal prosecutions against local officials for federal civil rights violations (except for cases involving peonage, or forced servitude). Further, there was as yet little cause to think this signaled any radical shift in administration policy on civil rights; the unit still had the smallest budget and the fewest number of attorneys (seven) of any Justice Department division (and the number would stay the same until 1951).[44]

White still kept his sights firmly set on Congress and the White House. He persuaded the NAACP board of directors to back another campaign to reintroduce the antilynching bill in 1939. He also released a pamphlet entitled *Can the States Stop Lynching?* to counter the South's argument that state courts were punishing lynchers. He examined each of the eight reported lynchings in 1937 (the NAACP believed there were many more) and found that the outcome was the same in each case: No arrests, no indictments, no convictions. White also went over the seven reported lynching cases in 1938 and reported that the states had not prosecuted anyone.[45]

White moved ahead. He was certain that he still had the votes in the House to get a bill through. New York Democrat Joseph Gavaghan, whose district took in Harlem, eagerly agreed to sponsor another antilynching bill in the House. But the problem was still centered on Roosevelt and the Senate.

Wagner considered reintroducing his bill in the Senate again but hesitated when Connally laid down an ultimatum that "any attempt to revive this bill will result in wasting half the time of the Senate and accomplishing nothing." In January 1940, the House passed the Gavaghan bill.[46]

White was hopeful that this might spur a reluctant FDR to support the bill. And indeed, there was some reason for hope. After years of rebuffs, the president finally agreed to see White in February. FDR probably consented to the meeting to appease Eleanor, who had publicly spoken in favor of an antilynching law. But White's hopes quickly faded when during the meeting, FDR cavalierly suggested that instead of pushing an antilynching law, the NAACP should get Congress to pass a bill authorizing the FBI to investigate lynchings.

An incredulous White reminded FDR that the attorney general already had the power to order the FBI to investigate lynchings. It would be ridiculous to suggest that the NAACP, in the middle of an intense fight over the Gavaghan legislation, should switch strategies and fight for a worthless bill. White probably knew that this was FDR's way of saying he would not help the NAACP fight for the Gavaghan bill.

Without White House support, the House action was nothing more than a symbolic gesture. The Senate Judiciary Committee, after months of wrangling, halfheartedly recommended the bill to the Senate floor, where it was ignored. In October, with no debate and not a dissenting word from any senator, the bill was tabled. Antilynching legislation was effectively dead for the remainder of the Roosevelt years.[47]

———•◆•———

By 1940, Roosevelt was deeply consumed with preparing America for war. Hitler had overrun France. Britain was on the verge of collapse. And the Japanese were challenging U.S. military and economic interests in the Pacific.

At a press conference in June 1940, one reporter, concerned that blacks were becoming increasingly disenchanted with Roosevelt's performance on civil rights, asked the president why he did not pay attention to "social needs first." Roosevelt blamed Congress. The reporter wanted a better answer and specifically mentioned antilynching legislation. But Roosevelt, not about to be pinned down, said that "we are going on it, but you won't get it this year." Only the president himself could decipher this cryptic answer.

Although the NAACP endorsed Roosevelt's reelection bid in November and black voters overwhelmingly supported him at the polls, the NAACP did not forget his capitulation to the South. *Crisis* surveyed Roosevelt's record after his reelection and gave him high marks on social and economic reforms, but when it came to lynching issues, he was rated worse than a failure. He was termed a hypocrite for "enunciating high sentiments of liberty, tolerance, and justice for the rest of the world, but [remaining] silent" while blacks died at the hands of white mobs.[48]

As Roosevelt worried about events in Europe and the Pacific, the domestic front was far from quiet. And NAACP officials, though thoroughly supportive of the war effort, realized that without federal protective legislation, blacks were still vulnerable to mob attacks.

In January 1942, while American troops prepared to hit the shores of North Africa and Sicily and the Allies battled Field Marshal Erwin Rommel in North Africa, a mob snatched Cleo Wright, a young black man, from a jail in Sikeston, Missouri, shot him, dragged him through the city streets, and burned his lifeless corpse. Wright had been accused of trying to rape a white woman. As in other lynchings, there was strong evidence that the local police chief and his deputies had helped the lynchers.

The publicity surrounding the Wright lynching quickly became headline news. Japanese shortwave broadcasters gleefully sent messages to the Dutch East Indies and India stating that the "Sikeston affair" was yet another example of the way the "white man" treated dark-skinned people. It was raw propaganda, but it put Roosevelt in the embarrassing position of fighting a war for freedom and democracy abroad while these same rights appeared to be denied to blacks at home. America might once more look like a hypocrite in the eyes of both its allies and its enemies.

By now, White had given up trying to appeal to Roosevelt on legal or moral grounds to bring action against lynchers. This time, he sent a telegram to FDR that tried to play on the president's war obsession: "Lynching will be used by Japanese propagandists" to subvert the war effort, his message said. White had found the magic formula.[49]

With the war on, FDR was willing to half-listen to White, and fortunately, there was finally an attorney general who would also listen. Frances Biddle, who had succeeded Murphy in August 1941 after Roosevelt appointed Murphy to the Supreme Court, had impeccable credentials. The son of a wealthy Philadelphia family, he was educated at Harvard and was considered an advocate of civil rights and civil liberties. He joined the Roosevelt administration in 1934 inspired by New Deal idealism and a spirit of reform. Biddle considered lynching a mockery of the very ideals for which America was supposed to be fighting. To FDR's credit, he recognized that Biddle could be an asset in his campaign to prevent racially motivated violence from disrupting the war effort.

In February, NAACP legal counsel Thurgood Marshall met with Biddle to discuss possible federal prosecution of the Sikeston lynchers. Biddle was receptive. But he also had to resolve a thorny problem. It was no secret even then that FBI director J. Edgar Hoover would do anything to keep the bureau out of civil rights cases. On occasion, he had even pestered Roosevelt not to issue orders that required the bureau to initiate investigations of such cases. Hoover's reasons were partly personal and partly pragmatic.[50]

Born and raised in the segregated, southern atmosphere of Washington, DC, Hoover was, at heart, a racist. However, he was also a pragmatist. Early in his career, he sensed that the Justice Department and the White House, based on their past performance, had deliberately done everything possible to avoid dealing with civil rights enforcement issues. Hoover was not about to damage the FBI's cozy relationship with southern police agencies or risk the bureau's prestige by tracking down lynchers when there was no real prospect that the Justice Department would prosecute.

The month before the Wright lynching, Biddle, perhaps in an attempt to rein in Hoover, issued a directive to all U.S. attorneys stating that they must have his approval to initiate civil rights investigations. The order actually played into Hoover's hands since it also meant that the bureau would not be required to independently investigate civil rights violations without Biddle's authorization.

In the short run, the order gave Biddle the authority he needed to make sure the reluctant director did not gloss over the Wright lynching. White and Marshall also did their part in this regard, sending Roosevelt a detailed memo that spelled out legal procedures and precedents for prosecuting police and local officials under the federal civil rights statutes.[51]

In May, the local grand jury ignored FBI reports that fully described the lynching and named mob members, and it refused to return any indictments. Biddle immediately convened a federal grand jury and, at Marshall's request, appointed a special prosecutor. The result was the same. Although the white jurors (who were mostly local townspeople), called the lynching "a shameful outrage" in their report, they refused to indict. Privately, a few jurors revealed their true feelings when they called Wright "a brutal criminal."[52]

Still, Biddle had made a good-faith attempt in the Wright case—a refreshing break from the prior federal indifference toward racial violence. But though Biddle was an idealist who was willing to use federal law to punish racist terrorists, the gnawing reality was that FDR backed him due to the war crisis and sheer necessity. Partly because of Biddle's influence and partly because of his own continuing resolve to prevent any disruption of the war effort, FDR told Biddle to investigate all lynchings. Cautious as ever on racial matters, Roosevelt did not put the order in writing. But it was enough for Biddle.

During the next two years, Biddle tried to get indictments in five more lynching cases. In each case, however, he failed to win either an indictment or a conviction. Ironically, the one case that Biddle did win would have profound and disastrous consequences for future federal criminal prosecutions of racially motivated violence.[53]

———— • ◆ • ————

On the evening of January 29, 1943, Baker County, Georgia, sheriff Claude Screws and two deputies dredged up a search warrant and arrested a young black man named Robert Hall for allegedly stealing a tire. As Hall got out of the police car at the courthouse, the three men began pummeling him with their fists and a two-pound, eight-inch-long, solid-bar blackjack. Hall never regained consciousness and died at the hospital an hour later. When word spread about the beating, NAACP members quickly got involved, collecting sworn affidavits from witnesses (including the ambulance driver) and pictures of Robert Hall's battered corpse. They sent the documents to Biddle and Georgia governor Ellis Arnall, demanding an investigation.

Biddle thought there was merit to the case under federal law. From the facts, it appeared the three officers had intended from the start to kill Hall. By committing murder, they had, in effect, conspired under color of law to deprive Hall of his due process rights. Therefore, they could be prosecuted under federal criminal civil rights statutes. But Biddle was wary. With the Sikeston fiasco still fresh in mind, he tried hard to get Georgia officials to prosecute the lawmen in state court. They declined.[54]

In April 1943, Biddle convened a federal grand jury. After listening to testimony from twenty-nine witnesses, including Hall's widow, the nearly all-white jury (there were two blacks) miraculously indicted Screws and two deputies on three counts of conspiracy.

Biddle tried to increase the penalties for conviction by charging the men under Sections 52 and 51 (formerly Sections 19 and 20). But the local judge claimed that the penalties were excessive and tossed out Section 51. Despite the setback, an all-white jury convicted the three men, and federal judge Bascom S. Deaver sentenced each to pay a $1,000 fine and serve a three-year prison term. For the first time since 1926, white Georgians had indicted white law enforcement officers for a crime against a black.

A month after the Screws verdict, Biddle told a black audience in Philadelphia that the conviction proved the government would enforce civil rights laws. NAACP officials, unaccustomed to this kind of victory, went along with Biddle. Wilkins agreed that "progress is being made in combating the evil" of police brutality. Both assessments were premature.[55]

Screws immediately appealed the ruling, and when a lower court rejected his appeal, the Supreme Court agreed to hear arguments in October 1944. Screws's defense was simple. He contended that he had made a legal arrest of Hall and that the federal statute he had violated was so vague that he did not even know that he had broken it. In effect, Screws turned the statute on its head and claimed that he, not Hall, was deprived of his due process rights.[56]

In May 1945, William O. Douglas, who spoke for the majority, was not willing to declare the statute unconstitutional (although Felix Frankfurter was), but he did agree that the trial judge had erred by not instructing the jury as to the specific charge. Douglas was saying that the men in fact did not know what crime they had committed and were being tried for "an unknowable something." Since murder was not a federal offense, the fact that Hall was dead was not enough to convict them even though the defendants, he said, "had a generally bad purpose." They had to have a specific intent to deprive Hall of his due process rights. Douglas cited the revised criminal code of 1909, which mandated that defendants must act "willfully" to deprive a victim of his rights; if not, there was no basis for federal prosecution.

Judge Frank Murphy, in a vigorous dissent, showed that he understood the disastrous consequences the decision would have on future federal prosecutions of civil rights violators. He feared it would give local police a license to kill suspects even if they had not committed a crime.

Given the southern states' horrible record of prosecuting racist murders, Murphy believed that the decision whittled away at the federal government's power to protect "unpopular minorities." As Murphy put it, states could not find "effective refuge" in federal law. Murphy's words were tragically prophetic. In the future, the case made the White House and the DOJ even more gun-shy about using the two federal criminal statutes to prosecute the perpetrators of racial violence.[57]

———— • ◆ • ————

Racial violence continued to be the one domestic policy issue that Roosevelt could not use his consummate political skills to predict or control. During the summer of 1942, blacks and whites fought bloody pitched battles in Mobile, Alabama, and Longview and Beaumont, Texas. The migrations of thousands of blacks from the South to escape racist terror, combined with the lure of wartime jobs in defense plants, had turned the North into a racial powder keg, too. In Philadelphia and Los Angeles, white servicemen attacked blacks and Mexican-Americans in the streets. FDR apparently was concerned enough about the L.A. violence to toy with the idea of asking Nelson Rockefeller, who then headed the Council of InterAmerican Affairs, to investigate. Nothing came of it.[58]

These disturbances paled in comparison to the much bigger and bloodier violence that erupted in Detroit in June 1943. The violence was touched off when a rumor spread that a black had raped a white woman. Within hours, white mobs roamed through downtown streets, beating and stabbing blacks at random. Scores of eyewitnesses later told NAACP investigators that the police did nothing to stop the violence and in some cases actually joined in the attacks.

Walter White was enraged that the police and local officials had deliberately let the attacks escalate. He asked FDR to make a radio appeal to the city to end the violence. White once again played down race and made his pitch to the president on the basis that the violence would "hamper war production."[59]

FDR did not need White to tell him that. Detroit was the major industrial key to Roosevelt's war plans. He had to keep the tanks, jeeps, and trucks rolling off the assembly lines, and any disruption could be a disaster. As the mobs still roamed Detroit streets on the second day, FDR issued a proclamation ordering the rioters to "disperse and retire" and immediately dispatched the first contingent of 1,000 troops to the city (later, the number would top 6,000).

The arrival of the troops was a mixed blessing. Several reporters observed that the troop patrols were confined to black neighborhoods. When police poured more than 1,000 rounds of ammunition into a black apartment house, allegedly in response to sniper fire, the troops provided the police with back-up.[60]

The violence left more than twenty-nine dead. Marshall rushed to the city to investigate. A seasoned and hard-bitten pro in civil rights battles who had several times braved southern mobs and violence, Marshall was shocked by the magnitude of the police actions. He spent two and a half weeks in the city, spoke with scores of eyewitnesses, and managed to piece together a graphic account of the violence. He bitterly concluded: "Yet the record remains: Negroes killed by police—seventeen; white persons killed by police—none."[61]

Marshall demanded to know why so many blacks had died from police bullets yet not a single white was killed, even though white mobs had burned cars and beat and stabbed scores of blacks. Roy Wilkins was even less charitable in his assessment. He flatly said that the police used the violence as an "excuse to murder Negroes in cold blood." White sent Marshall's report to Roosevelt.[62]

The Urban League conducted its own investigation. In its report, the league found it odd that, with the majority of the dead and wounded black, the police could only manage to round up 200 whites despite arresting more than 1,200 blacks. The Urban League saw no resolution to the problem until the police showed respect for the law.

Having no confidence in city officials, the league asked Roosevelt to keep the troops in Detroit for another three months to preserve the law.

White did not trust city officials to maintain order either and tried to get a meeting with FDR to urge him to keep the troops there for an indefinite period. Again, Roosevelt refused to meet with him. Frustrated, White asked New York City mayor Fiorello La Guardia to act as an intermediary to get his message to Roosevelt. La Guardia did, but FDR still declined to meet White.[63]

The Urban League and White had good reason to be skeptical about Detroit's officials. In August, for instance, the Governor's Commission issued a report that glowingly praised the police for dealing "adequately and properly with law violators" and blamed the black press for "inciting Negroes" with stories on discrimination. This probably didn't surprise many since the four individuals who sat on the commission were the Michigan attorney general, the state police commissioner, the Wayne County prosecutor, and the Detroit police commissioner.[64]

A few members of Congress also were troubled by the Detroit violence. New York congressman Samuel Dickstein thought there was ample evidence that the Klan was behind the violence; he noted that the KKK had recruited thousands of members in the Detroit area. This was, of course, no secret. During testimony two years earlier before the House Un-American Activities Committee, chaired by Texas congressman Martin Dies, Klan leaders openly bragged that they had signed up thousands of recruits around the city.

It was not beyond belief that some Detroit policemen were Klan members or sympathizers. But Dies dismissed the Klan threat. The Red-baiting congressman was too busy with his search-and-destroy mission against Communists and left-wing organizations. Perhaps to silence critics like Dickstein, Dies made a few soundings about conducting a probe on the Detroit violence. But given the congressman's obsession with the Red menace, few black leaders held their breath while waiting for him to act.[65]

With Congress and Detroit officials ignoring police violence and soft-pedaling the influence of Klan and racist hate groups, black leaders wanted Roosevelt to speak out. However, they knew that he would do anything he could to avoid getting involved in racial matters, so they continued to try to turn his fear of disrupting the war effort to their advantage. In Harlem, the Negro Victory Labor Committee drew more than 3,000 blacks to a victory-over-the-Axis rally and petitioned Roosevelt to condemn "the fascist incitement to riot."[66]

The rally had its effect. Roosevelt considered devoting one of his famed fireside chats to the subject of racial violence, but Biddle thought it "unwise" and talked him out of it. Meanwhile, Hoover, always on the watch for the slightest sign of any Communist involvement with blacks, urged Roosevelt to read his 714-page report entitled "Racial Conditions in the

United States." Hoover had spent two years compiling the report, mostly made up of clippings and articles from the black press. He claimed that the black press was a "provocateur of discontent" and blamed it for stirring up racial unrest. Hoover hoped that the report would spur Roosevelt to authorize the Justice Department to prosecute black editors for sedition.[67]

Roosevelt would not, however, go that far. A few months earlier, he had privately reprimanded Hoover for spending too much time investigating Communists while ignoring the fascists. Roosevelt did not mean the homegrown variety of fascists but rather the German and Italian varieties.

Roosevelt also reiterated to Congressman Vito Marcantonio that he had asked Biddle to "give special attention" to racial unrest. FDR was still being purposely vague. But some liberal church leaders and activists didn't wait for the attorney general to act. During a meeting with Biddle, they demanded that he "bring to justice" the KKK and others responsible for the Detroit violence.[68]

Biddle apparently had given some thought to doing that. He issued a circular explaining that blacks had a "right not to be lynched," that lynchings could be construed as a violation of the Fourteenth Amendment's due process and equal protection clause, and that lynchers could be prosecuted under federal statutes. But the language he used was odd. In the Orwellian world of federal civil rights enforcement, what should have been a simple human and legal issue had to be defined, justified, and defended for a reluctant public and White House—because this time it pertained to blacks.[69]

———— •◆• ————

White was not impressed with Biddle's arcane language or interested in the genteel debate over semantics between legal scholars. He wanted action. Since the Detroit riot, he had been closely monitoring the racial climate in Detroit, and he believed that white hate groups were still operating in the city with impunity and with the tacit aid of local officials.

White complained to Hoover that blacks in Detroit were still under siege and said that the director should act to stem the tide that was running high. Probably more to quiet Biddle than White, Hoover tapped the phones of the local leader of the United Klans of America and the state's shrill resident fascist, Gerald L.K. Smith.

White didn't know that Hoover also had other prey in mind. Hoover had decided that the real troublemakers didn't come from the ranks of the Klan but from the NAACP. In January, under the guise of searching for

Communists, he ordered his agents to conduct detailed background checks on all the officers of the NAACP's Detroit branch. Hoover, of course, found no NAACP-Communist link. But the search did accomplish his goal of diverting attention from racist groups. Ultimately, no Klan members (or police) were ever prosecuted for the Detroit killings.[70]

In the end, because Roosevelt and Congress refused to enact antilynching legislation and curb racial violence, FDR's administration left a sad legacy in this regard. While black soldiers died on foreign battlefields fighting Japanese militarism and Nazi tyranny, and while black Americans contributed millions in war bonds drives and loyally supported all patriotic activities at home during World War II, sixteen blacks were lynched in America during the war years. In FDR's thirteen years in the White House, a total of 109 blacks had been lynched.[71]

The death of Franklin Roosevelt and the defeat of fascism marked the start of the "American century." It would be a new era in which American ingenuity, backed by military muscle, would bring peace, prosperity, and capitalist-style democracy to the world. But black leaders were painfully aware that for their people, freedom was still an illusion. The violence directed at blacks, once largely a special trademark of the South, had spread to the North. The migration of thousands of blacks, the growing poverty of the urban ghettos in the North, and the danger of police violence were ominous portents. Black leaders gazed into the future and were not happy with what they saw.

3

Give 'Em Hell

The Truman Years

The young corporal loved to write letters to his wife, Bess, telling her about his experiences in the army. Later, when he became a circuit judge, he continued to ply Bess with funny anecdotes and observations he made while moving from town to town. As the newly elected senator from Missouri, Harry Truman continued the habit. And when he heard a Senate colleague use a "darky" anecdote to make a political point, Truman was sure that Bess would find the remark as amusing as he did.

He carefully wrote out the lines in what he thought approximated good "darky" dialect. This was not unusual for Truman since he loved to sprinkle his letters to her with references to "niggers," "darkies," and "niggahs. " None of this was surprising, for Truman won his political spurs in Missouri, a state that at that time was almost as southern in its racial customs and practices as Mississippi.[1]

In 1924, Truman had paid $10 to join the Klan in order to get reelected as a county judge. He later claimed that when he discovered what a rotten bunch they were, he promptly demanded his money back and told them to go to hell. The Klan didn't endorse him, and he didn't win. But did Truman repudiate the Klan because it was the morally correct thing to do? Or did he think that the Klan endorsement might shadow him for life and wreck any chance he might have for national political office? Even then, Truman, a savvy machine politician, realized the strategic importance of the black vote in Missouri. By 1926, there were more than 130,000 blacks in the key voting districts in St. Louis and Kansas City, and Truman openly courted them during his various state campaigns.

Walter White had followed Truman's rise from local political hack to senator and then Roosevelt's vice presidential running mate in 1944. White preferred to think that Truman had grown over the years. He had not forgotten Truman's reaction to the *Crisis* article on lynching that White had sent him in 1937. Truman had thanked him, told him he had read it, agreed that lynching was disgraceful, and said he supported a federal antilynching law. And indeed, this was true. Truman was one of only three senators to vote for cloture to cut off the southern filibuster of the Wagner–Van Nuys bill in 1938.[2]

With Roosevelt's sudden death in April 1945, Truman become president. NAACP officials wondered anxiously whether he had continued to mature in his political thinking on racial matters. Although White had pledged his personal support to Truman two weeks after Roosevelt's death, NAACP officials were still wary enough of the feisty border-state Democrat to warn that the organization "would resist the wiping out of any gains made in the past twelve years under Roosevelt."[3]

But Truman, like Roosevelt, was also a politician who could count votes. And black voters had grown in numbers, political strength, and sophistication since the 1930s. Blacks had been a key part of Roosevelt's support base. In fact, if they had not voted in big numbers for the Roosevelt-Truman ticket in eight of fifteen key nonsouthern states, Republican presidential contender Tom Dewey would have captured the White House in 1944. Also, helped by the Supreme Court's landmark ruling outlawing all-white primaries and by court decisions chipping away at the poll tax, blacks were beginning to register and vote in greater numbers in the South.

For the first time in nearly a century, a handful of southern politicians were forced to court the black vote. White was quick to pick up on the changing political realities. Even while the war raged, he called a political meeting in New York City before the 1944 elections and issued a "declaration by negro voters." The groups at the meeting hammered out a set of demands that included full voting rights, abolition of the poll tax, elimination of employment discrimination, and a federal antilynching law— White's pet project. This was the price they demanded for throwing their support to the Roosevelt-Truman ticket.[4]

Truman was also extremely sensitive to the fast-changing international political climate and understood that the Cold War between the West and Communist nations would be fought in Africa and Asia. As Truman noted, "We could not endorse a color bar at home and still expect to influence the immense masses that make up the Asian and African peoples." His secretary of state, Dean Acheson, warned that racial violence could also have "an adverse effect" on diplomatic relations with the newly emerging nations, most of which were colored. Acheson, ever the pragmatist, told Truman that the huge "gap" between America's professed ideals of freedom and democracy and its racist practices was making it "next to impossible" for him to sell American goodwill to Africans and Asians.[5]

Many southern Democrats were frightened by these developments. The war had barely ended and the ink on the treaty signed by General Douglas MacArthur and Japanese foreign minister Namoru Shigemitsu on August 2, 1945, was barely dry when southern vigilantes launched a new wave of terror against blacks. Between June 1945 and September 1946, fifty-six blacks were killed and hundreds more were beaten or severely harassed.[6]

Truman sensed that the issue of mob violence was becoming a huge test for him. White wasted little time trying to push the president to act. Beginning in November and on through the early spring, he repeatedly asked Truman to send a message to the NAACP annual conference in June. Truman agreed. There was, of course, no reason for him to resist: It was a token courtesy that even Coolidge, Hoover, and Roosevelt had extended.[7]

Neither Coolidge nor Hoover nor Roosevelt had done much to further civil rights, but the NAACP had reason to expect more from Truman. Black voters had become more politically sophisticated and aroused. They were spurred on by returning black veterans who had fought battles for democracy in Europe and the Pacific and were now restive and more militant. Moreover, the NAACP's membership rolls had swelled from 205,000 in 1943 to 395,000 in 1946. The group now had more branches, as well as more local political leaders and organizers experienced in political lobbying. When White sounded the call for action on an issue, the NAACP's branches could, on a moment's notice, generate thousands of letters, phone calls, and telegrams to the White House, Congress, and local public officials.[8]

In August 1946, Truman sent another small signal that he would do more than Roosevelt had on civil rights. When a reporter questioned him on the necessity of a federal antilynching bill, Truman didn't flinch. He boasted that as a senator, he had voted for every antilynching bill proposed. The events that had taken place on a secluded dirt road outside the small farming town of Monroe, Georgia, a week earlier made it even more gratifying to White that Truman gave the reporter that answer.[9]

———— •◆• ————

For more than a week, residents of the southeastern Georgia town of Monroe had talked about the incident. Some said that Barney Hester, a local white planter, had an affair with Middie Malcolm, the wife of his black hired hand Roger Malcolm. Others said that Hester owed Malcolm money. Still others said that Hester had tried to protect Middie from abuse. Whatever touched off the dispute, Hester now lay in the hospital recuperating from a knife wound allegedly inflicted by Malcolm.

The young black man was immediately arrested and held for several days in the county jail; bail was set at $600. The bail amount was absurdly low considering that a black man had assaulted a white man: This was still considered to be almost a capital offense in Georgia. Malcolm, who couldn't raise the bail money, might have stayed in jail except for Lloyd Harrison. The onetime convicted moonshiner had served time in federal prison. Since his release, he had become a respected farmer. Harrison needed workers, and since Malcolm was regarded by most as a good worker, Harrison agreed to post his bail. In the early afternoon of July 25, Sheriff E. S. Gordon told Harrison to go to the jail that evening to pick up Malcolm; he or his deputy, Louis Howard, would sign the release forms.

At five o'clock, Harrison arrived at the jail to pick up Malcolm. Middie, George Dorsey, and Dorsey's wife, who were close friends of Malcolm's, also went with him. Harrison had recently hired the Dorseys. George had been discharged from the army in February, having served in North Africa and Australia and won the Good Conduct Medal, the American Defense Service Medal, and the Bronze Star for his performance in combat. Coming back to Monroe was a painful adjustment for Dorsey. But he had plans. He would soon marry, work hard, and save enough to buy his own farm.

It was a relatively short drive back to Harrison's farm from the town, and the quickest route was on the paved highway. But for reasons he never explained, Harrison took a secluded dirt road. Halfway down the road, twenty heavily armed and unmasked white men stopped the car at gunpoint. The leader of the group stuck a shotgun to Harrison's neck (so he later claimed) and ordered Dorsey and Malcolm out of the car.

As the kidnappers marched Dorsey and Malcolm off to a clump of bushes, Malcolm's wife panicked and blurted out the name of one of the armed men. In the next instant, the two women were dragged from the car and shoved next to their husbands. Harrison claimed that he didn't see what happened next. He heard one man count to three and then heard the sound of repeated gunfire.[10]

When the sheriff arrived a few hours later, the scene wasn't pretty. The couples were found lying face down, their bodies riddled with more than sixty bullets. A student undertaker at Dan Young's funeral parlor, where the victims were taken, remembered working all night "to build a new face on what was left of the face of one of the women. " With the murders, Georgia had the macabre distinction of recording its ninth multiple lynching since 1892.[11]

As soon as the word of the lynchings reached NAACP headquarters in New York, White fired off a telegram to Attorney General Tom Clark. The Texas-born Clark, known generally as a legal conservative, had joined the Justice Department in 1937 and was appointed attorney general by

Truman in July 1945. White did not have the close relationship with him that he had had with Biddle, but he hoped that the shock of the Monroe massacre would move Clark to take action. White carefully made a case showing that local officials were complicit with the murderers. A few days later, he cited a report he had received that stated the police had ordered all blacks off the streets hours before the murders. He contended that the low bail and Deputy Howard's marriage to Hester's cousin were sufficient grounds for a federal investigation.[12]

Local officials acted fast to cover up the murders. Harrison claimed he couldn't identify any of the murderers and complained to neighbors that the FBI was badgering him to talk; "Why I'm mad as anybody, the way they killed my niggers, I need all the nigger hands I can get."

Sheriff Gordon and the Georgia Bureau of Investigation (BOI) officials insisted they couldn't find anyone who knew anything about the matter. A coroner's inquest, held at the site of the murders while the bodies lay uncovered in the open, found that the deaths were caused by "parties unknown." Herman Talmadge, leading contender for the governorship (he would win with the aid of more than 100,000 votes from Klan supporters), offered regrets that sounded more like a warning. "Nothing can be gained," he said, "by giving equal rights to someone with an artificial civilization."[13]

Talmadge probably spoke for many white Georgians. Given the state's violent racial history, his pronouncement might have been enough to bury the issue. But at the time, Talmadge did not yet sit in the governor's mansion. He was not sworn to uphold the law, and he did not have to answer questions from an increasingly indignant national public. Governor Ellis Arnall, on the other hand, did. He ordered the Georgia BOI to continue the investigation and offered a $10,000 reward for information on the murders. Although Arnall's quick actions showed good faith, the Monroe lynchings were brutal enough to spark a national outcry.[14]

Clark sensed that the case was politically explosive and ordered the Civil Rights Section to conduct "a complete investigation." He had barely gotten the words out when Harlem congressman Adam Clayton Powell took the floor in Congress to demand that Clark call on Truman to send in troops to protect blacks. Clark's preemptive move couldn't stop the flood of letters that poured in from black groups, religious organizations, civic groups, and labor locals across the country. Several congressmen proposed resolutions condemning the violence. The NAACP offered an additional $10,000 reward (eventually, the total would top $30,000).[15]

While the clamor for action grew, Truman remained silent. The National Association of Colored Women lost patience, and three days after the massacre, more than a hundred demonstrators paraded in front of the White House. One of the demonstrators' signs clearly stated what the group wanted: "SPEAK! SPEAK! MR. PRESIDENT."[16]

Other than a perfunctory statement from Truman's press secretary, Charles G. Ross, saying that the president would take "no direct hand" in the investigation, not a word was heard from the Oval Office. For the moment, the president preferred to let Clark do the talking. The attorney general took an unusual step and called two separate press conferences on the same day to talk about the case. At the afternoon press conference, he said that Truman had told him he was "horrified" by the murders and wanted the full resources of the DOJ used to solve the case. Clark also announced that more than twenty-five FBI agents had been assigned to the investigation.[17]

Privately, Clark was frantic to keep events from spinning out of his control while still appeasing J. Edgar Hoover. He reiterated the policy that Biddle had formulated in 1941 stipulating that the DOJ alone must initiate all civil rights investigations. Hoover certainly could not have been displeased. But the Monroe case was a high-profile matter with heavy political consequences. Hoover knew that he was being watched closely and that the prestige of the bureau was on the line. The next day, he announced that he was expanding the investigation of the Klan to seven states—New York, Michigan, Tennessee, Mississippi, Florida, Georgia, and California. Hoover promised that he would turn over any evidence of state and federal law violations to the DOJ for prosecution. What Hoover didn't tell the public was that he had been ordered by Clark in May to conduct the probe.[18]

Less than two weeks later, rumors began to circulate that FBI agents had conducted hundreds of interviews and could identify three of the Monroe murderers. Clark apparently felt confident that a breakthrough was near enough at hand to announce that he would convene a federal grand jury. Truman was also in an upbeat mood and told reporters that he was satisfied the investigation was going ahead with all the energy possible. Arnall, however, quickly put a damper on Clark's expectations when he described the progress as very slow. NAACP officials were more inclined to believe Arnall.[19]

Past experience with lynching cases had taught them to remain skeptical when public officials started expressing optimism about "cracking" a case involving black victims. Clark got a firsthand look at the NAACP's skepticism when he traveled to New York on August 10 to deliver the keynote address at the *New York Herald Tribune's* annual forum on "current problems." During his address, Clark painted a glowing picture of civil rights progress. But in the afternoon, he listened as the NAACP's publicity director, Ollie Harrington, attacked him for doing nothing on civil rights. Harrington didn't let up. He asked why the DOJ and the FBI could diligently track down and prosecute spies in this country and in Latin America during the war but couldn't find any lynchers. Clark, stunned by Harrington's attack, scrambled to defend himself. He claimed that the DOJ had prosecuted 23 civil rights cases and won 6 convictions.

What Clark did not tell the audience was that nearly all of these cases involved violations of the peonage statute. When it came to true civil rights cases, the government's record was embarrassing. Over the proceeding twenty-five years, the FBI had investigated 1,570 criminal civil rights cases and obtained only 25 convictions. The combined sentences for all the convictions totaled only thirty years and two months, and the total fines added up to a paltry $7,950. In the cases that exclusively involved civil rights violations, the FBI conducted 770 investigations between 1937 and 1947 and secured 15 convictions. But even this statistic was deceiving because most of the cases had been brought since 1942.

When it came to espionage cases, by contrast the FBI was a model of efficiency. From July 1939 to July 1942, the government got 54 convictions, with total sentences of 123 years and $35,000 in fines, for espionage cases, and it secured 327 convictions, 664 sentences, and $111,000 in fines for sabotage cases.[20]

Even as Clark was assuring the audience that the Justice Department was making good progress in civil rights matters, the FBI investigation was bogging down. Hoover still had not named any suspects. Worse, there was more violence. In Minden, Louisiana, John C. Jones, a black veteran, was lynched, and his companion barely escaped with his life. White immediately contacted Hoover.

White and Hoover had developed a grudging admiration for each other over the years. White shared Hoover's virulent anticommunism and occasionally passed on information about Communist Party activity among blacks to him. In their letters to one another, each used the other's first name. This was as personal as Hoover would ever get with any black leader.

White suggested to Hoover that he could get better results in Georgia if he used some black agents. He had been urging the director for some time to hire black agents, but Hoover was always evasive. To quiet civil rights leaders, he finally "appointed" his two black personal servants as special agents. White knew this was a cheap charade that Hoover used to stave off criticism: The director was a racist, and he was not about to "compromise" the lily-white standards of his bureau by hiring black agents. Hoover skirted the issue of black agents and assured White that he was committed to finding the killers. White tried to get a meeting, but Hoover put him off.[21]

White grew more impatient for a break in the case. He and civil rights leaders had Truman's promise that the president would act, and the time had come for White to cash in his political chips. In response to the Monroe lynchings, he and other civil rights leaders hastily pulled together the National Emergency Committee Against Lynching. White used the tactic that had become the trademark of past NAACP lobbying campaigns, rounding up influential leaders in business, church, and academic circles to endorse the campaign.

In early September, he asked for a meeting with Truman. On September 19, the president cordially received him and a small delegation of leaders from church, labor, and civic groups at the White House. Eleanor Roosevelt sent a telegram expressing her regret that she couldn't join the delegation but noting that she supported their aims. White approached Truman as an ally rather than an adversary. During the thirty-five-minute meeting, he reviewed the recent racially motivated murder cases and stressed the need for DOJ action.

Channing Tobias, director of the Young Men's Christian Association (YMCA), tried to play on Truman's fear that racial violence would damage America's international reputation. He told the president that he had heard loud complaints about America's racial problems during his recent trips to Europe and Africa. For his part, White wanted a pledge from Truman to support antilynching legislation and pressure the DOJ to prosecute lynchers. He urged Truman to break with his predecessors and not appease southern Democrats.[22]

When members of the delegation were finished, a flustered Truman blurted out, "My God, I had no idea it was as terrible as that! We have to do something." He told the group that "mob violence [is] one of [my] greatest problems." NAACP officials felt more and more comfortable with Truman. Other blacks were not so sure.[23]

Four days after the White meeting, Truman met with a delegation representing the American Crusade to End Lynching. The delegation was headed by radical singer and activist Paul Robeson. Truman certainly knew about the leftist ties of some of the delegation's members; Benjamin Davis, Jr., George Marshall, and Max Yergan, in particular, were well-known Communist Party leaders. At this meeting, there was little cordiality on the part of either Truman or the visiting group.[24]

Robeson was in no mood to exchange pleasantries. From the start, he went on the attack. He demanded to know how the government could be expert at prosecuting Nazi war criminals for human rights violations but "inept" when it came to prosecuting lynchers in the South. He tossed aside all restraint and warned Truman that "if the government fails to do something Negroes will." Robeson strayed far beyond the bounds of political propriety and told Truman to make "a formal public statement" on lynching within 100 days, to be followed immediately with a call to Congress for federal antilynching legislation.

Truman resented Robeson's tone, and he was determined not to be pushed around by him. He frostily told the activist that getting a law "was a political matter" and a matter of timing. Truman then brought the meeting to a close and quickly ushered the delegation out of the White House. But Robeson wasn't finished. In a meeting later in the day with Clark, he used even stronger words. He told the attorney general that forty-one blacks had been murdered since the end of the war and not one lyncher had been arrested, indicted, or convicted. He demanded that the DOJ "use all its authority" to prosecute lynchers.[25]

Robeson's "impudence" in the Oval Office attracted more than a passing interest from Hoover. For some time, the director had been using teams of agents and informers to track Robeson's movements. He told one informant who had sent him a clipping about the meeting from the *Des Moines Register* that he was well acquainted with Robeson's views on lynching. Hoover assured the informant that the information was being made "part of the official investigation."[26]

Although Hoover attempted to Red-bait Robeson, and Clark and Truman fumed at Robeson's impertinence, they all knew that racial violence was a volatile issue that could cause serious damage to Truman's domestic policies and future political ambitions.

With the public furor over Monroe continuing and the FBI having little luck in getting anyone there to talk, Clark begin to feel the heat. During a speech in California, delivered two days after his meeting with Robeson, he tried to shift the blame to local officials for not cracking down on mob violence. He claimed that the DOJ was "handicapped" by weak statutes that made it difficult to effectively enforce the laws. (Clark was partly right: The statutes were too vague, the penalties were inadequate, and the Screws decision had saddled the prosecution with the mountainous burden of proving "intent.") He also blamed local officials for their half-hearted or nonexistent prosecutions of lynchers.

But that was only half the story. The DOJ actually had ample opportunity to step in and prosecute lynchers, but it refused. Even if convictions were not obtained, selective prosecution could be an effective deterrent, as Biddle had shown, serving notice to local officials that the federal government took civil rights violations seriously. Still, the Monroe massacre and the political furor surrounding it convinced Clark that Congress had to take action. A week later, he announced that he would propose his own antilynching law.[27]

Days turned into weeks, and by October, the FBI was still no closer to getting any of the locals to talk. Civil rights leaders stepped up the pressure. By early November, the DOJ had received more than 30,000 letters and telegrams. DOJ officials sought to dampen any expectations of quick action. In a speech, Turner L. Smith, the CRS chief, told the Southern Regional Council in Atlanta that federal prosecutors would have "difficulty prosecuting civil rights cases as long as they had to prove intent." Turner was right, but civil rights leaders were less concerned with what happened in the courtroom than with the willingness of the DOJ to bring the cases to court in the first place.[28]

In December, Clark was finally ready to present his case to the grand jury. The only problem was that he did not yet have enough firm evidence to get indictments. After four months of work on this matter, the thirty-seven agents assigned to the case had conducted 2,700 interviews but had not succeeded in loosening a single tongue. Getting indictments appeared again to be a lost cause.[29]

For three weeks, jurors listened to more than 100 witnesses, including Harrison, testify that they didn't know a thing. The federal grand jury (which included two blacks and twenty-one whites) then concluded that it could not establish the identities of the killers and closed the case. Mostly to quiet the NAACP critics, Clark contended that it wasn't a "dead case" and vowed that he would continue to look for evidence. Privately, Clark ordered the FBI to terminate the investigation.[30]

Hoover was mad that Clark had tied up the bureau's resources only to come up empty-handed. The whole thing seemed to prove his point that civil rights cases were "a waste of time." Hoover privately gloated that the federal grand jury decision vindicated his contention that the federal government had no jurisdiction in these cases. He had always argued that they were simple murders that should be left for local officials to handle; if those officials didn't prosecute, there was nothing the federal government could do. Now, with the case shoved into the dead-letter file, Hoover was free to go after his critics. He wasted no time in attacking the NAACP for "playing up, exaggerating and extorting the facts" to criticize the FBI for its failure to investigate civil rights cases.[31]

There were several facts about the Georgia case that Hoover did not fully explain. If there was no involvement by local law enforcement, for example, how did the mob members know that Harrison would use the side road when the paved highway was the more direct route to his farm? There was also evidence that the sheriff had discussed Roger Malcolm's release time with unnamed visitors to the jail. In addition, the brother-in-law of the stabbing victim, Barney Hester, was the deputy sheriff who released Malcolm and was seen in the vicinity of the lynching half an hour before the massacre. On the witness stand, Sheriff Gordon frankly admitted that he did not intend to take any action in the case, and no one asked him why. All these matters were hardly secrets: They were prominently detailed in the *Chicago Defender* in August. Yet the FBI had apparently decided to let the loose ends dangle.[32]

The *New York Times*, which (like most of the press) regularly fawned over the bureau's "exploits" and had practically elevated Hoover to the status of demigod, marveled at how the FBI, with its "skills," its mastery of the "science of detection," and its "fabulous success in difficult cases," couldn't find one witness willing to talk about Monroe. But the *Times* stopped short of accusing the bureau of official malfeasance and blamed the failure to crack the case on the "timidity" of Georgia's law enforcement community.[33]

Thurgood Marshall was not as charitable in his assessment. During the year, Marshall had kept up a steady drumbeat of criticism of Hoover for the FBI's handling of assault cases against blacks in Tennessee and South Carolina. The Monroe travesty drove Marshall past the breaking point. In December, he unloaded a full broadside against Hoover and the DOJ. He repeated the NAACP's litany of complaints against the FBI and called it one-sided. He also marveled that the bureau could catch spies but not lynchers and charged that it had never taken civil rights cases seriously. Marshall noted that in the Minden lynching case, the NAACP, using inexperienced investigators and limited resources, had produced the names of the lynchers. To Marshall, the lynchings "demonstrate[d] the uneven administration of federal statutes."

In attacking Hoover, Marshall knew that he was treading on thin ice. To avoid getting into a public sparring match with Hoover, he tactfully noted that he had not publicly criticized the FBI and asked for a meeting with Clark and Hoover.[34] Hoover, stung by what he considered Marshall's effrontery, went directly to Clark and demanded that he straighten the jurist out. Clark was now caught between an irate director and a dissatisfied Marshall. He knew that nothing less than a full defense of the FBI would please Hoover. So, in a long and carefully worded letter to Marshall (which Hoover helped draft), Clark took the director's side. He claimed that the FBI had proceeded "carefully and thoroughly" with its investigation and told Marshall that the Justice Department would not prosecute civil rights cases without evidence that proved guilt "without doubt."

This letter was quite revealing. It basically confirmed Marshall's suspicion that the Justice Department handled civil rights cases differently than "routine" crime cases. Clark certainly knew that the evidence in many criminal cases was never ironclad, yet the DOJ still prosecuted.[35]

Hoover praised Clark for straightening out Marshall. Privately, though, he still seethed that "selfish forces" had "seized" on civil rights for "propaganda purposes" to criticize the FBI.[36] Hoover tried to get back at Marshall through White. He reminded White that they had an "understanding" to keep channels of communication open and complained that Marshall's "attitude" had caused a breach. Hoover undoubtedly hoped to create a rift between Marshall and White; perhaps White might even oust

Marshall from his post. White almost took the bait. In a brusque memo, he practically ordered Marshall to respond to Hoover in a "temperate and documented" manner.

White should have known better. Marshall was a no-nonsense veteran of many civil rights battles. He had no intention of knuckling under to Hoover or, for that matter, to White. He told White that Hoover "dodged the point" and had still not answered his questions as to why the FBI could not identify the killers. Marshall bluntly repeated that he had "no faith in Mr. Hoover or his investigators, and there is no use in me saying I do." (Marshall was never one to hide his feelings or mince words.) When White read a memo from Hoover denying his own accusation that the FBI had colluded with local police in South Carolina to cover up a beating case, Marshall shouted, "Bullshit." Privately, Marshall thought that White and Hoover were getting a little too chummy, which he felt was a bad mistake, for it might make White less likely to criticize the bureau's glaring lapses in civil rights cases.

White continued to try conciliation. He suggested that he, Hoover, and Marshall meet to reach an "understanding on both sides." But Hoover did not want a meeting; he wanted revenge. He would not soon forgive or forget Marshall's insolence. He filed the episode away, and from then on, the FBI's files on the NAACP would continue to balloon.[37]

The Marshall-Hoover flap, Monroe travesty, and continuing NAACP pressure convinced Truman the time was right to take more direct action. In December, he signed an executive order establishing the President's Committee on Civil Rights (PCCR). He promised that the blue-ribbon panel of liberals, moderate academics, and civic and religious leaders would welcome suggestions from the NAACP and other civil rights activists on legislation. In his brief remarks before signing the order, Truman specifically said that in some areas, "local enforcement of law and order had broken down." The president had finally spoken, and the committee had its mandate to make proposals to strengthen current federal statutes and develop a comprehensive antilynching law.[38]

The committee members were particularly interested in hearing Hoover's thoughts on racial violence. In March 1947, Hoover was called to testify before the committee, and it immediately became apparent that he had done considerable thinking about the issue. Smiling and unusually amiable, he was a model of decorum. He thoughtfully expressed his reservations about the liability clauses in prior antilynching bills, which he believed were unconstitutional. He also expressed worry that Congress might make murder a federal crime.

But Hoover left the impression that he generally favored an antilynching law, and committee members believed they had found an ally. Robert Carr, the executive secretary of the President's Committee on Civil Rights, dashed off a letter praising Hoover for his testimony. But Hoover was hardly a convert to civil rights. His criticisms, in fact, struck at the heart of the antilynching legislation. But the NAACP still believed that the liability clause was vital and that the law must cover private acts; if not, the law would be too limited.

The committee members would have been less than happy with the director if they had known what he really thought of them. Hoover had done his own bit of checking on the committee, and in a private memo, he had scribbled his very unflattering description of several of them: "Negress," "liberal," "ultra-liberal," and "communist leaning."[39]

While the committee worked on Truman's civil rights program, Roy Wilkins spent that spring lobbying Congress to begin hearings on antilynching legislation. Wilkins also kept the pressure on the White House. Following the acquittal of twenty-eight white cab drivers for the murder of a black cabbie in South Carolina, Wilkins wired Truman demanding that he support a federal antilynching law. By May, more than a dozen bills, some conflicting with each other, floated around in the House. But Wilkins waited for the bill from the White House.[40]

Truman continued to carve out his new role as the "civil rights president." On June 29, he accepted the NAACP's invitation to address its thirty-eighth annual conference in Washington, D.C. The NAACP played it up big: White boasted that there would be 75,000 to 100,000 people in attendance and that Truman's speech would be broadcast to the world by shortwave radio. The crowd was actually closer to 10,000, but numbers were less important than the event itself.

When Truman mounted the podium in front of the Lincoln Memorial on that hot early summer day and addressed the crowd, he became the first American president ever to speak before a civil rights rally. He expressed his outrage that blacks suffered "the threat of physical and mob violence" and promised to make the federal government a "friendly, vigilant defender of civil rights." When Truman finished his speech, he whispered to White that he "meant it." And from all appearances, he did.[41]

The PCCR delivered its sweeping report in October 1947. It called for a comprehensive civil rights bill to end discrimination in housing, employment, voting, and the armed forces. The PCCR also painted a woeful picture of civil rights enforcement. It ticked off nearly every criticism the NAACP had made for more than two decades, including the DOJ's failure to enforce federal civil rights criminal statutes, inadequate personnel, inaction by U.S. attorneys, the DOJ's total reliance on the FBI, and the CRS's lack of resources and ineffectuality. Despite the committee members' infatuation with Hoover, the report also took a swipe at the FBI for not conducting "immediate" investigations of lynching cases. Truman backed the report and was effusive in his praise for the committee.[42]

There was still a problem, however. Although the committee members called lynching "the most serious threat to civil rights," they had essentially bought Hoover's position. They recommended prosecutions of public officials for color of law violations but questioned the constitutionality of certain parts of the NAACP antilynching proposals, declined to recommend prosecution for private acts of violence, and did not endorse a liability clause. Their report also did not propose any additions to the federal criminal conspiracy statutes, Sections 51 and 52. Instead, it recommended increasing penalties, removing the "ambiguity" from the language of the statute, and specifying the violations. Perhaps some committee members honestly thought this was the best way to avoid controversy and not endanger congressional passage of stronger criminal civil rights statutes. But this was not what White had fought for.[43]

———— •◆• ————

The report was nonetheless a major boost for the NAACP, which now had a presidential endorsement and substantial support in Congress. Best of all, it had increasingly favorable public opinion on its side. The barbarism of Nazism had made many Americans aware and ashamed of racial practices in the United States. In July 1947, nearly 70 percent of white Americans supported antilynching legislation. More surprisingly, 56 percent of white southerners believed that such a law would provide a strong deterrent to lynching. NAACP officials had one more advantage, for 1948 was a presidential election year, and the Democrats (and a few Republicans) counted heavily on the black vote. NAACP officials felt they finally had the muscle to push Congress to seriously consider antilynching legislation.[44]

In January, NAACP legal counsel Charles Houston spent nearly a day before the Senate Judiciary Subcommittee lobbying for the Morse-Wagner antilynching bill. This was the only bill that contained all the features the NAACP wanted; the others were too severely compromised to be worth much. It was an uphill battle. Subcommittee members agreed that they had to recommend some kind of an antilynching bill but felt that they, not Houston, should decide what kind.

It was soon clear from the drift of the questions and objections that the county liability provision was likely to be a casualty. Even more damaging, the subcommittee argued that prosecutors had to be able to prove a conspiracy between law enforcement personnel and mob members. Houston tried to make the senators understand that this provision would cripple any law and make it practically unenforceable. He cited the

Monroe case as an example. The murders in Monroe were, in fact, summary executions: The killers had abrogated the authority of the law and the courts and denied the victims their rights to due process and equal protection, which should have been sufficient proof of a "conspiracy." Houston was uneasy as he left the Senate hearing room. He felt that the committee had not gotten the point. But Truman apparently had.[45] The next month, the president told Congress, "So long as one person walks in fear of lynching, we will not have equal justice under the law." He called for "decisive action" against lynching and promised that he would include an antilynching statute as part of his comprehensive civil rights legislative package.[46]

On hearing this, White tempered his enthusiasm with caution. He had seen and heard presidents make similar promises in the past and then renege on them when southern Democrats and conservatives objected. Would Truman do the same and sacrifice principle for political expediency? It was an open question. By the time the president spoke to Congress, his administration was in deep domestic trouble. Truman battled inflation, commodity shortages, rising unemployment, and labor strikes. He was also embroiled in a costly fight with Congress over reorganization.

Truman also contributed to the nation's raging anti-Communist fears. In March 1947, he signed an order requiring loyalty oaths from federal employees and then gave the green light to Justice Department efforts to stretch the Smith Act (passed in 1940) to include making membership in any group advocating the overthrow of the government illegal. The DOJ promptly indicted the top leaders of the Communist Party. The witch-hunt hysteria spilled over into the civil rights arena. Many Americans began to suspect that civil rights and civil liberties advocates had more than a little red taint. Soon, antilynching support began to slip badly in the polls, particularly among white southerners.

To make matters worse, Truman faced an open revolt within his own party. Southern Democrats were threatening to bolt over his civil rights program. By summer's end, his popularity had plunged to near record lows, and his White House days seemed numbered.[47]

At a press conference on March 11, 1948, a reporter asked Truman about his plans for the civil rights bill in Congress. Truman replied, "Congress [can] write its own bill." This didn't sound good to White. The next month, NAACP officials received more bad news: The Senate Judiciary Committee had ignored Houston, stripped the antilynching bill of the county liability clause and mandatory proof, and passed on a watered-down antilynching measure to the Senate floor.[48]

Just when the NAACP's fortunes seemed on the skids, there was a surprise. Truman hadn't gotten as far as he had in politics without learning that you don't sacrifice your base of support at the hour of greatest political need. On July 8, White spelled out the political facts of life to the Democratic platform committee. Black votes were concentrated in the twelve most important electoral states. In addition, black voters also were significant in seventy-five congressional districts and seventeen northern and border states. Truman took the cue. Three weeks later, he signed his famous executive orders desegregating the armed forces and prohibiting discrimination in federal employment.[49]

At the party convention, he grudgingly backed a strong civil rights plank, weathered the walkout of the southern Democrats, and staved off a challenge from Progressive Party rebel Henry Wallace. Three months later, Truman would "give 'em hell" and stun the nation with his "miracle" win over Republican Dewey. In reality, the victory was less of a miracle than it appeared. The Democratic coalition—labor, farmers, Catholics, and big-city ethnic voters—had prevailed again.

The segment that held firmest was the black vote. Seventy percent of black voters in twenty-seven major cities voted for Truman and provided the margin of victory over Dewey in the showdown states of California, Illinois, and Ohio.[50]

———————— ◆ ————————

A victorious Truman kept his promise to civil rights leaders. In April and May 1949, he introduced his antilynching bills in both the House and Senate as part of his omnibus civil rights package. Southern Democrats, still smarting from their political defeats during the convention and the elections, turned up the heat. They still held power in the Senate where it counted. A month earlier, on March 17, they had beaten back an attempt by civil rights proponents to revise the cloture rules and make it easier to kill a filibuster. Even so, there was still a chance that the antilynching measure could pass if the White House would throw its full weight behind it.[51]

But there was no evidence that Truman had worked out any coordinated plan or strategy with congressional leaders to push the bill through. This was made obvious when the House Judiciary Committee, following the Senate lead, rejected Truman's antilynching bill and approved a competing bill that did not provide for county liability and required that prosecutors prove conspiracy in order to convict lynchers.

Even this was not acceptable to southern Democrats. They immediately began beating the war drums and filled the Senate chambers with threats to filibuster. This time, they wouldn't have to fight. Despite a late-hour appeal from Clark to pass a bill and put the federal government in a position to prosecute lynchers, when the bill was suddenly called up for a vote, all it took for the senate to drop the measure was the objection of Florida senator Spressar Holland.[52]

Truman was silent, and NAACP officials once more felt they had been betrayed. A *Crisis* editorial noted that Truman had "merely announced" a civil rights program and added that "it has not been fought for." The meaning was clear. The NAACP officials felt that Truman's promise to support civil rights legislation was nothing but an election ploy to appease their organization and keep black voters in the Democratic camp. Were they right? The answer is, yes and no. There is little doubt that Truman wanted to pass a civil rights bill but not badly enough to risk permanent damage to his relationship with Senate Democrats; he believed they were just too important to his congressional legislation. The NAACP wasn't.[53]

The NAACP's forty-year campaign to secure a federal antilynching law was at an end. The organization had spent thousands of dollars, invested countless hours, pushed and prodded four presidents and dozens of congressmen, enlisted hundreds of prominent citizens, and rallied public opinion in pursuit of one clear goal: to get the government to protect black lives. Their campaign raised public consciousness and forced some state officials to bring more prosecutions and provide better protection for black prisoners. But in the end, there was still no antilynching law on the federal books. A year later, this would have tragic consequences in Florida and force Truman to face the horror of southern violence once again.

———— •◆• ————

By 1951, it was painfully obvious to White that southern terrorists had switched their targets and tactics. They had begun to bomb the homes and businesses of blacks (and Jews) who were active in voter registration or civil rights. Racist terrorists first struck in Birmingham, Alabama, in March 1949, bombing three black homes. By the close of 1952, the terrorists had struck in thirteen states and twenty-seven cities across the nation. There were more than sixty-eight bombings or attempted bombings, forty-nine against blacks.

White met with FBI officials on several occasions and demanded that they investigate the bombings. Each time, he was told that the FBI could find no evidence of federal violations and that the cases were local matters. NAACP officials did not know when or where the terrorists would strike next. As it turned out, the next strike would hit close to home.[54]

Rosa Moore's voice cracked as she choked back the tears. The middle-aged, frail black woman shook her head as she pleaded to a reporter that she had tried to get her son to quit the NAACP. But Harry T. Moore had shrugged off her pleas. He told her it was his duty "to help my race." His mother was not mollified. She was afraid that "something might happen to him." And now her worst fears had come true: Moore was dead. For more than five years, he had labored as NAACP state coordinator in Florida. In addition to leading voter registration drives, he had pressed hard to get the DOJ to prosecute a local sheriff for shooting two hand-cuffed black prisoners charged in a controversial rape case.

On Christmas evening 1951, Rosa Moore had traveled to Mims, Florida, one hundred miles north of Palm Beach, to celebrate the holidays with her son and his family. Other relatives were expected to arrive later. Moore and his wife had just gone to bed when a powerful blast shook the house. The explosion was triggered by nitroglycerin, a substance more powerful than dynamite. Rosa Moore was thrown to the floor in her bed-room. The walls on the side of the house where her son and his wife slept were obliterated. Moore was killed instantly, and his wife, Harriet, was seriously injured and would die a week later. The tragedy could have been even worse had not Moore's three children slept in another part of house; miraculously, they escaped injury.[55]

It was the eleventh bombing in Florida since June. Nothing, it seemed, was off limits. The bombers had attacked churches, synagogues, homes, community centers, and schools. Fortunately, there had been no deaths—until now. The day after Moore was killed, White asked Attorney General J. Howard McGrath, who had taken over after Truman appointed Clark to the Supreme Court, for a meeting to discuss the case. McGrath put him off and issued a terse statement saying that he would take "appropriate action" if he found that any federal laws had been violated.[56]

McGrath, sensing that the bombing case might have political over-tones, asked Hoover to send two FBI agents to examine the site. White didn't wait on Hoover. The NAACP board, in an emergency meeting, drafted a telegram to Truman, demanding that he direct the DOJ to con-duct a "relentless prosecution" of the murderers. White phoned McGrath almost daily, trying to get a meeting. In a *Crisis* editorial, Wilkins ham-mered on Truman. He asked what the federal government had done in the matter and then answered his own question: "nothing effective."[57]

McGrath moved to diffuse the anger. On January 8, he met with White and a select delegation at the DOJ. McGrath swore White to secrecy and then gave him some specifics on the investigation. He apparently hoped to pacify White by making him think that he was being given confidential information.

The next day, McGrath ordered Hoover to make the bombings his number one priority and not to worry about determining jurisdiction. He anticipated that Hoover would complain as usual that the federal govern-ment shouldn't get involved—his stock argument to keep the bureau out of civil rights cases. White was not satisfied. He wanted McGrath to ap-point a special prosecutor and impanel a special federal grand jury. But McGrath was not going to be rushed by White.

The bombings touched off panic and fear among blacks throughout Florida. Thurgood Marshall had wanted to hold two meetings in Jacksonville to protest the killings, but he hesitated after discovering that everyone was "jittery." He asked the FBI for protection. Hoover dodged the request by referring it to the bureau's Miami office.[58]

White wanted Hoover to speed up the investigation and tried to play on their "friendship." He phoned Clyde Tolson, Hoover's chief aide and personal confidant, and wrote Hoover, offering to assist in the investigation. Hoover politely turned him down, but Tolson assured him that the FBI was "working day and night" to solve the case. White tried another angle. He appealed to Hoover's anti-Communist paranoia and warned the director that the Communist Party was trying to "capitalize" on the case and that the NAACP was working to ward them off.

White's ploy backfired and served only to heighten Hoover's already considerable suspicions about the NAACP. Hoover thanked White for keeping the Communists at bay and then promptly ordered his special agent in charge (SAC) in Philadelphia to step up surveillance of the NAACP branches. Apparently, Hoover believed that the Philadelphia branch had been infiltrated by the Communist Party. FBI agents compiled secret dossiers on all the officers and monitored the finances of the branch.[59]

Despite Hoover's promises of quick action, the weeks dragged on with no breaks in the case. NAACP officials were getting impatient. At their annual conference in June, the board of directors passed a resolution condemning the Justice Department for failing to convene a federal grand jury. The board, however, avoided attacking the FBI. In July, the Oklahoma City branch, led by militant newspaperman Roscoe Dungee, had no such compunctions in this regard and fiercely assailed the FBI for its failure to bring the bombers to justice. Hoover was furious. He lectured White that the FBI had spent several hundred thousand dollars and assigned a large number of agents to the case, and he would not tolerate anyone "throwing brickbats" at the FBI. But White wanted results, and Hoover still had not produced any.[60]

In April, Truman fired McGrath for refusing to investigate corruption among federal officials. His new attorney general, James P. McGranery, seemed determined to pursue the Moore case. In October, McGranery told the press that he had found evidence of violations of civil rights statutes and other federal laws. He promised to present the case to a federal grand jury. It looked like White's persistence had paid off when three days later, McGranery impaneled a grand jury in Miami. White expected indictments.

Truman had been keeping an eye on the case. Campaigning in Harlem for Democratic presidential nominee Adlai Stevenson (Truman had declined to run again), he told a cheering crowd, estimated at 50,000, that the quick action by the Justice Department in the Moore case was an example of his "commitment" to combating racial violence.

Truman may have been sincere, but White's optimism quickly soured when the events in Florida took a bizarre turn. In December, the grand jury returned four indictments for the bombings in the Miami area but did not bring any indictments in the Moore case. The jurors ignored the testimony from FBI agents who had worked on the Moore case that clearly pointed to a conspiracy. But even though the Moore murders would remain unsolved, White did not blame Hoover for the failure. Instead, he praised him for doing a "diligent" job.[61]

Although the antilynching campaign had faded into history, the deaths of the Moores and the tightening legal restraints on the DOJ proved that terror was still a dangerous fact of life for southern blacks. Truman was a sincere man who genuinely wanted to help the civil rights cause, but good intentions were not enough. He faltered badly just at the critical moment when there was at least a chance of getting Congress to seriously consider a federal antilynching bill. Also, he did not pursue his own civil rights commission's recommendations to strengthen the federal statutes against racially motivated violence, nor did he order the DOJ to expand the scope of the federal investigations into the southern bombings. These failures only emboldened the terrorists in the South.

White later declared that the NAACP's antilynching campaign achieved its goal of stopping the "mass spectacle" of mob violence. But he noted that bombings, burnings, and beatings had replaced lynchings, and he warned that southern terrorism had not ended but had only gone underground.[62]

Racial violence would sorely test the new president, Republican Dwight Eisenhower. Civil rights leaders would demand that he commit the full resources of his administration to combat southern terrorism and resistance. If he refused, black lives would still be at risk.

4

The Big Chill

The Eisenhower Years

"I had lived for many years among the Southern people and liked them," Dwight Eisenhower wrote in *Mandate for Change*. And there was little reason to believe that Eisenhower's personal warmth and feeling toward southerners was anything but genuine. When the supreme allied commander, fresh from the battlefields of Europe, was busy planning his political future, he chose the South as his second home. He spent weeks relaxing and golfing with his chums at the Augusta National Golf Club in Augusta, Georgia. Ike loved that city so much that friends chipped in and made available a cottage, complete with a fishpond, for his permanent use. Later on, when Ike got restless, up north, he would head to Florida for some deep-sea fishing.

The general, riding the wave of public adulation, was courted by both Democrats and Republicans as a presidential candidate in 1952. When he chose the Republican Party, he was the odds-on favorite to become the first Republican president in the White House in twenty years. But Ike didn't just want to win. He wanted to be president of all the people. To do that, he urgently hoped to make a big political impact in his beloved South.

Ike's Republican strategists and advisers had already written off the South as unwinnable for the Republicans, but Ike ignored their predictions. He was not a traditional politician, and thus far, there was little to indicate where he stood on civil rights. There was, however, one clue. In April 1948, Ike had told the Senate Armed Services Committee that Truman's plan to desegregate the armed forces would get the country "in a lot of trouble" by "trying to pass a lot of laws to force someone to like someone else." Black leaders didn't like to hear that. The white South did.[1]

As Ike campaigned during the summer of 1952, he rarely said anything about civil rights, and when he did, his words were less than assuring to rights activists. At a press conference in June, Ike said that he did not believe federal laws could change the evil in men's hearts. Persuasion and goodwill, he believed, were the only things that could sway people, although it would take time. In September, Ike met a small group of black editors at his Denver campaign headquarters to discuss civil rights. He told the group that he was opposed to a "compulsory federal law" on civil rights.

The next month, at a Republican Party regional meeting in Cleveland, a black Ohio Republican candidate for Congress pressed him about his civil rights views. Ike said, "If I don't protect and support your rights, I will lose my own." Most black voters had heard enough of this kind of double-talk from past presidents and presidential hopefuls to know it usually meant they would do as little as they possibly could on civil rights.[2]

However, Ike's personal philosophy of benevolence and tolerance toward the South quickly paid political dividends. When he finally did go south in the early fall, his Republican doubters were shocked at the tumultuous crowds that greeted him. Ike's personal popularity gave the party a good shot at fulfilling its long-cherished dream of capturing substantial numbers of white Southern votes and making the party a real and perhaps permanent competitor with the Democrats in the region. But the price every Republican candidate since Rutherford B. Hayes had had to pay to get those white votes was to maintain silence on civil rights and keep federal hands off southern affairs. Ike knew the cost.

During his campaign swing through Texas, Arkansas, North Carolina, and Virginia, he did not mention civil rights. At a campaign stop at Columbia, South Carolina, Ike was greeted by a crowd of 50,000. The state's segregationist governor, Jimmy Byrnes, beamed as the University of South Carolina band broke into a rousing rendition of "Dixie." The *Charleston News and Courier* reported what happened next: "Ike had said he was one who could stand when the band played 'Dixie' [to show his southern sympathies]. He and Byrnes clapped through most of it."[3]

Ike's southern strategy also played well in the North, where he generally appeared before mostly white, suburban crowds and made almost no mention of civil rights. The one time he did, his words sounded like an apology: He told a suburban New York crowd that he would not "use civil rights as bait in elections."

But Ike also realized that if he was going to be president of all the people, he would have to speak to all groups, including blacks. So, barely a week before election day, he ventured into Harlem and was met by a modest crowd of several thousand. He spent most of his time telling old war stories, occasionally managing to toss in a platitude about equality and a perfunctory attack or two on the Democrats for taking blacks for granted.

The cool response he received was even more subdued when Ike said that he wouldn't "promise a law" on civil rights. The *Amsterdam News* took umbrage when Ike committed the ultimate racial faux pas and referred twice to blacks as "you people." Truman had visited Harlem a few days earlier. He spoke to a crowd that dwarfed Ike's and blasted the Republican candidate for "touring the South to woo the Dixiecrats."[4]

Ike's strategy, however, worked. For the first time since Reconstruction, the Republicans dented the solid South. Eisenhower won by huge margins in Texas, Virginia, Florida, and Tennessee and carried a number of congressional districts in Mississippi, South Carolina, and North Carolina. In the final tally, the Democratic contender, Adlai Stevenson, carried only one more southern congressional district than Ike (51 to 50). (Despite his generally progressive record as governor of Illinois, Stevenson had been as silent as Ike on civil rights during the campaign.)

Eisenhower's victory was the last bit of mortar needed to cement the alliance between northern Republican conservatives and southern Democrats that had begun in the Senate in the 1920s when the Republicans helped the South block antilynching legislation. In return, Republican conservatives demanded that southern Democrats help them tone down Roosevelt's New Deal programs, which they considered dangerously liberal, if not overtly socialist, tinkering.

But Ike could also count votes. Blacks were still effectively disfranchised in wide sections of the South, and in the North, Stevenson won the black vote in every one of the forty-five cities surveyed by the NAACP. Ike could see he had little to gain and much to lose by openly attacking segregation.[5]

———— • ◆ • ————

Ike's landslide victory gave him relatively free rein to shape the course of domestic policy in any way he saw fit. Black leaders nervously kept a close watch on his appointments, particularly at the Justice Department, for possible signs as to which direction he was going. He immediately moved to scotch the perennial rumors that Hoover would be ousted when a new president came into office.

Two weeks after the election, Ike called Hoover to the White House and assured him that he had his respect and confidence. Ike had asked Herbert Brownell, his new DOJ head, to sit in on the meeting. Brownell, a corporate attorney and longtime Republican Party politico, had served as Ike's chief preconvention campaign strategist. He was generally considered a liberal. Ike wanted Brownell at his meeting with Hoover so that the two men could get a feel for each other since they would have to work closely together.

During the meeting, Brownell praised the director, invited him to his home for dinner, and then flattered him by asking his advice on several men he was considering for the deputy attorney general spot. He buttered up Hoover for another reason as well. He was considering some changes in the Justice Department's civil rights enforcement procedures, and he needed the FBI director's cooperation. Brownell made the first change in January 1953, reminding all U.S. attorneys that the DOJ would act promptly and vigorously on all civil rights violations, whether committed by private individuals or police and public officials. Brownell also authorized the FBI to conduct preliminary investigations in civil rights complaints—a particularly critical move.[6]

A year earlier, Hoover had pressured McGranery to rescind Clark's directive requiring the FBI to conduct preliminary investigations in civil rights cases; the directive specified that Hoover would be "directly responsible" only to the attorney general.[7] Brownell's decision to get the FBI directly involved in criminal civil rights investigations was an important step that could have far-reaching consequences for future civil rights cases.

The decision had an immediate effect not in the South but in New York City. In December, NAACP executive secretary Roy Wilkins had demanded that the DOJ investigate the beating by New York police officers of two black prisoners being held in custody. Wilkins was stunned to discover that the DOJ would not investigate brutality cases involving the New York Police Department (NYPD). NYPD commissioner James P. Monaghan claimed that his department had a standing agreement with the DOJ that allowed all complaints of abuse or violations to be handled internally. Neither police officers nor witnesses could be compelled to talk with the FBI. The agreement gave the NYPD the power to investigate itself and usurped federal jurisdiction over civil rights violations. This policy was not only patently absurd but also illegal. However, Hoover apparently was ambivalent about the policy. He certainly was not unhappy that it kept the bureau out of civil rights cases, and he avoided the always sticky problem of investigating police. At the same time, the policy undermined his authority to determine when and what he would investigate—and this was a prerogative he guarded carefully. In January, McGranery, apparently with Hoover's consent, rescinded the policy.[8]

The public had known none of this. When the news finally broke, Wilkins exploded and called this an "incredible secret agreement." He also reminded Brownell that "it is the responsibility of the federal government to protect civil rights whether in New York City or Alabama." Brownell reacted quickly and reiterated to Monaghan that the DOJ could not be bound by that agreement. He told Hoover that it was the FBI's responsibility to investigate all civil rights complaints, including those involving police abuse.

The New York press continued to play up the story. After a torrent of fresh complaints of police abuse poured in from angry citizens, Brownell hinted that he might impanel a federal grand jury. The controversy quickly spilled over into Congress, and Congressman Adam Clayton Powell, from Harlem, and Senator Jacob Javitts angrily demanded that the House Judiciary Subcommittee investigate. At the House hearings in February, Powell was the first to testify. Although he blasted the NYPD for its "pattern" of brutality toward blacks, he was careful not to step on Hoover's toes. He claimed the "agreement" sullied the reputation of the FBI.

The subcommittee members, hardly needing a hint, gently deflected criticism from the FBI and the DOJ. Monaghan wasn't so lucky. The commissioner squirmed when the committee grilled him on the details of the agreement. He backed away and denied that the NYPD had any secret agreement or any "arrangement" with the Justice Department. In the end, even though the policy was patently illegal, the fact that an attorney general would strike such a bargain again highlighted the federal government's hands-off policy toward criminal civil rights abuses.

James McInerney, who had directed the criminal division of the DOJ's Civil Rights Section under Truman, confirmed that when he told the subcommittee the attorney general virtually prohibited the DOJ from introducing a remote federal authority to prosecute local racial violence cases.

Brownell did not carry through on his threat to launch a grand jury probe, but the committee praised him for scuttling the agreement and promising to vigorously investigate civil rights abuses. Powell and civil rights leaders were generally pleased and interpreted this as a strong signal that Brownell would make Hoover toe the line on civil rights cases.[9]

———— • ◆ • ————

The congressmen were premature with their praise. Brownell's policy looked good on paper, but in practice, it did not translate into more investigations or convictions for racial violence. In fact, the DOJ brought only seven criminal prosecutions in 1953, and these were all exclusively for minor voting rights violations.[10]

In his first year in office, Ike followed his own script on race matters and moved civil rights to the bottom of the White House policy agenda. In his first congressional address, he made only scant mention of civil rights, calling it a matter of persuasion and conscience. He vaguely promised to hold "friendly conferences" with state officials to speed up desegregation.

Later in the year, Ike's southern tilt seemed very obvious at a White

House dinner. Earl Warren was a special guest that night. Warren, who had recently been appointed to the Supreme Court and was in the midst of deliberations over the Brown school desegregation case, found himself sitting next to attorney John Davis, who was arguing the case for segregation. During the dinner, Ike repeatedly called Davis "a great man." When the guests were going for coffee afterward, Ike, speaking off the cuff, told Warren that he could understand why southerners would want to see that "their sweet little girls are not required to sit in school alongside some big black buck." The scent of magnolias hung heavy in the air at the White House that night.[11]

In the first months of 1954, Ike continued to stay far removed from the growing school desegregation battle. But he made a brief appearance in March at an NAACP legislative conference, where he delivered a short address praising the organization and tossed in a revealing line—that the White House would enforce civil rights only "wherever federal authority clearly extends." Ike had boxed civil rights into the narrowest limits.[12]

He could not, however, avoid getting caught in the swirling storm of national events. When the Supreme Court in May ruled unanimously to outlaw school segregation, southern governors expressed open defiance from their statehouses and on the streets. Within the year, White Citizens' Council chapters had sprung up throughout the South, claiming thousands of members. The members were businessmen, elected officials, and professionals—all "solid" citizens. They hid behind the facade of respectability and swore to use legal tactics to stop integration.

Others took another tack. They understood that racial terrorism would not be prosecuted and believed that any black who took the Supreme Court decision seriously and tried to exercise his or her rights would be a target, as the NAACP soon discovered.[13]

————— • ◆ • —————

It was difficult to find many blacks or whites in Humphreys County, Mississippi, who didn't like Reverend Herbert Lee, an amiable man. He was a familiar sight rushing about on Sundays as he preached at four separate churches. But Lee's stock dropped fast with many whites when the NAACP appointed him as its local director. The White Citizens' Council reportedly added Lee's name and those of two other local blacks to its list of individuals "to be made examples of."

Lee's first job with the NAACP was to get as many blacks registered to vote as possible—which he knew was a risky task. No one could even remember when blacks had last voted in the county. Whites kept it that way because blacks outnumbered them. In Humphreys, as in most Mississippi counties, whites had an iron grip on all elected offices, including sheriffs, court officers, and registrars. They also controlled the land and businesses. And any blacks who tried to register would quickly find themselves without jobs or their businesses without supplies; they were also likely to receive a warning to get out of the county or else. Black votes threatened white political domination.

Lee had to set an example. He knew that the only way to break the cycle of fear that trapped the county's blacks was to register and vote himself. He did. Respected and trusted by blacks, Lee finally persuaded some to take a chance and register. But he never got the opportunity to take them to the polls. Late in the afternoon as he left church and started for home, a car swerved next to him, and three shotgun blasts shattered the afternoon calm.

Bystanders said the car was filled with white men. When Lee died a few minutes later on the way to the hospital, he became the first lynching victim in the state since 1949. Within hours after the news of his death was released, Wilkins fired off a telegram to Mississippi governor E. B. Hunt. The telegram was merely political protocol. Wilkins, who had taken over as executive secretary of the NAACP after White's retirement, knew what to expect from the governor, and Hunt didn't disappoint him.[14]

The governor treated the murder as a joke. He told state officials that he had been "besieged" by NAACP telegrams and bragged that he had never answered one of them. While Hunt clowned and joked over the Lee murder, Wilkins demanded that Civil Rights Section chief A. B. Caldwell investigate. Caldwell told Wilkins that he would decide after "studying" the FBI report.[15]

Wilkins was not satisfied. Sensing that he was about to hit another official brick wall, he promptly went over Caldwell's head and wired Brownell. He cited the pattern of intimidation and harassment of blacks in the county that led to the Lee murder, blaming the death on the "indifference of local law enforcement." He repeated his demand that the Justice Department take action.[16]

At the NAACP's annual conference in June, Wilkins escalated the attack. He charged that the Lee murder was not just a simple racial murder but also part of a conspiracy by both Republicans and Democrats to disenfranchise blacks and stifle civil rights proposals. Plot or no plot, Wilkins still wanted Brownell to take action.

In July, Wilkins traveled to Washington to personally deliver a petition to Warren Olney III, chief of the CRS Criminal Division, demanding a stop to the violence. Olney promised Wilkins that if he found any violations, he would take "appropriate action."[17]

Wilkins knew that without Brownell's consent, there was virtually no chance that the DOJ would investigate the Lee murder. Wilkins did, however, manage to wring a minor concession from Brownell. In September, Brownell announced that the CRS had found evidence that Mississippi officials had engaged in "harassment" of black voter registrants. Brownell seemed to weigh the possibility of bringing suits but quickly dropped the idea. By failing to heed Wilkins's warning about the mounting terror, Brownell soon found himself drawn deeper into the vortex of Mississippi violence.[18]

————— • ◆ • —————

In August 1955, fourteen-year-old Emmet Till had traveled from Chicago for a summer visit with his grandparents in Money, Mississippi. The young man, who undoubtedly didn't know the customs in the town, allegedly whistled at a white woman. It was a fatal mistake. Till was soon abducted from his home at gunpoint by two white men. His badly mutilated body was found three days later floating in the Tallahatchie River near Greenwood.[19]

As soon as the story broke, the *Chicago Defender* wired Hoover and demanded a federal probe. The director told the *Defender* that no federal law was violated. When Till's body was shipped back to Chicago, thousands of blacks filed silently past the open coffin. With the Till case quickly turning into a cause célèbre nationally, local and state politicians in Illinois felt the heat from black voters. Chicago mayor Richard Daley and Illinois governor William Stratton made inquiries of Brownell about a DOJ probe, and Senator Paul Douglas reminded the press that he had introduced an antilynching bill in the Senate. When the French press carried some articles on the murder, *Crisis* noted that "crimes like this imperil the position of the U.S."[20]

When two men were arrested and indicted for murder, many whites and blacks breathed sighs of relief. It appeared that finally justice would be done. The *New York Times* hailed the indictment as a sign that "the people of Mississippi are against this form of murder." But ultimately, an all-white jury acquitted the alleged murderers, and blacks were outraged. The acquittal triggered mass demonstrations, rallies, and a flood of calls and telegrams to the White House imploring Ike to act. He was silent.

Wilkins demanded that the DOJ send a "team" (presumably of law enforcement personnel) to bring the lynchers to justice. Veteran civil rights and trade union leader A. Philip Randolph wired Brownell, demanding a DOJ probe.[21] Hoover was the next target. At an NAACP regional conference in Baltimore at the end of September, branch leader T.R.M. Howard angrily asked "why the FBI can't seem to solve a crime where a black is involved." It was unlikely that he would have risked openly attacking Hoover without Wilkins's and Marshall's blessing. Howard warmed up to the attack and demanded that Hoover and Brownell appear before a tribunal of black leaders and explain why there were no arrests.

To Hoover, Howard was another NAACP official who had gotten "uppity" and needed to be straightened out. Hoover sent Marshall a polite letter ticking off the cases that the FBI had successfully investigated, including the Moore case, and he reminded Marshall that the number of lynchings had dropped during the past decade. He implied that the FBI was responsible for this decline.

Behind the scenes, Hoover dropped the facade of sweetness and light and ordered another investigation of the NAACP under the guise of searching for Communist links. This time, Hoover tried to rope army intelligence into his scheme by pretending that the NAACP posed an internal threat to security.[22]

Hoover was not the only administration official worried about southern violence. Another official, E. Frederick Morrow, was caught squarely in the middle. Ike had tapped the one-time NAACP branch coordinator a year earlier to become the first high-ranking black staffer in the White House. Blacks expected him to push Ike to implement a stronger civil rights program.

Morrow was getting anxious. He told Maxwell Rabb, Ike's cabinet secretary, that he had heard blacks grumble that Rabb "was being cowardly" in not taking a more aggressive position with Ike. He also told Rabb that his "mail has been heavy and angry" about Till. Morrow was fighting on two fronts. He had to soothe black leaders while not antagonizing Ike and possibly risking his own career. He therefore told black leaders to be patient and that the attorney general "would act when and if federal laws are violated."

Morrow was playing for time, knowing there was little likelihood that Brownell would order an investigation. He cautiously floated a trial balloon past Ike. He proposed that Vice President Richard Nixon or presidential adviser Sherman Adams meet with a dozen or so black leaders at the White House to show that the administration "had a deep concern about this situation." Ike quickly vetoed the idea.

Morrow was not the only staffer who tried to prod Ike. White House aide Joseph Douglas also warned Rabb that the Till and Lee murders proved that "optimum relations with the Negro group had not been achieved." This was a huge understatement. The continuing violence had destroyed any goodwill that Ike had achieved with blacks, which wasn't much. To begin with, Douglas wanted the White House to "take the offensive," silence the critics, and play up its achievements on civil rights.[23]

While White House officials searched for a way out, NAACP officials were also in a quandary. Many blacks, angry and frustrated, demanded that the NAACP take action. Marshall patiently explained that the NAACP was "a private organization" that had no legal standing to prosecute anyone; it was up to the federal government to prosecute. He assured *Crisis* readers that the NAACP would continue to lobby the White House and the DOJ to investigate the murders.[24]

The Till case continued to send political shock waves across the nation. Labor organizations and numerous public officials appealed for an investigation. Even Tennessee's Democratic senator Estes Kefauver said that the Till murder pointed up the need for an antilynching bill. Kefauver had little to lose. Already contemplating a presidential bid and with an eye on the black vote, he was an outcast with southern segregationists due to his moderate (by southern standards) positions on civil rights. By then, the whole matter was a moot point anyway. A week earlier, on December 7, 1955, Brownell had written a terse note to Stratton saying no federal offense was involved in the Till lynching.[25]

Brownell later recounted that his "hands were tied" because of a lack of federal jurisdiction since the state had prosecuted the accused killers. This was a questionable position. There was, in fact, no evidence that the state had conducted a vigorous prosecution—supposedly one of the prerequisites to avoid federal prosecution in racial murder cases. It would be more accurate to say that Brownell's hands were tied by politics and expediency, not jurisdiction. He did not send a team to Mississippi.[26]

Wilkins was furious that the administration had "said nothing and [done] nothing." Meanwhile, in addition to Douglas's bill, two more antilynching measures were introduced in Congress. Hoping to use the Till murder as a springboard to launch another campaign for their passage, Wilkins complained that if there had been an antilynching law on the books, "there would have been no doubt as to federal jurisdiction." But antilynching legislation by now was passé, and although the NAACP could find a senator or congressman to introduce such legislation at each session of Congress, the bills were symbolic and intended more as a reminder that blacks still had no real federal protection against violence. Wilkins, in his year-end summary on the progress of civil rights, sadly noted that any progress had been blunted by the murders in Mississippi. He could have justifiably added "and the silence of the White House" to his report.[27]

———— • ◆ • ————

When Morrow later looked back on those years, he reflected that Ike had "missed the boat" on the Till case. But Morrow misread his boss's motivations. Ike hadn't missed the boat; he was aboard and deliberately steering the administration ship on a course away from troubled racial waters. At the same time, Brownell worried about the South's potential for violence and felt that any confrontation was too politically risky.[28]

Brownell believed that the administration should play a more visible role on civil rights issues. Under Brownell's influence and black pressure, Ike was considering civil rights legislation, particularly to protect voting rights. When Ike was absent due to heart surgery in December 1955,

Brownell presented his civil rights recommendations at a cabinet session. They included the establishment of a civil rights division within the DOJ, stronger enforcement penalties under Sections 241 and 242, and an anti-lynching amendment. Secretary of State John Foster Dulles immediately objected. Although he deplored the Till murder, he thought that federal intrusion in southern affairs would be a major mistake and only inflame southern opinion.

Brownell wavered. He agreed that DOJ investigations of the White Citizens' Councils would do more harm than good unless there was solid evidence that they were committing violent acts. He also didn't like the idea of a civil rights commission. In an odd twist of legal logic, he insisted that the White Citizens' Councils would regard such a commission as an open federal challenge. Why he expressed this strange and sudden concern for groups that were barely—just barely—walking the razor-thin line between law and lawlessness was a mystery.

In any case, Brownell stood by his recommendations that Sections 241 and 242 should be strengthened. Ike decided to take Brownell's advice, and with the Mississippi events obviously on his mind, he finally decided to speak out. In January, he told Congress that blacks were being deprived of the right to vote through intimidation and violence. Ike hedged, however, and did not mention either Mississippi or the South by name. Instead, he referred vaguely to "some localities."[29]

He was determined at all costs not to risk a major confrontation with southern Democrats or the conservatives in his cabinet over civil rights. Meanwhile, Brownell searched for ways to get the conservative cabinet members to agree to a workable civil rights bill without completely gutting the enforcement provisions.

At a meeting in February, Hoover and Civil Rights Section attorneys stridently opposed the antilynching amendment. They claimed that the Till murder was a "simple" murder case and should only be prosecuted by the state. Brownell agreed to drop the amendment. As Justice Department officials and cabinet members continued meeting through the remainder of the month, it became more evident that neither the cabinet nor the DOJ nor the congressional leaders would support stronger federal enforcement statutes.[30]

Ike groped for a unified administration position. In an effort to pull his fractious cabinet together, he asked Hoover for a briefing on the racial situation. Hoover had done some digging and had prepared a detailed report that mixed fact, gossip, and petty personal opinion. On March 9, 1956, Hoover told cabinet members there was nothing for the administration to be alarmed about; the KKK, he said, was "pretty much defunct."

Hoover prefaced his remarks on the White Citizens' Councils with the word *so-called*, dismissing these groups as minor irritants and assuring the cabinet that he could find no evidence that they had committed violent acts. He did not mention the Till or Lee murders, nor the fact that the White Citizens' Councils had recruited more than 200,000 members. The number would top 300,000 by the end of the year.[31]

Hoover, livid at perceived insults and criticism from NAACP officials, couldn't resist the temptation to take another jab at the black organization. He painted a lurid picture of conspiracy plots and violence orchestrated by the Communist Party and the NAACP. Hoover also claimed that the two groups were using the violence issue to promote a "rift" between Ike and his southern supporters and cause Ike to lose the election in 1956.

That was enough for Brownell. After consulting with Ike, who expressed his own doubts about the constitutionality of parts of the bill, Brownell announced at a meeting two weeks later that he had decided to drop the criminal enforcement sections.[32]

In April, the administration finally hammered out a compromise bill. As a formality, Brownell forwarded the complete text to Nixon and House speaker Sam Rayburn. He defended the administration's decision to drop criminal enforcement penalties, explaining that the "criminal cases in a field charged with emotion are extraordinarily difficult for all concerned." Brownell didn't elaborate, and certainly neither Nixon nor Rayburn were of a mind to ask him just whom he referred to by *all*—certainly, tougher enforcement statutes wouldn't be a hardship for blacks who were the victims of the violence, or for local sheriffs or public officials who were virtually immune from prosecution. Brownell of course was referring to those in the federal government who would be responsible for enforcing the tougher law.

The next day, when Brownell testified before the House Judiciary Committee, he quickly put the committee members at ease by stressing that the administration would not seek to strengthen the criminal penalties in the civil rights bill. Brownell was adamant that criminal prosecution would not be used "to forestall a violation of civil rights no matter how obvious the threat of violation may be." It seemed he was almost saying that the federal government would not attempt to prosecute racially motivated violent acts even if the state did not.

Brownell assured the committee that the administration was not "proposing any amendments to Sections 51 and 52" because to do it would be "so extraordinarily complex." He was certainly aware that the weak administration position was not acceptable to civil rights leaders. He recommended that Congress strengthen the conspiracy provision of Section 51 by including acts committed by a single individual, expanding the coverage to include persons other than citizens, and increasing penalties when death resulted.[33]

Did he really believe that Congress would do what the White House and the DOJ were too timid to accomplish? It was difficult to understand why Brownell would expect Senate Democrats who waged a yearlong battle to eliminate the weak, innocuous provisions for civil penalties in Ike's bill to even consider the far more stringent criminal enforcement penalties. This was almost certainly a face-saving tactic by Brownell, designed to cover all the political bases. But Emmanuel Cellar, Judiciary Committee chair, took him at his word and proposed an antilynching provision. His motion quickly died.[34]

Even though the White House had at last publicly committed itself to a civil rights bill, Ike and Brownell still tried to straddle the political fence between civil rights leaders and the conservatives. Brownell displayed the administration's balancing act on civil rights before reporters in June 1956 at a National Press Club luncheon. He assured the gathering that the administration believed that blacks must be safeguarded from the haters, but quickly stressed that the administration had taken meticulous care not to infringe on states' rights.

Brownell implied that he regarded black rights and states' rights, though separate and distinct, as equally important. But if White House performance on civil rights up to that time was any gauge, there wasn't much doubt about which right the administration would safeguard more vigilantly.[35]

———————— ◆ ————————

It was 1956, an election year. Although there was little worry among White House staffers about Ike's reelection, the Republicans still had a campaign to run. The task for the administration was to determine how to capitalize on the civil rights legislation and woo blacks while still maintaining southern support. The Republican National Committee believed the party could do both. With much fanfare, it issued an overblown, self-congratulatory, glossy handbook touting the achievements of the administration on civil rights. It hailed Ike's Negro appointments, his support of desegregation in the District of Columbia, and the civil rights bill. The handbook ended with the exaggerated declaration that civil rights progress during Ike's first four years was "unprecedented in American history."

The RNC distributed the handbook to all party workers for use in the campaign. The message it carried was good enough to sway Adam Clayton Powell to break ranks with the Democrats and campaign for Ike. The Republicans got another big boost in July when the House passed the civil rights bill by a wide margin.[36]

Ike moved to shore up his Southern flank. In September, he told reporters that he would not interfere in court-ordered school desegregation cases in the South. He had already come under some pressure from civil rights leaders to take a firmer stand on this issue. White mobs, goaded by local officials, had closed schools and defied federal court integration orders in Clinton, Tennessee, and Texarkana and Mansfield, Texas. When reporters pressed him, Ike sternly lectured that "when police power is exercised habitually by the federal government we are in a bad way."

The president seemed to imply that the federal government had been abusing its police power, which was hardly the case. Yet no one in the press corps asked Ike to cite examples of where or how the federal government had intervened to implement desegregation. He seemed confident that states could maintain law and order and protect black schoolchildren; he had not yet seen any evidence to the contrary. As events would soon show, Ike's optimism would soon be a thing of the past.[37]

Ike knew where the votes were. In late fall, he made a campaign swing through Virginia and Florida. One reporter noted that Eisenhower greeted crowds with his best homespun southern drawl—"ya all" and "ya folks." He mentioned civil rights only once and very briefly, in Miami; the relatively liberal political climate of that city made this fairly safe. He told an airport audience that equality had "to be achieved in the hearts of men, rather than the legislative halls." This was vintage Ike.[38]

The White House's dual-front strategy paid handsome dividends in November. Ike trounced Stevenson again, winning in forty-one of forty-eight states, including four southern states. And to the relief of RNC strategists, he registered a 5 percent increase in the number of black votes as compared to 1952.[39]

The administration had little time to bask in its decisive victory, for there was still much unfinished business in Congress. Senate Democrats had bottled up the civil rights bill for months following House passage, and they were demanding that the administration further water down key provisions. Black leaders were also worried about escalating southern violence. Each new court-ordered school desegregation decision brought more bombings, burnings, beatings, and assaults against blacks.

In January, sixty-nine black leaders from ten southern states held an emergency meeting in Atlanta to discuss the violence. The participants assigned Dr. Martin Luther King the task of presenting their two demands to Ike and Brownell. King had been propelled to national fame after leading a successful boycott of Montgomery buses. Now he sent two urgent telegrams to Brownell and Ike. He wanted Ike to make a major speech on civil rights in the South, and he wanted to meet with Brownell to "clarify" the DOJ's "responsibility" to prevent violence. Neither Ike nor Brownell seemed to be in much of a rush to respond.[40]

Three weeks later, King got a reply not from Ike or Brownell but from Warren Olney, who presumably spoke for both men. In a terse note, Olney ruled out a White House meeting, saying it would be neither helpful nor appropriate. Instead, he referred King to Ike's January 10 congressional speech in which he made a brief pitch for passage of the civil rights bill. According to Olney, Ike felt that he had said all that needed to be said. As for the DOJ's responsibility, Olney simply reiterated that the federal government had "no police power" to halt the violence and that King and civil rights leaders should look to local authorities for protection.[41]

Civil rights again was receding into the shadows in the White House—but not fast enough for some. Ike was coming under increasingly intense attacks from his white southern friends. The man with whom he had joyously sung "Dixie" in 1952 was among the harshest critics. James Byrnes, although no longer governor of South Carolina, believed that he spoke for most southern politicians and suggested that Ike's support of the civil rights bill was tantamount to a betrayal of the South.

Ike was doubly perplexed by Byrnes's attack. He considered the former governor a friend and believed that there were enough moderates in the South who were willing to go along with the bill's modest proposals. Although Ike gamely defended the bill, his reply sounded almost apologetic. He assured Byrnes that he had "no intent to recommend punitive legislation" or "to persecute anyone."[42]

Morrow and Val Washington, a chief Republican consultant on civil rights, struggled to prevent what Washington called a further White House "retreat" on the bill. Finally, after marathon debates and southern threats to filibuster, the Senate passed the bill in August. The final bill was largely brokered by Texas senator Lyndon Johnson. Although he had reinvented himself as a racial "moderate" and managed to win some southern support for civil rights, he still worked hard to gut the provisions from the bill that permitted the federal government to bring voter discrimination suits. In fact, the bill was so weak that the NAACP and King briefly considered asking Ike to veto it. In the end, however, they grudgingly resigned themselves to it; it was the best they could get for the moment.[43]

Ike and Brownell, on the other hand, were pleased with the bill. In fairness, the civil rights bill was a signal accomplishment that broke almost a century of impasse on civil rights. The fact that Ike and Brownell even fleetingly considered strengthening the two federal criminal civil rights enforcement statutes was also significant. However, there is no evidence that either man ever seriously considered including the statutes in the bill.[44]

Still, the effort they made paved the way for tougher civil rights legislation in the future. But Ike and Brownell were prepared to put the issue to rest, with hopes that racial peace would return. Unfortunately, they did not reckon on a defiant governor in Little Rock, Arkansas, who had his own ideas about what the federal government could and could not do on civil rights.

While the Senate wrestled with the civil rights bill in July, Arkansas governor Orville Faubus announced that he would defy a federal court order to desegregate Little Rock's Central High School. Whether he intended to or not, Faubus in one stroke made a shambles of Ike's carefully measured policy of racial persuasion and tolerance toward the South. Nightly newsreels of howling white mobs roaming the streets attacking blacks and jeering at black schoolchildren were beamed across the world. The naked, ugly violence of the South had spilled over into open defiance of the federal government.

As the situation worsened, Ike was torn. When civil rights leaders demanded that he send in federal troops to halt the violence, Ike at first tried to ignore them. At a press conference on July 17, Merriman Smith of United Press International (UPI) pressed him on the troop issue. Eisenhower testily told him that he "couldn't imagine any set of circumstances that would ever induce me to send federal troops into any area to enforce the orders of a federal court."[45]

Faubus, realizing that he had backed himself into a corner, groped for a way to save face. He asked for a meeting with Ike, and Ike agreed. In September, the president invited Faubus to his summer residence at Newport, Rhode Island. While the standoff continued, Brownell worked hard behind the scenes to craft a workable solution without using federal troops. The meeting in Newport was cordial, but Ike told Faubus that he would have to obey the federal court order. The meeting ended with Ike thinking that they had reached an understanding, but Faubus had no intention of knuckling under to federal pressure, at least not publicly. The impasse continued.[46]

Federal judge Ronald Davies seemed unsure on how to deal with the truculent governor. Instead of issuing an injunction and declaring Faubus in contempt if he violated it, Davies asked the DOJ to submit additional evidence and briefs to support its case. The delays were costly. The mobs continued to swell, and Faubus and other local officials refused to clamp down on the lawlessness.[47]

Brownell also didn't help matters. When Olney ordered the FBI to make on-the-spot arrests, an enraged Hoover pressed Brownell to rescind the order. He did. However, Brownell told Ike that there were ample grounds to pursue criminal action against Faubus, but Ike said no.[48]

Little Rock had turned into an international public relations disaster for the White House. The Russians were having a propaganda field day, rubbing America's nose in its racial problems before Africans and Asians. In a nationally televised speech, Ike noted that "our enemies are gloating over this incident and using it everywhere to misrepresent our whole nation." Yet the thought of using troops in Little Rock went against the very heart of his personal and political beliefs.[49]

As the crisis escalated, he and Brownell spent many hours huddled together, reviewing strategies. Morrow, who sat in on the meetings during those tense hours, recorded the agony Ike went through as he tried to find a way out of the mess. After Little Rock mayor Woodrow Mann confessed that he could not keep order and practically begged Ike to send in the troops, the president finally admitted that he had run out of options. White House adviser Sherman Adams remembered later that Ike called the decision to use troops at Little Rock "the most repugnant act in all his eight years in the White House."[50]

Despite his deep reservations, Ike did call in the troops, and black leaders were elated. Both King and Thurgood Marshall, merciless critics of the president's go-slow approach to civil rights, showered him with lavish praise. In his reply, Ike treated them almost like two lifelong pals, and the men congratulated each other for their success. But Marshall and King read more into the administration's actions then was really warranted.[51]

Ike simply did his duty. State officials had not only broken federal laws but also openly flaunted their defiance while the world watched. Not to act would have been a gross violation of the Constitution and of the president's oath of office. No matter what his personal beliefs, Ike had built his entire professional career as soldier and statesman on a strict obedience to law and duty to country. If Marshall and King had any illusions that Ike had changed, the president quickly laid them to rest.

The following May, in a luncheon address before the National Newspaper Publishers' Association, a black group, Ike advised blacks to be patient and "not to expect any revolutionary cures" for racial problems. He shoved the hand of the racial clock back a half century and paraphrased the conservative black educator Booker T. Washington when he told blacks to get "more and better education [rather] than simply rely on the letter of the law." The applause that greeted his remarks was restrained. Randolph, who spoke after Ike, was in no mood to be polite. He called the civil rights bill "toothless" and accused the White House of having "no will to enforce it."[52]

Wilkins and King felt that Little Rock had opened up opportunities to get more concessions from the White House. Wilkins had been trying since 1953 to get a meeting with Ike (as King and Randolph had been for more than a year). Finally in June, the White House agreed. Before the meeting, King, Wilkins, Randolph, and National Urban League director Lester Granger drafted a basic action plan to present to Ike. They were not overly optimistic; they knew the chances were slim that Ike would immediately commit to stronger civil rights legislation.

They latched onto Morrow's earlier suggestion that Ike call a conference of black and white leaders to seek ways to prevent more violent resistance to Supreme Court desegregation rulings. The meeting was not a placid affair. At one point, when Wilkins told Ike that blacks were "frustrated and angry," his words sounded like a veiled threat. Ike was having none of it. He bluntly told the group that he would not sponsor a meeting because he "didn't think much would really come of one."[53]

With the memory of Little Rock receding, Ike was content to say little about civil rights. But black leaders were plainly worried about more violent outbreaks. NAACP officials wanted the president to direct the DOJ to use the federal civil rights criminal statutes to prosecute terrorists who bombed and burned black churches and community centers. A *Crisis* editorial demanded, "We now want to see what the Eisenhower administration will do."[54]

As it turned out, it would not do much. The Justice Department followed the White House lead and also locked its gears in reverse. The CRD backed away from a policy directive Brownell issued in 1954 ordering it to investigate all civil rights complaints from any source, including newspapers. Under the new policy, CRD attorneys could not investigate unless they received a formal complaint. Although the DOJ took complaints from private citizens, those from public officials were given more weight. In a separate memo, the Civil Rights Division announced that it would not authorize the FBI to investigate complaints if there was even the remotest chance that the state involved would take action.[55]

This was probably meant to placate Hoover, who still wanted nothing to do with civil rights cases. In reality, the directive was almost meaningless since Hoover had, for all practical purposes, never complied with Brownell's 1953 directive ordering the FBI to investigate all civil rights complaints. In fact, Hoover did not even bother to conceal his insubordination. The bureau's annual reports for the prior three years had stated that "full investigations are not conducted in civil rights cases unless the Department or a United States Attorney so directs."[56]

The DOJ, despite its retreat, and Hoover's obstructionism, became a casualty of its own self-determined limits. In June, local police in Dawson, Georgia, went on a rampage, murdered two blacks, wounded two others, and beat another. The case fell into the lap of the new attorney general, William Rogers. Rogers had succeeded Brownell, who resigned immediately after Little Rock when it became clear that he had lost credibility with southern officials: They blamed him, not Ike, for sending in the troops. In his post as assistant attorney general, Rogers was generally regarded as the DOJ's point man on civil rights. He ordered Hoover to investigate the Dawson incident.

The director obliged and dutifully turned over a detailed report indicating police wrongdoing. But when Rogers sought indictments from a federal grand jury, he immediately faced the old bugaboo of trying to get white jurors to indict white men (especially police) who murdered blacks. When jurors in Dawson refused to do so, civil rights leaders feared that this would make DOJ officials even more reluctant to bring future prosecutions. Their fears weren't totally unfounded. Justice Department attorneys privately admitted that the case made them even more pessimistic about getting indictments in civil rights cases, and again, they advised that prosecution be left to state officials. This would be no comfort to the family and friends of a young black ex-serviceman in Poplarville, Mississippi.[57]

———— •◆• ————

In April 1959, Mack Charles Parker, accused of raping a white woman, was seized from the jail in Poplarville by a small group of armed white men. Ten days later, highway patrolmen and FBI agents fished his bloated, mangled corpse out of the Pearl River near Bogalusa, Louisiana. Parker had been shot and beaten. The incident touched off a national outcry.

The case seemingly met all the requirements for federal action. Parker was in police custody when he was kidnapped, and there was strong evidence that he had been transported across state lines. With the press churning out stories on the case and the NAACP demanding a federal probe, Ike had to move. In a telegram to Mississippi governor James Coleman, he promised "swift apprehension" of the lynchers and assured Coleman that he was receiving regular reports on the matter from Rogers.[58]

With Ike's approval, the Justice Department directed Hoover to conduct an investigation. Coleman, who was considered somewhat of a moderate by Mississippi standards, was embarrassed by the national attention and agreed to fully cooperate with federal authorities. But Coleman had other motives: He wanted to stave off any greater federal presence in his state. In later testimony before the Senate Judiciary Committee, Coleman admitted that he wanted "to keep the state from being engulfed in a torrent of federal civil rights legislation."[59]

Coleman specifically had in mind an antilynching measure proposed by Jacob Javitts that would increase penalties for mob violence. The horror of the Parker case had increased the sentiment in the House and Senate for the amendment, but would Ike endorse it? When journalist Robert G. Spivak put the question to him at a press conference, it was apparent that the president's laissez-faire approach to the South hadn't changed. He told Spivak that he didn't know how the law could be strengthened. He was confident that the state "would find some way" to punish the guilty. How, when, and where that punishment would come about was a subject Ike left to Spivak and others to ponder. By this point, Wilkins's patience with Ike had completely run out. In a speech, he angrily said that blacks felt "bitterness and anger" toward the justice system and the government's failure to protect black lives.[60]

If Wilkins was angry at Ike for refusing to endorse an antilynching measure, he was even less happy with events unfolding in Mississippi. Within three weeks of the Parker killing, the FBI had broken the case. Agents had identified Parker's assailants, knew how the murder was committed, had solid evidence that the murderers had indeed crossed state lines, and could make a good case that law enforcement officers had conspired with the killers. This should have been enough to bring federal charges against the killers under Sections 241 and 242 and the Lindbergh kidnapping law. After the FBI turned over its findings to the DOJ, nearly everyone from Hoover to the suspected lynchers expected that Rogers would seek indictments. But the DOJ claimed that it could find no evidence that federal laws had been violated. In an opinion that would have been comic if not for the tragedy involved, Rogers claimed that the Lindbergh Act did not apply since it referred to "persons" being kidnapped and, from the available evidence, it appeared that Parker was not a person but a "corpse" at the time of the abduction.[61]

Rogers, apparently lulled by Governor Coleman's cooperative attitude throughout the investigation, gave the evidence to the state for prosecution. Ike was satisfied. In a brief comment to the press, he stated that the DOJ had taken the appropriate action. Rogers would soon learn once again the hard truth about southern justice, for the local grand jury refused to indict the men. Rogers said he was "revolted and stunned" by the decision. But Wilkins wasn't, and he promptly challenged the federal government to not stand "idle" on the lynching. Rogers, feeling the heat, announced that the DOJ would convene a federal grand jury to secure federal indictments.[62]

In presenting evidence to a federal grand jury composed of local whites in Mississippi, Rogers was asking southern whites to indict other whites for killing a black. The jurors refused and returned a "no bill" against the men. The only consolation for Parker's family and those concerned about justice was that the alleged rape victim testified that she could not positively identify Parker as her attacker. If Parker had gone to trial, he probably would have been acquitted on the evidence or lack thereof. But Parker, like hundreds of other black men, would not have his day in court. And neither would his alleged killers.[63]

The fallout from the Parker case continued to be felt in Washington. Hoover was miffed that there were no arrests. This did not, however mean that he had softened his opposition to civil rights enforcement, but only that he still saw these investigations as a huge waste of FBI resources. In his annual testimony before the House Appropriations Subcommittee, Hoover said that he had employed sixty agents, spent more than $80,000, produced a 250-page report, and built a solid case against the alleged killers only to see everything go down the drain when the DOJ wavered on the issue.

This only confirmed his unshakable belief that it was a mistake for the FBI to get involved in civil rights cases since they almost always went nowhere. Rogers, however, when asked about the status of the Parker case, told the Appropriations Committee that "we do not have it closed." This statement was for press and public consumption only: The case, in fact, *was* closed.[64]

———————•◆•———————

The Parker case was hardly the dying gasp of southern resistance. Rather, it was part of a much bigger pattern of violence that had gone virtually unchecked since Little Rock. This violence was threatening to tear a deep gash in society and make a total mockery of the law. The Southern Regional Council gave a good overview of the devastating magnitude of the violence, documenting 530 cases, including 30 bombings, 6 murders, 29 persons wounded (including 11 whites), 5 stabbed, 54 beatings, and 1 black castrated. There were few arrests or convictions. The Council blamed the widespread terrorism on the "legislative and executive policies of evasion" in Congress and the White House.[65]

Ike's brand of goodwill diplomacy and "mutual understanding" was a failure. Under pressure, he had relented and proposed a new civil rights bill that mostly targeted voting rights violations. He added an amendment to make it a federal crime to cross state lines to escape prosecution for destroying an educational or religious facility and to obstruct court-ordered school integration.

For civil rights leaders and many in Congress, this was not enough. In fact, the measure was so inadequate that even Johnson and one staunch civil rights opponent—North Carolina senator Sam Ervin, who was prodded by Massachusetts senator John Kennedy—proposed an amendment that broadened the statute to include attacks on most public facilities. Arkansas senator John McClellan and Georgia senator Richard Russell tacked on a substitute amendment to make it a federal crime to resist any federal court order.[66]

The terrorist attacks also strengthened Javitts's efforts to get his anti-lynching measure through Congress. His amendment doubled the punishment (to $10,000 and imprisonment for twenty years). Javitts, a staunch Senate liberal and reliable civil rights supporter, was certainly driven by a sense of outrage, but he also paid attention to foreign opinion. He realized that with the Parker murder, "U.S prestige had suffered a huge blow." When the American image was on the line, this was, for many politicians, a powerful and persuasive reason to become concerned about racial violence.[67]

In any event, the motives of politicians were less important than the results of their efforts. Civil rights leaders welcomed any federal action to check racial violence. They knew that the Javitts measure would face stiff opposition from the same old enemies—southern Democrats and northern conservatives. If anything, the fight would be tougher than ever. The same tired old men had seniority and control over many of the key House and Senate legislative committees. Unfortunately, for example, the Senate Judiciary Committee was chaired by Mississippi senator James Eastland. A wealthy planter and cagey veteran of many civil rights wars, Eastland maintained a hawklike watch for any legislative matters that remotely touched on civil rights or social issues, and he did everything he could to bury them. He lost no time with Javitts's amendment, immediately asking the DOJ for an opinion on its constitutionality.

Deputy Attorney General Lawrence Walsh told Eastland that the amendment suffered "constitutional defects" and that the only way the federal government would have the authority to prosecute cases like the Parker matter would be for Congress to pass a constitutional amendment. Walsh, in effect, was asking the same Congress that refused time and again to pass antilynching bills or to strengthen federal criminal statutes to combat racial violence by passing a constitutional amendment.

This was absurd. Congress members from southern states refused to prosecute lynchers and opposed any federal protective laws as political meddling. They would never ratify such an amendment. But Walsh's ploy worked. He had given Eastland the ammunition he needed. In April 1960, the Senate dropped not only the Javitts amendment but also three other amendments to the civil rights bill that would have added stronger provisions to combat voting rights discrimination.[6]

---•◆•---

As his days in the White House dwindled, Ike increasingly retreated into the realm of foreign policy. He probably would have been perfectly content to hand over civil rights problems to his successor. But as the massive wave of student civil rights demonstrations, sit-ins, and protests spread throughout the South, white resistance escalated. Ike tried to ignore it.

When local police chased and pistol-whipped several black student protesters in Montgomery, Alabama, in March, the police chief threatened to close off the local college. King wired Ike demanding that he direct Rogers to intervene and stop the "reign of terror." King got his answer a week later. At a press conference, reporters asked Ike what the administration intended to do about the racial violence. He nonchalantly claimed that the government had too much interference in private matters. Ike may have been counting his days in the White House, and perhaps he wanted to leave with as little controversy as possible.[69]

In the spring, civil rights leaders were mildly pleased when the civil rights bill passed. Although most of the attention was focused on the bill's voting provisions, the two criminal enforcement titles empowered the Justice Department to apprehend and prosecute fugitives in connection with terror bombings. The law provided for penalties from $1,000 to $10,000 (for death or injury) and prison sentences from five years to life (or even capital punishment). The administration tried to claim credit for the law but did not deserve it.

Ike did little lobbying for the law (privately, he admitted he thought it was too broad). And in his 1959 congressional speech, he made only a vague reference to "equal protection of the laws." In his final congressional speech, he failed to call on Congress to pass any further civil rights legislation. Thus, the laws passed in spite of his dubious support.[70]

Civil rights leaders hoped that the CDR, created in the DOJ with passage of the 1957 civil rights bill to replace the toothless Civil Rights Section, would push investigations and seek more indictments for civil rights violations. But the numbers told another story. In 1958 and 1959—the division's first two years of existence—it did little. It received 2,430 complaints of racial discrimination or violence but investigated only 908 and sought indictments in just 27 cases.

During Eisenhower's eight years in the White House, the DOJ obtained convictions in only 21 cases. Only one defendant actually served a jail term; the others received light fines, probation, or suspended sentences. And the sole jailed offender was sent to jail in Nevada, not in the South. In sum, then, the DOJ's dismal performance was hardly enough to strike terror in the hearts of the perpetrators of race violence.[71]

In his farewell address to the nation, Ike warned of the danger of a military-industrial complex and the threat it posed to individual rights and freedoms. Millions heard his speech, remembered it, and praised it. But one man in Georgia perhaps wondered about Ike's sincerity—Martin Luther King.

Several months prior to Ike's speech, King had been sentenced to four months of hard labor at Georgia's Reidsville State Prison after being arrested on a trumped up traffic warrant and for violating probation. The second charge stemmed from an earlier arrest at a sit-in. Lawrence Walsh had prepared a report for Ike to read that called King's arrest "fundamentally unjust." Walsh wanted the president to order Rogers to intervene with local police and secure King's release.[72]

With Kennedy and Nixon locked in a tight election race and thousands of black votes on the line, Walsh thought this was a golden political opportunity for the Republicans. But Ike didn't read Walsh's report, and

Nixon, who knew about the plan to free King, declined to act. Over Morrow's objections, Nixon's campaign aide answered "no comment" when asked about the King case.

Two years later, a more talkative Nixon claimed that he had called Rogers and asked him to intervene, but Ike said no. Nixon couldn't have been too disappointed that he had refused. In the next sentence he said that he thought that intervening in the case on behalf of King would have been a breach of the "canon of the legal ethic." Nixon thought like a lawyer. But Kennedy thought like a politician.[73]

On October 26, Kennedy made his much publicized call to King's wife, Coretta. He told her simply that he was thinking about their welfare and safety. That was enough: The Democrats soon turned the call into a giant public relations coup. Kennedy's action was credited with tipping large numbers of blacks toward the Democrats.[74]

Ike's and Nixon's inaction probably did not cost the Republicans the White House in 1960. An election rarely hinges on any one event—there are just too many other variables. Privately, however, many Republican officials thought that it had. A bitter Nixon later reflected that Democrats painted him as a "villain" and destroyed the good relations he thought he had established with civil rights leaders. On this, he was right.[75]

This was one more lost opportunity during a decade of lost opportunities for the Republicans. Perhaps this was a fitting close to the "quiet" years of the 1950s, a decade in which a reluctant White House did everything it could to avoid facing racial conflict. Ike acted only when events swirled out of control, when world public opinion became a harsh judge of the nation's racial practices, and when America's image as the champion of the free world was in danger of being badly tarnished.

Still, reluctant or not, Eisenhower must be given credit for taking the initiative on civil rights. The two civil rights bills passed on his watch opened the door for the passage of future legislation that battered down legal segregation. Equally important, the developing national consensus on civil rights might, in future years, force the White House to use federal power to aggressively prosecute racially motivated violence. As events would prove, this was crucial.

The next decade would be anything but quiet. A new generation would come forth to assault legal segregation, and as always many southern whites met the assault with their most reliable weapon—terror. That was the challenge that faced the new young president. But this time, it would take more than a campaign phone call to Coretta Scott King to meet it.

5

"Don't Lean Toward the Negroes"

The Kennedy Years

Clarence Mitchell was embarrassed by the boos and catcalls that greeted the young senator as he took the podium. The NAACP's Washington bureau chief frantically waved to the crowd and shouted, "We don't boo guests, that is not the NAACP way." But if John F. Kennedy was ruffled, he didn't show it. He appeared to take the crowd's reaction in stride. The mostly black crowd of 6,000 had packed the Shrine Auditorium in Los Angeles for the NAACP-sponsored civil rights rally, which had been timed to coincide with the start of the 1960 Democratic National Convention.[1]

Kennedy and the other Democratic contenders had been invited to address the rally. All the major civil rights leaders, including King, Adam Clayton Powell, A. Philip Randolph, and Roy Wilkins, were present. During his few brief moments at the podium, Kennedy did manage to get a few cheers from the crowd, especially when he said, "The next president cannot stand above the battle by engaging in vague sermons on brotherhood." Kennedy promised to oppose discrimination in education, housing, and employment. He kept his poise, turned a bad situation around, and impressed many skeptical blacks that he sincerely supported civil rights. But as the initial crowd reaction demonstrated, blacks were deeply worried about the Democrats. After all, for nearly a century, powerful southern Democrats had condoned racial violence against blacks and opposed all civil rights legislation.

With Ike out of office, the Democrats had a fairly good shot at capturing the White House. But King told reporters that in his travels through the South, black voters repeatedly expressed doubts about the Democratic candidates. King couldn't offer them much hope. To him, "no candidate [had] measured up." That certainly included Kennedy, who was the clear front-runner for the nomination.[2]

There was much in Kennedy's past that troubled civil rights leaders—
his ambivalent views on civil rights, his cozy relations with southern
Democrats, and now his tilt toward Texan Lyndon Johnson as his running
mate. Black leaders could hardly forget that Johnson, before turning congressional statesman in 1957, had voted against every piece of civil rights
legislation for nearly two decades.[3]

——————— • ❖ • ———————

Kennedy had grown up in the wealthy, racially sheltered world of
Boston's patrician society. By the time he entered Harvard, he had ac-
cepted much of the historical mythology about America's racial past.
Historian Arthur Schlesinger once sighed in exasperation that "alas
[Kennedy] had been taught by the Harvard history department."
Schlesinger was clearly peeved that his former student could write in his
Pulitzer Prize–winning *Profiles of Courage* that the Reconstruction period
was "a black nightmare for the South." It was obvious to Schlesinger that
Kennedy had swallowed whole the southern view of Reconstruction.[4]

Kennedy wasn't completely to blame. Historians had taught genera-
tions of high school and college students in the North that the South was
a tranquil land of mint juleps, genteel southern ladies, and chivalrous
gentlemen who had fought an honorable battle against the greedy, evil,
corrupt northern carpetbaggers and ignorant blacks who were out to subvert their way of life.[5]

Kennedy's congressional and Senate years in the early 1950s were fairly
unobtrusive. Like most Americans, he basked in the relative racial quies-
cence of the early Eisenhower administration and apparently gave little if
any thought to racial problems. The 1954 *Brown v. Board of Education* school
desegregation decision abruptly thrust the racial issue onto the nation's
table. Kennedy, already being groomed by his father, Joseph Sr., for the
presidency, couldn't avoid the issue. But he had to move with caution. As
a Democrat, he had to delicately balance the sharply competing interests
of the party's two major constituencies—southern whites and blacks.

He made it clear that he supported the Brown decision. But during debate over the 1957 civil rights bill, Kennedy, observers thought, revealed
an underlying sympathy for the South when he voted to send the bill
back to the Judiciary Committee. This would have been fatal. It would
have dropped the bill into the hands of Eastland, Ervin, and the other
southern Democrats who dominated the committee. Fortunately, the
move was defeated. Kennedy later explained that he recommended the
bill to the committee purely for procedural reasons and not because he
opposed it.

At the 1956 convention, Kennedy got his first real taste of national exposure and was almost selected as Adlai Stevenson's vice presidential running mate. Directly on track for a White House bid in 1960, he continued to maneuver politically between blacks and the South. Blending idealism and political pragmatism, he carefully cultivated the image of a political moderate to attract black support, but at the same time, he was careful not to take any political positions that might cost him southern white votes. He also maintained cordial relations with the governors of Georgia, Mississippi, and Alabama.[6]

This confounded Wilkins. In May 1958, he had criticized Kennedy for his vote to send the 1957 civil rights bill back to Eastland's committee. After Kennedy sharply reprimanded him, Wilkins changed his mind and two weeks later praised JFK for having the "best voting record in Congress."[7]

Kennedy soon found the ideal issue to establish his credential as a civil rights advocate without jeopardizing his relations with southern politicians. By 1958, the wave of bombings had alarmed southern moderates, who deplored the injuries and deaths but also feared that the violence would bring direct federal intervention into local affairs. Kennedy proposed his own antibombing bill that made interstate transportation or possession of explosives a federal crime. This was a tougher bill than Ike's.

Kennedy telephoned Ervin and shrewdly coaxed the "moderate" segregationist and states' rights champion to cosponsor his antibombing measure. But Ervin had more in mind than protecting black churches, homes, and community centers. He insisted that the measure also cover labor conflicts and that it clearly state that the federal government would not exclude "existing state laws." In a sharp exchange with New York senator Kenneth Keating over federal jurisdiction, Ervin revealed his true concern. He told Keating that he wanted to ensure that a "man who commits a local act" would not be subject to federal prosecution. Ervin did not want the federal government prosecuting anyone under Sections 51 and 52. Kennedy agreed with him: It was a win-win situation. He needed the senator, for Ervin's name carried tremendous weight with southern Senate Democrats.[8]

Throughout the spring of 1960, Kennedy continued his drive for the presidential nomination and effectively worked both political sides. In June, he told reporters that the student sit-ins in the South were "not to be lamented" but welcomed. On the eve of the Democratic convention the following month, Kennedy discussed the demonstrations again. This time, instead of applauding rebellious protest, he told the press that he would only support the sit-ins "as long as they were peaceful and legal."[9]

For black leaders, it was touch and go with Kennedy. They were shocked and angered when he chose Johnson as his running mate but pleased when he announced his support for the Democratic platform that called for new civil rights legislation.[10]

During the campaign against Nixon, Kennedy was low-keyed. He said little of significance on civil rights issues. Civil rights leaders were particularly annoyed that he refused to speak out against the racial violence in New Orleans. In the fall of 1960, local officials there had defied a federal court order to integrate the city's schools. Mobs of whites took to the streets, attacked blacks, and threatened parents who sought to comply with the court order. NAACP and Congress of Racial Equality (CORE) leaders appealed to Kennedy to go to the city and urge racial peace. He ignored them as well as a Louisiana legislative committee that tried to sound him out on his position on school integration.[11]

It was a risky proposition for civil rights leaders to back Kennedy, but after the King call and Nixon's silence, he seemed to be the lesser of two evils. On election day, Kennedy grabbed 68 percent of the black vote, 7 percent more than Stevenson had in 1956. In their postelection assessment, NAACP officials noted that blacks were "in no mood to consent to a 'cease fire' in the field for full civil rights." The words sounded less like a congratulations than a warning.[12]

Still, Kennedy, unlike Ike, was young and vigorous, and he seemed open to change. In March, he told a reporter that he would recommend civil rights legislation the moment that he thought there was "a chance of getting that congressional action." His promise was vague and perhaps intentionally evasive, but civil rights leaders wanted to think the best about Kennedy. They were hopeful that part of his civil rights package would include stronger enforcement provisions to deal with racial violence.[13]

Kennedy, however, was cautious. Elected by the barest of margins over Nixon, he did not have a popular mandate to make sudden social changes and certainly not racial change. As a Democrat, he felt that he had the same problem as Roosevelt and Truman: He could not afford to openly oppose southern Democrats. They controlled the key congressional committees and could block key legislation if he pushed too hard on civil rights. More important, he needed their support to be reelected.

Wilkins didn't have that problem. He had generally taken a wait-and-see attitude toward Kennedy during the first few months of 1961. As the months passed and JFK still had not delivered on his promise, Wilkins grumbled that the Kennedy administration was the same old story. It had put civil rights at the bottom of the legislative agenda. Wilkins marveled at how Kennedy, by contrast, could practically order the presidents of the major steel companies not to raise prices and threaten them with congressional and federal grand jury investigations when they protested. NAACP officials sarcastically noted how JFK demonstrated what federal power can do. What they wanted to know was why the president couldn't do the same to enforce civil rights violations. What Wilkins did not know, since Kennedy did not see fit to tell him, was that JFK had privately decided to postpone indefinitely introducing a civil rights bill.[14]

————— • ◆ • —————

Congress was only one front in the civil rights battle. Black leaders knew that civil rights enforcement rested heavily on the Justice Department as well, and the key there was the attorney general. The president picked his brother Robert for this post. This was a slightly puzzling choice, for, unlike the president, RFK was not a professional politician. He had left no paper trail of public statements and he had no voting record by which he could be judged.

RFK had achieved some public notoriety during his brief stint witch-hunting Communists and liberal "fellow travelers" when he served as committee counsel to Wisconsin senator Joseph McCarthy. Later, he hounded racketeers as counsel to Arkansas senator John McClellan's Permanent Subcommittee on Investigations. There was no indication that RFK knew anything more about race problems than his brother did during his early congressional years.[15]

In January, RFK entered the chambers of the Senate Judiciary Committee accompanied by his wife, Ethel, for his confirmation hearing. Smiling and waving to admirers, he hardly seemed worried about doing battle with southern Democrats like McClellan and Louisiana's ever-vigilant Allen Ellender. The senators were gracious and even deferential as they tossed soft questions at him.

The only questions that even remotely touched on the sensitive issue of civil rights enforcement came not from a southern senator but from Nebraska Republican senator Roman Hruska and New York Republican senator Kenneth Keating. Hruska asked Kennedy whether he would bring civil rights suits and seek court injunctions against local officials in voting rights cases. Kennedy easily deflected the question, telling Hruska that such decisions would be made by his brother.

Keating tried to pin him down on his views on the Democratic Party's civil rights plank. RFK said he supported the plank but quickly added that problems could not be solved overnight. He gave a solid performance. The Kennedy light had begun to glow brightly. At the very least, the honeymoon with the South was not over. RFK left enough for both sides, while not allowing much room for criticism.[16]

Civil rights leaders, still unclear about the direction of the "new" Justice Department, were no more enlightened in February when RFK tapped corporate antitrust attorney Burke Marshall to head the Civil Rights Division. Marshall was described by colleagues as a calm and deliberate man who had a penchant for facts and never went off half-cocked. But other than his work on the voting rights referee plan that became part of the 1960 civil rights law, Marshall, by his own admission, was a novice in the civil rights field.[17]

Robert Kennedy admired Marshall's personal qualities, but he admired his legal philosophy even more. It mirrored his own. Both men believed that the federal government should play a restricted role in local affairs. Kennedy was particularly sensitive to the charge from southerners that the federal government wanted to set up a "national police force" that would usurp state powers over courts, law enforcement, and governmental functions. Marshall and Kennedy talked only about federal separation of powers. The South talked about civil rights enforcement.

During the first round of confirmation hearings in early March, Marshall stole a page from Hoover's book. He told Ellender and Ervin that he didn't think the Department of Justice should initiate investigations of voting rights violations unless there was a prior formal complaint. Marshall also assured them that he would refer all civil rights violations "to the states first."[18]

Ellender and Ervin weren't satisfied. They knew that with the South's die-hard attempt to maintain political and economic dominance over blacks, the Civil Rights Division would be under intense pressure from civil rights leaders to bring more suits, seek more injunctions, and prosecute more racially motivated criminal acts. They wanted reassurance from Marshall that the CRD would remain above the fray. Two weeks later, they called him back for more testimony.

This time, RFK accompanied him, sitting conspicuously in full view of the TV cameras—an obvious sign that Kennedy badly wanted Marshall confirmed. Marshall, who almost surely had discussed strategy with his boss-to-be beforehand, was conciliatory. He promised that the DOJ would always defer to local officials on enforcement of civil rights abuses: "That is the procedure we are going to follow in all kinds of cases."[19]

RFK emphasized the same point later in the month when an interviewer asked him what he would do if faced with another Little Rock–type crisis. In words reminiscent of Ike, Kennedy confidently predicted that he couldn't "conceive of this administration letting such a situation deteriorate to that level." Like Ike, Kennedy would soon find that his words would come back to haunt him.[20]

In May 1961, the nation watched in stunned disbelief as white thugs burned buses and bloodily assaulted white and black freedom riders in Alabama and Mississippi. The freedom rides were organized by CORE to challenge segregation in transportation and public accommodations. During the attacks, local police and sheriffs stood by and watched or were conveniently away from the scene while the violence took place.

Kennedy told a graduating class at the FBI National Academy that local law enforcement personnel must "do their job." But they did not and would not.

The White House, shamed by the violence and the international outrage that ensued, ordered federal marshals to protect the demonstrators. Some CORE and Student Nonviolent Coordinating Committee (SNCC) workers were skeptical of Robert Kennedy's action. They thought his motives were politically cynical and that the marshals were used less to protect demonstrators than to maintain public order, which Alabama state officials had deliberately allowed to break down.[21]

———— • ◆ • ————

Throughout the summer of 1961, RFK and Marshall were flooded with letters from CORE and NAACP leaders throughout the South that described new atrocities. Again and again, civil rights workers and local blacks in the South were attacked while picketing, shot at while traveling down open highways, assaulted while trying to register to vote, or beaten while in jail or police custody. CORE director James Farmer complained repeatedly to RFK that police and local officials openly condoned or openly initiated the violence.[22]

During the Eisenhower years, it was relatively easy for Brownell and Rogers to ignore civil rights abuses except in extreme cases like the Parker lynching, which provoked worldwide criticism. Civil rights demonstrators weren't in the streets marching, picketing, demonstrating, and threatening to disrupt local functions during most of the 1950s. In 1961, things were different. The civil rights movement was bigger, stronger, and better organized.

Moreover, civil rights leaders and the young student protesters were more conscious that the federal government was doing virtually nothing to protect them. When a voter registration center was bombed, when a church was burned, or when protestors were shot at or beaten, FBI agents would stand nearby, casually writing on notepads and amiably conversing with local police. Civil rights activists began to feel that they were fighting two battles—one against violent white racists, the other against the indifference of the federal government.

Charles Jones was one of these activists. An early convert to SNCC in 1960, Jones, like most of the young activists, believed that the DOJ was on his side. When the Klan threatened to take SNCC leader Bob Moses from jail in McComb, Mississippi, Jones feared that Moses would be murdered, and therefore, he called the local FBI agent. The agent politely told him, "Oh, I don't think they'd do that." Next, Jones called Marshall to urge him to "get on the FBI man." Marshall told him, "It's a matter of jurisdiction." The final straw for Jones came when John Doar, Marshall's top troubleshooter, arrived. Jones believed that he would finally get some action, but Doar quickly dispelled that notion when he said, "Well, I'm sorry but there isn't anything I can do."[23]

Marshall was not indifferent to Jones's plight, nor did he intentionally underestimate the danger to local blacks and civil rights workers. Rather, he was convinced that he could reach an understanding with southern law enforcement officials to get them to protect those individuals. Yet when a group of white toughs attacked civil rights demonstrators in Jackson in March 1961, local police watched and made no effort to make any arrests. Several of the demonstrators were white students from Michigan and Pennsylvania.

The attacks prompted a flood of letters from angry parents to Pennsylvania senator Joseph Clark and Michigan senator Phillip Hart. The senators promptly demanded that Marshall take immediate steps to prevent further violence. Marshall assured them that Jackson police officials promised the FBI they would arrest the assailants. But even though no arrests were ever made, Marshall was satisfied that his approach of negotiation and persuasion worked. "It was a practical matter. I wasn't trying simply to talk police out of beating people up. I wanted them to take responsibility for law enforcement."[24]

Marshall was not naive. Since FBI offices generally would not respond to personal phone calls from SNCC and CORE activists, RFK had given out his and Marshall's personal phone numbers. Often, Marshall received frantic calls at home in the middle of the night from terrified civil rights workers in some backwoods town in Mississippi or Georgia who had been beaten or jailed and wanted help.

When he got such calls, Marshall listened sympathetically and promised to contact the sheriff or refer the matter to local officials. However, the attacks on the freedom riders had certainly made him aware that there were occasions when local officials and police operated beyond the pale of laws. In those instances, he could not intervene effectively.[25]

In July, Marshall had to deal with two potentially explosive and dangerous situations. New Orleans faced a second year of turmoil over school integration. Local officials, still as defiant and determined to resist court orders as ever, incited white mobs to take to the streets again. At the same time, SNCC announced that it would begin a voter registration drive in Mississippi. Marshall had nightmares of a repeat of the freedom rider violence. He told Deputy Attorney General Byron White that Kennedy might be forced to send federal marshals to Mississippi and New Orleans if mob violence broke out. Marshall was relieved that the city remained relatively peaceful.[26]

The lull, however, was temporary. On September 25 on a back road outside McComb, Mississippi, State Representative E. B. Hurst shot and killed Herbert Lee. Hurst claimed that Lee had attacked him with a tire iron, but witnesses said Lee was unarmed. Some speculated that Lee, a young black farmer, was killed because of his volunteer work in SNCC's voter campaign. Hurst claimed he acted in self-defense and was not arrested.

Marshall sent Doar to investigate, but Doar hit a snag when local officials refused to cooperate. Lee was buried before the FBI received instructions at its New Orleans office to examine his remains. Despite SNCC protests, Marshall declined to order an FBI investigation. Two weeks later, black high school students and two white reporters were assaulted in the area. Marshall expressed concern but again refused to order an investigation.[27]

———— • ◆ • ————

Many academic and religious leaders, appalled by the lawlessness in Mississippi and other areas of the South, did not share Marshall's faith in the ability and willingness of local police and officials to keep order. The Civil Rights Commission (CRC) held hearings on civil rights enforcement and police abuse issues in several cities. Dozens of witnesses told horrific stories of violence and the indifference of local officials.

At the end of the hearings, commission members came to believe that the civil rights activists were correct. In its final report, the commission issued a stinging rebuke of RFK for letting Hoover get away with doing virtually nothing to stop the violence and called on the White House to propose legislation toughening the federal criminal statutes, Sections 51 and 52.

Hoover was livid that the CRC had the audacity to attack him. He hated the comission anyway, and thought it was an "unwitting tool" of King and other civil rights leaders. Hoover promptly sent an angry letter to CRC chairman John Hannah saying that he resented the suggestion that he was derelict in his duty. Marshall, when he got wind of the dispute, sided with Hoover. Marshall and RFK earlier had put pressure on Hannah to cancel the hearings, fearing that they would antagonize Mississippi whites.

Marshall had read a draft of the CRC report before it was issued and thought that it overstated the police brutality picture. He told Deputy Attorney General Byron White that he had found many "errors" of fact and misstatement in the document and had convinced Hannah to correct them. Marshall generally believed that law enforcement officials in the North and South were doing a good job, and he resented the CRC's blanket indictment. He also saw his own tilt toward Hoover as tactical diplomacy rather than appeasement. "Hoover," he noted, "didn't like to have anything to do with complaints against police officers if there was a racial element involved."[28]

RFK made a small concession. He quietly directed Hoover to initiate preliminary investigations immediately whenever the FBI received a civil rights complaint. In reality, this simply meant that RFK was returning to a policy that was standard practice before Brownell changed it in 1958.[29]

During the early months of 1962, SNCC and CORE activists still had not seen much evidence that the Justice Department was willing to do more to halt the violence against local blacks. Farmer continued to bombard Marshall and the Kennedys with letters and telegrams. If a CORE worker was beaten in Alabama, a black church was bombed in Georgia or Tennessee, or a demonstrator was assaulted by police in North Carolina, Marshall or Kennedy was sure to receive an urgent telegram from Farmer or a CORE leader demanding an investigation.

Marshall's reply was almost always the same: The attack "does not indicate any violation of federal law." Or he would challenge Farmer to produce "more facts." Marshall continued to tell his critics that "the government cannot provide protection in a physical sense for everyone who is disliked because of the exercise of his constitutional rights." He believed that he was acting in accord with sound constitutional and philosophical principles but also for pragmatic reasons. A strong federal presence, he insisted, "would have encouraged a stronger backlash from segregationists."[30]

Farmer and other civil rights leaders questioned his logic. They weren't asking him to arrest sheriffs, or to send troops to protect and serve as bodyguards to SNCC and CORE field-workers. They would have been more than satisfied if federal prosecutors brought occasional indictments against local officials for inciting racial violence. Even if authorities didn't succeed in getting a conviction, a criminal prosecution would at least serve as a warning that the federal government was willing to enforce federal statutes. The CRC essentially agreed that "every assault or murder which goes unpunished reinforces the legacy of violence–the knowledge that it's dangerous for a Negro to depart from traditional ways." Marshall took a more jaundiced view. "It would have been largely an exercise in futility," he noted, "since it was nearly impossible to get white juries to convict anyone."[31]

By reducing racial violence to personal antagonisms and demanding that civil rights leaders undertake the near impossible task of proving that federal statutes applied when they were victimized, Marshall created a straw man. He also could not satisfactorily explain why the White

House and the DOJ promptly sent in troops or sought injunctions during labor strikes or riots to protect property and maintain order, often without a formal request from state or local authorities.

Didn't the same constitutional limits apply in those situations, too? When local law enforcement could not handle certain types of crime, Congress simply created new federal laws. In fact, Congress had passed the Mann Act, the so-called white slavery law, in 1910 to stop the interstate trafficking in prostitution; the Auto Theft Act in 1919, to stop the transport, sale, and receipt of stolen cars; and the Federal Bank Robbery Act in 1934.

Twenty years later, when Congress made it a crime to deliver and sell fireworks in states that prohibited or regulated their use, neither Congress nor the White House raised a major outcry about states' rights or constitutional violations or federal limits of power.

There was another problem as well. Marshall was hamstrung by a skimpy budget, a scarcity of personnel, and Congress's refusal to increase spending for criminal civil rights enforcement: "There simply wasn't enough staff. We had only fifteen attorneys to work on civil rights cases. I asked the House Appropriations Committee in 1962 for a modest increase of $200,000 in 1962 and was turned down."[32]

———— • ❖ • ————

Beyond the philosophical debates and pragmatic issues of limited resources, RFK and Marshall had to contend with Hoover. The DOJ was almost totally dependent on the resources and personnel of the FBI for gathering information and submitting reports on racial violence. But Hoover's hostility toward the black movement (and King in particular) only intensified with the increase in protest marches and demonstrations. He had not changed his view that civil rights cases were dead-ends and counterproductive since such cases seldom led to arrests, indictments, or convictions. He was even more determined to avoid investigations.

Hoover's attitude and racism filtered down to the field agents, many of whom were at best indifferent, if not openly hostile, to civil rights workers. This could not be dismissed as black paranoia. Even Marshall acknowledged, "The FBI wasn't much good at civil rights investigations. Blacks didn't trust them or want to talk with them. More often than not, I had to use my attorneys to gather evidence."[33]

CRC staff director Berl Bernhard rode from Jackson to New Orleans with an FBI agent in 1962. Bernhard became more and more uncomfortable as he listened to the agent spout his racial views. He thought, If we who were also in the government didn't feel the FBI men were our friends, how must blacks feel?

For years, Hoover had loudly protested that when it came to civil rights, the FBI was not a national police force and did not have the power to intervene and make arrests in civil rights cases. He had a grab bag of excuses for the policy. According to him, agents didn't have the experience or expertise to make on-the-spot decisions as to what specific laws were being violated. If agents got directly involved in the action, it would cloud their objectivity, and, moreover, agents needed warrants to make legal arrests, or so he claimed.[34]

This was nonsense. The DOJ office of legal counsel ruled that agents could make arrests if they observed "a crowd of white citizens pursuing and beating a Negro student." Even without a specific DOJ ruling, FBI agents routinely arrested bank robbers, car thieves, individuals who possessed illegal weapons, and anyone else who broke federal laws without warrants. All they needed was "probable cause."[35]

ACLU director Charles Morgan, an outspoken Hoover critic, constantly marveled at Hoover's verbal gymnastics on this point. He watched the FBI immediately spring into action time and again to nab auto thieves, bank robbers, and kidnappers. The prohibition against on-the-spot arrests for civil rights violations was not statute but merely Hoover's personal policy. RFK had the statutory authority to make Hoover change the policy and make arrests. But he did not.[36]

Hoover feared that if the bureau made on-the-spot arrests, he might have to arrest some law enforcement officers who committed acts of violence. This was unthinkable to him. He believed doing that would have seriously damaged the working relationship and trust that he had spent decades developing with local police. Meanwhile, that relationship may have had a more sinister and dangerous consequence for some civil rights workers. Although Hoover may not have been personally aware of it, there was inferential evidence that many local police officers and public officials were Klan members or sympathizers. The FBI routinely passed on information and shared intelligence reports with local police departments on SNCC and CORE activities. Some of this information was passed on to Klan leaders, enabling them to track the movements and monitor the plans of civil rights workers, thus endangering their lives. RFK certainly knew this, for Southern Christian Leadership Conference (SCLC) fieldworkers repeatedly complained of the collusion between the FBI agents and local law enforcement. However, he ignored their complaints.[37]

If Kennedy had ordered Hoover to take more aggressive action against racist terrorists, Hoover would have had to obey. And judging by his past practice, he would have. Despite his personal bigotry and megalomania, Hoover was a career civil servant and a loyal bureaucrat. He could not have survived for very long in the cutthroat world of Washington politics if he didn't understand his limits and respect authority. He had served eight presidents and twelve attorneys general precisely because he knew how to follow orders. In 1959, when Rogers ordered him to compile evidence in the Parker lynching, his FBI conducted a diligent and professional investigation.[38]

Despite the press reports of mutual hatred, allegations of sexual blackmail, and personal feuds between Hoover and the Kennedys, RFK found Hoover to be a model of cooperation. He noted, "Anytime I'd call and ask him to do something, which wasn't very frequent, he was the most enthusiastic person you ever talked to. When the president gave an order," RFK said "either you had to do it or you'd have to get out."

RFK grudgingly ordered Hoover to increase the number of FBI agents assigned to civil rights cases in the South only when confronted with massive racist violence. But he did not reverse the informal arrangement established by Brownell and Rogers, which permitted Hoover not to investigate civil rights complaints unless specifically directed to do so by the DOJ.[39]

————— • ◆ • —————

While Kennedy and Marshall tried to reconcile their legal strategy and philosophy with the hard realities of southern violence, SNCC activists ran out of patience. In March 1962, a small band of SNCC activists, led by Stokely Carmichael, invaded the offices of RFK. For several hours, they staged a sit-in at the attorney general's outer office, and they told police they weren't leaving until they met with RFK. They demanded that the DOJ press Louisiana officials to drop the prosecution of two SNCC workers arrested on criminal conspiracy charges and to investigate the beatings of SNCC workers by local police. Moments earlier, Kennedy had left the office to attend a scheduled meeting with Defense Secretary Robert McNamara, just missing the protesters.

Marshall was anxious to avoid an ugly incident. He hurried over to talk with the activists and listened patiently for nearly thirty minutes as Carmichael and others took turns haranguing federal officials for their inaction. When they finished, Marshall coolly told them that the DOJ could not intervene in a state prosecution. He promised that he "would investigate" all violations. The angry SNCC activists were in no mood to listen to any more promises. That weekend, several hundred other demonstrators circled the DOJ building, demanding immediate action. On Monday, they returned. This time, they sat for two and a half hours in a reception area outside Kennedy's office. But neither Kennedy nor Marshall would meet with them.[40]

Carmichael's bold action attracted considerable press attention and put the DOJ in an embarrassing position. In fairness, Marshall's and RFK's method of gentle persuasion and behind-the-scenes negotiating with state officials had produced some important breakthroughs. More blacks were voting. More schools were desegregating. And more businesses were hiring and promoting blacks. But the violence had not stopped. Despite widespread criticism that he was too soft on local law enforcement, Marshall tried to maintain some credibility with civil rights groups. He boasted in an interview, "I never met with Klan or bigoted police officials."[41]

Privately, though, Marshall was worried that police violence could endanger the tenuous, fragile relationships the administration had with civil rights leaders. He and Robert Kennedy searched for a way to appease civil rights activists without jeopardizing JFK's cautious legislative timetable. A week after the SNCC sit-in, Marshall and Kennedy floated a trial balloon.

They prepared a bill that would toughen penalties for police misconduct. It was a halfhearted gesture since neither man really believed that the bill had any chance of being passed. After police chiefs got wind of it and mounted a brief but furious letter-writing campaign opposing the measure, Marshall quickly backed off. Congress never scheduled any hearings. Marshall did not push for them, and the bill died.[42]

CORE leaders, like SNCC activists, had also run out of patience with the White House. Instead of sitting in or picketing, they decided to investigate the federal government. They announced plans to hold hearings in Washington, D.C. CORE also convinced Eleanor Roosevelt to serve as chair of their "Committee of Inquiry into the Administration of Justice in the South."

For two days, a panel composed mostly of civil rights activists and academics listened to a parade of activists from Louisiana, Mississippi, Alabama, Tennessee, and South Carolina tell harrowing stories of beatings, jailings, and threats by local rednecks, sheriffs, and public officials. In addition, affidavits and briefs submitted by local blacks who had been beaten or jailed were read.

Their stories were all too familiar. After a beating or a bombing, FBI agents or DOJ attorneys were notified. They would take statements, file reports, and then nothing more would be heard from them. The committee hoped that the drama and novelty of the hearings would be enough to draw the media, but all the major dailies ignored them. Eleanor Roosevelt, incensed by the media no-shows, promptly sent angry letters to the *New York Times*, the *Washington Post*, and the major TV networks accusing them of being "indifferent" to the violence.

The only official who attended was New York congressman William Ryan. Marshall was curious and decided to send an observer to the hearings who would report back to him. As a pro forma courtesy, he requested that Farmer notify him if any facts or information about criminal violations were revealed to the hearings.[43]

Meanwhile, King increasingly shared the frustrations of the young militants regarding the DOJ and the White House. During much of 1961 and 1962, his campaign to desegregate transportation and public facilities in Albany, Georgia, had hit a stone wall. Hundreds of protestors had been jailed, and yet King had little to show for his efforts. Albany sheriff Laurie Pritchett, determined not to resort to violence and give King ammunition to drum up national sympathy, scrupulously followed legal procedures in making arrests. But he could not control the area's toughs who assaulted demonstrators and local blacks.

Desperate to stop the jailings and harassment and force city officials to negotiate, King endorsed a study by SNCC activist Howard Zinn that accused the FBI agents of racism: "One of the great problems is that the agents are white Southerners who have been influenced by the mores of the community." King was even more troubled by the attitude of the Kennedys, whom he felt had done nothing to encourage local officials to cooperate with civil rights leaders. The day before he was arrested, a frustrated and tired King lashed out at RFK, "I'm tired. We're sick of it." King's lieutenant, Wyatt Tee Walker, bitterly complained that the Kennedys "had not raised a finger to protect the rights of Negro citizens." At the end of August 1962, a disappointed King finally admitted defeat and announced that Birmingham was his new campaign target. When he left Albany, most of the major media packed up and went with him. They left too soon. The racial terror that had just begun would present another dilemma for the Kennedys.[44]

———— • ◆ • ————

For a quarter century, Mount Olive Baptist Church had been a popular meeting place and the center of social activities for blacks in Sasser, Georgia. But for several months in 1962, the pastor had allowed SNCC workers to use Mount Olive as the headquarters for a voter registration drive and now, almost nightly, SNCC held rallies at the church to encourage local blacks to register.

Sasser was located eighteen miles north of Albany in Terrell County. The region was known for its rich soil, cattle, cotton, and peanuts. Some area farmers had become wealthy and lived on vast estates worked by poor white and black farm laborers. Terrell County had a particularly bad reputation for violence and intimidation against blacks. Although blacks made up nearly half of the county's population, only 51 out of 8,209 were registered to vote. White planters and local officials had for decades had an ironfisted control of county politics. They feared that large numbers of black voters would threaten their dominance.

Mount Olive's pastor generally ignored the numerous threats and warnings he had received since SNCC began its voter campaign. But he couldn't ignore Sheriff Z. T. "Zeke" Matthews. On the evening of July 25, Matthews and a contingent of gun-toting deputies stormed into the church during a small voter registration meeting.

New York Times reporter Charles Siton, who recorded the whole incredible scene, overheard one of the deputies tell a black registrant, "I know you, we're going to get some of you." Matthews's outrageous action was too much for Marshall. Two weeks later, the DOJ filed a voting rights complaint against the sheriff. SNCC also tried to get an injunction to stop him from intimidating and harassing black registrants.[45]

The threats of violence were not idle threats. On the evening of September 9, Mount Olive was burned to the ground; the only thing that remained was the brick chimney. The arsonists also struck the same evening in nearby Chickasawatchee, where Mount Mary Baptist Church, which had also been used for voter rallies, was also burned to the ground. SNCC workers were hardly surprised when Matthews quickly ruled out arson as a motive. The sheriff did, however, concede there was a problem: "The niggers are upset about it." SNCC organizer James Forman immediately sent a telegram to RFK and JFK and demanded that the DOJ take action to "stop the Nazi-like reign of terror." The two church burnings brought the total of churches burned that summer to three. Shady Grove Baptist Church in Leesburg was also burned to the ground three weeks earlier. The violence quickly escalated.[46]

Within days, the racists fired shots into five black homes. Donald Harris, who spent several months in Terrell in the voter registration campaign, later remembered that the homes where SNCC workers lived had been shot into on at least six occasions. Although he couldn't prove it, he was convinced that the attackers weren't local rednecks but "officials who were carrying out most of the intimidation." In another attack, three blacks who had joined the SNCC registration team were wounded.[47]

Forman could make a convincing case that the violence was part of a bigger, organized pattern of violence. The FBI found evidence that the Mount Olive burning was arson and determined that the fires at the other churches were also set. The day after Forman sent his telegram, RFK made a verbal report to JFK on the burnings and the shootings.

If RFK could show a direct connection between the violence and voting rights, he had the authority to seek federal criminal conspiracy indictments against the terrorists, under the provisions of the 1957 Civil Rights Act. White House press secretary Pierre Salinger reiterated to the reporters that the Kennedys were staying in touch with each other on the case.

The following day, JFK underscored the importance of the case when he told RFK that he wanted daily reports on the progress of the investigation sent to him during his visit to space centers in Florida and Texas. The president sensed that the church burnings were a sensitive issue that could stir the outrage of most Americans. There was little political risk for him in taking a tough stance against this type of terrorism.[48]

At a press conference two days later, JFK made his toughest statement on racial violence, noting that "I don't know any more outrageous action." He warned that "we will arrest them, we will bring them before a jury." JFK even dropped a hint that he would be willing to provide the "extra legislation and extra force" needed to uphold federal laws.[49]

King and moderate civil rights leaders applauded him. But SNCC workers such as Harris did not simply distrust the government; they also saw it as "the enemy." Harris savagely attacked the FBI, claiming that it had made no attempt to investigate the shootings or offer protection. "Very often," he said, "they did their best to work against us."

Though King did not see the FBI as an enemy, he was not satisfied with the bureau's performance. He had returned to the area to lead a prayer service at the site of the charred remains of Mount Olive. Afterward, at an impromptu press conference, he said that the "FBI investigation had been all too slow." King challenged the Kennedys to turn "investigating action into prosecuting action."[50]

King had barely gotten the words out when terrorists struck again. In Valdosta, Georgia, two firebombs were found inside one church, and the next day, the I Hope Baptist Church in the area was burned to the ground. It was the fourth church torched in three weeks, and this, too, was arson. Forman sent another telegram to JFK, again demanding that the federal government put an end to the terror.[51]

King and SNCC workers were understandably skeptical. So far, the DOJ had sought only a handful of criminal indictments for civil rights violations and only after mass pressure. But JFK's well-timed pronouncement at least guaranteed that the DOJ would not abandon the case. The FBI announced that it was setting up a twenty-four-hour surveillance of all roads and churches in southwest Georgia. The next day, the bureau announced that it had arrested four white men seen near the Mount Olive Baptist Church the day it was burned. RFK was relieved and immediately phoned Hoover to congratulate him.

He was premature, for the FBI's action was hardly an investigative coup. The four men were questioned by an FBI agent who spotted them sitting in a car directly across from the church. They admitted that they had been drinking beer and were angry about the voting rights rallies. They were so inebriated that they virtually confessed and were arrested.

RFK quickly announced that he would not seek federal indictments and would turn the evidence over to Georgia authorities for prosecution. The men pled guilty and were sentenced only for the burning of the I Hope church, not the others. The DOJ in a prepared statement claimed that the FBI did not prove that the men had burned the church specifically to intimidate blacks from registering to vote. RFK seemed to forget that, a week earlier, he had promised to apply federal statutes to prosecute the arsonists. The timing and pattern of the fires, in conjunction with the voting registration campaign and Sheriff Matthews's actions, certainly pointed to the possibility of a conspiracy. If RFK had sought indictments, he probably would have uncovered solid evidence linking the burnings with the voter registration efforts.[52]

The Kennedys were satisfied that the state had done its job. The few reporters who bothered to cover the story left the area, and the public shifted its attention to the battle brewing at the University of Mississippi over the admission of James Meredith. Five days later, another church was burned down—the fifth in one month. The pattern was the same. But this time, the FBI immediately discounted the possibility that there was any racial motive to the burning.[53]

————— • ◆ • —————

At Ole Miss, the nation watched as howling mobs of whites, egged on by defiant state officials, fought pitched gun battles with federal marshals to prevent James Meredith from enrolling at the school. The violence pushed JFK into a corner and left him no alternative but to use federal troops and marshals to maintain order.

The Kennedys were still not willing to heed King's plea to turn investigations into prosecutions of racial terrorists. In January, when CORE picketers were assaulted in Tennessee and an attempt was made to bomb a CORE voter registration project center, Marshall lamely reminded Farmer that the DOJ couldn't investigate unless the explosives had been transported across state lines.

He was technically correct, but Farmer probably wondered how Marshall could know whether the bombing met that legal "prerequisite" without conducting an investigation. Farmer and the civil rights leaders continued to be trapped in the DOJ's convoluted legal logic.[54]

Farmer was not the only one annoyed with Marshall's timidity. Civil Rights Commission members were openly rebellious against the DOJ for failing to halt the near anarchy in Mississippi. They wanted to return to the state and hold more public hearings. Robert Kennedy hit the ceiling. He called Bernhard and demanded that the CRC cancel the hearings. He claimed that his strategy of bringing selected voting rights lawsuits against county officials and negotiations with Mississippi officials was succeeding in opening up the voting rolls to more blacks. CRC hearings, RFK insisted, would only antagonize state officials.

Bernhard didn't agree. The few suits that the DOJ had brought against county officials for voting discrimination had been complex and time-consuming efforts. Mississippi officials were using every dodge to resist black voting registration, and the violence in the state hardly seemed an indication that state officials had become more conciliatory on civil rights. The commissioners concluded that Kennedy was just cuddling up to the southern white power structure.

Bernhard wanted to hold the hearings anyway, but this would have meant risking an open break with RFK, a step he wasn't prepared to take. Although the CRC bowed to RFK's wishes and postponed the hearings, it nonetheless issued a pamphlet in January 1963 condemning the deplorable conditions in Mississippi. Three months later, the CRC released an interim report that strongly urged the administration to suppress existing lawlessness and provide federal protection to blacks and civil rights workers in the state.

The White House did not officially comment, but RFK turned to Marshall for advice on how to respond. He dutifully tried to refute the CRC's claims point by point. He contended that the FBI investigated all bombings and burnings, and he downplayed the number of injuries involved. More incredibly, he insisted that the FBI and DOJ found no evidence that local police and other officials had taken part in any violence against blacks and civil rights workers. Marshall's tone was accusatory. He blamed the CRC for exaggerating the threat of violence. But Kennedy believed that the report was simply another instance of the errant commissioner crying wolf.[55]

In early May, JFK's policy of using racial diplomacy to curb racial violence was severely tested in Birmingham. Following weeks of mass protests and a citywide boycott led by King to force city officials to desegregate public facilities and end employment discrimination, local vigilantes launched a wave of assaults and bombing attacks. Kennedy was convinced that the city's business and political leaders could end the violence by sitting down with civil rights leaders and talking out their problems. Although King agreed to negotiate, he also demanded federal protections against violence. JFK followed the situation closely. On May 8, he told reporters that the DOJ did not detect any violation of federal civil rights or other statutes. RFK agreed. He did not think that federal protection was feasible or acceptable.[56]

Within a week, the situation had deteriorated. Following a series of violent police attacks against civil rights demonstrators, young blacks hurled rocks and bottles at police. For two nights, the air crackled with the sound of gunfire. Marshall, RFK, JFK, and several top aides held marathon strategy sessions at the White House. Again, they debated whether to use federal troops to quell the violence.

As the hours wore on and the violence continued, JFK reluctantly prepared for the worst and ordered army units at Fort Benning, Georgia, placed on alert. His plan called for 3,000 troops to move into the area. Kennedy played for time as Marshall placed calls to King, Birmingham's mayor, and the city's top business and political leaders to try to get the negotiations back on track. Toward evening, local officials gradually restored order. King and his aides, local black leaders, had worked through the day to calm the situation.

As order gradually returned, JFK directed Marshall and other assistants to draft a press statement. When the president and his chief adviser, Ted Sorensen, scanned the statement, Kennedy complained that "it leaned too much on the side of the Negroes." He was wary of doing anything that would upset the fragile peace. Hours later, a somber JFK told reporters that the civil rights leaders and city officials had reached "a fair agreement" and that he would not permit it to be "sabotaged by a few extremists on either side." Kennedy was pleased by the results. Eventually, businesses hired more blacks, and public facilities were desegregated. The agreement held—but only at the point of federal bayonets.[57]

Kennedy's "threat" to use federal force to stop racial violence followed the same pattern. Mass demonstrations and violence would lead to a crisis that would garner the attention of the media and spark national outrage. At the same time, however, the routine daily acts of racial terror against blacks and civil rights workers beyond the public eye generally went unpunished.

———————— • ◆ • ————————

The violence in Birmingham increased the sense of urgency at the White House. JFK was now in a hurry to introduce his civil rights package. In June, he gave two national addresses, barely a week apart, on civil rights. He candidly admitted that "continued federal legislative inaction will continue, if not increase racial strife." When Kennedy introduced his long-awaited civil rights bill, it contained eight provisions on education, employment, public accommodations, and voting rights but no provisions to increase criminal penalties against mob violence.[58]

RFK was adamant that criminal sanctions should not be included in the civil rights bill. In July 1963, Wisconsin senator Robert Kastenmeier, angered over the continuing southern violence, tried to insert an amendment into President Kennedy's bill that toughened criminal penalties for assaults on civil rights workers while they were in custody. Kastenmeier got no encouragement from the White House or the DOJ. RFK objected that saddling the bill with strong enforcement provisions would only increase the already considerable resistance of southern Democrats to the legislation.[59]

Civil rights leaders and their Senate allies did not agree. Since his private meeting with RFK two years earlier, Wilkins had repeatedly urged

JFK to include a Title III provision in his civil rights package. Brownell had dropped a similar provision from the 1957 civil rights bill. Title III would empower the attorney general to bring suits and seek injunctions against southern public officials to end segregation and voting discrimination. RFK refused. Civil rights leaders persisted.

When Jacob Javitts agreed to introduce an enforcement amendment, RFK immediately sprang into action. In a dramatic appearance before the House Judiciary Committee in October, he warned that a Title III amendment "would reach too many things" and make it difficult "to control in advance the actions of local police." Some thought that Kennedy was merely trying to appease the conservatives. In fact, his motives were not purely pragmatic. He feared that Title III, like the Kastenmeier amendment, would turn the federal government into a national police force.

This ran contrary to RFK's interpretation of federal power. Javitts tried to persuade Kennedy to compromise. He even offered to drop Title III in the Senate if Kennedy would support a narrower amendment that would strengthen penalties against police abuse. Kennedy refused. Clarence Mitchell, NAACP's Washington lobbyist, was disgusted and called Kennedy a sellout and accused him of joining the ranks of those who opposed civil rights enforcement.

Mitchell spoke in anger, and his comments were unfair. RFK didn't think like Ellender, John Stennis, and southern segregationists, but his arcane defense of federalism seemed to play into the hands of the conservatives. In the final version of the bill, which the Kennedys approved, the Kastenmeier amendment was eventually deleted and no Title III provision was included. The issue of stronger criminal civil rights enforcement was effectively dead. This was not necessarily a major disappointment for Marshall, for he continued to have serious problems with the "complexity" of the existing federal criminal enforcements provisions: "The legal difficulties in bringing prosecutions were much more complicated than people realized."[60]

The debate on the bill dragged on, and the tension was felt at the DOJ. When Gilbert Harrison, editor of the *New Republic,* mildly challenged the DOJ's enforcement policies, Marshall icily reminded him that the federal government did not have a national police force and ridiculed any such idea as "an extreme alternative."[61]

———◆———

The assassination of JFK in November 1963 shocked and saddened civil rights leaders. Despite the squabbles they had had with him and despite the indecision and at times opposition he expressed to some of their goals, they had come to regard Kennedy as a friend—a man who had grown in office and who sincerely grappled with the complexities of America's racial dilemma. But they were also aware that Kennedy did not fully understand the dangers inherent in southern violence.

Although the Kennedy civil rights bill was a landmark in civil rights legislation and would permanently ban segregation in American public institutions, it did nothing to strengthen federal law against racial terrorism. RFK and Marshall stuck to their belief that sheriffs and local officials, not the federal government, were responsible for protecting blacks. As a result, the reality for most blacks was that their churches, schools, homes, and ultimately their lives were still at risk. Except in the cases of the highly publicized violence at Ole Miss and Birmingham and the attacks on the freedom riders, the White House never brought federal power to bear against racial violence.

During Kennedy's last year in office, the DOJ filed fewer criminal civil rights cases (16) than Eisenhower had in his final year (19). Marshall blamed this more on scarce resources than on his limiting philosophy of federalism: "If we had unlimited funds and staff we would have pushed for more prosecutions."[62]

John Kennedy's death snuffed out the Camelot dream. With the nation in deep mourning and undergoing intense soul-searching, all eyes now turned to the man who replaced JFK. Lyndon Johnson, a southerner and a man who had spent most of his political career battling against civil rights, worried black leaders. The South was even more defiant and violent than ever, and civil rights leaders wondered whether Johnson could fulfill the Kennedy promise and lead the nation away from its dreary racial past—a past that he had done so much to perpetuate.

6

Did We Overcome?

The Johnson Years

A crowd of nearly 10,000 gathered at Wooldridge Park in Austin, Texas, on the warm spring evening of May 22, 1948. They came to hear the tall, lanky, ex-schoolteacher turned politician from the small central Texas county of Blanco. They weren't disappointed. The crowd whooped it up when Lyndon Johnson said Truman's civil rights proposals were "a farce and a sham—an effort to set up a police state in the guise of liberty. I am opposed to that program."[1]

The rally was the official kickoff for Johnson's 1948 Senate campaign. Locked in a tight primary race with Texas governor Coke Stevenson, Johnson moved to firmly establish his credentials as a bona fide states' righter and champion segregationist. He assured the mostly white crowd that he would not betray the cause of white supremacy. In campaign stops in east Texas, which had a strong Deep South air, Johnson occasionally tossed in a line or two about vowing to fight against federal domination and preserving states' rights. His words were cheered by delighted crowds.

From the day he was elected to Congress in 1937 and throughout most of his Senate years in the 1950s, Johnson kept his word. Twenty-seven times, he voted against civil rights legislation, including three votes against antilynching legislation and nine votes against the repeal or reform of the poll tax. He also voted against Roosevelt's Federal Employment Practices Committee; withholding federal funds for housing, colleges, and schools; nonsegregated railway labor unions; armed forces integration; and nonsegregated selective service registration.

Mississippi senator John Stennis, leader of the Senate's segregationist bloc, considered Johnson a loyal ally and a good friend. Johnson was flattered and sent Stennis a warm note pledging to always reciprocate the friendship.[2]

117

A lot had happened since Johnson's early Senate days. Always a fast study, Johnson ingratiated himself with the Senate power brokers and became a master at deal-making in congressional chambers. With his eye on national office, Johnson soon rose in his party's ranks. By the mid-1950s, he had become a Senate statesman and even somewhat of a moderate on racial issues. He received high praise from Senate liberals and the Eisenhower administration for playing the key role in brokering a compromise with southern Democrats on the 1957 and 1960 civil rights bills. Johnson's name had luster and political marquee value to northern party moderates.

At the Democratic convention in July 1961, Johnson got his payoff. The presidential nominee, John F. Kennedy, needed southern votes to win, and Johnson could deliver them. Over the loud protests of party liberals, civil rights leaders, and his own brother, RFK, John Kennedy selected Johnson as his vice presidential running mate.

Two-and-a-half years and an assassin's bullet later, Johnson was president himself. To the relief and joy of civil rights leaders, LBJ moved quickly to assert leadership in Congress on civil rights. He effectively used the skills and tricks honed over a quarter century in politics to break the Senate stalemate on Kennedy's stalled civil rights bill and win its congressional passage in June 1964. It appeared that he had finally buried the ghosts of his segregationist past.

———— • ◆ • ————

Johnson, however, now faced an even tougher problem. In June, the world's attention was riveted on Mississippi, where SNCC activists Michael Schwerner, Andrew Goodman, and James Chaney had disappeared while traveling on a lonely highway north of Meridian. For eight weeks, a small army of FBI personnel, Navy Seabees, and state and local police searched frantically for the young men. Civil rights leaders and many government officials (including Hoover) were fairly certain that the men would never be found alive. But civil rights leaders also wondered whether the massive federal machinery that Johnson had set in motion to find the men would also be used to end the daily campaign of terror waged against blacks and civil rights workers. Doubts persisted.[3]

In late June 1964, two reporters from the *New York Herald* talked with Johnson about federal intervention. They said that Johnson "recognizes the rights reserved to the states to uphold law and order." Johnson apparently held the same tightly restricted view of the role of federal law enforcement in the South as the Kennedys had. But events were forcing Johnson down a different path.[4]

During that same week, the president told reporters at the White House that he had ordered Hoover to send more agents to Mississippi. While Johnson guaranteed that the killers would be brought to justice, he also cautioned that he would not turn the FBI into "a federal police force." He felt that this was "inconsistent with the tradition of the country." He would look first to "governors and local officials to keep the peace and to protect its citizens." In these sentiments, Johnson echoed RFK.[5]

Marshall, who stayed on for a brief period at the DOJ after John Kennedy's assassination, was deeply shaken by the disappearance of Schwerner, Goodman, and Chaney. To make matters worse, there was a fresh wave of bombings near McComb, Mississippi. Wondering what kind of people and system he was dealing with in the state, Marshall described Mississippi as a "frontierlike society and atmosphere."

If local law enforcement personnel and officials interpreted the law as they saw fit, then, Marshall concluded, this created "a law enforcement problem to which there is no satisfactory answer." Mississippi teetered on the brink of anarchy, and local officials were doing nothing to stop the process. The answer may not have been satisfactory to Marshall, but based on his federalist convictions, it was inescapable: The federal government would have to take even stronger action.[6]

After an extensive fact-finding tour of the state, NAACP executive secretary Roy Wilkins and a small delegation met with RFK. They demanded that Johnson declare the state in rebellion, impose martial law, and send in a contingent of federal troops to restore order. RFK would have none of that. He told Wilkins that responsibility for containing the violence was a local matter for law enforcement. He promised to send more federal marshals and to request more FBI agents, but that was it.

A week later, RFK hadn't changed his mind. Before boarding a plane for West Germany, he told reporters that the federal government "lacks power to take preventive police action in Mississippi." The attorney general left the distinct impression that the federal government's hands were tied.[7]

Kennedy and Marshall were lone wolves in the legal community on the question of federal enforcement. Twenty-nine leading constitutional experts were troubled by the "misleading simplicity "of RFK's statement. In an open letter, widely quoted in the media, they stated they were appalled that RFK was so ill informed about the law and seemingly dense about history. They cited specific federal statutes that empowered the federal government to act and named presidents who had moved to restore order in the states. If the attorney general had been their student, they would have flunked him in constitutional law.

The debate spilled over into Congress. New York representative John Lindsay inserted the experts' letter in full into the *Congressional Record* and requested that RFK explain his position. Three weeks later, the battered and beleaguered attorney general was clearly on the defensive. He assigned Nicholas Katzenbach to respond to the critics. Under Kennedy, the assistant attorney general was increasingly handling more of the civil rights load at the DOJ. He claimed that RFK's remarks were not an accurate and complete statement of his views.

Katzenbach reminded Lindsay that Kennedy had sent federal troops and marshals to protect the freedom riders in Alabama and to Ole Miss to restore order. He insisted that Kennedy had also increased the number of marshals, FBI agents, and DOJ attorneys in the South. But he did not agree that the Mississippi situation had deteriorated to the point that federal intervention was necessary. Katzenbach said the DOJ would continue "to seek the cooperation of state officials" to prevent further violence.[8]

RFK was not totally oblivious to the extreme menace of Klan violence. He suggested to Hoover that the FBI keep a closer watch on Klan chapters and perhaps even use more informants. But he did not push Hoover. And for some black Mississippians, that was a costly error.[9]

———————— • ◆ • ————————

For Mazie Moore of Meadville, Mississippi, the grief began two months before Schwerner, Chaney, and Goodman disappeared. On the evening of April 24, she reported to Sheriff Wayne Hutto that her son Charles was missing. Hutto told her not to worry. Charles, age 19, and his friend Henry Dee, also 19, worked part-time at a sawmill in Meadville. They were last seen standing by the side of the road near a gas station on the outskirts of town. Hutto said they had probably gone searching for a job and would turn up soon.

Mazie Moore still worried. Four days earlier, Charles had been expelled from Alcorn A&M, the all-black state university, for taking part in a student demonstration. That was enough to typecast her son as a troublemaker in the eyes of many local whites.

The weeks dragged on, with no sign of the pair. Hutto told Moore that the owner of the sawmill where Dee worked owed Dee money that he hadn't picked up. The mill owner had cracked, "It's not like colored people not to come for their money."

John Bowles finally cleared up the mystery. While fishing in the Old River, near the town of Tallulah, Louisiana, a hundred miles west of Neshoba County, his line got tangled up on an object that turned out to be the lower torso of Moore's bloated body. Moore was identified by the Alcorn room key in his pocket. FBI agents rushed to the area, hoping that perhaps they had gotten the first break in the search for the three civil rights workers. A day later, a search party found the lower part of Dee's body. FBI agents and navy frogmen spent the next two days in boats borrowed from Mississippi's and Louisiana's fish and game commissions scouring the muddy river bottom looking for other bodies. None were found.

The case was not a priority for the FBI, but it was not hard to piece together the facts. FBI informers and agents had begun to infiltrate the Klan factions. For several weeks before the murders, a rumor had been floating around that black militants were coming to the area to attack whites. Because it was generally known that Moore had been active in student demonstrations, he automatically became a prime suspect in the alleged "black militant plot."

Klansmen who spotted Moore and Dee standing by the side of the road trying to hitch a ride put out the word. Soon, two white men pulled up and offered them a lift. Their overly friendly attitude apparently made Moore suspicious. He noted that a pickup truck with several white men inside was trailing close behind their car. One of the men claimed that he was an Internal Revenue Service (IRS) agent and shouted at them, "Dammit, you niggers get in this car." Moore and Dee complied and were taken to the Homchitto Woods. The men ordered them out of the car at gunpoint, tied them to a tree, and took turns beating them until their flesh was broken and bloody. Supposedly, they were trying to get the youths to tell where the guns were hidden.

The kidnappers wrapped the unconscious boys in tarpaulins, drove to the river, loaded their bodies down with heavy chains, and dumped them in the water. The story of black militants and guns was a concoction that the Klansmen themselves probably didn't believe. But in the climate of racial terror that gripped the state, any excuse—no matter how flimsy— was enough to commit murder.

Dee and Moore were only the latest black victims. During the prior eight months, five other blacks had been murdered, and others were beaten or driven from nearby towns on even the faintest suspicion of being involved in civil rights activity. Most of the attacks were done with the knowledge or connivance of local police, and no arrests were made. Furthermore, the FBI had generally shown little interest in the violence. As one official noted, there was "no link to the civil rights workers."[10]

Local civil rights leader Charles Evers bitterly asked about the FBI, "What are they doing here? What good are they?" With national attention focused on the search in nearby Neshoba County, the Dee and Moore case did cause a ripple of concern among law enforcement personnel. The FBI identified the alleged murderers, and four months later, James Ford Seale, a truck driver, and Charles Marcus Edwards, a papermill worker, were ar-

rested. The men could have been brought up on federal charges, including kidnapping, but the DOJ instead turned the evidence over to the state
for prosecution. Local prosecutors did not even bother to seek indictments. And despite the army of reporters in the state, no mention appeared in the press when local officials refused to indict Edwards and
Seale.[11]

---------•◆•---------

The murders of Dee and Moore were the latest in the tragic and continuing saga of Mississippi violence. The murders of Schwerner, Chaney, and
Goodman, however, were a different story. Marshall was now worried
that Mississippi was fast slipping into a no-man's-land where lawlessness
prevailed and local officials did nothing about it. He candidly told
Katzenbach that many law enforcement officials in the state were helping
the Klan. He did not blame Hoover for the breakdown.

This was risky and would seriously jeopardize the shaky relationship
between the FBI director and the Civil Rights Division. Marshall tried to
finesse the situation. He suggested that the FBI should develop better
methods of identifying violent individuals and groups. He also advised
Katzenbach to assign more DOJ attorneys with organized crime experience to civil rights cases. Marshall's final stop was at the White House. "I
went to Johnson with a memo stating that it was time to energize the
Bureau and move into action."[12]

Marshall tried another tack to get Hoover's cooperation. He played on
the director's penchant for spying and covert operations against a favorite
target, the Communist Party. In a follow-up memo to Johnson, Marshall
suggested that Hoover could use "specially trained, specially assigned
agents" for intelligence-gathering inside the Klan. Marshall didn't know it,
but he had planted the first seed of what would soon become the FBI's supersecret (and illegal) Counter-Intelligence Program (COINTELPRO)
against white and black radicals. Marshall realized that Johnson was the
only person who could really make Hoover act in Mississippi.

Hoover respected and feared Johnson, probably because he viewed
him as someone as tough and in his own way as ruthless as he himself
was when it came to wielding power. At the time, Johnson was beginning
to consider taking stronger action in Mississippi. As the search for the
three men dragged on and as more burnings and bombings occurred, he
ordered Hoover to go to Jackson, open an office, and send more FBI
agents in. Hoover obeyed. With much press fanfare, he told reporters that
he was assigning fifty-three additional agents to the state. He claimed
that this was ten times the number of agents assigned to any other southern state.[13]

Hoover had few qualms about his task. Despite his thinly veiled racist views and his contempt for the civil rights movement, he regarded Klan members as low-life white trash who operated outside the law. The Klan sullied his purist ideal of an orderly, law-abiding, Christian American society. Hoover drew the line between the Klan riffraff and Mississippi state officials and law enforcement personnel for whom he had a healthy respect.[14]

In Jackson, Hoover had cordial meetings with Mississippi governor Paul Johnson Jr. and local officials. He praised them for their integrity and assured them that he would rely on them to maintain law. At a press conference with the governor, he emphasized that the FBI "most certainly will not protect civil rights workers." This did not satisfy Charles Evers, who had taken over as NAACP state secretary after the murder of his brother, Medger Evers. At the close of the press conference, while Hoover prepared to leave, Evers stepped in front of him and berated him for not investigating more cases of violence. Hoover quickly recovered his composure and motioned him to a conference room, where the two men talked for ten minutes. Evers later told reporters that "we wanted to give him our side of the story."

He knew that theirs was a story that Hoover would not hear—nor probably want to hear—from Governor Johnson or any other white Mississippi official. But somebody had to tell him. Ironically, while Hoover praised Johnson, terrorists firebombed a black church in nearby Greenwood. Officials claimed they could find no clues, and no arrests were made.[15]

———— •◆• ————

The search for the missing civil rights workers continued through July. Hoover and his aides wrestled over strategies to attack the Klan. Some FBI officials felt that the responsibility for the investigations should logically fall to the General Intelligence Division, which handled mostly common criminal matters. These officials saw the Klan as a criminal group that should be broken up by employing orthodox criminal investigation procedures. Others argued that the job should go to the Domestic Intelligence Division (DID), which handled covert operations.

Hoover agreed with these latter officials. The kind of campaign that he had in mind would be a no-holds-barred assault patterned after the deep-cover campaign he had waged against the Communist Party. He promptly assigned the job to the DID, which had developed wide experience in the penetration of subversive organizations.

The Inspection Division of the DOJ backed Hoover, and on July 30, 1964, the DID got approval to begin preparations. Katzenbach knew about the secret plans and supported them, but he also apparently thought along traditional law enforcement lines. He knew that the FBI manual directed agents against "wholesale investigations" of individuals who "merely attend meetings." But Hoover didn't follow the book, and Katzenbach did not really know that. Former agent Robert Wall did and later quit in disgust over Hoover's spy policies. He told how agents, using the pretext of the Red menace, placed wiretaps and mail covers, compiled dossiers, amd maintained surveillance on the established civil rights organizations.[16]

When the bodies of Schwerner, Goodman, and Chaney were found in August, Hoover kicked the FBI's destabilization campaign into high gear. He targeted seventeen Klan organizations and nine "hate" organizations, "which he would expose, disrupt, and otherwise neutralize." Hoover also used the full array of informers, wiretaps, mail covers, poison-pen letters, and harassing phone calls against the Klan leaders.

He ordered duplicate Klaverns to be set up, most of which were led by FBI informants or agents. By November, the director, in a self-congratulatory mood, bragged that they had done a good job on them and vowed that the FBI would soon put the groups out of business. Hoover was praised like a conquering hero by the press, public officials, and some civil rights leaders for attacking terror. There were, however, some dissenters. The Council of Federated Organizations reported that the number of incidents of racial violence in Mississippi actually increased between June and September despite the heavy FBI presence in the state.[17]

Although Hoover's secret methods were known only to a few government insiders in those days, they paled in comparison with the methods used in FBI operations against the Communist Party and black radicals. Hoover approved 287 operations (an average of 40 per year) against the Klan, compared to more than 100 per year against the Communists. Against the Black Panthers, Black Muslims, and assorted black nationalist groups, Hoover employed more than 7,500 "ghetto informants" and hundreds of FBI agents in a well-coordinated national campaign to annihilate these organizations.

Federal investigators probing FBI abuses during congressional hearings in the 1970s marveled at the scope of Hoover's program. Not even the Communist subversive and counterespionage programs matched it. In all, Hoover had approved more than 2,411 COINTELPRO proposals, virtually all of them against black or leftist groups. The discrepancy in results was fairly easy to understand. In part, Hoover warred against the Klan because he personally loathed them, but in larger part, he did so because he was ordered to by Johnson. By contrast, he warred against the Communists and black radicals because *he* wanted to.[18]

King, like other civil rights leaders, was skeptical of Hoover. In September 1962, King had publicly blamed the FBI for not diligently investigating civil rights abuses in Georgia. Hoover was especially angered at King's assertion that the majority of the FBI agents were southerners and by inference racists.

Technically, King was wrong. The majority of the agents were not from the South. The problem was that many FBI agents stationed at southern posts thought and acted like white southerners, and many of their superiors did, too.

FBI agent Arthur Murtaugh, who worked on civil rights cases in several southern cities during the 1960s and later quit the bureau in protest over FBI practices, told the House Select Committee investigating the King assassination, "I never knew of the situation where someone who wasn't a good local boy wasn't assigned to the senior resident post." Their job was to send all reports and communications to the Washington Bureau headquarters by AIRTEL. Murtaugh also noted that one senior agent he worked under had routinely tailored all reports he made on civil rights complaints to minimize their seriousness. That way, the DOJ would consider them frivolous complaints and take no action.[19]

Hoover bided his time and did not respond to King. It wasn't just that Hoover objected to the criticism of the bureau. He had also developed a hatred of King that bordered on the pathological. It was grounded in Hoover's complex blend of racism, puritanism, and plain jealousy. He saw King as the Antichrist.

————— ◆ —————

By 1964, Hoover had moved from keeping a standard surveillance of King to employing the full arsenal of dirty weapons against him. This included mail covers, phone wiretaps, hidden microphones in motel rooms, informants, and eventually poison-pen letters. Previously, Hoover had worked quietly behind the scenes to get King. But that was no longer enough. Now he wanted to destroy King publicly.

The moment he waited for came in November 1964, a few weeks after King had been awarded the Nobel Peace Prize. At a press conference, Hoover dropped his infamous bombshell, calling King "a notorious liar."[20]

The "feud" between King and Hoover, as the press quickly tagged it, was out in the open at last. A meeting was arranged on December 1 to clear the air. The press and public much later mistakenly latched on to the tale that Hoover used the confidential information about King's alleged sexual improprieties and the Communist ties of his associates to force King to back away from his criticism of the FBI. However, neither FBI officials nor King aides who were present at the meeting said that Hoover did any such thing.[21]

During the three-hour meeting, Hoover delivered a fifty-five-minute rambling monologue that confirmed many of the worst fears and suspicions that King and other civil rights leaders had about FBI practices and Hoover's own racism. He admitted knowing that sheriffs and local officials had Klan ties and that they directly participated in or worked to cover up crimes of violence. Hoover also knew that it was almost impossible to get white juries and judges in state courts to convict white defendants who committed violent crimes against blacks. Yet he told them he would not "jump the gun" and recommend that the DOJ prosecute a case unless the department had solid evidence to get a conviction. Hoover also repeated his claim that the FBI had no authority to make on-the-spot arrests; it could only investigate cases, he said.

As soon as the news broke that Hoover had criticized King, Burke Marshall enthusiastically defended Hoover against his critics. He assured Katzenbach that the reports about the reduced number of FBI agents in Mississippi were false. Marshall thought Hoover was right in resisting those who wanted an even more expansive federal role, and he advised the White House that he would not support an "investigative" grand jury to probe the ties between local sheriffs and Klan bombers in southern Mississippi. He counseled patience and predicted that "change is going to come accompanied by disorder."[22]

Meanwhile, Hoover basked in the public limelight after his attack. He used the media as a personal forum to vindicate his views. He repeated his stock line: The FBI was not a police force but only an investigative agency. He carved out for a suddenly attentive public his role as the guardian of the gate and swore that as long as he was director, the FBI would "never become a lackey to self-serving individuals or pressure groups." Civil rights leaders knew whom he meant.[23]

While Hoover was in the midst of his noisy press campaign, he also inadvertently confirmed one of his critic's suspicions. In January, he made his annual appearance before the House Appropriations Committee to justify his standard request for more money (which was always approved). He spoke glowingly of the FBI's crime-fighting record and tossed out big numbers. According to him, agents had arrested more than 13,000 fugitives, recovered more than 20,000 stolen autos, and taken in more than $203 million in fines, savings, and recoveries.

He was particularly proud that bureau investigations had resulted in more than 12,850 convictions. Perhaps through oversight or simply unconcern, he also confirmed all the civil rights activists' charges about FBI obstructionism, noting that the bureau had investigated fewer than 1,000 civil rights cases.[24]

In December 1964, nineteen Klan members and two local sheriffs were charged with civil rights violations in the murders of the three civil rights workers. Much of the general public believed the FBI had turned the corner in its battle against the Klan. Even some civil rights leaders applauded Hoover. SCLC's Andrew Young thought that the meeting with King had forced Hoover to take more aggressive actions against the Klan, "so in a sense we were reassured that the FBI was doing its law enforcement job."[25]

Young's assessment was premature. Hoover's dirty little war against the Klan was still in its skirmishing stages. On March 25, 1965, Viola Liuzzo, a white suburban housewife and mother of five from Michigan, was shotgunned to death on an open highway outside Selma, Alabama. She had been ferrying marchers between Selma and Montgomery. National attention was already focused on the SCLC-led freedom march from Selma to Montgomery, which had drawn thousands. The murder of Liuzzo touched off a wave of national revulsion over the murderous power of the Klan.

Hoover had no problem solving this case. Within hours, Hoover had the names of the killers, using information supplied by Gary Rowe—the FBI's deep plant in the Klan who rode in the murder car. Johnson knew he had scored a public relations coup, and he intended to take full advantage of it. He checked with aides to make sure he could get prime network time for a national address. The next day, flanked by a stony-faced Hoover and Katzenbach, who had taken over as attorney general when RFK decided to run for the Senate, Johnson told a national TV audience that the FBI had arrested four Klansmen for the murder of Viola Liuzzo.

During the course of the talk, he publicly revealed that he had ordered the FBI to go after the Klan and promised to introduce proposals to strengthen federal criminal statutes against racial violence. Although Johnson gave no specifics about the legislation, civil rights leaders were ecstatic. King immediately wired Hoover to praise him for his prompt arrest of the Klansmen. Publicly, Johnson was the first Democratic president to fully support legislation that would give the federal government solid legal weapons to use in prosecuting and punishing civil rights violations.

What the nation did not see was that, behind the scenes, Hoover had tried everything he could to discourage Johnson from getting involved in the case. In one memo, he referred to King as "this character" and urged Johnson not to acknowledge his telegram.[26]

———— • ◆ • ————

There were, however, several indications that Johnson and the general public had not moved as close to racial enlightenment as first appeared. The murders of Jimmy Lee Jackson and the Reverend James Reeb illustrated the glaring contrast in how the administration handled cases of violence against blacks and cases against whites.

Jackson, a young black laborer, was gunned down in February by an Alabama state trooper during a demonstration in Marion, Alabama. Jackson was unarmed and was not threatening the officer. Less than two weeks later, Reeb, a young white Unitarian minister from Boston, in Alabama to aid SCLC's voter registration drive, was severely beaten by white thugs on a Selma street. Three white men were immediately arrested and charged with the beating. The DOJ considered filing civil rights charges against the men.

Johnson sent flowers to Reeb in the hospital, and when he received news of the minister's death a day later, he and Vice President Hubert Humphrey stopped in the middle of a White House meeting to call Reeb's widow and express their condolences. A week later, Johnson sent an air force plane to fly Reeb's widow and four children to her family's home in Casper, Wyoming. Memorial services for Reeb were held in dozens of cities. Humphrey and Senator Robert Kennedy, along with a parade of other dignitaries, attended the service in Washington, D.C..

In the Jackson case, by contrast, state officials refused to identify the Alabama state trooper who had shot him. Jackson's family did not receive any calls from Johnson or Humphrey, and no public officials attended his memorial service in Marion. King understood the differences in how the two men were treated. During the eulogy he delivered before a mostly black crowd of about four thousand, he blamed Jackson's death on the "timidity of the federal government unwilling to protect the rights of its citizens."

For many blacks, Jackson was yet another addition to the long list of black victims of violence and official indifference. Their anger was reaching the flash point, but unlike King, they were not willing to turn the other cheek nor rely on the good graces of the federal government to solve the problem of racist violence.

A short time later, President Johnson did order troops and federal marshals to protect civil rights marchers during the march from Selma to Montgomery. But it would have been difficult for him not to take aggressive federal action, because the nation had reacted in horror to the clubbing and trampling of peaceful marchers a few days before by Alabama state troopers. Meanwhile, to many blacks, the federal government was still the problem. And as the summer of 1965 approached, Johnson had a new worry.[27]

————— • ◆ • —————

When the smoke cleared in August 1965, thirty-four people were dead, 1,000 were wounded, 4,000 were arrested, and more than $40 million in property damage had occurred during five days of black rioting in Los

Angeles. Nearly all the victims were blacks, most were unarmed, and most had been killed by police or National Guard bullets. Four years earlier, the Civil Rights Commission had held special hearings in Los Angeles and listened as civil rights groups and local blacks denounced the LAPD for its alleged brutal treatment of the city's minorities.

With the explosion in Watts, police violence had suddenly become a major issue in the North for the first time since World War II. But the media and public officials rushed to absolve the LAPD of any responsibility. The McCone Commission, appointed by California governor Pat Brown to investigate the violence, flatly rejected demands for a civilian police review board. Instead, the commission weakly called for an "inspector general" to review citizen complaints.[28]

Johnson was terribly shaken by the violence. He took it as a personal affront by ungrateful blacks whom he had made a special effort to help by pushing civil rights legislation and implementing an array of Great Society social programs for the poor. For days, he refused to read the cables from his advisers on the situation in the city.[29]

Johnson was not simply reacting like a petulant child; he also feared that the violence so far confined mostly to the South would now spill over into the urban North and bring more confrontations between white police and the black poor. When he finally recovered his senses, he searched for the appropriate federal response. Johnson seemed to understand that the riot was not the handiwork of "outside agitators" or Communist subversives. Hoover had dispelled that notion the summer before.

Following the July 1964 riots in Rochester, New York, and Philadelphia, Johnson had ordered Hoover to prepare a report specifically detailing the involvement of subversives. To the president's disappointment, Hoover found no evidence of a conspiracy. Johnson was convinced that the riots could cost him white votes, damage his hard-won popularity with blacks, and increase the already considerable resistance among congressional conservatives to his Great Society programs. White House aide Walter Jenkins called the riots Johnson's Achilles' heel.[30]

Between hunting for subversives and searching for scapegoats, Johnson came to see that there were deep social reasons for the rising black anger. He told reporters that many blacks felt that "justice is not open to them." He dispatched Deputy Attorney General Ramsey Clark to head a federal task force to recommend resolutions. For the moment, Johnson preferred to deal with urban violence by modest increases in government spending on social programs and by developing better community relations.[31]

Johnson ordered that the Community Relations Service be moved from the Department of Commerce to the DOJ, and he directed it to take a more active role in relations between police and the community. This was essential. Polls showed that it was a politically volatile and controversial issue and that there was a gaping disparity between white and black perceptions of the problem; in April 1965, 35 percent of black males viewed police abuse as a major problem, while only 7 percent of white men did. Hoover had no sympathy. He complained that blacks "cry police brutality on the slightest provocation." He didn't have to worry, though, for Johnson did not intend to involve the DOJ in any full-scale investigation of police abuse.[32]

King believed that this was a mistake. He had already gotten a first-hand glimpse of the destruction and anger. During a brief "peacekeeping" mission to Watts, King had been jeered by some young blacks. He warned that conflict was inevitable when blacks confront law enforcement that is "as totally prejudiced as it is totally white." He urged Johnson not to ignore the deadly consequences of police violence for the ghetto poor.[33]

By the end of the year, Johnson's political troubles had already begun to mount. His Great Society programs were under attack as ineffectual and wasteful, and the Vietnam War occupied much of his attention. Civil rights leaders continued to press him to keep his promise to push for new legislation ending housing and employment discrimination and a stronger statute to curb racist violence. Johnson tried to keep his pledge.

———————•◆•———————

In January, Johnson called on Congress to give the federal courts the power "to try those who murder, attack or intimidate civil rights workers and others." But he did not specifically mention blacks. He knew that the mood of Congress was changing. In the wake of the Watts riots, more and more House representatives were opposed to any new civil rights initiatives, which they viewed as unnecessary appeasements of civil rights leaders and rewards for black lawlessness.[34]

This created a huge dilemma for DOJ attorneys. They were divided over exactly what kind of criminal sanctions amendment would be palatable to Congress. Louis Claiborne, assistant solicitor general, argued that Congress should not modify or eliminate the intent provision in Section 242. He felt that, by themselves, racial attacks on blacks did not interfere with due process rights and that Congress did not have the power under the Thirteenth or Fourteenth Amendments to make racial assaults federal crimes. These were individual acts that the states should punish, Claiborne insisted, and the intent provision in the federal conspiracy statutes was a valid measure to determine if an individual's rights had actually been violated.[35]

If Claiborne had prevailed, the DOJ would have had almost no leverage to get Congress to substantially alter the enforcement statutes. Fortunately, the Supreme Court rendered Claiborne's argument moot at the end of March 1966. The members of the Court unanimously ruled in two civil rights cases that the federal government had the right to prosecute individual acts of violence and that Congress could legislate against racially motivated violence.[36]

In a side note, Judge Thurgood Marshall, whom Johnson had appointed solicitor general, presented the government's case and found himself on the same side with his onetime adversary, former Attorney General Tom Clark, who still sat on the Court. Clark added a final touch of irony when he wrote in his opinion that there was "no doubt that Congress has the power to enact laws punishing all conspiracies with or without state action that interfere with Fourteenth Amendment rights."[37]

With the legal path clear, DOJ attorneys now began trying to shape a workable enforcement amendment. Title V strengthened penalties, eliminated the proof of intent provision, and specified nine "protected activities"—from housing to education. Violators were subject to federal prosecution. In April 1966, Johnson sent his entire legislative package to Congress.

Almost immediately, SNCC and CORE militants began attacking the bill as weak and ineffectual. At a stormy White House conference on June 1 and 2, CORE activists attacked the DOJ and the FBI for failing to protect blacks and civil rights workers (SNCC had refused to participate in this meeting). Some called for Hoover's resignation. They claimed that Title V was badly flawed since it did not specify that law enforcement officials could be prosecuted for denying an individual's due process rights.

The conferees demanded that Johnson add further provisions to Title V to toughen the penalties for police abuse. But the DOJ had invested too much time in drafting the title to bow to pressure. Johnson realized that he would have a hard enough time getting the bill passed. Southern Democrats and conservatives were gearing up for a prolonged battle against a controversial provision that would outlaw discrimination in housing sales. The conservatives also denounced the antiviolence statute, resurrecting the ancient argument that it infringed on the Constitution and violated state sovereignty.[38]

The proposals had barely arrived when the conservatives tried to make deletions, change the wording, and use stalling tactics to water down the amendment. North Carolina senator Sam Ervin, who had staked out the high ground as a self-appointed constitutional watchdog, led the attack. He claimed that the Fourteenth Amendment "did not confer on persons of any race special privileges." He contended that Congress had no authority to pass legislation that infringed on state jurisdiction. Ervin was a formidable roadblock because the legislation would first have to clear the Judiciary Committee on Constitutional Rights. As committee chairman, Ervin was in the perfect position to gut the amendment. He scheduled hearings for June.[39]

On opening day, an all-white audience packed the hearing room. Katzenbach, the first witness, gamely tried to explain the complex amendments, but Ervin repeatedly butted in with objections. For the better part of two hours, Katzenbach had to sweat under hot TV lights listening to Ervin tick off a long list of objections to each of the provisions in the bill. When it came to Title V, he told Katzenbach that he would not "sacrifice" criminal law for a "newfound infatuation with sociology."

The administration got a momentary reprieve when news reached Washington that James Meredith had been shot on a Mississippi highway while making his one-man march against terror. With racial violence back in the news, Ervin backed off slightly. He told reporters that he would propose his own constitutional amendment to give Congress authority to punish private acts of violence. The cagey veteran was really playing for time. He knew that such an amendment would require ratification by three-fourths of the states—which would require a hopelessly costly and time-consuming effort. The DOJ was opposed.[40]

---·◆·---

During the summer of 1966, rioting broke out in Chicago, Cleveland, and Omaha. SNCC and CORE renounced nonviolence and integration, kicked whites out of their organizations, and embraced the rhetoric of Black Power and self-defense. As liberals and moderate sympathizers beat a wholesale retreat from both groups, the momentum swung back to Ervin and congressional opponents of civil rights.

Politically, Johnson was vulnerable. In August, he watched helplessly as House members grabbed at the chance to show that they could get tough with the black militants. The representatives overwhelmingly passed an amendment to the civil rights bill that made it a federal crime to cross state lines to "incite to riot." Johnson was displeased with the antiriot provision. He knew it would alienate civil rights leaders, but the bigger risk he faced was alienating Congress. He felt he had no choice but to support the measure. The day after passage, Johnson congratulated the House.[41]

Johnson had also begun to hear the first rumblings of a white backlash. A Gallup poll in October 1966 showed that nearly 75 percent of whites felt that blacks were getting too much. During off-year elections in November, Republicans—who had hammered away at Johnson for permissiveness, the breakdown in law and order, and economic wastefulness—rolled up big gains. The Democrats lost forty-seven seats in Congress.[42]

The backlash was being felt in an even deadlier way as well. Hoover, perhaps forgetting his boast the year before that he would wipe out the Klan, reported that the KKK was making a comeback. By summer's end, there were nearly 15,000 hard-core Klan members and tens of thousands of sympathizers. There were fourteen separate Klan organizations nationally and active chapters in Maryland, Delaware, New Jersey, New York, Pennsylvania, Ohio, Indiana, Michigan, Wisconsin, and every southern state. But Hoover reassured the public that "FBI investigations of Klan organizations and their activities are, of course, strictly limited by law."

In truth, they were not. Hoover was still busy running his backroom, covert campaign against Klan factions, but beyond a few high-profile murder cases, the DOJ had not increased the number of indictments and prosecutions it brought for civil rights violations in 1965 and 1966. The numbers weren't much different than those during the Kennedy administration. Unless a prominent murder case with a white victim was involved, Johnson and Katzenbach, albeit reluctantly like the Kennedys, also bowed to political expediency and refused to wield federal law to aggressively prosecute racial assaults against blacks. Worse, in approving the antiriot act to crack down on black violence while merely slapping the Klansmen's hands, Johnson became a reluctant partner in the congressional hypocrisy.[43]

In September, Johnson suffered another setback in Congress as Ervin, who had stepped up the attack on Title V, got his first victory. The Senate caved in to pressure from southern Democrats, who threatened to filibuster, and tabled the bill.

This was Johnson's first loss on civil rights legislation in nine years. At his subsequent press conference, the president looked dejected and physically spent when asked whether he would try to "salvage" Title V. Johnson simply answered, "I don't know." The confidence and decisiveness that had been his trademarks over the past two years in dealing with the press and Congress had suddenly disappeared. All he could add was that he "wasn't sure what Congress would do." For civil rights leaders, the future seemed murkier than ever.[44]

The increasing disarray at the White House had filtered over to the DOJ. Ramsey Clark, who succeeded Katzenbach as attorney general, had the near impossible job of trying to please Ervin and save Title V. Internally, CRD attorneys tinkered with and debated the various points of the amendment. Stephen J. Pollack suggested that the bill should have a "proof of purpose" provision. John Doar, who followed Marshall as CRD chief in January 1965, shared Marshall's view about the limits of federal power and agreed that the intent clause should be eliminated to avoid constitutional difficulties. Doar argued that the amendment should be redrafted to require prosecutors to prove that for an act to be punishable, it had to be the result of intentional interference with the exercise of a right. This was largely a semantic exercise. Doar would still keep the intent restriction in without actually calling it by that term. CRD attorney William Taylor thought the best way out of the morass was to simply design a race-neutral amendment that punished only acts of economic coercion.[45]

Doar still wasn't satisfied. Given the law-and-order mood in Congress, he was convinced that the Senate would never approve any amendment that it perceived would punish police officers and public officials accused of committing civil rights abuses while "doing their job." Doar wanted Clark to assure Congress that the statute could not be used to prosecute law enforcement officers. He believed that the two federal conspiracy statutes were sufficient weapons against police brutality.

Personally, Clark was unequivocal. He wanted the DOJ to become even more active in prosecuting racially motivated violence: "I believed that the federal government should have made more frequent use of the criminal statutes." But Clark knew that the attitudes in Congress against black lawlessness were hardening. Getting a strong Title V provision would be a tough sell.[46]

For his part, Doar read the mood in Congress correctly. During the summer, the House Judiciary Committee scrapped Title V after sharp debate and redrafted its own amendment, H.R. 2516. This amendment retained most of the White House's provisions but exempted all law enforcement and local officials from any prosecution for acts committed during civil disturbances. Ervin took the cue and drafted an amendment that pared from the list of "protected rights" jury trials, state elections, private schools, and state-financed facilities—all of which directly affected police and public officials in the South.[47]

Ervin wasn't finished. Waving high the states' rights flag, he railed that the White House simply had too many "misinterpretations" of the Constitution. He accused the administration of trying to turn the federal government into a federal police force. Ervin had no difficulty convincing the senators that he was right.[48]

All this debate was mostly hyperbole. There was no evidence that Johnson had exerted strong pressure on the DOJ or Congress to push or consider the tougher federal criminal statute. Ervin's best ally in trying to get Congress to water down or scrap the statute altogether was still the long hot summer. In July, the nation would experience the worst racial violence in U.S. history.

———————— • ◆ • ————————

By summer's end in 1967, nearly 100 American cities had experienced "civil disturbances." Eighty-three people were dead, hundreds were wounded, and thousands had been arrested. The property damage totals were in the millions. Nearly all the dead were blacks. And most were killed by police gunfire.

Johnson had basically ignored King's prophecy that police and blacks in the urban areas of the North were hurtling down a collision course. Now that prophecy had come back to haunt him and the nation. But this time,

King was in a much less conciliatory mood. While obligingly criticizing blacks for looting and destroying property, he blamed the police for the violence: "It is wrong for white armed forces to shoot to kill for larceny."[49]

Johnson faced his worst domestic crisis. His Great Society programs had failed miserably to satisfy black needs or stem the rising tide of violence. And much of the white public, appalled by the violence, demanded a halt to social spending and a crackdown on lawless blacks. Johnson's options narrowed.

In a national TV address, Johnson commanded that the police "should and must be respected" and obeyed. Yet his political instincts, which had accounted for much of his success in civil rights, told him that something was terribly wrong in America's ghettos. Get-tough solutions might temporarily appease a frustrated and anxious public, but they would not solve the deep-seated social and economic problems. "It would compound the tragedy if we should settle for order that is imposed by the muzzle of a gun," he noted. Johnson announced that he was appointing a blue-ribbon panel to study the causes of the violence. He went to great lengths to create the impression that the commission had free rein to make any kind of recommendations it deemed appropriate.

But Johnson hedged his bets. His handpicked commissioners, starting with the chairman, Illinois governor Otto Kerner, were considered reliable party stalwarts. John Lindsay, the commission vice chairman, though a Republican, had solid mainstream liberal credentials. The other eleven members were established politicians and leaders from labor, business, and moderate black groups. Johnson expected them to come back with mildly reformist recommendations that would not be too costly nor too condemning of the system, let alone his administration.[50]

While the commission began its arduous job of sifting through mounds of reports and listening to the testimony of hundreds of eyewitnesses and experts, Johnson tried to contain the rage in Congress over black violence. One of his tactics was to downplay civil rights. In his annual congressional address in January, he made only passing reference to civil rights legislation, drawing just scattered applause from his audience. But when he thundered that "the American people have had enough of rising crime and lawlessness," Congress's response was deafening.

Johnson reeled off a long and costly ($100 million) laundry list of anti-crime measures. They included drug interdiction, gun control, and additional FBI personnel. Congress interrupted him with more applause. Johnson's bow to the law-and-order frenzy of Congress worried some civil rights supporters. Indeed, Phillip Hart, Senate sponsor of the civil rights bill, wondered whether Johnson still backed his own bill. Although Johnson assured Hart there was no doubt that he was still committed to the bill, but he also knew that the bill was doomed if he did not change his tactics.

Five days later, Johnson went back to Congress, this time with a carrot-and-stick strategy. He lashed out at the "criminal conduct" of the rioters and promised to support tougher laws. Then he evoked nostalgic memories of past civil rights glories, cited the recent convictions of the Mississippi Klansmen, and noted that "federal laws can reach those who engage in conspiracies against law abiding citizens."[51]

Johnson's political tightrope act was masterful, but Congress was only half listening. Many Congress members weren't concerned about the conspiracies of racist southern sheriffs or brutal northern police, but they did worry about black militants. DOJ attorneys were caught in the middle. They were determined to craft a statute to punish racial violence even though most Congress members believed that the DOJ should go after the black militants.

The day after Johnson spoke, Ervin won another partial victory when he persuaded the Senate Judiciary Committee to strike out any reference to racial designation as the determining criterion for enforcing the statute. Pollack was willing to concede the point. He believed that even without specifying the race of the victim the statute would still be adequate to protect black rights. The next month Pollack had second thoughts and suggested that the word *race* be reinserted into the statute.

The debate caused another delay and played into Ervin's hands. Johnson tried to break the stalemate by tossing in his own antiriot statute, which made inciting to riot a felony that carried a mandatory five-year sentence. This was a blatant reversal of Johnson's previous position, for a year earlier, he had opposed the House antiriot amendment as a violation of free speech and civil liberties. Johnson consoled himself that his statute, unlike the House amendment, would not punish "advocacy" but only "incitement." The Senate Judiciary Committee, however, rejected both Johnson's reasoning and his amendment.[52]

While Congress wrangled over civil rights, Johnson faced another ticklish situation. Following months of investigation, members of the Kerner Commission had become deeply sensitive—even a bit radicalized—about the problems of poor blacks. They listened as speaker after speaker harshly condemned the police for their brutal practices. The commissioners concluded that the ghetto poor, locked in a vicious downward spiral of economic neglect, regarded the police as a cruel "occupying army."

On March 2, the Kerner Commission released its report. The recommendations put much of the blame for the riots on police violence and called for a massive urban renewal program that would cost billions. Johnson was enraged. Days passed with no official word from the president. White House adviser Joseph Califano spent hours arguing with Johnson, trying to get him to send a courtesy acknowledgment to the commission, but Johnson refused. He said that he would have nothing to do with it. He wouldn't even accept a private copy of the report.[53]

Meanwhile, presidential candidates Richard Nixon, Eugene McCarthy, Robert Kennedy, and Ronald Reagan, along with mayors, governors, and nearly everyone else with an official opinion, took turns praising or condemning the report. Finally, at a news conference three weeks later, Johnson was pressed for his reaction. He talked around the report and gave the impression that his reservations pertained solely to costs and implementation matters.

This was partially true. Under pressure from congressional opponents, Johnson had begun to slash spending for domestic programs and redirect more funds from social programs to police, law enforcement training, and weapons. But the basic reason why Johnson distanced himself from the report was, as Califano claimed several months later, because he thought that the commission's emphasis on white racism was overdramatized. In his memoirs, Johnson hinted at the same reason.[54]

Johnson and Hoover had no such problem with one of the minor recommendations buried in the appendix of the Kerner report, which involved the creation of police intelligence units to gather information on black organizations. The commission had in mind social data collection. Hoover had in mind political spying.[55]

This recommendation gave Hoover an even wider opening through which to pursue black militants. With Johnson's approval, he escalated his campaign of political spying and harassment against black organizations. None of this, of course, had anything to do with protecting civil rights, and both Johnson and Hoover knew it.

———— ◆ · ————

The urban upheavals marked a new departure for America and the White House. The public and Congress demanded tougher laws and crackdowns on the violence. The pressure was on to pass new antiriot laws and constitutionally questionable crime control acts, to expand wiretapping, and to beef up spending for police and military armaments. Police departments launched their own arms race. They built up their arsenals with armored cars and trucks, machine guns, battering rams, bulletproof vests, helicopters, and Special Weapons and Tactics (SWAT) teams. They were also armed with new shoot-to-kill directives. The riots also sparked a wild spree of militant organizing among the police rank and file.

Within a year, the Fraternal Order of Police had chapters in thirty-seven states and more than 130,000 members. They lobbied, protested, picketed, demonstrated, leafleted, and even threatened strikes to get politicians to change laws and police procedures in order to gain a free hand in dealing with crime. Clark was alarmed by the new "fortress America" mood: "The DOJ opposed the massive arming of the police. I personally felt that the whole country—Democrats, Republicans, the President and Congress—overemphasized police force. It doesn't solve problems."[56]

Even as the nation's political chill on civil rights deepened, black leaders continued to lobby Congress to pass the civil rights bill. The bill included the weakened antiterrorist amendment that virtually exempted police and public officials from prosecution for acts committed while they were engaged in official functions or on duty. The price was high. The Senate passed its own tough antiriot statute, introduced by South Carolina senator Strom Thurmond. But the bill was still not law. It would have to go to a joint Senate-House conference committee to have the differences ironed out. Civil rights opponents would have had another chance to water the bill down or kill it completely if tragedy had not intervened.[57]

On April 4, an assassin's bullet tore through the neck of Martin Luther King. Renewed rioting in dozens of cities erupted, and when the rioting came within a few blocks of the White House and Capitol Hill, even the most stubborn conservatives realized that something had to be done. As troops circled the White House and the Capitol, Johnson was desperate to get the civil rights bill passed. Throughout the weekend, he sent urgent letters and made frantic calls to congressional leaders and met with a steady stream of black leaders, House representatives, and cabinet officials. At one point, he invoked King's memory, even telling one group that "I know what he would have wanted," as if he had been personally communing with King.

This time, his tactics worked. Congressional leaders and Roy Wilkins preferred to attribute the progress to the NAACP's hard lobbying effort. But the truth was that the public's mixture of guilt and revulsion over King's murder shamed many Congress members into taking action. Within a week, Johnson had his civil rights bill. At a news conference the day after passage, a tired but relieved president praised Congress for "striking the shackles of an old injustice."[58]

The bill was a victory for civil rights enforcement, but it also reflected the deep anguish of a divided White House, the DOJ, and the obstructionist Congress. The antiterrorist amendment kept intact the provisions increasing penalties for color of law violations under Sections 241 and 242, and it specified the types of violations that could be punished. A new Section 245 was added, which made it a crime to commit violence against persons based on race, color, religion, or national origin and specified the types of activities that were punishable. Civil rights leaders rightly considered this a victory.

After nearly a century of protest, they had finally gotten Congress to strengthen the only two statutes that could be used to prevent racial violence. But their victory was not complete. U.S. attorneys could not prosecute civil rights violations without a "certification in writing" from the attorney general or deputy attorney general, who would authorize prosecution only if, "in his judgment," it was in "the public interest." Thus, criminal enforcement of civil rights statutes still depended on the political whims of the attorney general. Clark was only partially pleased: "I still didn't think they were adequate." But under the circumstances, it was the best he would get.

Although civil rights leaders rejoiced, the bitter fact was that the bill passed because Congress and the White House were motivated as much (if not more) by the desire to punish black "rioters" than to prosecute racist attacks against blacks. Many senators were still convinced that federal power should be used only in the most extreme cases to protect rights. In the closing moments of the Senate debates on the bill, RFK clung as tightly as ever to his federalist ideals of noninterference in local affairs. He admitted that he would not have "even thought of sending this kind of legislation up [to Congress]" during his days in the DOJ. This attitude practically guaranteed that the tough new criminal civil rights statutes would be used as sparingly as their predecessors had been.[59]

———— •◆• ————

The retreat from civil rights issues during the waning months of Johnson's final term was especially painful for Ramsey Clark. A civil libertarian and strong civil rights supporter, Clark had to balance the public and political demand for tough law enforcement against alleged black lawlessness with his obligation to investigate and prosecute civil rights violations. He also had to appease Johnson. This was becoming more and more difficult, for Johnson was increasingly unhappy with Clark's less than enthusiastic attitude about implementing the new repressive legislation.

After a particularly stormy cabinet meeting in which officials criticized Clark for not finding a way "to get" black militants Stokely Carmichael and Rap Brown, Johnson angrily told Califano, "If I had ever known that he didn't measure up to his daddy, I'd never have made him Attorney General."[60]

On February 8, Clark was on his way to address a meeting of thirty mayors and police chiefs on riot control techniques when he received word that South Carolina highway patrolmen had killed three black students and wounded twenty-nine on a small hill outside Orangeburg, South Carolina.

The killings followed a series of demonstrations by students at all-black Orangeburg State College over segregation at a local restaurant and bowling alley. The initial reports Clark read indicated that the highway patrolmen, thinking they were under attack, had fired on the students in self-defense. The press, the governor, and state officials all backed the police version. The fact that, aside from scattered protests from black organizations, there was no national outcry over the shootings testified that the times were indeed changing. Clark had doubts about the police version of the shooting and immediately ordered the FBI to investigate.[61]

Clark didn't know it, but the FBI was at the scene during the violence. Three agents had actually witnessed the shootings. The cover-up began almost immediately. Two days after the FBI began its official investigation, Special Agent in Charge Charles DeFord, one of the three agents who had been present, shared the same motel room with South Carolina Highway Patrol director J. P. Strom, who was also at the scene during the shooting. When questioned by an attorney from CRD, DeFord lied and said that he hadn't been present. When the FBI finally submitted its report to the DOJ two months later, it made no mention of the fact that the agents had been on the scene.

This was a disaster. The DOJ had wasted precious time and squandered valuable resources trying to piece the story together. Why the agents withheld the information became much clearer when reporters Jack Nelson and Jack Bass confronted DeFord. He angrily told them, "I don't want to get in a pissing match with the civil rights attorneys." The traditional sweetheart relationship between the FBI and southern police officials had again nearly torpedoed justice at a critical moment.

The DOJ had to rely initially on police reports of the shooting. It would take weeks of painful investigation before the DOJ could get the full story. But Hoover barged into the act. He claimed that his agents were not guilty of wrongdoing. When Bass and Nelson published their book on the incident, Hoover fired off an angry letter denying that his agents had been present.

Meanwhile, local officials, police, and the state governor had closed ranks. They stuck to their story that the patrolmen had only fired at the students after they heard a gunshot. They insisted that officers had given the students an order to disperse before opening fire. The state refused to bring any charges against the patrolmen. The surviving students and other eyewitnesses at the scene disputed the police version. They denied that they had received any warning and said that their demonstrations had been peaceful until the patrolmen arrived. The final FBI report backed the students. It noted that there was no provocation, that no warning had been given, and that the students were unarmed. The most damaging piece of evidence was that each wounded student had been shot in the side or the back.[62]

Clark was under intense pressure from black leaders at this point. Immediately prior to his assassination, King had wired Clark insisting that the shootings should not go unpunished. Clark sought indictments against nine highway patrolmen under federal civil rights statutes.

When the mostly white federal grand jury refused to indict, Clark was in a quandary. He felt strongly that the evidence required the government to prosecute the patrolmen. Meanwhile, civil rights leaders continued to press the DOJ to bring charges. Finally, after weeks had passed and charges were made that the government would whitewash the case, Clark took a rare and courageous step and filed a "criminal information charge" against the nine patrolmen. This permitted the DOJ to prosecute the case without a formal grand jury indictment. The officers were charged under Section 241.[63]

Clark knew that the chances of getting a conviction against them in the racially charged atmosphere of South Carolina was slim. But he had other reasons for his actions: "From a law enforcement standpoint, I would say that it would have a stabilizing effect on law enforcement." This represented a radical departure from the traditional DOJ practice of bringing a civil rights case only when there was a reasonable chance that it could be won. Clark gambled that even if the case lacked legal soundness, it was morally and politically correct to take the matter to court. Prosecution, even without a conviction, was enough to send a message to law enforcement officers that the government took police abuse seriously.

However, conviction was not in the cards. Thirteen months later, a jury took less than two hours to acquit the patrolmen. The only reason it took the jurors that long was because the two blacks on the jury had some doubts about the officers' innocence. The ten whites, from the very start, were unanimously in favor of acquittal. The White House was silent through it all. Clark would comment, "My office had no communication with the White House, so in that sense there was no support or lack of support for our efforts."[64]

By the time the verdict came in, neither Clark nor Johnson was around. Six months earlier, a beaten and politically spent Johnson had departed the White House, frustrated over his Vietnam failure and with his Great Society programs in shambles. Perhaps the cruelest blow of all was that Johnson could no longer make the claim that he had broken the back of the Klan and other violent racists.

Hoover told the House Appropriations Committee that "many thousands of sympathizers lend their support to Klan programs and activities." Despite the much publicized civil rights enforcement activism of the Johnson years (with the exception of 1964, when twenty-one Mississippi Klansmen were indicted), the DOJ actually filed fewer criminal cases yearly during Johnson's term than during the Kennedy years.[65]

The new head of the Civil Rights Division, Jerris Leonard, a Republican, later observed that "the Division really had no capacity to prosecute criminal civil rights cases. The fact is they were reticent to bring them and the ones they brought they lost in almost every case." It was a partisan and perhaps politically self-serving observation, but, sadly, it was correct.[66]

There was much to admire about Lyndon Johnson. He was a man who had overcome his racist past to become a powerful and effective advocate of civil rights. But there was also much that was tragic. Johnson was perhaps an undeserving victim of the rising black anger and white resistance of his era. His fall from grace over Vietnam, which ultimately drove him from the White House, unfortunately overshadowed much of the great good that he tried to accomplish with his domestic agenda.

Tragically, this was true with civil rights as well. Johnson, more than any other president, had shown a willingness to use federal power to punish racial violence. But this said less about Johnson's political commitment than it did about that of the other presidents. LBJ also had the advantage of his times. The shock of the Mississippi violence, the power of the civil rights movement, and the murder of JFK created a national consensus that segregation was wrong.

Yet at crucial moments, Johnson, like Truman, shrank from using the full force of executive power to budge an increasingly resistant Congress to strengthen old and enact new federal criminal statutes against racial violence. It took the murder of Martin Luther King and the ensuing black rioting for Johnson to push Congress to pass new civil rights legislation containing the tougher criminal statutes. But even this was compromised by Johnson's and Congress's determination to pass an antiriot statute to punish black militancy.

Despite Johnson's ambiguous legacy in enforcing federal law against racial violence, the civil rights bills of the 1960s were far-reaching, and they forever changed America's racial landscape. They also represented the climax of four decades of struggle by civil rights leaders to get the federal government to strengthen the criminal civil rights statutes. Klan violence and terror receded into history, and southern states became more efficient and effective in enforcing the laws.

A decade earlier, then NAACP executive director Walter White had tempered his joy over the end of the lynching era with the sober warning that with the escalation in the bombings and burnings of black homes and churches, southern violence had merely changed forms. Now, at the close of the 1960s, civil rights leaders tempered their joy over the end of massive and unpunished Klan violence with the sober realization that blacks could still be assaulted and murdered—this time under color of law.

7

Deadly Force

The Nixon-Ford Years

Nearly 30,000 Texans packed Houston's Miller Memorial Amphitheater on the evening of September 6, 1968. Many wore Texan trademark ten-gallon hats, cowboy boots, bolo ties, or bangled wide skirts. But many more wore tailored business suits and formal dresses. The crowd—southern, conservative, and mostly white—smelled of the new money made in real estate speculation and the state's booming oil industry.

They stomped, whistled, and hooted as the big guns of Texas Republican politics took turns blasting the Democrats for their big spending and social permissiveness. This was just the warm-up. When the thin, smallish man entered the arena, flanked by an entourage of local and state Republican officials, the crowd exploded.

Richard Nixon was the man they had come to see. They expected him to be the next president. For several minutes, Nixon smiled, waved awkwardly, and basked in the adulation of the crowd. He brought along Senator Ed Brooke, the Senate's only black member, to dispel criticism that he was running a racist campaign. Still, the audience knew that Nixon would hit hard at Democrats for the liberal social and economic policies that the crowd believed had opened the floodgates of lawlessness and economic ruin in America.

He didn't disappoint them. Nixon lambasted his Democratic opponent, Vice President Hubert Humphrey, for the failed Great Society programs and for big-government spending. Next, Nixon attacked the Warren Supreme Court, which had become the conservatives' favorite target. When he shouted that the Court "had gone too far in strengthening the criminal forces," the cheers were deafening. Nixon's "southern strategy" was paying off. Texas, Virginia, and Florida were already considered shoo-ins for the Republicans. Nixon was also gaining support from many disgruntled southern Democrats repelled by their party's pro–civil rights positions.[1]

Two weeks later, Nixon was in politically friendly and equally conservative Orange County in southern California. This time, he was specific about his domestic concerns. He told reporters that he resented anyone who said that law and order was a code term for racism. The majority of Americans, he explained, were decent, hardworking, law-abiding citizens. They were sick of the lawlessness and violence in the cities. They were angry at the courts for coddling lawbreakers. Nixon claimed he was the candidate who spoke for white ethnics and blue-collar workers, whom his campaign strategists had deftly labeled the "silent majority." He counted on these voters to rescue him from the political wilderness he had roamed for nearly a decade after his defeat by Kennedy in 1960.

Nixon accurately gauged the mood of the silent majority. The urban riots had convinced many whites in the South and in the northern suburbs that the ghettos were out of control and that their lives and property were threatened by the menace of black violence. In speeches to northern suburban audiences, Nixon hammered on the twin themes of law and order and Great Society permissiveness. His strategy worked. On election day, Nixon parlayed the silent majority's smoldering discontent and fear into enough votes to eke out a narrow victory over Humphrey.[2]

———— • ◆ • ————

During his first year and a half in the White House, Nixon tried to back up his words. He called on Congress to pass a tough, omnibus anticrime bill that contained controversial and, some charged, openly repressive "no-knock," stop-and-frisk, and preventive detention provisions. The bill authorized the expanded use of wiretaps. Nixon received a further boost from the presidential commission appointed by Johnson in June 1968 to study the causes of violence.

Stung by the Kerner Commission's recommendations that blamed the ghetto riots on police violence and white racism, Johnson had played it safe. He packed the commission with politically safe moderates and conservatives. The chair was a Republican, Milton Eisenhower. In December 1969, the presidential commission delivered its final report to Nixon. It ignored the Kerner Commission recommendations on police reform and urged sharp increases in federal spending on weapons, training, and riot preparation.[3]

Police departments promptly went on the largest weapons-buying spree and personnel buildup in American history. From 1971 to 1974, federal and state spending on criminal justice jumped 42 percent, from $10.5 billion to $15 billion. The number of employees in the criminal justice system rose 22 percent, from 862,000 to 1,051,000. The police garnered more than half of the funding, or $8.5 billion. By 1975, police personnel had doubled, rising from 371,000 in 1965 to 653,000. Police power in America now became a dominant and ominous new political force. Even as the commission was putting its final stamp on its report, the consequences of the police militarization had become frighteningly evident.[4]

———— •◆• ————

In the fall of 1969, J. Edgar Hoover intensified his secret war against the Black Panther Party. The party's "pick up the gun" rhetoric and call for socialist revolution fed Hoover's worst paranoia and his hatred of blacks. He called the Panthers America's greatest internal threat to security. When the FBI and local police raided Panther offices in twelve cities, more than ten Panthers and two policemen were killed in the ensuing gun battles.

Hoover's goal was not simply to destroy the Panthers but also to "prevent the rise of a black messiah." He was plagued by the horrific prospect that a black leader might emerge who possessed the charisma and organizational talent to unify and energize the black masses. In his half-century reign as bureau head, Hoover had already leveled the FBI's full arsenal of weapons to "neutralize" Marcus Garvey, Elijah Muhammad, Martin Luther King, and Malcolm X. The FBI had played a huge role in harassing, surveilling, and obstructing these black leaders' organizations. Garvey had been deported. King and Malcolm X were dead. And Muhammad was a broken old man. Hoover was determined that no other black leader would follow in their footsteps.

He closely watched one black teenager in Chicago. At age sixteen, Fred Hampton had become an NAACP youth leader in the suburban town of Maywood. Hoover immediately authorized a tap on Hampton's mother's phone and planted an informer in the NAACP office to keep tabs on the youth.[5]

The energetic Hampton quickly found the NAACP too politically moderate and confining. When the Black Panther Party opened a chapter in Chicago, Hampton was one of the first recruits in the door. He quickly rose to become the chairman of the party's Illinois chapter. A galvanizing speaker, cast in the mold of King and Malcolm X, Hampton forged alliances with the Young Lords, militant Puerto Rican activists, the Young Patriots (who were organizing poor whites), and the radical Students for a Democratic Society.

During the summer of 1969, he was close to signing a unity pact with Chicago's largest street gang, the Blackstone Rangers (P Nation). Negotiations hit a brief snag when Hampton was convicted of theft and sentenced to two to five years in prison. In August 1969, he was released on appeal bond. Hoover apparently wasn't content to rely on the courts to dispose of Hampton. He had a better idea.[6]

Hoover knew that his covert and illegal war against the Panthers had the tacit support of Nixon. More important, the campaign had the active approval of Attorney General John N. Mitchell. The dour-looking, balding, pipe-smoking Mitchell, formerly a municipal bond and investment counselor, had served as Nixon's campaign manager before being picked to head the DOJ. During the presidential election, he had worked closely with Fred LaRue, the Republican national chairman from Mississippi, to craft Nixon's southern strategy. Even after LaRue relinquished his post, he still was a frequent visitor to Mitchell's office. Mitchell vowed to "vigorously" carry out Nixon's law-and-order mandate and implement "no-knock" raids, wiretaps, preventive detention, and other repressive measures.

While Hoover worked under deep cover to destroy the Black Panthers, Mitchell worked out in the open. In May 1969, he elbowed aside the nation's only black U.S. attorney, Cecil Poole, and sent a team of DOJ attorneys to San Francisco to convene a special grand jury. Mitchell wanted to nail Panther leaders for violating the Smith Act and conspiring to overthrow the government.[7]

On December 4, a special squad of Chicago police, assembled by Illinois state's attorney William V. Hanrahan, charged into Hampton's apartment in the early morning hours. The police poured more than ninety rounds of ammunition into the rooms. Hampton and Mark Clark, the Panther defense captain from Peoria, were shot to death while they slept. Seven other Panthers were arrested. William O'Neal, one of sixty-seven paid FBI informants in the Chicago Panthers, had provided Hanrahan with the apartment's floor plan and tipped him that the Panthers had illegal weapons. Chicago SAC Marlin Johnson immediately informed Hoover that Hampton and Clark were dead.[8]

The confrontation fell into what had by then become a familiar tragicomic pattern. Police officials would claim that they conducted a raid looking for illegal weapons, they then came under attack and returned the fire, and a "bloody shoot-out" followed in which Panthers (and sometimes police officers) were wounded or killed. City officials would then congratulate the police on their bravery, and the press would run sensational stories on the shoot-out based on the police version of the clash.

This time, however, Black Panther leaders in Chicago turned the tables on city officials. In something resembling agitprop theater, they held press conferences and denounced the police attack. They ushered reporters, local officials, community leaders, and thousands of local residents on tours through the bullet-riddled apartment. The Panthers scored their biggest coup when they persuaded a delegation of black Congress members to tour the apartment. At a press conference afterward, a visibly shaken John Conyers, a Michigan Democrat, called the police attack "murder" and demanded an immediate federal investigation.

The Panthers were succeeding in turning public hatred into public sympathy. When the Civil Rights Commission sensed the rising anger among blacks and formally asked Mitchell to investigate, the attorney general was boxed into a corner. The case was politically explosive. Police and city officials had clearly bungled the raid, and the federal government's involvement might be discovered. On December 19, Mitchell announced that he would convene a special federal grand jury. He dispatched the Civil Rights Division chief, Jerris Leonard, to Chicago to head the investigation.[9]

Nixon administration critics were uneasy. Although Leonard, a former Wisconsin corporate attorney, was considered a "moderate conservative," he also had a reputation as a deeply partisan Republican loyalist, one observer called him a "politician." Leonard had kept the political fires going for Nixon in 1964 in Wisconsin during Nixon's wilderness years. He also had worked closely with Mitchell on bond problems in his home state.

Members of the Ripon Society, a liberal Republican activist group, smelled a cover-up. They demanded that Mitchell drop Leonard from the investigation, convinced that he would find "political considerations" to sabotage the investigation. Mitchell was livid. On CBS's *Evening News*, he called the society members "little juvenile delinquents."[10]

Leonard ignored the critics and moved ahead. To the surprise of almost no one familiar with the labyrinthine world of Chicago machine politics, a Cook County grand jury ruled the killings "justifiable homicide" in January. By then, the official version of the raid had begun to unravel. Investigators determined that the Panthers had fired only one bullet at the police and that Hampton had died from two gunshot wounds to the head fired at close quarters while he slept. In addition, all the Panther guns were found to have been purchased legally and registered.[11]

———————•◆•———————

Hoover took his cue and ducked for cover. The whitewash that critics had feared had begun. In February, SAC Marlin Johnson swore to the federal grand jury that the FBI had played only a "peripheral" role in the raid. This was hardly the case. Johnson did not mention the role played by O'Neal, the FBI's sketch of the Panther apartment, or the bogus report about illegal weapons. He could not mention that the FBI had kept constant pressure on Hanrahan to conduct the raid. Behind the scenes, Hoover, Mitchell, and Leonard maneuvered hard to defuse the crisis.

In April, Leonard and Hanrahan worked out a deal at a secret meeting. Leonard promised that the federal grand jury would not indict Hanrahan or the Chicago police involved in the raid in exchange for dropping the charges against the seven Panthers. Apparently to avoid arousing suspicion, Leonard set a thirty-day timetable for dropping the charges. Hanrahan kept the bargain and on May 9 dutifully dismissed the charges. Hoover completed the elaborate little charade with help from the House Appropriations Subcommittee. Also on May 9, the subcommittee conveniently made public Hoover's March 5 testimony in which he blamed the violence against the Panthers on their "intense hatred and vindictive hysteria against local police."[12]

A week later, Leonard kept his part of the bargain. In a deft bit of legal choreography, the twenty-member federal grand jury (there was only one black juror even though Chicago was one-third black) issued a 250-page "narrative report" mildly criticizing the police for the "ill-conceived" attack. When it came to the Panthers, however, the jurors dropped their polite restraint. They railed against the Panthers for "political posturing" and virtually blamed them for bringing on the attack. No police were indicted.

In defending the grand jury's nonaction, Leonard stated that the Panthers were also culpable: "The jury refused to indict the police officers mainly based on the fact that the first shot was fired by Hampton." Yet other than police testimony, there was no independent corroboration that Hampton had fired any shots at police. In fact, he was asleep during the assault.[13]

When critics screamed about a fix, Leonard simply retorted that "case law gives the grand jury the right" to issue a report in lieu of indictments. Technically, Leonard was correct. But this was a right that grand jurors almost never exercised, and many legal experts deeply questioned the practice. Several federal court rulings held that the "narrative report" violated the secrecy of grand jury proceedings and breached the separation between the executive and judicial branches. In the Kent State shootings, for example, a federal court tossed out the Ohio grand jury report on the grounds that in not returning indictments against the guardsmen, it acted "as a trying body and determine[d] guilt."[14]

The federal grand jury nonaction was a tough sell even for Senator John McClellan. The Arkansas senator was a hard-line anti-Communist and sworn foe of civil rights. As chair of the Senate Permanent Subcommittee on Investigations, McClellan had conducted a three-year investigation of black radicals. He also worked hand in glove with Hoover in trying to link the ghetto riots to a "Communist conspiracy."

But McClellan also was a ranking member of the Senate Judiciary Committee, and his respect for legal proprieties momentarily overcame his hatred for the Panthers as he questioned the legality of the report by the grand jury. Leonard, rather than quieting critics, only enraged them.

The ACLU charged that the government had cut a deal to cover up the murders.[15]

Leonard's angry denial rang false to NAACP executive secretary Roy Wilkins and former Supreme Court justice Arthur Goldberg. In December, they agreed to head a task force of attorneys, civil rights activists, and community leaders that would conduct a private investigation into the shootings. They revealed that in January, Mitchell had arranged for Leonard to meet with Goldberg at his Manhattan law office. At the meeting, Leonard bluntly told Goldberg that the investigation would prejudice the evidence and strongly implied that if Goldberg's task force backed off, there would be indictments.

The revelation was too little too late. Mitchell closed the case and in June refused to release a complete transcript of the grand jury report. The next month, he was back on the attack. At his first news conference in a year, he defended Hoover's attacks on the Panthers. In 1971, civil rights and legal groups won a Pyrrhic victory when Hanrahan and eight Chicago policemen were indicted. All were acquitted in a nonjury trial.[16]

A decade later, the federal government, together with Chicago and Cook County officials, agreed to shell out $1.85 million to Hampton's and Clark's families and to the other Panthers. Assistant U.S. Attorney Robert Gruenberg admitted no government guilt and chalked the settlement up to "court weariness" and cost-saving concerns. The mountain of federal documents released during the years of court battles proved overwhelmingly that the FBI and the DOJ had conspired with Hanrahan to "neutralize" Hampton.

Judge John Grady obliquely confirmed this when he imposed a monetary sanction on the FBI for obstructing justice by hiding their COINTELPRO case files. The files told the sordid tale of the deceit and betrayal of Hoover, Mitchell, and, by extension, the Nixon administration, not to mention a ruthless and illegal use of federal power to wage war on black activists. COINTELPRO also made a mockery of Nixon's, Mitchell's and Hoover's sanctimonious promises to restore law and order to America and protect its citizens from racial violence.[17] Hoover, Mitchell, and Nixon justified their criminal abuse of power by skillfully turning the Panthers' violent rhetoric against the group. They convinced much of the public that the Panthers operated outside the framework of law and society and consequently deserved not federal protection but repression.

———— • ◆ • ————

During the same May week in which Leonard and Hanrahan cut their deal, Nixon faced yet another crisis, this time in a state that still symbolized America's hideous legacy of racial violence for many Americans. On May 19, 1970, Nixon issued a terse, one-paragraph statement from his Key

Biscayne vacation retreat stating that he and his wife were "deeply saddened" at the deaths of Phillip Gibbs and James Green at Mississippi's
Jackson State University. Gibbs and Green were killed and twelve other
black students were wounded at the all-black college when Jackson city police and state highway patrolmen opened fire on a student demonstration.

Police claimed that snipers had fired on them from Alexander Hall, the
women's dormitory. Nixon perhaps intended his message to be a simple
human gesture of sympathy, but the *New York Times* found that his words
were "shamefully lacking" and that the time was past for empty gestures.
The paper demanded that the White House issue "persuasive orders"
that police violence would not be tolerated and blamed Nixon for creating a climate of repression by openly exploiting white fears of crime and
black violence.[18]

The Jackson State killings came on the heels of the first campus strike in
American history following the National Guard shooting of four students
at Kent State. The turmoil was another crisis for Nixon. The day after the
shooting, Nixon met with the presidents of fifteen black colleges. Although the presidents had asked for the meeting to talk about civil rights
and educational issues, Jackson State was no doubt on their minds.

Nixon sat at an oval table and listened intently as the men told him that
blacks felt "alienated" by his policies. Reporter Jack Nelson, who was present, noted that Nixon grew more uncomfortable as the criticism continued. Finally, Dr. Herman Branson, the president of Central State University in Ohio, read off a list of recommendations to defuse the situation.
The presidents urged Nixon to meet with black students, issue guidelines
on the use of weapons for crowd control, and prohibit police from carrying weapons on college campuses. Nixon refused to make any promises.
He quipped, "Judge me by my deeds."[19] Although the presidents left the
White House empty-handed, Nixon realized that empty platitudes would
not quiet the national outcry. He had to act. Therefore, on June 13, he announced the appointment of a commission to study the campus violence.[20]

Also, with the polarized and precarious state of racial politics in
Mississippi, there was the strong likelihood that Jackson officials would
try to suppress any evidence that implicated the police in wrongdoing. If
Nixon authorized an investigation, the FBI and the DOJ would have to
gather the evidence. This presented a problem, given Mitchell's and
Hoover's hard-line attitude on "black radicals." In fact, at that very moment, Hoover was waging his COINTELPRO war against black activists
in Mississippi.

Since the days of the war on the Klan, FBI agents in Jackson had spent
much of their time spying on and harassing black student groups, sometimes with the connivance of local police who, with FBI prodding, made

"nuisance arrests" of black students on various trumped up charges. At Tougaloo College, for instance, FBI agents deliberately conducted a series of high-profile interviews with students involved in a campus political action committee. The college administration quickly disbanded the group. In another case, a local SAC decided that one student was a "black nationalist organizer." The student was evicted three times from apartments he rented after FBI agents "interviewed" his landlords. Despite the FBI's dubious record in this arena, however, the prospects were good that it would be called into the present case.[21]

Three days later, Nixon ordered the FBI to investigate the Jackson State killings. Leonard was dispatched to gather evidence at the shooting scene. Nixon announced that he directed Mitchell, previously scheduled to speak to the Delta Council in nearby Cleveland, Mississippi, to visit Jackson to confer with the mayor and the president of Jackson State. Mitchell was worried. Before he left Washington, he had asked Hoover whether he might be picketed by local blacks. Hoover calmed him down and assured him that the situation was under control. But as a precaution, Hoover got Mississippi governor John Bell Williams to place the National Guard on standby alert.

Arriving in Jackson, Mitchell gave the appearance that he was all business and that Nixon regarded the Jackson State shootings as a real crisis. When a reporter shouted to him at the airport, "Is this the most serious one yet?" Mitchell replied as he jumped into a waiting sedan, "It could possibly be." He headed directly downtown for a two-hour meeting with Jackson mayor Russell Davis and Jackson State's president John A. Peoples.

He assured Peoples that he was "deeply concerned about this tragedy." After the meeting, Peoples escorted Mitchell to the campus. Photographers at the scene snapped away as Mitchell squinted into the midday sun, pipe in hand. At one point, he stared hard at the bullet-shattered windows in Alexander Hall. Bewildered, he turned and innocently asked Peoples, "And only twelve were struck?" An hour later, Mitchell was on his way to Cleveland.[22]

The attorney general was in a hurry to keep his speaking engagement with the Delta Council, a largely white association of wealthy planters and businessmen. The council had only recently admitted blacks as members, which black leaders suspected was only a public relations gesture for Mitchell's benefit. Police kept a group of about 100 black demonstrators at a safe distance from the entrance of the Delta State College football stadium, where Mitchell was scheduled to speak.

The mostly white crowd of several thousand cheered warmly when Mitchell praised them for backing Nixon's invasion of Cambodia. When he mentioned the Jackson State shootings, he seemed to place the blame equally on both the students and the police. He noted that the administration would not condone "violent demonstrations, nor unrestrained reactions." But with black anger over the shootings at a fever pitch, Mitchell would have to do more than issue vague reprimands to law enforcement personnel and protesters.[23]

A few days after Mitchell's visit, Minnesota senator Walter Mondale, Indiana senator Birch Bayh, and several other Democratic congressional leaders trooped to Jackson to get a firsthand look and to talk to local officials. When they later visited the campus, they, unlike Mitchell, weren't bewildered at what they saw. Both senators angrily denounced the police for overreacting. Bayh practically called the police account of snipers a lie, noting that "I've heard no evidence of a sniper."

Mondale thought it peculiar that police always blamed the "unfound sniper" when they opened fire on blacks. Bayh and Mondale were mindful of the Kerner Commission report that found absolutely no evidence of the sniper fire that police claimed had prompted the use of massive firepower and the resulting deaths during the upheavals in Detroit and other cities in 1967.[24]

Two days later, Mitchell surprised reporters by sternly lecturing law enforcement officials that they were responsible for protecting the public. He promised that the DOJ would issue new guidelines for the police on weapons and crowd control. Senator Ed Muskie, on his way to the funeral of James Green, told reporters that Nixon should conduct more than a departmental investigation.[25]

Mitchell seemed determined to avoid the blunders the FBI and the DOJ had made at Orangeburg. This time, FBI agents questioned dozens of police, city officials, students, and college administrators. They carted off the shattered panes of glass from Alexander Hall to an FBI lab for examination. Agents quickly determined that the police version of the events was a fabrication. In truth, the police had given no warning, and all the shots had come from police weapons. Moreover, the students had been unarmed.

Despite the FBI findings, Nixon's opponents were still worried that the DOJ would whitewash the Jackson State shootings. Katzenbach and Clark had not changed RFK's directive authorizing the FBI to initiate its own investigation of allegations of racial violence and police abuse upon receiving initial complaints, but in 1969, Leonard reversed that policy. Now the DOJ would not authorize the FBI to investigate civil rights cases unless the complaint came from a person who had knowledge of the case—presumably, an official or an agency. This was ostensibly intended to cut down on the time and resources CRD attorneys spent investigating "frivolous" complaints. Leonard insisted that he had "reorganized" the CRD and had a staff of prosecutors who "were extremely expert in the prosecution of criminal cases." He pledged that there would be no slackening in criminal enforcement.[26]

Still, there were deep suspicions that the DOJ had reversed prior policy to avoid conducting serious investigations of civil rights violations. This change might have been designed to free up DOJ and FBI resources for fighting crime and tracking down black militants. Certainly, Hoover was not opposed to the policy reversal. Since the majority of civil rights complaints concerned police abuse, he had always worried that investigations of such complaints could jeopardize the FBI's close working relationship with police departments.

In any case, the FBI findings in the Jackson shootings gave Democratic leaders fresh ammunition. They demanded that Mitchell convene a special grand jury and seek indictments. Nixon and Mitchell had little choice. Although a biracial committee, appointed by Mayor Davis, confirmed that snipers had not fired on police, the committee did not recommend that Jackson police be prosecuted.[27]

In June, Mitchell presented his case to a federal grand jury. He immediately hit a snag, for the hearing would be held in the courtroom of Harold Cox. A controversial Kennedy appointee in 1961, Cox was a militant segregationist who had a reputation for hurling derogatory insults at black defendants. Cox quickly set the tone for the proceedings when he reminded the jurors that there had been a "riot" at Jackson State and that the officers had been in danger. The jurors got the message and refused to indict. But Mitchell was not Ramsey Clark. This time, the DOJ would not file a "no criminal information" bill against the Jackson police or the highway patrol. Meanwhile, the White House was silent, and Leonard was conciliatory: "It was simply not possible to identify those police officers who had actually fired at the two persons who were killed."[28]

The failure of federal officials to take further action was compounded in August. Members of Nixon's Presidential Commission spent three days in Jackson listening to testimony from police, local officials, and students. They also found no evidence of student provocation. Ultimately, the commission called the shootings an "unreasonable, unjustified overreaction." But it also found that Gibbs and Green might not have died from their wounds if the Mississippi highway patrol officers had used birdshot instead of the more lethal buckshot in their weapons. Shortly before the shooting, the highway patrol had revised its policy authorizing the use of buckshot. The commission concluded that police weapons guidelines were "violated in every respect at Jackson State."[29]

The families of Gibbs and Green and the injured students had one last opportunity to get justice. They filed a civil lawsuit in federal court against the city of Jackson and the state of Mississippi. Nearly two years later, when the case was finally heard, five FBI agents and numerous supporting witnesses for the plaintiffs testified that the shootings were un-provoked. But their testimony was not enough. An all-white jury absolved the city, the state, the police, and the highway patrolmen of any liability in the students' deaths.

When the verdict was read, no Jackson State students or black leaders were in the courtroom to hear it. Conditioned by a century of Mississippi injustice toward blacks, they knew that the verdict was a foregone conclusion. Charles Evers, now mayor of Fayette, said, "It is just another episode in what is happening to black people in Mississippi." Leonard had far more faith in state officials than Evers. He believed that in future years, state officials "would be capable of prosecuting common crimes, i.e., murder perpetuated by police officials."[30]

———— • ◆ • ————

The shootings at Jackson State and the FBI's continued assault on black organizations were added deadly reminders that despite the passage of civil rights laws, racial violence was not a thing of the past and that black lives were still at risk. By the time the exposure of Watergate crimes drove Nixon from the White House in disgrace, more blacks than ever were dying from police bullets. In fact, blacks made up the following percentages of those killed by police fire in prominent cities in 1973: Chicago, 75 percent; Oakland, 79 percent; New York, 60 percent; Atlanta, 76 percent; Newark, 78 percent; Birmingham, 79 percent; and Los Angeles, 55 percent. As sociologist Paul Takagi noted, it seemed that the police had "one trigger for whites and another for blacks."

Takagi actually tempered his criticism of the police. He acknowledged that they were under stress and conceded that police officials had a point when they claimed that more blacks than whites were shot because blacks committed more felonies and were more likely to have violent confrontations with law enforcement personnel. At first glance, this seemed like a good argument. The high incidence of shooting deaths seemed to match the crime index figures, felony arrests of blacks were higher, and police work in poor inner-city neighborhoods was perceived as riskier. The problem was that many of the black victims of police bullets were *not* dangerous felons: Many were unarmed, and some were shot in circumstances that could hardly be called life-threatening to the officers.[31]

Civil rights leaders were worried that police killings along with racial violence could spark more racial explosions. But the political focus at the White House and the DOJ did not change following Nixon's departure. The civil rights views of his successor—the solid and bland Republican team player Gerald Ford—were best described by NAACP legislative analyst Clarence Mitchell as "restricted."

While Ford dutifully fulfilled his role as Nixon caretaker and pressed for more and tougher anticrime legislation, the number of complaints of racial violence and police abuse soared to record levels. In the last year of Ford's two-year tenure at the White House, the DOJ received more than 13,000 civil rights complaints; in the same period, the number of investigations dropped, and the DOJ managed only to secure 30 indictments.[32]

The Nixon years were largely remembered for the political triumphs in China and the Middle East and the political tragedy of Watergate. But the shootings at Jackson State, the assaults on the Black Panther Party, and Hoover's escalating secret war against the black movement were ugly reminders that, for blacks, federal law still was not a shield of protection but a dagger of repression. As Americans prepared to celebrate the bicentennial in 1976, black leaders hoped that the newly elected Democratic president would initiate an aggressive federal enforcement policy against racial and police abuse.

8

"The Only Rights You Get Are Right Fists"

The Carter Years

"Johnny Reb," as the upperclassmen called him at the U.S. Naval Academy in the 1940s, had made a decision. "No sir, I wasn't going to sing that one." Underclassman Jimmy Carter would rather take any punishment the upperclassmen dished out to him for defying their hazing rituals rather than sing "Marching Through Georgia." The song was the old Yankee tribute to General William Tecumseh Sherman's devastating and victorious march that broke the back of Confederate resistance in Georgia, Carter's home state, during the Civil War. As one biographer noted, if Johnny Reb Carter had sung the song, it would have betrayed his "Confederate sensibilities."

During the 1950s, Johnny Reb shed some of the prejudiced thinking he shared with most Georgia whites about blacks. He even refused to join the local White Citizens' Council. Over the next decade, he rose steadily in state politics. As governor of Georgia, he had a fairly progressive civil rights record and generally maintained good relations with the state's black leaders and politicians. He considered this a crucial asset in his bid for the Democratic Party's presidential nomination in 1976.[1]

In the closely contested spring party primaries, Carter openly courted and heavily depended on the black vote to provide him with the margin of victory. In November, a large black voter turnout in the key swing states of Florida, North Carolina, Illinois, Pennsylvania, and Michigan put him over the top. Blacks expected a lot from him. Whether the new president could meet those expectations was questionable. He was, by his own admission, inexperienced and politically naive in the ways of Washington.[2]

Still, Carter seemed to understand that the vast expansion of police power, the tougher laws, and the longer prison sentences established during the Nixon-Ford years deepened black resentment toward the police and courts. Carter promised that "he would not have innocent people going to jail who happen to be black."[3]

Carter-watchers paid close attention to the DOJ in this period, for one measure of his commitment to civil rights enforcement would be the number of prosecutions the DOJ brought in police abuse cases and for racial hate crimes. From the start, there were problems. Griffin Bell, Carter's pick for attorney general, was also a wealthy Georgian, but unlike Carter, he was not considered a racial moderate. Liberals on the Senate Judiciary Committee were deeply troubled that Bell had given a legal memo that appeared to support school segregation to Georgia governor Ernest Vandiver in 1959. They also probed Bell's membership in an all-white country club. The committee took six days to confirm his appointment.[4]

Bell's first months on the job weren't promising. In March, he announced that the DOJ would not bring "dual prosecutions" for civil rights violations, which would directly impact police abuse cases. The DOJ's long-standing rule was to leave it to the states to prosecute police officers accused of excessive force violations. After all, it made little sense to bring state and federal charges at the same time if local officials diligently prosecuted police officers guilty of excessive force violations. The problem was that local officials generally did not.

There were several reasons for this. Many police departments had not developed clear and enforceable guidelines on the use of deadly force. Local prosecutors depended heavily on the police to gather evidence and collect testimony from witnesses in criminal cases, and they did not want to jeopardize that relationship. Also, prosecutions seldom brought convictions. Many jurors simply refused to believe that police officers abused their authority.

Bell's directive seemed to close the door on any follow-up prosecution of police officers by the DOJ. The new attorney general would consider prosecution only if there was solid evidence that the local prosecutors handled a case poorly or if it was "necessary to advance a compelling interest of the federal government." Since he didn't explain what the federal government considered "compelling," the question of police violence would remain a murky, confused, and contradictory legal issue.[5]

Some within the DOJ recognized that the problem of police violence was a time bomb waiting to explode. In March 1978, Gilbert Pompa, director of the DOJ's Community Relations Section, told an NAACP conference that "there is no single issue which [more directly] provokes both majority and minority resentment, and [has] the potential for community conflict" than police shootings.[6]

---◆·---

Bell's constricting decision on investigations put Carter in an embarrassing political position. Following a series of controversial police shootings of blacks and Hispanics in Houston and Dallas in 1977 and 1978, black and Hispanic leaders pressured Carter to take action. In July, the president told reporters, "There is a duality of culpability to those who commit some crime." Though this was an impressive moral and philosophical argument, it had little meaning in law or policy as long as local prosecutors did not bring charges against police officers accused of committing crimes.

Despite the rash of questionable killings in his city, the district attorney in Houston had prosecuted only one police officer. He claimed it was too time-consuming and costly to review police files to determine if other incidents of police brutality had occurred. Black and Hispanic leaders were outraged and requested that the Texas attorney general take action at the state level. This would, however, be a largely symbolic move, for the attorney general had no power to prosecute police abuse cases. After reviewing ten such cases, he referred four to the DOJ for investigation.[7]

The DOJ came under even greater fire in Dallas after failing to win convictions of police officers who had allegedly killed a Hispanic teenager. And in Houston, the DOJ seemed helpless to do anything when officers convicted of abuse received ridiculously light sentences. The cases sparked mass demonstrations in Dallas and rioting in Houston.

The CRC was soon drawn into the mounting controversy. Since 1971, commissioners had held public hearings in several cities nationally and had issued nearly a dozen reports on police abuse, all of which concluded that such abuse was pervasive. In September 1979, the CRC decided to hold a public hearing in Houston following the most recent killings.[8]

The CRC grilled city officials on Houston's policy regarding the police department. The city charter conferred statutory authority on both the mayor and the city council to hire and fire police personnel and review police procedures. But the city officials were loath to exercise that authority, fearing repercussions from business people and members of the chamber of commerce who continually pressured the council to appropriate bigger budgets. They were also terrified that they would be accused of political tampering. Former Houston mayor Louis Welch, who now headed the chamber of commerce, was adamant that "whenever city hall tries to run the police department it almost always gets into trouble. This is the sort of thing that destroys police departments."[9]

By the end of the first day of the hearing, the commissioners had a fairly good picture of a department that had run amok while city officials looked the other way. Given that local controls over the department were virtually nonexistent, the commissioners sought to determine how the DOJ would respond. On the second day, the commissioners called Drew Days, director of the Civil Rights Division, to testify. A former NAACP Legal Defense Fund attorney and the first black to head the CRD, Days could do no more than repeat Bell's directive and emphasize that the federal government "would not become the law enforcement body of the first resort." Days, sounding very much like Burke Marshall and his other predecessors, insisted that federal prosecution would usurp state authority. The DOJ's policy, he said, was "to encourage local authorities to police themselves."

He leaned heavily on the argument about the limits of federal authority to try and convince the commissioners that the DOJ had a bona fide legal reason for not moving more aggressively to prosecute police abuse. Days did not tell them that the DOJ's policy of deferring prosecutions was due not to fixed policy or statute but simply timeworn custom and practice. During the 1950s, CRD chief Arthur Caldwell had made it clear that deferring prosecutions in racially motivated violence cases to local prosecutors was "not authorized by law." It was a gratuitous decision, designed to maintain good working relationships with local officials. But Caldwell noted at the time that, contrary to the impression Days gave, the DOJ was "obliged" to investigate and prosecute all civil rights violations if there was any indication that federal laws had been broken.[10]

The CRC also worried that Bell's restrictions on independent investigations by local U.S. attorneys severely handicapped prosecutions of civil rights violations. Former U.S. attorney J. A. Canales told the CRC that he and other U.S. attorneys were never prohibited from acting on their own to prosecute white-collar fraud, embezzlement, public corruption, or drug cases; the attorney general had always left the decision to prosecute these crimes up to U.S. attorneys. Indeed, U.S. attorneys had wide latitude to prosecute these types of crimes based solely on the evidence they uncovered during their investigations. Canales also noted that getting approval to prosecute civil rights violations was a torturous process that involved five different layers of review. Often, Canales said, the U.S. attorneys would wait for months before getting the approval to go ahead, only to learn that the CRD had rejected their requests. Even if the CRD approved prosecution, the long delay often damaged a U.S attorney's case by making it more difficult to secure evidence and testimony from witnesses.[11]

The Houston hearings further added to the perception among black and Hispanic leaders that the administration was indifferent toward police abuse. Carter tried to salvage a bad situation. In July, he sent his newly appointed attorney general, Benjamin Civiletti, on a peacekeeping mission to Texas to talk to black and Hispanic leaders about the administration's civil rights enforcement policies. Civiletti seemed uniquely suited for his job. Before joining the DOJ he had worked mostly in civil litigation. Described as a rather colorless "technocrat," he was a cautious, competent manager who wouldn't rock any political boats.

During a series of emotionally charged meetings, community leaders in Houston reminded Civiletti that blacks and Hispanics had worked hard for Carter's election and delivered the votes he had needed. Now they expected reciprocation. Before departing, Civiletti told reporters that he would instruct all U.S. attorneys in the Southwest to make police abuse cases a priority. Unfortunately, neither the White House nor Civiletti placed the same political weight on the issue of police violence against blacks. "During this period there was not the same prevalence of violations against blacks as in the Nixon years." The administration was wrong, as events would soon show.[12]

Carter also tried to repair the political damage. In May 1978, he told the Los Angeles County Bar Association that there was still "a disturbing trend" toward police harassment of minorities. He promised that the DOJ would take prompt action in police abuse cases. The Texas violence and the revelations in the CRC hearings about local indifference to police abuse forced Carter and Civiletti to recognize that officials in many cities were unable or unwilling to clamp down on police violence. Although the situation in Houston was a prime example, it was not the worst.[13]

———— • ◆ • ————

The occasion was the 1977 canonization ceremony of Saint John Neuman in Rome. It was a holy and festive event, and the mayor of Philadelphia had made a special trip to Italy to attend. But Frank Rizzo was in a sour mood. Rome had recently been rocked by a series of violent street demonstrations by leftist students, traffic had been tied up, and some businesses had been forced to close. Rizzo thought the Italian *carabinieri* were treating the students too softly. After the ceremonies ended, he told Amitore Fanfani, president of the Italian senate, how he would handle such protestors in his own city. It was simple: "Spacco il capo." Loosely translated, this meant, "Break their heads." Fanfani didn't laugh; he knew Rizzo meant it.[14]

Before becoming mayor in 1971, Rizzo had publicly staked out his claim as the "toughest cop in America." From the moment he took over the reins as Philadelphia's police commissioner in 1967, Rizzo ran the Philadelphia Police Department (PPD) as his own private army. Under Rizzo, the PPD had built a fearsome reputation with its savage assaults on the Black Panthers and black militants in the city. Black leaders were outraged at the widely publicized crackdowns, street sweeps, and head-knocking that Rizzo ordered in black neighborhoods. He and his department, which was 80 percent white, seemed to be at perpetual war with the city's blacks, who made up about one-third of the population.

If the city's business and political leaders had reservations about his roughshod methods, they kept them mostly to themselves. They could not argue with the results Rizzo obtained. Philadelphia, as Rizzo liked to boast, had the lowest crime rate of any major city in the country. Beyond that, the press seemed to have a love affair with the "big bambino." He was flamboyant, and he made good copy. Some reporters called him the "Cisco Kid" because he often packed two pistols. Rizzo was a special favorite of Walter Annenburg, a powerful media mogul and owner of the city's major daily, the *Philadelphia Inquirer.* Annenburg delighted in riding through the streets with Rizzo in his police cruiser. To preserve Rizzo's tough, incorruptible image, Annenburg instructed his editors to screen all calls the paper's reporters made to the police chief.[15]

In 1971, Rizzo waged a no-holds-barred law-and-order campaign to win the mayor's race that would have made Nixon envious. His department continued his "kick butt first and ask questions later" policies. But by the late 1970s, things had begun to change. Rizzo, whose antics city officials and the press had long applauded or at least tolerated, was increasingly regarded as an embarrassment. In addition, the city had acquired a nasty reputation in the national press for corruption, political cronyism, and mismanagement. In the fall of 1978, voters rejected a city charter measure that would have waived the two-term limit for the mayorship and allowed Rizzo to run for a third term.

In part, the measure was rejected because the police department was out of control. During Rizzo's years in office, Philadelphia led the nation in police shootings, averaging 75 per year. There were 300 fatalities during his term. In 99 of the shooting deaths, no criminal activity was alleged. In 99 others, the victims were charged only with misdemeanor offenses. Most of the victims were young black or Hispanic males. Furthermore, during interrogations, police routinely beat suspects with lead pipes, blackjacks, brass knuckles, handcuffs, chairs, and table legs. Other suspects were forced to watch the beatings and threatened with the same treatment unless they talked. One detective admitted that he had told a black suspect, "The only rights you get are right fists." Many Americans were shocked at a picture in *Time* magazine of a shirtless young black man lying on the ground in Philadelphia being kicked and punched by four officers, while another stood over him with a machine gun.

The *Inquirer,* sold by Annenburg in 1971, now had a new staff of young reporters and editors who were encouraged to be aggressive in their work. The paper began printing lengthy exposés of police abuse and eventually garnered the Pulitzer Prize for this reporting. Rizzo and the department were enraged by the stories. The police union boycotted the paper and persuaded some building and trade union locals that depended on city business contracts to join their protest. The conflict came to a head one afternoon when picketers, egged on by the police, began pummeling employees as they emerged from the building. On-duty officers made no move to intervene and make arrests.[16]

Rizzo's strong-arm tactics did not scare David Marston, a tough and able U.S attorney. The *Inquirer* exposés convinced him that police officials had an "official blind spot" in regard to police abuse. Marston asked Bell for permission to convene a federal grand jury to investigate abuse in the PPD. In June 1978, Bell agreed, and Marston, assisted by five other U.S. attorneys aided by the FBI, began preparing evidence. A concerned group of civic and church leaders met with Days, who assured them that the Carter administration backed the probe.

Marston's diligence paid off. The grand jury indicted six officers and gave strong indications that indictments would be returned against at least a dozen more. But Marston could not leap the hurdle that had blocked all conscientious federal prosecutors in the past. Despite presenting solid evidence corroborated by eyewitness testimony, Marston watched as an all-white jury, drawn mostly from the outlying suburban areas, acquitted three officers charged in the beating of a young black. Marston got some satisfaction when six homicide detectives were convicted for beating and torturing suspects. However, Rizzo not only refused to fire the officers but also promoted one of them. He loudly declared that the officers were still innocent until the Supreme Court ruled on their appeal.

Marston ignored a gloating Rizzo and vowed to bring more cases to trial. Rizzo wanted Marston's head. He screamed of "plots" and "conspiracies" by the DOJ to get him and the police. In a bizarre twist, he demanded that Bell investigate officials in his own DOJ. Rizzo did not get his investigation, but he got something even better. On January 17, Carter fired Marston. The president had bowed to pressure from state Democrats who were beginning to fear that Marston's investigation of the corruption of city politicians and Pennsylvania's Democratic House members would bring indictments. Marston's firing was a major blow to police reform efforts. The federal grand jury probe virtually ground to a halt. There were no more indictments.[17]

———— • ◆ • ————

If Rizzo was relieved, his relief was only temporary. On April 16, 1979, the CRC opened two days of hearings in the city. Commissioners listened as city and federal prosecutors told how police officials systematically stonewalled police abuse probes—shredding complaint files, burning records, and forbidding officers to talk to investigators. Even when the police department cooperated, the DOJ required FBI agents to complete their investigations of civil rights complaints within twenty-one days. This was a Herculean task, for an agent who faithfully followed bureau procedures would have had to interview witnesses; obtain medical records, photographs, and a description of physical injuries; compile police reports and criminal records of the victim and officers; and track down records of other complaints against the officer. The DOJ did permit agents to file interim reports if they could not complete their full reports on time. U.S. Attorney John Penrose told the commission that the stall tactics of the police made it almost impossible for agents working under pressure to meet the deadline to fully document their cases.[18]

On the second day of the hearings, reporters packed the room to hear the commission's star witness. Rizzo entered the room accompanied by an entourage of supporters. He shook hands, smiled, and waved to cheering fans, many of whom were off-duty police officers. He seemed determined to turn the hearings into a sideshow. He was defiant, combative, and mocking as he gave sarcastic and wisecrack replies to the commissioner's questions. CRC Chairman Arthur Fleming, whom Rizzo derisively called "doctor," had his hands full trying to contain the boisterous crowd. At one point, Fleming threatened to use federal marshals to clear the room.

Frustrated and exasperated, the commissioners sat back and listened as Rizzo, for nearly one and a half hours, railed against militants, anarchists, and reporters "who scream first amendment" and were out to wreck his department. There was one amusing moment when Rizzo momentarily slipped and said, "As long as I'm police commissioner." He quickly stopped to correct himself: "As long as I'm mayor," he amended, "no one will take advantage of a policeman doing his job."[19]

The commissioners didn't get much further with Police Commissioner Joseph O'Neill. CRC Vice Chairman Stephan Horn asked O'Neill what would happen to an officer who violated department policy by using deadly and excessive force. This was the exchange:

Horn: "Well, I just wondered if you'd shoot or not shoot if you were that officer."
O'Neill: "I don't know. But I'll tell you this, that if he did shoot, if he felt that he was doing that which is right, most certainly I'd defend him."

O'Neill said he would go to bat for the officer since the department had never devised a clear policy on the use of weapons. In fact, the Philadelphia Police Department's manual hadn't been changed since 1963.[20]

The department presumably adhered to the guidelines outlined in the general statutes the state had incorporated seven years earlier. The decision on when to use deadly force essentially fell back on the individual officer. Since Rizzo's word was practically law on the streets, the results were hardly a surprise. The commission reviewed thirty-two killings by police. Seventy-five percent involved black males; the remaining victims were Hispanic, Indian, or of an unspecified race. Only two of the victims were white. Nearly all were under age twenty-five. Nineteen were unarmed. One was killed while handcuffed, and an innocent bystander was shot while lying on the ground.

Only one of the victims was shot during the commission of a known felony. The rest were shot while fleeing police after committing a minor offense or during a car theft. According to the statute in the Pennsylvania Constitution, this was not sufficient cause to use deadly force. The rule clearly stated that officers could only discharge their firearms when a suspect had committed a felony or was in the act of committing a forcible felony and the officer presumably was in physical danger. In 1975, the Public Law Center reported that the Police Board of Inquiry (PBI) investigated only 6 of the 170 shootings between the years 1972 and 1974. The PBI held hearings in only 2 cases. The rest were summarily dismissed.[21]

———— • ◆ • ————

The CRC hearings gave the DOJ the opening it needed to get itself out of the predicament that Marston's firing had created and the police violence had exacerbated. Days announced on August 13, 1979, that the DOJ had conducted its own probe (based mostly on the findings from the hearings and Marston's investigation) and found that the PPD engaged in illegal searches of homes, seizures of property, stops of motorists and pedestrians, and detentions and also used excessive force.

The DOJ filed a lawsuit to stop the police from engaging in practices that "inflict summary punishment by use of force beyond that which is reasonably necessary to serve legitimate ends." Days claimed that the department violated four federal statutes and six amendments to the Constitution.

Did the suit indicate that the Carter administration finally meant business on police violence? Or was it merely a time-consuming public relations gesture that let the DOJ dodge the call to push for criminal prosecutions? Days countered that indictments of individual officers could only scratch the surface; the department's "practices were too ingrained."[22]

DOJ officials went out of their way to head off the inevitable complaint from Rizzo that the department was waging a vendetta against the PPD. U.S. Attorney Peter Vaira said, "It's not a vindication or attack on anyone."

Still, the suit presented a dilemma for Rizzo. If the DOJ got an injunction against the PPD's practices, and if he defied it and refused to initiate substantive reforms, he would risk losing $4 million in federal grants from the Law Enforcement Administration Agency. But Rizzo, defiant as ever, shot back that "I've never seen any police brutality."[23]

Most observers believed that if the DOJ won its suit, a strong message would be sent to police departments in other cities that the federal government would not tolerate police brutality. The DOJ was even considering filing similar suits against police departments in other cities. But Judge J. William Ditter abruptly quashed that prospect. Without hearing arguments or even a defense motion to dismiss, he tossed out the suit against the PPD on the grounds that the attorney general had "no standing to advance the civil rights of third persons."[24]

Ditter implied that a favorable ruling would place too much power in the hands of the attorney general. He fell back on the old federalism argument, suggesting that the government had overstepped its constitutional boundaries in bringing the lawsuit against a sovereign municipality. Congress, Ditter said, would have to pass legislation permitting the attorney general to take injunctive action under Title 42, and since Congress had stricken those proposed federal statutes from the civil rights bills in 1957, 1960, and 1964, Ditter concluded that the issue had become a dead letter.

Ditter had made an incredible legal leap over a wide body of court rulings, congressional decisions, legal opinions, and history to arrive at his decision. Civiletti was not seeking any power that Congress had not already given the attorney general. The Reconstruction Acts passed by Congress in April 1870 were explicit: "The Attorney General may, whenever he deems it in the interest of the United States, conduct and argue any case in any court of the United States." In March 1875, Congress gave federal courts jurisdiction over all legal and constitutional cases in state courts, specifically for the redress of issues that pertained to civil rights matters and violations when state courts refused to consider them.[25]

Ditter confused congressional intent with political mood and trends. But whether Congress passes or rejects a particular piece of legislation is hardly a gauge of the measure's constitutionality. Bills are shaped and fashioned through political horse trading, deal making, and compromise. There are dozens of examples of legislation that Congress initially rejected only to pass later when public sentiment or the political alignment of Congress changed. The civil rights bills that Ditter cited to bolster his argument were examples. In 1957 and 1960, southern Democrats and Republican conservatives were able to water down key enforcement provisions in those bills.

By 1964, a powerful civil rights movement had forced a new public consensus on civil rights. Johnson vigorously supported the 1964 civil rights bill, and Congress passed it. The final bill included the very provisions that Congress and the White House had earlier rejected.

In claiming that the attorney general had no legal standing, Ditter apparently ignored prior Supreme Court rulings. Between 1888 and 1947, the Court had ruled in five cases that interstate commerce, land rights and disputes, public fraud, water rights, and foreign commerce were all legitimate areas of federal interest and that the government had the right to bring suits in such areas.[26]

If Ditter's decision stood, it would effectively strip the DOJ of a potentially powerful enforcement weapon to compel local officials to curb racially motivated police violence. *New York Times* columnist Tom Wicker scoffed at Ditter's contention that only an "aggrieved person" should be allowed to file a civil rights suit. This assumed, said Wicker, that there were enough individuals out there with the legal know-how, resources, and courage to bring a civil rights suit against police officers. Days immediately announced that the DOJ would appeal the decision. But a jubilant Rizzo told reporters that the case was built on nothing but "sensationalist statements." As always, the Big Bambino believed that he should have the final word on police matters.[27]

This time, he was right. In February, the Third District Appeals Court borrowed Ditter's language and claimed that the suit was really a power grab by the attorney general. The judges warned the government to stay out of an "area that is manifestly the concern of the states." Civiletti remained optimistic that some good would come out of the suit, saying that "it may have had a lasting effect" on police practices in the city.[28]

Although Civiletti and Days made a sincere effort to break Rizzo's deadly stranglehold on police policies, their work did not signal a new departure for federal civil rights enforcement efforts. Despite Carter's assurance to black leaders that it was standard operating procedure for the DOJ to require the FBI to investigate civil rights cases, the percentage of cases involving criminal civil rights enforcement brought by the DOJ in 1979 was much lower even than during the Nixon-Ford years. The DOJ did an even worse job in handling complaints. From 1976 to 1980, it received more than 50,000 civil rights complaints and investigated less than 25 percent of the complaints it received.[29]

At the close of the decade, Carter was politically adrift. The embassy seizure in Iran, the prolonged hostage crisis, the continuing Mideast difficulties, escalating unemployment, steep rises in gas and oil prices, double-digit inflation, and a major recession had made a shambles of his foreign and domestic policies. With the 1980 elections fast approaching, Carter was in big trouble. In June, his popularity rating plunged to 29 percent, a record low for an American president.[30]

However, Carter's political assets were not completely depleted. Black leaders were generally pleased with his civil rights record, his appointments, and his support of increased federal spending on employment, education, and small-business development. He still might use that support to rescue his failing presidency. But a routine traffic incident in Miami soon spelled more political trouble for him.

———————— •◆• ————————

The week before Christmas, Arthur Lee McDuffie was in an especially jovial mood. Everything seemed to be going right in his life. The thirty-three-year-old ex-marine had recently been promoted to associate manager of the Coastal States Life Insurance Company. "Duff," as his friends called him, had another reason to smile: Coastal States had just given him a free trip to Hawaii as a reward for being the company's top salesperson. Duff had a reputation in the community as a man who cared. In his spare time, he worked as a volunteer with unemployed and troubled youths in Liberty City, one of Miami's two major black ghettos.

Duff had also worked out some of the problems with his ex-wife, Fredericka, that had led to the breakup of their marriage the year before; now they were seriously talking about remarrying. Duff was determined to be a real father to his two young daughters, Dewanna and Shederica. He did not want them to grow up in a fatherless home like so many other black children. The only thing that marred his nearly unblemished driving record was an unpaid $35 traffic fine. When his license was temporarily suspended after the check he wrote to pay the fine bounced, Duff didn't think much about it. It was a fatal oversight.

In the early morning hours of December 17, Duff had borrowed his cousin's motorcycle and was on his way home when he ran a red light. Two Miami traffic cops immediately gave chase. Duff probably panicked, fearful that he might be arrested, and tried to outrun the officers. According to police, the chase reached speeds of 100 miles per hour, and Duff ran an estimated twenty-five red lights. Twelve other officers quickly joined in the chase. Duff was eventually apprehended, but it was not an ordinary arrest.

When the fire department paramedics arrived seven minutes later, Duff lay on the ground, battered and beaten. His skull, in the words of Dade County chief medical examiner Ronald Wright, was "cracked like an egg." Four days later, Duff died from injuries that police rated 29 on the 1 to 30 scale they used to rank injuries. Police officers had a simple explanation: Duff had sustained the injuries after he crashed his motorcycle and fell to the pavement. It seemed plausible enough. It was dark, and there were no eyewitnesses.[31]

But local blacks were suspicious. McDuffie's was not an isolated case. For nearly a decade, black leaders had complained to city officials about the brutality of Miami police officers. The situation had reached a dangerous flash point. In 1976, the Civil Rights Commission, fearing civil disturbances, issued a report that backed the black community's charges and

called on police officials to take immediate steps to identify problem officers and counsel or discipline them. Miami police officials ignored the report, and the rift continued to deepen.

In February 1979, the police conducted a drug raid on the home of a
black schoolteacher; the man and his son were beaten. Although it turned
out the police had the wrong address, no action was taken. In December,
an off-duty officer killed a young black, claiming that his gun had acci-
dentally discharged. Again, there was no action. The same year, a highway patrol officer was convicted of molesting an eleven-year-old black
girl. He was sentenced to one year of probation. During the prior two
years, six blacks (and several whites and Hispanics) had died after en-
counters with police under suspicious circumstances. There were too
many accidental falls and mysterious accidents. Miami blacks felt that
they were under siege by the police.[32]

The police report of McDuffie's death would have been routinely
closed and forgotten had it not been for Charles Veverka. One of the first
officers to arrive at the arrest scene, Veverka had signed the police report.
But the young officer's conscience bothered him. While he was playing
with his young son and daughter on Christmas, he kept thinking of
McDuffie and the grief that his family must be feeling.

A few days later, he told internal affairs investigators he had lied about
the incident. McDuffie hadn't fallen from his motorcycle; rather, he was
held at gunpoint while the officers savagely beat him. Veverka said that
one officer, Alex Marrero, bashed McDuffie in the head and the shins
while he lay handcuffed and motionless on the ground. Another officer,
apparently sickened by the savagery, only shrugged and said, "They
looked like animals fighting for meat." Investigators quickly confirmed
Veverka's story. Six officers were charged with second-degree murder
and falsifying a report. The district attorney later agreed to drop charges
against two officers, and three others were granted immunity in exchange
for cooperating with the prosecution.[33]

Meanwhile, city officials were sitting on a time bomb. Feelings in
Miami's black community were running high. On December 29, Duff's
funeral became a rallying point for Miami blacks, and the media, sensing
a big story, gave it widespread coverage. The front page of the next day's
edition of the *Miami Herald* showed a photo of Duff's tearful mother and
his former wife, Fredericka. Inside the church, McDuffie lay in a flag-
draped casket, resplendent in his full marine corporal's uniform, as hundreds of mourners filed past. The next day, demonstrators marched
around the Dade County Courthouse demanding that the district attorney prosecute the officers.

The controversy grew more heated when the *Miami Herald* reported
that 5 of the officers involved were among 196 officers on the department's "watch list." These officers were frequent targets of citizens' com-

plaints and internal investigations. Between them, the 5 had accumulated 47 citizen complaints, 13 internal review investigations, and 53 use-of-force reports. Some justified their actions by explaining that they worked in Miami's central business district, an area called the "combat zone" due to its high rates of crime and violence. But to many blacks, this was only an excuse police officials used to cover up the violence.[34]

NAACP executive secretary Ben Hooks closely followed the McDuffie case. He charged that police in Miami and other cities used crime as a pretext to summarily punish blacks. Immediately after the indictments, Hooks met with DOJ officials and urged them to recommend that police departments across the nation adopt a firearms policy to control the use of deadly force.[35]

———————◆———————

As the police officers' trial date approached, Miami officials grew more jittery. Miami circuit judge Lenore Nesbitt agreed to move the trial to Tampa, but black leaders were wary. They pointed out that in an eerily similar case a few months before, an all-white jury had acquitted a white Tampa officer for the beating death of a black motorcyclist. But Nesbitt's decision stood. In early April, after defense attorneys challenged and removed every prospective black juror, an all-white, all-male jury was selected. The trial dragged on through seven weeks.

On May 16, 1980, the jury took less than three hours to acquit the four officers. Black leaders and some city officials blamed the state's attorney, Janet Reno, for the fiasco. Reno, already under attack for doing little about prior police abuse cases, was accused of presenting a weak and incompetent case. She made matters worse when speaking to reporters, for she sounded as if she herself wasn't convinced about the officers' guilt; "People aren't sure who did what," she said. But people *were* sure what happened the next day. Miami exploded. Within three days, more than eighteen people were killed, hundreds more were injured, and more than $100 million worth of property was damaged.[36]

Before the fires had cooled, black leaders Jesse Jackson, Andrew Young, Ben Hooks, and Joseph Lowry toured the devastated areas and demanded federal action. But Carter was concerned about restoring order. He telephoned Florida governor Robert Graham, congratulated him on his handling of the violence, and delivered a stern message; "Violence can contribute nothing to the resolution of problems."

Carter's get-tough message created even more friction with black leaders. In recent months, they had sharpened their criticism of his policies. Facing a stiff challenge from Republican Ronald Reagan, Carter had drifted to the right to appease conservatives. He announced big cuts in domestic spending programs and paid less attention to civil rights. But the president realized that without the black vote, he would have little chance at the polls in November.

Carter dispatched Civiletti and Pompa to Miami to assess the damage. Civiletti was shaken by the destruction and pleaded with community leaders "to give the U.S. government a chance to rectify whatever injustice that has occured here." He said that he was shocked by the verdict and that he had expected some convictions. It was time for damage control. At a hastily called press conference at the U.S. Customs Building, he announced that he was assembling a team of twenty-five to thirty-five investigators, including federal prosecutors, FBI agents, and U.S. marshals, to investigate all allegations of police abuse leveled against the Dade County Police Department. He promised to subpoena any police official who had any connection to McDuffie's beating.[37]

But why did Civiletti wait so long to conduct his probe? Pompa had earlier warned that racial tensions were increasing. Blacks were feeling squeezed by rising unemployment, growing Cuban political power, and a predominantly white, male police force. But until recently, the DOJ had refused to authorize any money to open a CRS office in the city.

Miami's civil disturbances opened up old wounds. Hispanic leaders, smarting over what they considered Civiletti's whitewash of police shootings in Texas in 1977 and 1978, climbed all over Carter. At an emotionally charged press conference in Washington, Ruben Sandoval, of the La Raza Legal Alliance, shouted, "What does it take to get these DOJ people off their asses?" He answered his own question, "It looks like it takes burning, looting and killing." Was that what Civiletti meant by "a compelling federal interest"?

The inescapable conclusion was that the DOJ would only act when lives were lost and property was destroyed. But getting the DOJ to aggressively prosecute civil rights abuses, including those committed by police officers, within the limits of federal law was still problematic. Civiletti had barely gotten his investigation under way when blacks began to whisper that the officers would not be punished.[38]

It was easy to dismiss this as the anger and frustration of a black community skeptical of white law. But a week later, Pompa and Civiletti did nothing to allay the fears. Pompa saw the DOJ as a facilitator and not a prosecutor. The tensions in Miami were a public relations problem, he explained, that could be resolved by better communication between the police and the minorities. Pompa believed that the police and local officials could work out their difficulties with minimal federal intervention. Back in Washington, Civiletti told reporters that the Miami situation was "unique" and that he didn't think that relations between the police and blacks were all that bad.[39]

While the controversy in Miami continued to swirl, Carter was practically invisible. Black leaders were running out of patience. Hooks sent a letter to Civiletti and Carter criticizing "official insensitivity." He said that blacks were fed up with being "targets" of the police and demanded that the DOJ foot the bill to establish law enforcement "sensitivity training programs" nationally. He suggested that Carter appoint a panel to follow up on the old Kerner Commission recommendations for reforms in jobs, housing, and the police.

It was politically expedient for Carter to do what Hooks wanted; by doing nothing, he risked further alienating his increasingly restive black supporters. A week after the Miami riots, he invited Hooks and other black leaders to the White House, and for more than an hour, he listened intently to them lambast the administration for its failures. Congresswoman Cardiss Collins warned him that there was "a Mount Saint Helen's in every black community in this country." If Carter didn't take action, Collins intimated there would be political reprisals in November. But the president brushed off her threat and refused to make any commitments. Black leaders called the meeting "disappointing."[40]

Although Carter may not have had a specific plan to deal with the Miami crisis, he could not afford to totally ignore the black community's criticisms. The next day, the politically vulnerable Carter flew to Miami to get a firsthand look at the damage and discuss relief efforts. The real issue that was on nearly everyone's mind in the black community was the police. In a brief meeting with twenty city officials and local black leaders at the James E. Scott Community Center, in the heart of the riot area, Carter refused to second-guess the verdict. In response to a question, he said that "we must all share the responsibility for the guaranteeing of equal justice."

These were puzzling words. The president seemed to equally blame blacks and whites for racial injustice. Carter added to the muddle when he tried to mix themes of social justice and law and order, reminding the group that he was sworn to establish justice and ensure domestic tranquility. He succeeded in doing neither. If he believed that he had won friends, he was immediately slapped back to reality.

As Carter emerged into the muggy Miami afternoon, smiling and waving, a soft drink can bounced off the roof of his pastel blue limousine. A group of young blacks at a market across the street mocked him by dumping peanuts on the street and stepping on them. More bottles and cans were thrown by the crowd as Carter and his entourage of Secret Service agents beat a hasty retreat from the area. Later, the president downplayed the incident to a reporter, noting, "I didn't consider it significant." Carter regarded himself as a strong president bravely treading into hostile territory to "show leadership and concern."[41]

At a subsequent press conference, Carter again performed his racial balancing act. Everyone, he insisted, "must share the responsibility for guaranteeing equal justice." He had barely finished his opening remarks when reporters started in on him. When they demanded to know why it had taken him so long to come to Miami, Carter lamely explained that he had relied on reports from his aides to keep him updated on the situation. He still seemed determined to absolve the justice system of any blame. He could understand how blacks could "sense" that the system was unfair, he said, but it was still better than that in "almost any other nation on Earth."[42]

Carter's "almost" bothered many blacks. And apologetics did nothing to cool their anger. In July, the Civil Rights Commission again tried to bail out the beleaguered administration. Following a brief probe, it issued another report critical of police practices. The commission again called on the White House and Congress to stiffen federal penalties for police and public officials who committed color of law violations. The CRC, perhaps mindful of the DOJ's failure to win its suit against the Philadelphia Police Department, recommended that Congress authorize the attorney general to bring civil suits against local officials for police misconduct. CRC chairman Arthur Fleming admitted that the recommendations were "hastened" by the McDuffie killing. But they could not substitute for a successful federal prosecution of the officers. Moreover, Carter gave no indication that he would act on the recommendations.[43]

In a bizarre twist, the federal grand jury returned a five-count indictment in July against Charles Veverka for civil rights violations; the four officers who actually beat McDuffie were not indicted. Blacks weren't sure whether to be glad or sad. Why did the DOJ indict the man who had turned state's evidence and testified against the other four? Civiletti refused to answer. Veverka was also mystified by the indictment. He correctly pointed out that if he hadn't come forth, there would have been no McDuffie case at all. It appeared that the DOJ action was designed to punish a cop who told the truth rather than punish the guilty. At least, that's what Veverka concluded: "I can't see any cop going forth and telling the truth after this." If this was Civiletti's idea of how to get officers to report misconduct, the DOJ certainly had a funny way of going about it.[44]

The DOJ waited until the close of the trial to explain why it only indicted Veverka. Brian McDonald, the chief prosecuting attorney, said that the evidence against him became readily available first. That evidence consisted mostly of his self-incriminating admission that he participated in the beating. Since the shield of immunity Veverka got from the state technically applied only to state charges and did not extend to federal charges, he was easy pickings. His attorneys tried unsuccessfully to argue that a federal trial would violate his Fifth Amendment rights against self-incrimination (based on his testimony against the officers in the state trial) since no charges were ever brought against him in the McDuffie killing. Although Carter did not comment on the indictment, the Miami events were very much on his mind when he addressed the National Urban League's annual conference in August. He defended Civiletti's claim that he had acted promptly in the case.[45]

In December, Veverka went on trial in San Antonio (the trial had been moved there because of fears of riots). Federal prosecutors rehashed the evidence and testimony from the first trial. The only new revelation came from a former Miami officer who stated that police routinely beat people in the central business district if those people "gave them trouble." The jury quickly acquitted Veverka. However, there was one more twist. Veverka offered to cooperate with federal prosecutors if they agreed to prosecute the other officers. When they decided not to do so, the book was closed on what Miami Urban League director T. Willard Fair called a "farce."[46]

————— •✦• —————

By the time the Veverka verdict came in, Carter was out of the White House. Despite his political fumbles on racial problems, he still got high marks from civil rights leaders for his support of affirmative action, minority political appointments, small businesses, and job and housing programs. The performance of the DOJ during Carter's final year in office, however, was not nearly as admirable. Days's strategy of relying on police administrators and local officials to police themselves was a disaster. Days admitted that the DOJ received 12 "serious" police brutality complaints daily and that more than 1,600 cases were under investigation.[47] A frustrated Days agreed that local officials still had the tendency to shield brutal police officers. Under Carter, the DOJ was run by moderate Democrats who were sympathetic to civil liberties and civil rights issues. Yet they came no closer to reducing the use of deadly force by police against blacks than the Republicans had during the Nixon and Ford administrations. During the four Carter years, 1,428 police killings were ruled justified homicides, and more than 60 percent of the victims were blacks. The numbers far surpassed those of the Nixon years.[48]

Bell, Civiletti, and Days had made a fair effort to challenge the corrupt and racist policies of a runaway police department in Philadelphia. If they had won their suit, police administrators and local officials in other cities might have been forced to implement major reforms. But they did not win. And the riots in Miami only deepened the frustrations of black leaders and ensured that the Carter administration would be permanently scarred by an ambiguous legacy on criminal civil rights enforcement.

9

Rolling Back the Clock

The Reagan-Bush Years

In 1889, they traveled in covered wagons and on horseback to the Neshoba County Fair. Nearly a century later, they arrived in station wagons, campers, and family cars. The fair, held on an expansive campground outside Philadelphia, Mississippi, had grown bigger each year, drawing thousands of visitors from throughout the South.

Under dozens of Confederate flags that hung limply on flagpoles in the humid August air, visitors reveled in the week-long festivities, including dog races, square dancing, cakewalks, and beauty contests. Visitors wolfed down mounds of fried chicken and ham, massive slabs of barbecued ribs, pecan pie, and coconut cake. Children romped freely throughout the campgrounds, and camp lodgers left their doors unlocked. No one seemed to know or at least speak of Philadelphia's grim and violent past. It was the place where three civil rights workers had been murdered in 1964.

The Neshoba County Fair was more than just fun and games. In 1980, Mississippi governor William Winter called it the premier showcase for politicians. Men and women who aspired to be senators, governors, and congressional and state officials trekked to the fair, seeking votes. It was said that visitors could hear some of the best political stumping in the country at the fair. In 1980, fair visitors were expecting two special guests—Ronald and Nancy Reagan. From the time of their arrival at the small Meridian airport nearby, they would be treated like conquering heroes. Neshobans regarded the Reagans as their native son and daughter. Deep South Neshoba was Reagan country.

Reagan was the first presidential candidate in the ninety-one-year history of the Neshoba County Fair to speak at the event. As the Reagan motorcade headed to the fairgrounds, thousands of cheering whites chanted,

"We want Reagan." Buoyed by the crowd's enthusiasm, the candidate shouted back, "There isn't any place like this anywhere." Before the speech, the fair sponsors presented a beaming Nancy with a rocking chair and other gifts. She was so gratified by the down-home southern hospitality and warm welcome that she just stood in the center of the stage with a rapturous expression on her face.

Reagan warmed up the crowd with a few jokes and what had become a stock routine of his campaign—a football story. The only thing he regretted, he said, was that John Wayne couldn't be there, "God rest his soul." That brought thunderous applause and a chorus of rebel yells. Reagan then got down to business, tearing into the Washington bureaucrats, big government, and welfare.

Sensing the moment was ripe, he shouted to the crowd, "I believe in states' rights. I believe that we've distorted the balance of our government by giving powers that were never intended in the Constitution to the federal establishment." Reagan pushed all the right political buttons, and from then on, his campaign played even bigger throughout the old Confederacy than that of his Democratic opponent, Jimmy Carter—a true native son of the South.[1]

———•◆•———

The Reagan revolution was an attempt to return America to a world in which God, patriotism, rugged individualism, anticommunism, and family values ruled supreme and minorities and women knew their places. Reagan, even more adroitly than Nixon, parlayed this "forgotten America" sentiment and a sanitized image of the past into a powerful ideological movement. During the presidential race, he closely followed the strategy laid out by campaign architect Richard Wirthlin, who reminded Reagan to "appeal to the Republican/conservative political base" and "the undecideds and Middle America."[2]

White southerners joined with blue-collar ethnics who were fed up with busing, affirmative action, and black crime and deserted the Democratic Party in big numbers to put Reagan in the White House. Civil rights leaders braced themselves for the onslaught.

From the beginning, Reagan had attacked affirmative-action programs as the tender Achilles' heel of Democratic liberalism. Since 1970, the federal government had secured agreements from 15,000 companies with 23 million workers to submit modest plans to encourage the hiring of more minorities and women as a condition for receiving government contracts. By the mid-1970s, conservatives had stepped up their attacks on the plans. They managed to convince growing numbers of whites that affirmative action forced employers to hire a set "quota" of "undeserving, unqualified" blacks, while excluding whites. In a Gallup poll in 1977, only 11 percent of whites supported affirmative-action hiring.

Reagan wasted no time in fanning the flames of white anger. At his first press conference, held a week after his inauguration, he told reporters, "I'm old enough to remember when quotas existed in the United States for purposes of discrimination and I don't want to see that again."[3] To carry out his battle plan, Reagan needed a tough but uncompromising soldier to head the Justice Department's Civil Rights Division. And he did not want his candidate to be "tainted" by a background in civil rights. Drew Days, the outgoing director of the CRD, had been a legal counsel for the NAACP Legal Defense Fund and was anathema to conservatives. Erwin Griswold, Nixon's solicitor general, thought he knew the right man—Bradford Reynolds. When Reagan announced the appointment of Reynolds as head of the CRD in May 1981, Griswold told reporters, "If he had been a lawyer with the ACLU or the NAACP they wouldn't have wanted him."

Previously, during his three years as Griswold's assistant, Reynolds had impressed his boss with his discipline and intensity. A graduate of Yale University and Vanderbilt Law School, Reynolds was an heir of the DuPont family fortune and was comfortable with old money. Best of all, (from Griswold's perspective), he did not have any experience in civil rights law. Rather, he had handled commercial and government contract cases with the Washington law firm of Shaw, Pittman, Potts & Trowbridge. Moreover, Reynolds was not a hard-nosed, rigid ideologue.

Reynolds gave an early tip on what his approach to civil rights enforcement would be. When a reporter asked him about affirmative action, he said it was counterproductive to dwell on historical background. But during his confirmation hearing, Reynolds, like most nominees, skirted controversial issues and revealed little about his views. What he did say sounded moderate enough to please the senators. He promised to enforce all civil rights laws and not attempt to reverse prior court decisions on discrimination. Reynolds breezed through the hearing.

At a press conference the next day, the moderate image Reynolds had carefully cultivated in the confirmation process faded quickly. He emphatically stated, for example, that he opposed quotas and timetables to end discrimination. It soon became clear that the lines were sharply drawn between the Reagan administration and black leaders. Civil rights enforcement from then on would be under full attack.[4]

Even before Reynolds took over in August, the Justice Department had drastically scaled back the number of criminal prosecutions it pursued for civil rights violations. During the first six months Reagan was in the White House, the CRD filed only twenty-one criminal cases for civil rights violations, compared to twenty-eight filed by Carter during his first six months in Washington. Many CRD attorneys, especially the holdovers from the Carter administration, were in virtual rebellion and had begun a quiet campaign to counter the rightward drift within the Justice Department. Seventy-five attorneys had signed a petition opposing Reynolds's policies. Morale soon sank so low that one attorney said, "When we lose in court, we go up and down the hall cheering because we feel we really won."[5]

The public got wind of the infighting in September when Justice Department dissidents leaked a memo prepared by Robert D'Agostino, deputy attorney general, that claimed black students were disruptive in classrooms and recommended that they be placed in programs for the "emotionally disturbed." Reynolds called an emergency meeting, and during the stormy session, lawyers, paralegals, and secretaries listened as Reynolds reprimanded the staff for leaking information. However, he did not repudiate D'Agostino's views. Everyone present knew that the department's real issues were Reagan's civil rights policies and Reynolds himself. But Reynolds's boss, Attorney General William French Smith, made it clear that Reynolds was doing nothing wrong. Many Justice Department attorneys, particularly the black attorneys, saw the handwriting on the wall. Private practice suddenly looked more appealing: By the end of 1981, more than half of all the DOJ's attorneys had quit the CRD.[6]

By February 1982, civil rights leaders were in a near panic over Reynolds. The Leadership Conference on Civil Rights, an umbrella group of 160 civil rights organizations, issued its own 75-page report that not only condemned the CRD for its obstructionist role but charged that the division was deliberately conspiring to become the "locus" of all attacks on civil rights. Reynolds was hardly troubled. He had the complete blessing of the White House to pick his own target, which he soon did.[7]

———— • ◆ • ————

In 1970, of the nearly half million police officers nationally, only about 23,000 were black. For civil rights leaders, this situation was intolerable. Since the 1960s, they had contended that police departments were bastions of white male power and were insensitive and even hostile to poor blacks. Most of the racial explosions of the 1960s were triggered by conflicts between the largely white police forces and generally poor blacks in the inner cities.

As the numbers of blacks in major cities grew, it was crucial that urban police departments employ and promote more black officers; if not, the prospects for further civil disturbances were good. To stave off costly and time-consuming lawsuits by the Carter administration, officials in several big cities negotiated consent agreements to hire and promote more minorities and women.[8]

New Orleans was an unlikely location for the ideological battle between the Reagan administration and civil rights leaders. The city had a
well-deserved reputation as a fun-loving place where a good time could
be had by all. Moreover, by southern standards, New Orleans had been
an oasis of racial enlightenment. With the exception of the school desegregation battles in the early 1960s, the city had been spared much of the
racial violence that tore the rest of Louisiana apart. In 1980, New Orleans
had a black mayor, black school board members, many black city officials,
and a prosperous black business establishment. The city population was
55 percent black.

The New Orleans Police Department was a different story. The department did not hire any blacks until 1950, and it did not have a black super-
visor until 1966. By 1980, only 7 of 283 supervisors were black. In 1973,
black officers, assisted by the NAACP Legal Defense and Education
Fund, filed a discrimination suit against the city. The case had dragged on
for years, with little prospect of a settlement. While city officials and the
NAACP tried to sort out the legal tangle, events in the city took a deadly
and tragic turn that would soon embroil the Reagan administration in
controversy and test the DOJ's commitment to using federal criminal civil
rights statutes in cases involving police violence.[9]

Twenty-three-year-old New Orleans police officer Gregory Neuport
once told his brother, "I love it," and indeed he had a passion for police
work. In 1978, he graduated first in his class from the police academy. He
thought nothing of putting in extra time in the evenings and on weekends
for the department. But Neuport was restless and bored. He had spent
two years patrolling the relatively quiet Fourth District. His brother later
remembered, "He wanted to be where the action was." In early 1980,
therefore, Neuport requested a transfer to the Sixth District.

The district took in the Algiers section, a thickly populated area of low-
slung homes and tenement-style apartments located just across the
Mississippi River from downtown New Orleans. The majority of the residents were black and poor. The Algiers section long had a reputation as a
high-crime, drug-ridden, and dangerous area. In the center of the district
was the densely packed Algiers-Fisher housing project, which showed all
the familiar signs of urban neglect and decay. For the residents, many of
whom were welfare recipients, poverty, drugs, and violence had become
a disturbing way of life.

As a patrol officer, Neuport saw the pain and suffering of the residents
and wrestled with their problems every day. He also lived with the dangers. And sometime during the early morning hours of November 9, the
dangers caught up with him. Neuport's blood-splattered body was discovered near his squad car, adjacent to the Algiers-Fisher project.
Residents later reported that they had heard a shotgun blast.

The brutal murder sent shock waves through the New Orleans Police Department: A fellow officer had been killed (the second in two years). The murder looked like a difficult case with no eyewitnesses, clues, or suspects. The only thing the New Orleans police were sure of was that he was killed next to the project. Police Commissioner James Parsons immediately announced that the entire homicide unit was working on the case. Parsons had barely finished the announcement when residents began complaining that the police were conducting sweeps and shakedowns of all black males in the project. Some residents claimed police broke down doors, searched apartments, and made mass arrests.

Parsons denied that the officers had committed any wrongdoing and promised that if they did, they would be punished. He suggested that if residents had complaints, they could take them to the FBI. Gloria DeGruy, a project resident, decided to take Parsons up on his suggestion. She complained to police officials that she had heard some police officers shout, "You niggers know who killed that policeman." The watch commander at the Sixth District told her curtly that he didn't know anything about that. Residents, wary and scared, knew they would have no peace until the police had the suspects in hand.[10]

They were right. The first victim was Raymond Ferdinand, 38, an ex-addict, petty thief, and recent parolee. Friends said that Ferdinand was trying to straighten out his life. He planned to marry and was searching for a job. But Ferdinand's dreams of a better life ended in a hail of gunfire the evening of November 10, when he was shot by Officer John Marie, a member of the tough Felony Action Squad. Marie claimed that Ferdinand tossed a bag of drugs in a bush and then lunged at him with a knife when Marie went to retrieve it. Ferdinand's fiancée told a different story. She said that Ferdinand did not have a knife, did not resist Marie's search, and was shot in the neck. The day after the killing, six men reported that they were taken to the local district station and beaten (two reported that they were taken out to a nearby woods and beaten).

FBI special agent Cliff Anderson was disturbed by the reports of abuse. Within a week, he opened up a case file to investigate the complaints. As reports of the police harassment reached Washington, the CRD announced that it would begin an investigation. Parsons denied that his officers had committed any violations and reiterated that they were under strict orders to conduct a "professional" investigation. Despite Parsons's assurances, however, events were racing toward a tragic and deadly conclusion.[11]

———— • ◆ • ————

Friends and neighbors called James Billy Jr., 26, and Reginald Miles, 29, the "boogie brothers." They were a happy-go-lucky pair who liked to spin records at dances and bars. The police, however, said the two men were criminals with numerous arrests for drug-dealing. And both had been fingered by informants as the triggermen in Neuport's killing. In separate early-morning raids on their apartments near the Algier-Fisher project, Miles and Billy were killed in what police described as a "wild shoot-out." Sherry Singleton, Miles's girlfriend who was at his apartment at the time, was also killed. Police said she was shot when she pointed a small-caliber pistol at the officers.

At a hastily called press conference, Parsons congratulated the officers involved in the raids for acting with "self-control." He was satisfied that Miles and Billy were Neuport's killers and declared the case closed. But Parsons had badly misjudged the depth of the community's anger over the shootings and previous beatings and harassment. Many blacks did not believe the police version of the killing. And they noted that all but one of the officers involved in the killing of Miles, Billy, and Singleton were white.[12]

Anderson also thought there were too many loose ends: "We read the newspapers too." Residents of an apartment next to Miles's swore that they heard Singleton begging officers not to shoot her before the fatal shots were fired. The coroner's preliminary report noted that Singleton was found in a fetal position in the bathtub and that there was no weapon present. An independent pathologist reported that Miles was shot in the back of the neck.

Reporters made a more detailed check of Miles's and Billy's backgrounds and discovered that they had only been arrested for minor offenses and had not served any jail time. Furthermore, both men had held steady jobs for two years as housepainters. One resident who knew them scoffed at the depiction of Billy as a dangerous criminal: "Anybody could knock him down, that dude was a disc jockey." Drew Days, who had also been following developments, now directed Anderson to open an official probe. But Anderson would not be able to follow through. In a few days, he would be out as head of the CRD, and the case would fall into the lap of his successor, Bradford Reynolds.

The city's first black mayor, Ernest N. Morial, who had made his mark as a civil rights attorney, was also feeling the heat. He asked Parsons "for a full report" on the shootings. With the storm of protest, planned marches, and demonstrations and with the police version of the shooting unraveling fast, Parsons was on the spot. In a surprise move, he offered Morial his resignation, effective immediately. Morial accepted and announced that he wanted the Justice Department to speed up its investigation.[13]

Local civil rights leaders were not satisfied. They wanted indictments. In April 1981, a local and a state grand jury spent several weeks sifting through the evidence. The jurors listened to testimony from more than 100 witnesses, but they refused to indict any officers. New Orleans Parish district attorney Harry Connick was incredulous at the decision; he believed that many of the acts did occur. Morial, obviously disappointed by the grand jury action, sought to cool public anger by proposing to create the Office of Municipal Investigation.

Morial realized that even this modest proposal would face stiff opposition in the city council. He tried to make it appear that he was not singling out the police. The new department, he said, would investigate misconduct in all city offices. Local black leaders regarded the measure as a weak compromise.

Morial had accurately gauged the mood of the council as well as that of the rank-and-file police officers. After a stormy marathon session of the city council, during which several council members and police union officials roundly attacked the proposal as antipolice and tried to shout down supporters, Morial's measure barely squeaked through. Morial, Connick, and other city officials now hoped that the controversy would die out. They were wrong. In May 1981, the Justice Department, mostly because of Anderson's persistence, indicated that the evidence of police misconduct was compelling enough to warrant impaneling a federal grand jury.[14]

In July, reporters jammed the federal building for a press conference called by U.S. Attorney John Volz. Volz severely criticized the state for not returning indictments against some of the officers. He announced that the federal grand jury had returned indictments against seven officers, all white. But the joy of many local black leaders was short-lived, for Volz said that the officers would be prosecuted solely for the beating of two men—the alleged informers, Robert Davis and Johnnie Brownlee.

The jurors concluded that there was "insufficient evidence" to indict any of the officers on civil rights charges in the shootings of Miles, Billy, and Singleton. The jurors' actions puzzled many. Did Volz present all the evidence? Or did the grand jury simply take the most expedient way out to quiet the clamor for federal action?

Two months later, the questions were partly answered when federal judge Adrian Duplantier stunned the city by dismissing all charges against the seven officers on the grounds that Volz had been "overzealous" in seeking the indictments. Duplantier, in explaining his decision, gave the public a glimpse into the secret grand jury deliberations. He said that the jurors had been hopelessly deadlocked, ten favoring indictments against officers involved in the shootings and ten opposed.

Fearing that he might completely blow the government's case, Volz had backed off and instead pressed for indictments in the beatings of the informants. But even this was a tough sell. Volz continued to present evidence while refusing to release the jurors until indictments were returned. He immediately appealed Duplantier's decision to the Fifth District Appeals Court. Nine months later, the Fifth Circuit Court overturned Duplantier and reinstated the indictments.[15]

The beatings and shootings of local blacks had attracted national publicity and stirred black anger. This was a high-profile case and thus a political case. The DOJ had little choice but to press for reinstatement of the indictments.

———— • ◆ • ————

Just when it seemed that the legal turmoil between the New Orleans police and local blacks would be resolved, events took another turn. On October 11, after nine years, black officers who had sued the department to get more blacks hired and promoted finally got their day in court. On opening day of the trial, NAACP officials demanded a substantial cash settlement for the officers and asked the city to agree to hire or promote one black officer for every white officer hired or promoted until the department reached parity.

City officials, backed by the police union, balked, and it looked like a bitter struggle was shaping up. But despite their bluster, the city officials were in a hopeless position. They faced towering litigation costs that could severely strap the city's tight budget; in addition, they had no real prospect of winning, and it was possible that federal funds would be cut off.

A prolonged court battle coming on the heels of the shootings would be a public relations nightmare. And the case would surely open up even deeper hostilities between the police and local blacks. Two days later, city officials caved in and agreed to the settlement. On December 17, 1982, a three-member panel of the Fifth Circuit Court approved the settlement plan.

Reynolds now had the perfect test case. Three weeks later, he announced that the CRD would ask the Fifth Circuit Court to overturn the settlement. Reynolds said that the plan discriminated against the white officers by establishing a "race-conscious quota system," and he argued that quotas violated Title VII of the 1964 Civil Rights Act and the equal protection clauses of the Fourteenth Amendment. This was the standard conservative attack on affirmative action, and legal scholars shot holes through it.

While the Civil Rights Act and the Fourteenth Amendment did not specifically mention blacks, it was clearly understood by the framers of the amendment and by Congress that these were race-conscious measures designed to explicitly protect the rights of blacks and minorities. Charles Fried, who a year later would take over as Reagan's solicitor general, thought Reynolds had gone overboard in insisting that everything must be victim specific (Fried eventually swallowed his doubts, however, and dutifully made a case for the Reagan administration's "reverse discrimination" suits before federal courts.)

In the case of the New Orleans Police Department, if Reynolds had succeeded in getting the court to overturn the settlement, the chances were
good that white males would continue to formulate and implement the
policies and practices that had fueled much of the fear, hostility, and ultimately violence between police and local blacks. Within a week, the Civil
Rights Commission skipped past Reynolds's legal objections and blasted
the Reagan administration for failing to enforce civil rights laws.
Commissioners accused the White House of fostering a climate that
spawned racial and religious hate.[16]

———————◆◆◆———————

With Reynolds's intervention, New Orleans officials had two potentially
explosive and controversial court actions on their hands. Morial and city
council members undoubtedly remembered the riots that had occurred in
Miami three years earlier following the acquittal of four white police officers charged with killing black insurance executive Arthur McDuffie.
They requested that the trial be moved out of the city. A federal judge
agreed and ordered the case moved to Dallas.

As federal prosecutors prepared their case, events took yet another
strange turn. On January 16, 1983, CBS's *60 Minutes* planned to air a special segment that featured interviews with black men who claimed they
had been beaten by New Orleans police. Defense attorneys immediately
cried foul, declaring that the program would prejudice their case. They
filed a motion to prevent the showing of the segment in Dallas. Supreme
Court Justices Byron White and Warren Burger denied the motion, and
CBS executives hailed the decision as a victory for the First Amendment.
But federal prosecutors were not celebrating. The likelihood was that the
officers would be tried by a mostly white jury. Many whites, deeply
mired in racist thinking, believed the stereotypes about black criminality
and were reluctant to take the word of a black defendant over that of a
white officer. In Dallas, white police officers would be on trial. It would
be a stiff test.[17]

But the prosecutors were well prepared. Although they lost the opening round and failed to get any blacks on the jury (six blacks were
promptly eliminated from the panel), they presented a strong case that
documented the abuses. The jurors listened to gruesome tales from witnesses of prisoners being beaten with heavy books while their heads were
wrapped in plastic bags to cut off their air supply.

The prosecution's star witness was Oris Buckner, a black police officer.
In exchange for immunity, Buckner tearfully admitted that he had taken
part in the beatings along with the other officers. After two days, the jury
convicted three police officers on the charges; the three later received five-
year prison sentences. The lead federal prosecutor, Michael Johnson, was

elated that "justice has been done" and stated that the verdict sent a message to New Orleans city officials to clean up their department.[18]

Johnson certainly had every right to congratulate himself on the verdict, considering the Justice Department's timidity about prosecuting police abuse cases. The victory was a tribute to the competence and tenacity of the prosecution team. But in truth, the verdict could have easily gone the other way. Seven women jurors later told reporters that they didn't believe the police had beaten the victims and that the witnesses had lied. In a twist, this time the white male jurors had pushed for conviction. Federal prosecutors again confronted the old bugaboo of white jurors' reluctance to convict white police officers when the victims were black. Johnson had won—but just barely.[19]

———— •◆• ————

While Johnson was sending his message, his bosses in Washington were busy trying to send their own. Two weeks after the verdict, Smith, Reynolds, and other administration officials huddled at the White House to figure out how to pressure the Equal Employment Opportunity Commission (EEOC) not to file a counterbrief against the Justice Department in support of the New Orleans Police Department's affirmative-action plan.

Smith was blunt. There was no room on the Reagan team for dissenters; The "Reagan administration must speak with one voice." But he could not browbeat the Civil Rights Commission. It issued yet another broadside calling the Justice Department's position "legally and constitutionally incorrect" and sent two letters to Reagan demanding that he stop trying to bully the EEOC.[20]

The political mess that Reynolds stirred up got even messier in June when Reagan met with a delegation of black Republicans at the White House. These men and women, who had spent three years deluding themselves and the Republicans into thinking they could sell blacks on Reagan's brand of laissez-faire conservatism, tried to explain to the President that his political strategies had caused "self-inflicted damage" with black voters.

To repair the damage, they wanted Reagan to fire Reynolds. But the "Great Communicator" was no more inclined to listen to them than to those whom Reynolds contemptuously branded as the "usual critics" (civil rights groups and liberal Democrats). Reagan would stay the course. The same day, Reynolds began presenting his case to the appeal judges. He got nowhere.[21]

The Fifth Circuit Court rejected Reynolds's arguments and upheld the police settlement. Although Reynolds came up empty-handed, he saw the defeat as only the opening skirmish in a bigger war. The affirmative-action plans "imposed" on police departments by the courts remained high on his list of targets. He wouldn't rest until the courts and public officials reflected his own racially constricted view of how departments should conduct their business.

Though Reynolds had not won a single court victory, as CRD chief he was still in a powerful and strategic position to affect civil rights enforcement. When Reagan's first term ended in 1984, the number of civil rights suits brought by the CRD in housing, education, and voter discrimination matters was 66 percent lower than the number the Justice Department had brought in Carter's first three years in the White House (124 for Carter, 42 for Reagan).[22]

Reagan still tried to maintain the appearance that criminal civil rights enforcement was a high priority for his administration. In June 1984, he boasted at a news conference that "he felt no higher duty than to defend the civil rights of all Americans." He claimed that the Justice Department had filed more cases under the federal criminal statutes for civil rights violations that year than in the past few years.

His presentation was tragicomedy of the highest order—comic because the president who had done so much to gut the cause of civil rights was pretending to be its champion, and tragic because he was almost right. The Justice Department actually had filed more criminal civil rights cases in 1983 than during Carter's last year. By the end of Reagan's first term, the DOJ had brought more criminal civil rights prosecutions than during Carter's four years. However, this said less about Reagan's commitment to civil rights than about the past abysmal performance of the Justice Department in combating racial violence.

In April 1985, Reynolds stepped up the attack. He petitioned the Supreme Court to overturn affirmative-action plans in fifty-one cities. Most of them, like that for New Orleans, involved either the police or the fire department. Reynolds specially targeted hiring and promotion plans in Chicago, Detroit, St. Louis, Miami, Milwaukee, and Philadelphia that resembled the plan in New Orleans. It was hardly coincidental that these were the very cities that had the longest histories of lethal racially charged conflict between local blacks and police departments that were run by white males.[23]

————————◆————————

Philadelphia continued to be a painful example of how tough and resistant to change the old-boy network was in big-city police departments. The Philadelphia Police Department was still haunted by the ghosts of the Frank Rizzo era. During his reign as police commissioner and mayor in the 1970s, the department was a disgraceful national symbol of the brutal and murderous treatment of blacks and minorities. By the early 1980s, not much had changed. Throughout 1984 and 1985, police officers had been engaged in a series of deadly confrontations with the black separatist group MOVE. The ongoing conflict was marked by arrests, allegations of beatings and harassment, and a shoot-out that left one officer dead.

The conflict reached an even deadlier end on May 14, 1985, when police dropped a bomb containing C-4 explosive (an unauthorized military explosive reportedly supplied by the FBI) on the roof of a home that MOVE called its headquarters. The blast incinerated 6 adults and 5 children and wiped out 61 homes in the neighborhood, leaving 350 homeless.[24]

A local grand jury, after sifting through evidence and hearing testimony from numerous eyewitnesses, concluded that Mayor Wilson Goode and the police administrators were grossly negligent, and it branded the killings unjustified homicide.

The FBI and the Justice Department made weak promises to investigate. But there was every reason to expect that the promises would remain just that—promises. Reagan's presidential adviser and confidant Ed Meese now ran the Justice Department. Meese, who had replaced the comparatively moderate William French Smith in March 1984, was known as a combative and immovable ideologue. He had already managed to infuriate civil rights leaders when he advised Reagan to rescind an IRS policy denying tax exemptions to private schools that discriminate on the basis of race.

Three days after the MOVE bombing, Meese told the California Peace Officers' Association that the bombing was "a good example for us all to take note of." He reminded the officers that the bombing was "caused by the criminals, not the police." Meese did not, however, tell the association exactly what crimes the children who were killed had committed or if the 350 residents made homeless by the incendiary bombing thought the action was "a good example" for police to follow. These were the fine points that Meese left to Justice Department press spokesman Terry Eastland to explain. Eastland tried to clear up any misconceptions that his boss condoned the killings. He assured the reporters that Meese didn't applaud the bombing and the loss of life but referred only to the "willingness of Mayor Wilson Goode to explain it to the public."[25]

Meese was the first attorney general in fifty years to publicly hold such a narrowly constrained view of federal powers. He kept up a running battle with civil libertarians over the meaning of the Constitution and insisted that the Bill of Rights applied only to the national government. Literally, he was correct. But fundamentally, his was a ludicrous position. A citizen of a state was also a citizen of the United States and thus protected by the Bill of Rights. What Meese really wanted was to further reduce federal intervention in state affairs on racial and economic matters.

His idea of asking the Supreme Court to reverse or modify the Fourteenth Amendment so that state and local governments would not be held to the strict provisions of due process and equal protection was part of his ploy. Meese apparently saw no contradiction in encouraging Reynolds to use federal power to tamper with affirmative-action plans that were voluntarily agreed to by local governments to end discrimination in police departments.[26]

Meese and Reynolds could not turn back the legal clock completely. Federal courts continued to turn aside Justice Department challenges and uphold affirmative-action plans within police departments. But while Reynolds still held the reins at the CRD, he kept the racial pot stirred up.

Following the murder of a young black by a gang of young whites in the Howard Beach section of Brooklyn and the attacks on black families by the KKK in Forsyth, Georgia, in February 1987, Reynolds addressed the Florida Bar Association in Orlando. He lashed out at civil rights groups for making an issue of the violence. He considered the incidents in Forsyth and Howard Beach to be isolated cases and not part of any national pattern. Reynolds based his assertions on an informal survey of U.S. attorneys and the number of complaints CRD received.

In truth, this was pure guesswork by Reynolds, and it badly understated the magnitude of racial violence. The Southern Poverty Law Center, a civil rights watchdog group, reported forty-five cases of violent attacks in 1985 and 1986, including cross-burnings and assaults on black families who moved into white neighborhoods. In addition, there were hundreds of incidents of vandalism and intimidation aimed at minorities in these neighborhoods. The center demanded that Meese set up a special unit to monitor and prosecute civil rights violations related to "move-in" violence.

Reynolds apparently was unfamiliar with the report commissioned by the National Institute of Justice (the Justice Department's own in-house think tank) that documented the sharp rise in hate crimes during the 1980s. He understated the violence partly for partisan political reasons and partly because no federal agency, including the CRD, had compiled and published any data on these types of attacks.

He also did not tell the Florida bar members that the CRD failed to investigate the majority of the complaints it received. FBI deputy director, Floyd Clarke told a House congressional appropriations panel that the FBI only "concentrated on the cases that have the greatest regional or national impact and the greatest prosecutorial potential."

Oddly, Reagan indirectly confirmed the suspicions of civil rights groups that Reynolds had deliberately downplayed racial violence. In a Lincoln Day talk to junior high students, Reagan, although he did not specifically refer to the attacks in Forsyth or Howard Beach, said that "racism is still with us, North and South." He did not, however, tell the students what his administration would do to change that.[27]

Black leaders were more convinced than ever that the president would not do much. By the end of 1987, although the CRD had received 7,348 civil rights complaints, it had investigated only 2,826. The Justice Department prosecuted only 57 criminal civil rights cases. Of that number, 36 defendants pled guilty, and 17 were convicted.

In his last message to Congress before departing the White House, Reagan cast one eye on history and the other on the "usual critics" (meaning liberal Democrats and black leaders) of his civil rights policies. He claimed that the Justice Department had filed more criminal cases for civil rights violations than any other administration in American history. The irony is that Reagan was right. And this only underscored the Justice Department's weak history of criminal enforcement in cases involving civil rights violations.[28]

Civil rights groups and black leaders considered the eight Reagan years as the single worst period for racial progress in recent U.S. history. The Reagan legacy was terribly marred by the gutting of social programs, the escalation in poverty, the rollback of civil rights laws, and the widening of racial divisions. Conservatives, however, reveled in the aura of Reagan and confidently made plans for a smooth and quiet transition of power to the man who had nestled so long and quietly in Reagan's considerable political shadow—Vice President George Bush.

———————•◆•———————

For a brief moment, it seemed that Republican plans for a Bush White House might go astray. The vice president had an identity problem. Many voters perceived Bush as a weak, indecisive politician. Moreover, just eight years earlier, he had been considered a Republican liberal. During the 1980 campaign, for example, he attacked Reagan for his conservative economic policies. But that didn't last. Instead, he joined the Reagan team as vice president, rediscovered his Texas roots, and moved quickly to the political right.

Following the Democratic convention in July 1988, Democratic presidential candidate Michael Dukakis, from Massachesetts, held a commanding lead in the polls over Bush and seemed a good bet to break the Republican lock on the White House. But Republican strategists found a trump card for Bush. A black convict named Willie Horton, who was serving a term for first-degree murder, had been released on a work furlough program from a Massachusetts prison. Shortly after, Horton was accused of raping and torturing a Maryland woman. Bush used the incident to stoke the latent fears of many whites about black crime and violence. His standing in the polls quickly shot up, and by November, he had turned the election into a rout. The Reagan revolution was still in safe hands.[29]

In his first few months in office, Bush said almost nothing about civil rights. But in September, he made his first cautious remarks on racial violence. At a White House press briefing, a reporter was curious as to what Bush intended to do about the rise in racial attacks by white supremacist Skinheads, Klansmen, and Aryan Nation members. Bush seemed to think the problem could be solved by moral appeals, "I don't think there's a federal statute that is going to take care of an incident of that nature." He was wrong. There were three federal criminal statutes on the books to criminally prosecute civil rights violations. Two had been there for more than a century, the third since 1968. And they had been at the disposal of every president. Bush, at least for the time being, ignored them and apparently thought it was enough that he "speak out" against racism.

Presidential goodwill did not do much to check the spread of KKK Klaverns and Nazi and Aryan Nation branches. In December, the membership of these groups topped 20,000, and their followers had committed at least a dozen racially motivated murders in 1988.[30]

Bush was finally forced to confront the threat of armed white terrorists in December 1989, when federal judge Robert Vance and Robert Robinson, an NAACP legal counsel, were blown up by mail bombs. Within the week, NAACP offices in dozens of cities had received bomb threats. Under pressure from civil rights leaders, Bush ordered FBI and Justice Department investigations.

The FBI tapped its network of agents and informers for leads, with little luck. After three months, bureau officials announced that the investigation had hit a stone wall. The failure to get immediate results raised the old suspicions among civil rights groups about the FBI's diligence and the White House's commitment when it came to bringing criminal prosecutions in civil rights cases.

FBI agents and U.S. attorneys involved with the case met in Atlanta in April 1990 to discuss strategy and to pump new life into the investigation. They began rechecking their leads and putting more pressure on informants. Eventually they turned up a name, and seven months later, FBI agents arrested Walter Moody Jr., a former Klansman. When Moody was convicted in June 1991 and sentenced to a life term, federal officials quickly closed the book on the case. But several questions were left unanswered. How could one man acting alone manage to concoct an elaborate plot and carry out actions in dozens of cities nationally? Where did Moody get his funds? To what organizations did he belong? Who were his associates? Nonetheless, the government had its "lone nut" and felt there was no need to dig any further.[31]

The bombings and the murders exposed the continuing weakness in federal civil rights enforcement methods. First of all, it was a difficult and time-consuming task to hunt down racial killers without a formal system to measure or track racially motivated hate crimes. For five years, civil rights leaders had lobbied the Justice Department to keep records of these crimes. Reagan had resisted, and the attorney general said he didn't have the resources. But the bomb threats to the NAACP and the two murders in December 1989 had some political impact. In April 1990, the House and Senate passed the Hate Crimes Statistics Act. But Congress still seemed unsure about how much weight to place on racial violence and made the law effective for only four years.

In remarks during the signing ceremonies, Bush seemed to rethink his earlier belief that appeals to moral conscience were enough to counter racist violence. Now he promised to see "if new law enforcement measures" were needed "to bring the hatemongers out of hiding." But Bush's metaphor hardly fit. The hatemongers were already out in the open. By the start of 1990, there were more then 3,000 racist Skinheads and the Order, Aryan Nation, the White Patriots' Party, Nazi factions, and the Klan claimed to have thousands of supporters.

Borrowing generously from the terror methods of the old Klan, members of these groups cut a bloody swath through the nation, committing dozens of bombings, murders, and bank robberies to bring about their apocalyptic vision of a white, Christian America. Many experts believed that official crime statistics greatly understated the magnitude of the crimes since four out of five victims of hate crimes did not report them because they were too fearful or felt they had little legal recourse or protection.[32]

The FBI and the Justice Department tried to assure an increasingly nervous public that they were cracking down on these crimes, and the FBI formed a special task force to track hate crimes. But despite the federal government's new public get-tough stance, there was no guarantee that more terrorists would be prosecuted. Floyd Clarke warned that the Justice Department would move cautiously in these cases due to the extremely "sensitive nature of the constitutional issues involved in applying federal law."[33]

The Justice Department continued to apply the old states' rights litmus test exclusively to the prosecution of criminal abuses in civil rights cases. It was hard to imagine FBI deputy director Clarke attaching the same "sensitive nature" precondition to the prosecution of a drug-trafficker, bank robber, car thief, or kidnapper.

Like Reagan, Bush claimed that he was making headway in attacking race terror and that the Justice Department "had vigorously prosecuted hate crimes." Federal prosecutors had convicted several dozen Klan,

Skinhead, and Aryan Nation members in 1989 and 1990. On the surface, it seemed that the Justice Department was making a big effort to nail racial terrorists.[34]

The DOJ was certainly in a self-congratulatory mood. Linda Davis, chief of the CRD's criminal section, proudly noted that the department's "overall success ratio increased from a low of 10 percent to as high as 80 percent" in prosecuting racially motivated crimes. Although the department deserved credit for hauling more violent hatemongers into court, the truth was that most of the convictions came in a handful of high-profile cases; in other instances, the defendants pleaded guilty.[35] In each of the cases, either there was overwhelming evidence against the defendants or prosecutors got the cooperation of informers to win convictions. The figures made Bush look good only because they were measured against the meager criminal prosecution record of the Justice Department in past years. Bush also failed to add that his administration's record on civil rights enforcement against voting, housing, and employment discrimination violations was just as dismal as that of his predecessors.[36]

In early 1991, Bush was busy trying to shore up the fledgling democratic parties in East Europe that had replaced the defunct Communist parties, as well as unleashing U.S. military might against Iraq's leader, Sadam Hussein. These were satisfying victories that demonstrated America's power and dominance. By March, Bush seemed politically secure and comfortable as he rode the crest of public popularity. Things might have stayed that way if not for an amateur photographer and his video camera.

———————— • ◆ • ————————

In March, Bush was vacationing in Bermuda when he saw the first news reports. He watched four Los Angeles Police Department officers mercilessly beating a black man lying prostrate on the ground while a small army of other officers stood and watched. The assault on black motorist Rodney King was captured on film by George Holliday, who stood on the balcony of his nearby apartment. TV stations across the nation, sensing a hot story, quickly snatched the tape and began broadcasting it. Soon, it was beamed worldwide. Bush's press secretary, Marlin Fitzwater, immediately issued a statement on the president's behalf. Bush said that he was "sickened" as he watched the tape; he called the beating "a pretty shocking thing."[37]

The ninety seconds of raw brutality captured on the Holliday tape touched a deep nerve in many blacks who perhaps had momentary, horrific visions of lying on the cold ground that night and being beaten themselves. They could feel King's agony. The beating symbolized the legacy of lynchings, beatings, and assaults that blacks had suffered at the hands of vigilantes for more than a century.

Even though charges were quickly filed against LAPD officers Stacey Koon, Laurence Powell, Ted Briseno, and Timothy Wind, the events in Los Angeles were now careening out of control. As TV stations continued to play the tape, national and world indignation mounted. The White House worried that the King affair could turn into a public relations fiasco.

The King beating held special dangers for Bush. He had to express his moral indignation at the incident, but at the same time he dared not appear too critical of the police. His election and his administration had been carefully crafted on law-and-order themes and the promise to crack down on crime. One of Bush's first acts as president had been to retain Richard Thornburgh as attorney general.

Picked by Reagan in July 1988, Thornburgh had solid conservative credentials but was considered "less ideological" than Meese, who had resigned under a cloud of scandal. The former two-term governor in Pennsylvania had been a successful federal prosecutor whom Reagan praised "as a tough-minded crime buster." Thornburgh, who was expected to be the Bush administration's point man on law and order, admitted that he "was more sympathetic to U.S. attorneys." By that, he meant he intended to give U.S. attorneys near absolute power to prosecute criminal cases. Unfortunately, that did not translate into more prosecutions of police violence cases.[38]

Bush also seemed to have a genuine admiration for the LAPD's bellicose police chief, Daryl Gates, who was under intense fire in Los Angeles following the King beating. Gates was hardly a stranger to controversy. For years, he had been the target of attacks by blacks, women, and Hispanic and gay groups because of his inflammatory racial and sexual remarks and the alleged brutal policies of the LAPD toward minorities. During the 1988 presidential campaign, photographers snapped photos of Bush and Gates grinning and hamming it up together after a raid on a local crack house. The raid was a showy photo-op stunt clearly staged to shore up Bush's image as a tough law-and-order candidate. In September, after Bush challenged his ACLU membership and implied that he was soft on crime, Michael Dukakis spoke to cadets at the Los Angeles Police Academy. Gates, who sat stoically during the speech, was in no mood to help the beleaguered Dukakis. Afterward, he warned him, "I'd burn that ACLU card so fast . . . you can't be strong on law and order and be a member of the ACLU." The press immediately took this as a sign that Gates was "noticeably warmer" toward Bush.

Two days after the King beating, Bush described Gates as an "all-American hero" and refused to join the steadily growing chorus of critics calling for him to resign. Fitzwater told reporters that his boss had no intention of getting embroiled in the growing controversy: "It's not our role to comment on individual police departments."[39] The next day, Bush told a joint session of Congress that it was "time to stand up for America's police and prosecutors." Since 1989, Bush had been locked in a fight with Congress to get his omnibus anticrime bill passed. The bill included provisions to expand the death penalty for dozens of federal crimes, put limits on appeals for federal prisoners, impose mandatory sentencing for violations of firearms laws, and allow illegally seized evidence in court "if police acted in good faith in seizing it."

The measure was a civil libertarian's nightmare. After liberal Democrats had stalled the bill, Bush issued an ultimatum to Congress to pass it in one hundred days. He also threw in a little saber-rattling jingoism by tying it into the Gulf War, and in a blatant attempt to shame Congress, he implied that if they didn't pass the bill, they were less than patriotic.

At an informal press briefing in the White House cabinet room, Bush tried to straddle the line. He again called the King beating "sickening" and promised that he "would go the extra mile" to see that justice was done in the case. Then he switched tracks. He praised Gates as an "exemplary police chief" and played on the memory of the eighty-three police officers killed in the line of duty in 1990 to boost support for the police. They "need the faith and support" of citizens, he said, before making another pitch for passage of his crime bill.[40]

It was never clear why Bush felt he had to defend the police since critics had not accused the nation's police departments of misconduct; only the officers who beat Rodney King were criticized. Bush also didn't explain what the King beating had to do with the crackdown on street crime—unless he was suggesting that there were provisions in his crime bill that would specifically punish police who committed criminal acts, which he certainly was not.

———— • ◆ • ————

Black leaders ignored Bush's political posturing. They were satisfied with his pledge to take action in the King case. The next day, a group of black and Hispanic House members, along with NAACP officials who earlier had called for a federal probe of the beating, met with FBI director William Sessions and Thornburgh. Congressman John Lewis told Sessions that the King beating was "symbolic of what is happening around the country." Benjamin Hooks chimed in that "police brutality is one of the recurring, persistent themes that has never died down."

Congressman John Conyers was angry that the Justice Department and

FBI had rejected his modest suggestions that they keep records on the number of police abuse complaints. For years, Conyers had been practically a lone voice in Congress warning that tensions between blacks and the police had dangerously increased. He fully exploited the King beating and told Sessions that the federal government must "explore this ugly phenomena."

Sessions was clearly uncomfortable with the sharp reaction of the black elected officials, but he mostly listened. He knew that the King case was a minefield and that any misstep could damage the reputation of the FBI and further anger black leaders. He decided that the best approach was to minimize the wider consequences of the case for law enforcement. Sessions told the representatives that the beating was an "isolated" incident and that the bureau would investigate the King case just as it did any other. But Sessions probably knew that the King case was scarcely just another "routine" case. The FBI's performance would be watched closely.

Later the same day, Congressional Black Caucus members met with Thornburgh and repeated their demand for a federal probe. Thornburgh apparently was genuinely peeved with police conduct in L.A. He warned that "those engaged in law enforcement must be among the first to assure the observance of civil rights." Two days later, Thornburgh announced that the Justice Department was considering filing charges against the dozen or so officers who watched and did not intervene in the beating.[41]

Following the meeting with the Congressional Black Caucus, Thornburgh promised to conduct a nationwide review of the more than 15,000 complaints of police brutality that the department had received between 1984 and 1990. Although the figure seemed staggering, it badly understated the true problem. Like hate crimes, many cases of abuses went unreported because many people feared legal reprisals or even arrest. Since most departments handled police abuse complaints internally, an individual would have to go to the local station house, where the officers who committed the alleged abuse worked, to report it. This further discouraged filing.

Even when complaints were filed, attorneys were extremely reluctant to take such cases unless the injuries were severe and there was a good chance of winning a large damage settlement. Most police departments simply regarded police abuse complaints as a nuisance and assigned them the lowest priority. Martin Rosenthal of the Harvard Law Criminal Justice Institute was frank in stating, "They just don't care enough about them."

Other than dealing with a handful of carefully selected, high-profile cases, the Justice Department had done virtually nothing to solve the problem. Since no other federal agency kept a systematic record of the numbers of complaints, it was impossible to measure the scope of police abuse or pinpoint a pattern to it. But using the crude yardstick of Thornburgh's numbers, it was possible to glean some insight into the problem. The bulk of the complaints came from eight states—California, Louisiana, Texas, New York, Georgia, Florida, Alabama, and Mississippi. These states had heavy concentrations of blacks and Hispanics, and they filed the largest number of civil rights complaints.

Since police abuse was not its priority, the Justice Department had investigated only about one-third of the complaints. This seemed to fly directly in the face of testimony that Sessions had given a year earlier before a congressional oversight committee. He gave the impression then that police abuse was a major concern of the FBI. He told committee members that "ninety percent of all civil rights investigations involved law enforcement."

But how important did Sessions really consider civil rights investigations? Although he asked Congress for hefty funding increases for the FBI units that handled organized crime, drug enforcement, counterterrorism, white-collar crime, crimes of violence, and foreign counterintelligence, he did not request more money for the bureau's civil rights unit.[42] Thornburgh probably realized that the figures didn't look very good. But he got ahead of the critics and said that during his three years as attorney general, he had prosecuted forty-six police officers for civil rights violations. He also hinted that he might bring more cases.

While Thornburgh was assuring the press that he was determined to put an end to police abuse, others within his department presented a far different picture. CRD chief John Dunne raised the standard argument that members of the Justice Department were not the "front-line troops" to combat police brutality; that was the job of local authorities. Dunne said the Justice Department was just a "backstop." The department was firmly convinced that there was no percentage in directly confronting police agencies with excessive force complaints. Instead, it took the more expedient and politic approach. In some cases, it tossed out a few dollars "to assist police agencies in reviewing alternatives to the use of deadly force," according to Linda K. Davis, assistant director.

A week later, Sessions tried to drop the expectation level of the public in regard to the King beating. He reiterated that his "gut reaction was that the investigation will settle into the King affair."[43] It did. FBI agents in Los Angeles questioned only the officers and supervisors at the Foothill Division station where the officers who beat King worked. Even this was too much for Gates. He fumed and ranted about the "stupidity" of the bureaucrats at the Justice Department. The officers who were questioned rushed to the L.A. Police Protective League and protested they were "under duress" from the FBI. The league offered to supply attorneys. Gates and the officers finally relented when federal prosecutors threatened to get a federal subpoena to release all records.[44]

———————— • ◆ • ————————

The federal investigation became narrower each day. During congressional hearings on police abuse in May, Oregon congressman Michael J. Kopetski wondered how the Justice Department could wage a vigorous battle against racial violence without committing more resources or personnel to the effort. He noted that although the department had increased personnel overall by 55 percent since 1981, the number of attorneys assigned to investigate and prosecute civil rights violations remained the same.

In June, Thornburgh announced that not only would he not prosecute the officers who watched the beating but also he would probably not prosecute the four officers charged if they were acquitted in state court. Protecting his flank, he said that the Justice Department might reconsider prosecution if it was convinced that the state had not been "vigorous" enough in its case.[45]

While Thornburgh prepared to settle into his armchair and join millions of Americans as passive spectators in what promised to be the most closely watched trial in years, the events in L.A. seemed to awaken the Civil Rights Commission from the deep slumber it had fallen into during the Reagan-Bush years. The CRC had barely survived Reagan's major attempts to emasculate it by cutting its funds. (Congress cut its budget by $3 million in 1990.) Reagan had effectively neutralized the commission by packing it with conservative, anti–affirmative action appointees.

The CRC, sensing more trouble ahead, made some barely audible noises about examining L.A. police practices. William Allen, an archconservative college professor, took over as commission chairman following the death of rabidly conservative and controversial chairman Clarence Pendleton in 1988. Allen said he considered police abuse a "question of urgency and sensitivity." These were strange words coming from Allen. Like his predecessor, he hadn't seemed in much of a hurry to investigate civil rights abuses. In fact, he had barely taken over as chairman when he found himself under fire from civil rights leaders for a speech that belittled blacks and gays.[46]

A prudent person might ask why Allen was now so concerned about police misconduct in Los Angeles. The CRC had had plenty of opportunities during the 1970s and 1980s to probe the LAPD, which had been the focus of several FBI investigations regarding questionable shootings and beatings. Allen also must have read the Christopher Commission report issued in July 1991. The commission, appointed by Los Angeles mayor Tom Bradley in the wake of the King beating, revealed the wide pattern of abuse, racism, and sexism rampant within the LAPD. It had made sweeping recommendations for reform.

Given the CRC's recent dormancy on civil rights, few expected the CRC to do much about the problem. Besides, the time for more studies or hearings had passed. Blacks and much of the general public now expected concrete action against police abuse, starting with the convictions of the four police officers. Would it happen?

Many had deep doubts. The "new Right" politics of the Reagan and Bush years had bred a deep cynicism in many Americans about their justice system. The rollback of civil rights gains, the assaults on social programs, the erosion in civil liberties protections by the Reagan courts, and the fear of crime on the part of millions of Americans had created a deadly climate that seemed to make abuses like the Rodney King beating almost inevitable.

The beating, however, had touched a raw nerve in many blacks. These men and women were angry, and they demanded justice. For an administration that many believed was adrift and out of touch with the nation's problems, this spelled big trouble.

10

A Compelling Federal Interest

The Reverend Thad Garrett was one of the most respected members of the clergy in Washington, D.C. Over the years, he had been an adviser to many prominent persons in Washington business and political circles. Among them was President Bush. Garrett had grown close enough to Bush that the president regarded him as both an adviser and a personal friend. On the morning of May 2, 1992, Garrett was worried about the president. He had just spent more than ninety minutes closeted in the Oval Office with Bush, members of the Congressional Black Caucus, NAACP officials, and senior administration officials. Garrett told reporters afterward, "In all the years I have known him, I have never seen a session like this."

Two days earlier, a jury with no blacks had acquitted Wind, Koon, and Briseno of all the charges in the King beating and deadlocked for acquittal for the fourth defendant, Powell. Within hours, Los Angeles exploded. When the smoke cleared, there were forty-five dead, and $550 million in property damage. It was the most devastating urban upheaval in America in the twentieth century.

Bush faced his worst domestic crisis. With the economy in shambles, unemployment spiraling, and Congress gridlocked on White House legislative proposals, Bush's popularity had sunk fast in the public opinion polls. One of his Republican advisers, perhaps trying to find a philosophical meaning to the president's woes, called the L.A. riots Bush's defining moment. To the black leaders who met with Bush that Friday, he suddenly seemed very vulnerable.

These were the men and women that Bush, like Reagan, had spent most of his White House years keeping at arm's length, rarely meeting with them and rejecting their demands for civil rights reforms and greater spending on social programs. Now for the first time, he looked to them for advice on how to curb the violence.

During the meeting, he scribbled furiously on a notepad while the NAACP's Benjamin Hooks and other black leaders took turns telling him that blacks felt the justice system had failed. Bush could send a strong signal that the White House cared by instructing the Justice Department to bring federal charges against the four officers. Later that evening, Bush had regained his composure. He sternly lectured the nation on law and order and pledged massive military force to restore peace in Los Angeles. But Bush then struck a note of compassion and understanding as black leaders had urged. He said he could understand why blacks "felt betrayed" by the verdict. That was the signal for the Justice Department to act.[1]

———— • ◆ • ————

A high-profile case, a failed prosecution, the Los Angeles riots, and massive international media attention gave the federal government the "compelling interest" it claimed it needed to intervene. The only thing left was for the attorney general to work out the legal strategy and procedure. Much depended on William Barr. Bush had chosen Barr in October 1991 to replace Richard Thornburgh, who made an unsuccessful bid for the U.S. Senate in Pennsylvania.

Thornburgh's contentious style had often drawn criticism from political opponents, but Barr had no such problem. He had the right political credentials—he was a career government official, an ex-Central Intelligence Agency legal staffer, a loyal Republican party man, and a dedicated conservative. As deputy attorney general in 1989, Barr had authored the Justice Department's ruling that permitted the FBI to kidnap fugitives from foreign countries without the permission of the other government. Federal officials promptly used this to nab Panamanian ruler Manuel Noriega. Team player Barr had his orders from Bush.[2]

Fortunately, Barr's deputies within the Civil Rights Division had prepared for the possibility that they would have to bring charges against the officers. Alan Tiegar, CRD attorney, had sat in the Simi Valley courtroom daily taking copious notes on the proceedings. When the verdict was announced, Tiegar and CRD director John Dunne rushed into Barr's office and requested permission to reopen the investigation. Barr immediately agreed. Both men also anxiously watched the fast-deteriorating situation in Los Angeles. They wanted Barr to issue a public statement saying that the Justice Department was investigating the King case, hoping this could help calm the situation in L.A. Barr readily consented, and within the hour, he announced that he would "now undertake a review of the incident to determine what if any action may be taken under federal civil rights laws."

The cautiously worded statement masked the frenzy within the CRD. Over the next few days, attorneys scrambled to plan their strategy. They quickly agreed to argue legal issues and nothing more. They were determined to avoid making the case seem like a political vendetta by the government against the officers. Barr did not want it to appear that the Bush administration was prosecuting the case because of the riots: "We can't allow the process to be dictated by mobs."

Barr also played it tough with the Congressional Black Caucus, which had pressed the Justice Department to release the 700-page report on police brutality ordered by Thornburgh the year before. Claiming the report was "just raw data," Barr said he was turning it over to the National Institute for Justice for study and refused to give any timetable for completion or release.

Appearing on the CBS News program *Face the Nation* a week later, Barr kept up the appearance that the rioting had nothing to do with the Justice Department's decision to prosecute. "I think the last thing the American people would want is for us to precipitously rush to indictments and then not be able to win that case." Barr knew better. The violence in Los Angeles was continually discussed within the CRD. It was on everyone's mind.[3]

Two days after Bush spoke, the Justice Department announced that it would convene a federal grand jury and subpoena all the LAPD records pertaining to the King investigation. The DOJ threw a small army into the case; seventeen investigators worked around the clock, collected thousands of documents, subpoenaed more than 200 witnesses, and conducted an additional 500 interviews. On July 30, the DOJ notified Briseno, Wind, Powell, and Koon that the "grand jury was close to bringing in an indictment." With the riots, Bush's pronouncement, and the tense racial climate, the four officers had pretty much resigned themselves to their fate. They refused to testify before the grand jury.[4]

Two weeks later, the grand jury made it official: Koon, Powell, Briseno, and Wind would stand trial again. This time they would be prosecuted under Sections 241 and 242 for violating Rodney King's civil rights. If convicted, each of the officers could be sentenced to five years in prison and a fine of $10,000.

———————•◆•———————

Barr and Dunne realized that a federal trial presented mountainous challenges. They could not trust the case to just anyone. They needed the best. Dunne turned first to the man known affectionately as the "pit bull." Barry Kowalski, deputy director of the CRD, got the nickname because of his tenacious, relentless techniques in court. Once he sank his teeth into a case, he wouldn't let go until he won. In several celebrated trials, Kowalski had won convictions against white supremacists and wayward cops.

The second member of the team was Richard Clymer. Young and aggressive, Clymer had made his mark by putting away corrupt politicians, drug kingpins, and money launderers. He was considered an up-and-comer within the Department of Justice. Over the next few months, Kowalski and Clymer would be an inseparable duo, spending long hours together pouring over documents and discussing strategy. They became so close that a reporter who spotted them in a deli noted that when Clymer ordered apple pie, Kowalski promptly did the same to be, as he said, "in unanimity."[5]

Clymer and Kowalsi knew they were in a high-stakes game. If they won convictions, the public and the press might easily expect the Justice Department to successfully prosecute more police abuse cases in the future. If they failed, the department would almost certainly be accused again of not presenting a diligent and forceful case against the police officers. Many critics practically blamed the riots on local prosecutors in the Simi Valley trial, after accusing them of presenting a weak, halfhearted case.

Federal prosecutors faced the same problem that state prosecutors did. They would have to convince a jury to convict white police officers charged with beating a black man. In the Simi Valley trial, local prosecutors badly underestimated the hidden pro–law enforcement, antiblack bias that some of the white jurors harbored.

Two jurors later spoke to a reporter on the condition that their names not be used. The first, a retired real estate broker, said, "Powell could have called King the worst name in the world [presumably "nigger"] and it wouldn't have made any difference. It didn't show that he was a racist or hated black people." The other juror, a cable technician for California Edison Power Company, added, "Most of us believe in law and order, and we haven't been in trouble with the law." He obviously referred to King's prior brushes with the law. The juror reflected the sentiments of much of the general public toward the police. The King beating hadn't changed that.

A survey of 114 court cases after the King beating in which police were sued for injurious acts showed that law enforcement won two out of three times. One attorney who failed to win convictions in three police abuse suits said, "People have a fear of saying the police are out of control—that the guys in blue aren't who you thought." But it was not just a matter of public perception about the infallibility of police officers. In five cases since 1967, the Supreme Court had thrown an almost impenetrable cloak of immunity around police departments by sharply restricting the grounds on which private citizens could sue state and municipal governments, thus making recoveries difficult.[6]

John G. Davies, the trial judge, certainly had deep doubts about the case. The Australian-born Davies, a silver medalist in swimming at the 1952 Olympics, had been appointed to the federal bench by Reagan in 1986. Davies, who had the air of a British lord judge, was a stickler for formality and impatient with attorneys who violated the decorum of his courtroom. At a pretrial hearing on August 6, Davies said, "There are good and equitable reasons why the case shouldn't be tried, but the government has the right."

Federal prosecutors repeatedly explained that the four officers were not on trial for assaulting King, the charge for which they were acquitted. Assault and murder were not federal offenses. The civil rights violations were totally separate, and they carried their own specific penalties and procedures. Three weeks later, Davies laid the issue to rest when he reluctantly ruled that the officers could stand trial again.[7]

Wind's attorney, Paul DePasqualie, correctly sensed the Justice Department's dilemma. He called the prosecution a "political case" and claimed that if L.A. and other cities hadn't blown up and Bush hadn't criticized the verdict, the four would not be back in the courtroom. Briseno's attorney, Harland Braun, was even more vociferous in blasting the prosecution. Braun frequently and loudly declared to anyone who would listen that the officers were "political scapegoats." Braun had a point; "There were the riots, and the video. To the public it looked like four white guys were beating up a black guy. It had all the symbols of racism, so they felt they had to do something."[8]

———— •◆• ————

With the preliminary legal skirmishes now past, Clymer and Kowalski cautiously prepared for the real battle. The prosecutors and Davies were sensitive to the charges made by DePasqualie and Braun that this was a "political case" and that the officers were being prosecuted only because the government feared more riots. They bent over backward to avoid any suggestion of legal unfairness. The first issue was bail. Federal prosecutors made a major concession when they went along with a recommendation by the Federal Courts Pretrial Service that the officers be released on unsecured bail of $5,000. Davies agreed. Local black leaders immediately raised a howl of protest. CORE chairman Celes King called Davies's decision "tantamount to no bail at all." King saw the bail decision as a glaring example of the double standard that existed within the justice system—"one white, one black." He referred to the case of four young black men charged with beating white truck driver Reginald Denny during the riots.

The Denny beating was captured on newsreels and shown repeatedly to millions of horror-struck TV viewers. The press and much of the public compared the incident to the King beating. The four men had languished in jail for months, unable to post the bond, which exceeded $500,000. The defense attorneys for the officers, mindful that the two cases were being compared, defended the low bail. They argued that the circumstances weren't the same. Unlike the four blacks, their clients had not committed any crimes, posed no risk of flight, and had strong community ties. Federal prosecutors did not challenge this.

It was an invidious comparison. Although three of the young blacks did have prior convictions (mostly misdemeanors), they all had dutifully shown up for their court hearings and sentencing. They also still lived in the same neighborhood where they grew up and were well known by community residents.[9]

Even more disappointing, federal prosecutors did not seriously question the defense attorney's assertion that the officers had simon-pure conduct records. Three of the officers had been found guilty of assorted charges of misconduct in past arrest cases. In September 1986, Koon received a 5-day suspension for kicking a juvenile car theft suspect twice in the chest. In June 1987, Briseno was suspended for 66 days for stomping on the back of a man who was handcuffed. Powell was disciplined twice, the first time in October 1989 for breaking the elbow of an El Salvadorian factory worker (Powell's own partner testified that there was no provocation). The city council shelled out $70,000 to the victim to settle the lawsuit. A year later, Powell was charged with beating a handcuffed teenager he had arrested for jaywalking.[10] If Powell, Koon, and Briseno had committed these same acts as private citizens they would have been arrested and charged with felonious assault. The decision to grant the officers low bail came back to haunt the prosecutors in November when they tried to have the officers' disciplinary records admitted as evidence. They hoped to show that a prior pattern of violence proved the officers had intended to do physical harm to King. Davies rejected the motion and admonished the prosecutors for "reaching."

The second week of November 1992, Davies handed the defense another huge plum. He agreed to a motion by defense attorneys to postpone the trial for two months to allow two attorneys who had recently joined the defense team to familiarize themselves with the case. With the intense media and public interest in the case, the delay worked to the defense attorneys' advantage by increasing their chances of getting an unbiased jury.[11]

Davies made another important concession to the defense. He refused to allow prosecutors to question Powell about a controversial radio transmission he sent shortly before the King beating. Several hours earlier in that evening, Powell had broken up a domestic squabble involving a black couple. In a radio report to the precinct station, Powell referred to them as "gorillas in the mist." (The term was taken from the title of a popular movie about the fight to preserve Ugandan gorillas from extinction.) The prosecutors wanted to use this to bolster their contention that Powell was a racist and, therefore, that the King beating was racially motivated.

Davies disallowed the transmission tapes as evidence and lectured the prosecution that they "had a high and heavy burden" to prove that the officers had acted willfully. Davies's well-timed rebuke was a reminder that the court intended to give the defense the benefit of any legal doubt. The significance of the judge's actions was not lost on the defense. Braun jubilantly exclaimed, "I've died and gone to heaven."

Prosecutors did not mention that Koon had also made derogatory references to blacks in an unpublished manuscript on his LAPD exploits. The FBI had earlier obtained a manuscript copy. Some months later, when prosecutors tried to get it admitted, Davies refused. By then Koon's manuscript had been sanitized by his publisher; gone were the references to "Mandingo." In the book, he came off as a misunderstood liberal on race relations.[12]

There was more bad news. On November 19, reporters on National Public Radio's *Morning Edition* revealed that in early August, Michael P. Stone, Powell's attorney, received a memo in the mail from an anonymous source in the Justice Department detailing the prosecution's strategy. The memo, intended for Deputy Attorney General Linda Davis and U.S. Attorney Lourdes Baird, known as an "order of proof," focused on the reliability of two of their prospective witnesses. The first witness, Melanie Singer, a California Highway Patrol officer, witnessed the beating and testified against the officers in the Simi Valley trial. The other witness, Bryant Allen, was a passenger in King's car the night of the beating.

Prosecutors were worried that the jurors would find their testimony less than credible. In the memo, the prosecutors also seemed to question their ability to win the case. When the memo was leaked, Davies immediately held two secret hearings with defense attorneys and the prosecutors to determine how badly the leaked memo jeopardized the prosecution's case.

Legal expert Abbey Lowell thought it did: "Whoever did it wanted the defense to take advantage of the government's weakness." But Justice Department officials moved quickly to try to mend the damage. They claimed that the leak wasn't a serious problem and that prosecutors had plenty of time to readjust their strategy. While they were busy putting a cheerful face on a potential disaster, no explanation was offered about why or how the memo was leaked in the first place. Was it the work of a disgruntled employee or someone higher up in the department who did not want the case to go to trial? Federal officials constructed a "lone individual" theory to explain the leak.

Most insiders and defense attorneys thought the most likely culprit was an FBI agent who worked closely on the investigation. A spokesperson in the Justice Department claimed that whoever did it "betrayed" the government out of misplaced loyalty to fellow law enforcement officers.[13]

This sounded a little too pat to some Democrats who had been forced to take a back seat to what had so far been a Bush administration show. Conyers and Joseph Biden, chairman of the Senate Judiciary Committee, spotted an opening and called for congressional hearings and the appointment of an independent prosecutor. This was mostly political talk that quickly ended when the Justice Department promised to turn the matter over to its Public Integrity Section for an internal investigation. Black leaders, suspicious of the Bush administration's civil rights policies, saw the leak as part of a conspiracy by high governmental officials to sabotage the trial. Danny Bakewell, chairman of the L.A. Brotherhood Crusade, screamed, "Justice is always twisted when it comes to African-Americans."

The government's fumble could not be attributed solely to racial double standards. The King beating case was a political case. And the federal government rarely prosecuted police officers unless there were dire political consequences if it did not. Prosecuting police officers simply went against federal policy and tradition. The Justice Department clung to the belief that education and cooperation with police departments would blunt the use of excessive force. Davis was emphatic, "We meet with local and state police officials to discuss the nature of police misconduct. The consensus has been that all levels of law enforcement must address this problem together." The sentiments were noble, but the continuing negative fallout from the King case indicated that the DOJ's approach still left much to be desired.[14]

As the start date for the trial neared, Davies continued to cause prosecutors some anxious moments. For a brief period, it seemed that he was seriously considering making the prosecutors prove that the attack on King was racially motivated in addition to proving intent. If Davies followed through on this, the prosecutors would have been in a deep hole. Many experts were puzzled by Davies's legal logic.

In 1941, the Supreme Court ruled in *U.S.* v. *Classic* that a prosecutor did not have to prove that attacks on blacks were racially motivated in order to win a conviction. That certainly was the understanding of the CRD. "The statute," Linda Davis contended, "does not require proof of racial motivation." But Davies had latched on to the second part of the *Classic* decision, which stated that a victim abused by a police official because of his or her color or race was subject to "different punishments." He apparently took this to mean that the prosecution should be required to prove that a defendant acted from racial animus. This was judicial hairsplitting that would have made Clymer's and Kowalski's jobs almost impossible. Fortunately, Davies, with no explanation, dropped the matter.[15]

Despite the mild setback, defense attorneys continued to hammer away at the federal government for prosecuting the officers. During jury selection, Braun aggressively questioned prospective jurors on whether they believed the federal government was politically persecuting the officers. After one exchange, Davies angrily cut Braun off and reminded him "that it was not an issue." But it was, and Braun, perhaps not so skillfully, tried to suggest to the jurors that the defendants had done nothing wrong.

Davies's quick intercession did not solve the biggest problem that the prosecutors faced. They would still have to convince a jury—likely to be mostly white, middle-class suburbanites—to convict white police officers for beating a black man. This was the main hurdle that had repeatedly blocked prosecutors in past racial violence cases.

Clymer and Kowalski spent five days trying to get the right racial and gender mix of jurors. The twelve jurors selected were somewhat more representative of L.A.'s diverse racial makeup than the Simi Valley jurors had been. They included two blacks and one Hispanic. But the nine whites were drawn not only from Los Angeles County but also from the mostly white, middle-class bedroom suburb communities in Orange, San Bernardino, and Ventura Counties.

Prosecutors were uneasy. With the media constantly fanning fears of another riot, the trial would be held in a crisis atmosphere, and prosecutors could not be certain what effect this would have on the white jurors. The names of the jurors were so closely guarded that their identities were described as a "state secret." They were identified only by their seat numbers.

The attitudes of three white male jurors were particularly troubling. They seemed to be anything but objective. One juror, who had immigrated from Denmark in 1963 and worked as a welder, said of the police, "I think they do a good job" and their "job can be stressful." Another white male juror was just as candid: "I would give more weight to testimony from a police officer."

Another juror, a security guard, admitted that he had used forceful methods to subdue troublesome individuals on more than one occasion. He made no effort to hide his feelings about the decision in the Simi Valley trial: "I don't think the verdicts were unjust." Clymer and Kowalski might have been even less happy if they had known then that a forty-year-old white male engineer had beaten out a female insurance executive for the post of jury foreperson. The jurors voted exclusively along gender lines.[16]

To counteract juror bias toward the police, the two prosecutors would not make the same mistake state prosecutors in the Simi Valley trial did by relying exclusively on the videotape. They would build their case on eyewitnesses and the testimony of use-of-force experts and medical personnel. "They learned from the state's mistakes," Braun observed, "and were trying to make sure that there were no surprises."

They also planned to call as a witness the one person whom the state prosecutors had not—Rodney King. This strategy was risky, but they felt the jurors needed to see King as a real person who was sensitive and intelligent rather than as the criminal that the defense had depicted him to be. Although some legal experts second-guessed Clymer and Kowalski's decision, Daniel Rinzel, former director of the criminal section of the CRD, thought it was a good move; "Even if he had been impeached they don't rely on him for evidence."[17]

———————

After thirteen days, the prosecution and defense finally rested their cases. Clymer and Kowalski had called thirty-four witnesses, introduced volumes of documents, and shown the jurors a superenhanced videotape of the beating. Yet they still could not be sure that they had convinced the jurors that the officers did anything wrong to the black motorist. And then there was Judge Davies, who continued to have doubts about the trial. He briefly considered giving the jurors an "Allen charge." This seldom used legal maneuver was based on a century-old ruling in which the Supreme Court gave judges authority to instruct jurors who are preventing a jury from reaching a verdict to change their opinion and make the verdict unanimous. If the judge in the Simi Valley trial had given the few jurors that held out for conviction of Powell on one count an Allen charge, they probably would have been forced to change their decisions. All four officers would have been acquitted. Clymer immediately saw the danger this posed for the prosecution's case and jumped to his feet to protest. Davies relented on this point.[18]

Seven days later, on April 17, 1993, the jurors delivered a split verdict, convicting Powell and Koon and acquitting Briseno and Wind. After the verdict, federal prosecutors were still very mindful of the weighty political consequences. When a reporter asked Kowalski, "Did you feel pressure?" Kowalski snapped, "Of course I did."

In Washington, federal officials breathed a huge sigh of relief at the verdict and immediately rushed to hail it as a victory. Attorney General Janet Reno declared, "Justice was done." President Bill Clinton interrupted a speech in Pittsburgh to pronounce that the system had been vindicated; "The courts are the proper forum to resolve our deepest legal disputes." Reno's and Clinton's reactions were predictable. The verdict in the high-profile, politically charged case seemed to vindicate the justice system and quiet racial anger. It was the ultimate in political damage control.

But if Clinton thought that the King case was merely a "dispute" that the trial had resolved and if Reno believed that justice had triumphed, they hadn't paid very close attention to the jurors.[19]

At no time during the jurors' week of deliberation was the final verdict assured. In early straw votes, the jurors actually split 7 to 5 to acquit Koon. One juror said that they took as much time as they did because they "wanted to be fair to the defense and prosecution." If this had been a standard criminal trial, with the amount of compelling evidence the prosecution had presented it would probably have been an open-and-shut case for conviction.

The length of time the jury took deliberating suggested that the jurors had questioned every piece of evidence the prosecution presented, looking for weak points. After the trial, an embittered Powell claimed that the jurors "lacked integrity to listen to evidence that easily allows a finding of reasonable doubt." He was wrong.

Another juror revealed that they disregarded the testimony from witnesses and much of the evidence, including the videotape. He was convinced that "some of the blows [King suffered], may or may not have been caused by a fall." This was exactly the point defense attorneys had labored to prove from the beginning. They contended that King incurred facial injuries not from the officers' blows but when he fell to the pavement as the officers subdued him. The videotape clearly showed King being struck in the face.

Juror #9 said that even though on the tape he saw Powell striking King across the chest with his baton, only about one-third of the jurors believed that this was excessive force. The jurors also revealed their prodefense bias in deciding the fate of Wind and Briseno. In an initial straw vote, the jurors voted 8 to 4 for acquittal even though Wind had inflicted the second greatest number of blows on King, after Powell.

Briseno had been the most vociferous in protesting his innocence and had even tried to sever his case from the others. Jurors never questioned Braun's contention that the only reason Briseno had put his size 8D shoe on King was to protect him from being beaten further. On the tape, it appeared that he was stomping on King. Braun was amazed that the government couldn't do better; "They had massive resources, and they still came within a whisper of not getting any convictions."[20]

The week after the trial, another development cast even more doubt on the objectivity of the jurors. In an attempt to cash in on his newfound notoriety, Koon made the rounds on the TV talk show circuit. During his $25,000 paid appearance on the *Donahue* show (earlier, he had been paid $10,000 for appearing on *A Current Affair*), one of the jurors confronted him. The beefy, tattooed juror, who might have been the security guard, lived in the predominantly white Orange County suburban enclave of Fullerton. He angrily pointed at Koon and tried to get him to admit that he "screwed up." When Koon tried to defend himself, the man tore into him; "I think you owe the police department an apology."[21]

The juror evidently saw Koon as a rogue cop who broke the rules. He was wrong. Koon came closer to the truth when he claimed that he had acted the way he did because there were no clear policy rules or training procedures on the use of force by the LAPD when subduing suspects. The Christopher Commission obliquely confirmed Koon's charge; the commission found a widespread pattern of abuse within the department. Nearly 1,800 officers were the targets of citizen complaints of excessive force or use of improper tactics between 1986 and 1990. Even more damaging, 44 of the officers were tactfully called "potential problem officers." These officers had six or more charges of excessive force or complaints of improper tactics lodged against them. These were not "frivolous" complaints by hard-core criminals or malcontents. They involved serious incidents—alleged beatings, shootings, and the kicking of suspects. The commission observed that although the officers' violent acts were well known, the department did nothing "to control or discipline" them and that their supervisors "were not held accountable" for their actions. Indeed, the men had garnered numerous commendations, awards, and promotions.[22]

When the Christopher Commission released its report in July 1991, three months after the King beating, all of the officers were still at their posts. The commission recommended that the officers receive more counseling and retraining. A year and a half later, despite a new chief's pledge to implement the reforms, only three of the officers had been fired. Four had resigned, and the rest were still on the job. There was no indication that these men had undergone the counseling or training the commission recommended. In 1993, two and a half years after the commission investigation, the number of police abuse complaints was only marginally lower than that in 1990. The DOJ was well aware of the reported complaints. Yet in ten years, it brought only three prosecutions against police officers for misconduct. Not one of the cases involved a black victim.[23]

If the statements made by some LAPD officials were any guide, it seemed unlikely that more officers would be prosecuted. Charles Duke Jr., the LAPD's expert on the use of force, vigorously defended Koon, Powell, and Wind. He insisted that they had not violated LAPD use-of-force guidelines. Duke implied that the officers had been sacrificed by top LAPD officials who sought to cover their backsides; it was a "tragedy the police department orchestrated, and the federal government carried out." Duke would soon discover that he was not the only one bothered by the federal government's action against the officers. Davies ordered Koon and Powell to return to court on August 4 for sentencing.[24]

———————•◆•———————

Many expected or at least hoped that the sentencing would finally draw the curtain on the most tumultuous and bitter case in recent legal history.

Prosecutors had asked for sentences of seven to nine years for Powell and nine to ten years for Koon, fines of $15,000 to $150,000, financial restitution to King (who had incurred medical costs of $189,000), and immediate imprisonment. Clymer and Kowalski were fairly confident that they would obtain the sentences. The federal sentencing guidelines approved by Congress in 1984 had been repeatedly criticized as too rigid. But in this instance, they might actually have worked against the police officers. The guidelines assigned mathematical values to offenses. A felony conviction for a crime of violence in which there was substantial bodily injury to the victim dictated a maximum sentence.[25]

Davies seemed to have little choice in the matter. Ira Saltzman, Koon's attorney, demanded probation, and Michael P. Stone, Powell's attorney, pushed for the minimum sentence of ten to eighteen months. Both asked that the officers remain free on bail pending appeal. But neither realistically expected that Davies would agree to the reduced sentences. Saltzman noted, "I'm a realist, Stacey is prepared to go to jail if he has to." Both men, however, were in for a pleasant surprise. During the three-hour sentencing hearing, Davies described the officers' lives, families, and careers in warm, almost idolatrous terms. He agonized over their plight and said he felt they had suffered enough. He also expressed deep concern over their safety if they are incarcerated.

Davies again implied that the federal government should not have brought the case, and he complained that it "had a specter of unfairness to it." Davies turned his anger on King. He claimed he was drunk at the time of the incident and blamed him for "provoking" the officers. Davies sentenced the policemen to thirty months, one-fourth of the term the sentencing guidelines mandated. Prosecutors won a small victory on the bail issue—but only barely. For a moment, Davies actually toyed with the idea of granting the defense motion that the officers remain free on bail while they appealed. Prosecutors vehemently protested that the judge would be in direct violation of federal law stipulating that an individual convicted of a violent crime cannot remain free on bail. There were exceptions, but neither Powell nor Koon met the criteria. Davies was in a quandary and took a forty-five-minute break to think about it. After apologizing and again offering his sympathies to the pair, he reluctantly told them that "the court [was] bound by the law" to deny bail continuance.[26]

U.S. Attorney Teree Bowers, in a huge understatement, criticized the downward departures in their sentences and announced that he was considering an appeal. The DOJ was even more guarded. It asked the Ninth Circuit Appeal Court to determine whether the federal guidelines were properly applied. But the department was not completely blameless. The federal probation office normally prepared a presentencing report with a recommendation and a rationale for sentencing that federal judges usually followed. For some unexplained reason, this time the probation office did not. Instead, the office simply outlined two "options" for Davies, neither of which clarified whether the King assault was "minor" or "aggravated."

If the report had clearly called the attack "aggravated," Davies would have been almost duty-bound to impose the longer sentences. The judge fully exploited the loophole and apparently accepted the defense attorneys' contention that the attack was "minor." Finally, there was King himself. Davies practically admitted that King's conduct influenced him to whittle, as one reporter put it, the biggest piece off the sentences. This was a revealing observation. Joseph Duff, president of the Los Angeles NAACP, denounced the sentencing as a "travesty." He spoke for most blacks.

But he did not speak for the jurors. Although several did express doubts about the decision, they still praised Davies as a man of integrity. One juror, who likely spoke for the majority, went further, stating that he was pleased Davies shared his feeling that Rodney King was to blame for the beating. The perceptions of many blacks and many whites about the justice system still remained wildly at odds.

It took more than a year for the Ninth Circuit Court to decide that Davies had indeed erred in sentencing Koon and Powell and order him to resentence them. The court mildly rebuked him for "departing" from the guidelines, but it still bought Davies's and the prosecution's argument that King had provoked the officers. There was not a shred of proof beyond the officers' claim that he had. During the state trial, the prosecution, for some inexplicable reason, did not call eyewitnesses to the beating. They told reporters that King was cooperative. But in the eyes of much of the legal world, it still seemed that a black man could not be an innocent victim of police violence.[27]

<hr />

Following the acquittal of the officers in the Simi Valley trial, the King case might have quietly receded into the shadows of history. But the fires of L.A. and the national outrage created the "compelling federal interest" that forced Bush and Barr to heed the advice of black leaders and bring federal charges against the officers. Despite the honest effort of two federal prosecutors and the DOJ's promise to push for stiffer sentences, the reality was that blacks' faint hope that justice would be done was quashed—this time by a man, Judge John G. Davies, who symbolized the failure of the federal government to protect black lives. This proved that the King case, tragically, had not resolved the issue of racial violence within federal law.

Conclusion

Federal law gave Rodney King a victory, but it was a tarnished victory. Clinton and Reno gladly hailed the verdict as vindication of the justice system. Yet they were silent on the leniency of the sentences. Although Reno approved an appeal of the sentences and was successful, there was no real indication that the DOJ would bring more prosecutions to stop the use of excessive force by the police. The likely scenario would be that the DOJ would continue to rely on negotiation and persuasion with wayward police agencies. Civil Rights Division official Linda Davis was optimistic: "Hopefully this will provide a constructive response to address the issues of police misconduct and racial violence."[1]

The administration's attitude was no surprise. Like Clinton, Reno's political ties and sentiments were rooted in the conservative Deep South. For two decades, she had been a tough, no-nonsense state prosecutor in Miami. For a time, she was haunted by the ghost of Arthur McDuffie. A former prosecutor said that her failure to convict the police officers accused of killing McDuffie in 1980 had "traumatized" her. She exorcised the ghost, the prosecutor noted, by "choosing to be non-controversial and low key."[2]

During the 1980s, Reno played it close to the legal vest when it came to prosecuting police officers accused of racially motivated violence. In 1983, a county judge chastised prosecutors in Reno's office for acting as defense counsel for police in abuse cases and not fully presenting evidence at inquests. Despite two major riots in Miami during the 1980s sparked by police killings, Reno dodged police prosecutions by simply referring all cases to county judges; they then determined whether a case should be filed. But Dade County judges are elected and are heavily dependent on support from police unions. The results were predictable. By the close of the 1980s, Reno had filed only one case against an officer. Police applauded her system as "fair."[3]

Even as Clinton eyed her for attorney general, she did not change her policy regarding police prosecutions. Sociologist Marvin Dunn, a long-time Reno-watcher, observed that although there were several questionable beatings and killings in her area in 1992, no charges were filed against officers. A few critics challenged her crime-fighting toughness at the confirmation hearings, but Republican conservatives, as Utah senator Orin Hatch put it, were "impressed" with her credentials.[4]

Even if Clinton were not a southern Democrat and Reno an aggressive prosecutor, there was still little reason to expect more federal prosecutions of Klan, Nazi, Skinhead, or police violence. Reno and Clinton were trapped by the inelastic federal policy followed by their Democratic and Republican predecessors. Put simply, racially motivated violence should have been prosecuted by state and local officials. If local officials didn't do the job, the DOJ and the White House were loath to intervene.

They *do* have the power. Sections 241 and 242, passed by a Reconstruction era Congress, were solidly based on the equal protection and due process clauses of the Fourteenth Amendment. These sections gave presidents the legal right to protect blacks from racially motivated attacks. They also gave attorneys general the legal weapons to prosecute those who committed such acts. Linda Davis was clear that legal authority was not an issue within the DOJ: "The Department of Justice is authorized to prosecute the incidents of official misconduct, which frequently involve police brutality."[5]

Authority was one thing, but action was another. Presidents and attorneys general generally ignored or sparingly used the federal statutes to prosecute criminal civil rights abuses. This had less to do with the personalities, individual preferences, or even racial bigotry of the men and women in the White House and DOJ than with political expediency. The men in the Oval Office were determined not to offend the politically powerful South. They rationalized their hands-off policies by slavishly adhering to a misguided and narrow interpretation of federalism. The only exceptions occurred when a violent act triggered a major riot, generated mass protest, or attracted major press attention. Even then, black leaders had to pressure the federal government to take action.

That has been the pattern throughout this century. Although NAACP officials pleaded with Harding, Coolidge, Hoover, Roosevelt, Truman, Eisenhower, and Kennedy to endorse or actively support federal laws to end lynching or strengthen criminal penalties for racially motivated violence, the presidents refused. Johnson, though certainly the most conscientious president on civil rights, took decisive action to strengthen the federal criminal statutes primarily when confronted with massive white anarchy in the South, destructive black urban violence, and heavy pressure from the civil rights movement. But DOJ prosecutions were still confined mainly to high-profile cases of Klan violence. The irony is that in the end, Johnson may have harmed as much as helped civil rights enforcement when he bowed to the white backlash in Congress and the public and approved new repressive laws that eroded civil rights and civil liberties. This set in motion a dangerous and seemingly irreversible conservative trend that would become the trademark of American politics through the 1980s and the 1990s.

Civil rights leaders pressed Nixon, Carter, Ford, Reagan, and Bush to vigorously use federal statutes to curb police violence. The presidents refused. They pressed the attorneys general to bring prosecutions. The attorneys refused. They pressed the FBI to investigate civil rights complaints. The bureau refused. They pressed federal grand juries to promptly return indictments against racially motivated violence. The jurors refused.

The federal prosecution of the four LAPD officers in the Rodney King beating case did not alter White House or Justice Department policy. It took a major riot and international outrage to force Bush and Barr to act.

The failure of presidents and their attorneys general to vigorously enforce criminal civil rights statutes against racially motivated violence has had dangerous consequences for American society. In October 1994, the Southern Poverty Law Center warned Attorney General Reno that the failure to investigate and prosecute white supremacist hate groups was a "recipe for disaster."[6] The terrorist carnage that claimed 169 lives in the blast at the Oklahoma City federal building in April 1995 was tragic proof that white terror was very much alive in America. But the federal government had done a masterful job in making the public think otherwise.

On March 26, 1965, a somber Lyndon Johnson, flanked by FBI director J. Edgar Hoover, announced the arrest of four Klansmen suspected of murdering civil rights worker Viola Liuzzo on an Alabama highway. Johnson promised the national TV audience that he would break the back of racist terrorism. He gave Hoover the green light to wage a no-holds-barred battle against the Klan. Hoover had already secretly riddled Klan chapters in Mississippi with a small army of informers and undercover agents.[7] During the racist terror campaign of bombings, burnings, and shootings between 1955 and 1965, more than forty blacks and civil rights activists were murdered, and dozens were injured. The media, much of the public, and civil rights leaders took Johnson at face value and believed that the government would finally end the violence. Hoover knew better. A year later, he told the House Appropriations Committee that "many thousands of sympathizers lend their support to Klan programs and activities."[8] With the exception of 1964, when twenty-one Mississippi Klansmen were indicted, the number of criminal civil rights cases Johnson's Justice Department filed overall did not match the pathetic number of cases filed under Eisenhower and Kennedy. It was enough, however, to convince many Americans that the end of racist violence was in sight.[9]

There were more prominent warning signs during the Reagan years that made-in-America terrorism had not gone away. In 1987, the Southern Poverty Law Center warned the Justice Department that terror attacks on blacks had risen. The warning fell on deaf ears. The Reagan administration marginally increased the number of criminal civil rights prosecutions of police officers on excessive force charges. Hate terrorists were still virtually ignored. Klan Klaverns, and Nazi and Aryan Nation branches continued to spread. These groups had more than 20,000 members, and they had committed at least a dozen racially motivated murders.[10]

In the 1990s, white supremacists made a strategic shift that further confused the public. They exchanged their white sheets for camouflage fatigues, called themselves militias and patriots, and depicted themselves as red-blooded, patriotic citizen-soldiers fighting to preserve American freedom. Their enemies became the Bureau of Alcohol, Tobacco, and Firearms (BATF), the IRS, the FBI, federal land agents, international bankers, and the United Nations. Although their publications still read like a who's who of white supremacy and were crammed with the standard racist and Jew-baiting articles, they cleverly exorcised derogatory references to blacks and Jews from their public statements and writings.[11] They borrowed the technique politicians perfected during the quarter century since the 1960s to win white votes, using racial and gender-loaded doublespeak, code words, and code concepts. In the 1960s, it was law and order, crime in the streets, rampant permissiveness, and out-of-touch federal bureaucrats. In the 1970s, it was busing, high taxes, crime, and the Organization of Petroleum Exporting Countries (OPEC). In the 1980s, it was heavy-handed government, welfare cheats, drug-dealers, and gang-bangers.

In the 1990s, Republican conservative icon Newt Gingrich, rightist talk show hosts Rush Limbaugh and G. Gordon Liddy, corporate-backed foundations, and think tanks refined, massaged, and spruced up the racist code concepts and presented them to the nation in the Contract with America. They promised to increase defense spending, cut education costs, kill national health reform, hire more police and prosecutors, build more prisons, and hack up what remained of the federal safety net for welfare recipients and the poor.[12]

Accused Oklahoma City bomber Timothy McVeigh punched all the code concepts in angry letters in 1992. He railed against crime, high taxes, corrupt politicians, government mismanagement, and the "eroding American dream." McVeigh made only a passing comment on race. More wasn't necessary. Many whites understood that "evil government" had become the conservative's surrogate code term for blacks and the poor.[13]

The anger, violence, and ultraparanoia of many white males was grounded in racism. Their prime targets, as always, were blacks and other people of color. The new white supremacist groups were helped by the storehouse of dodge tactics that many Americans employed to mask their racism. Many Americans accused blacks of always making an issue of race. They avoided having any physical or personal contact with blacks.

They got angry or defensive when racial issues were raised. They resisted programs for ostensibly nonracial reasons if they perceived the programs directly or indirectly benefited minorities. They voted for candidates who promised to eliminate the welfare state. They supported organizations and leaders who promised to restore religion, moral values, and personal freedom and to battle "federal tyranny."[14]

The media was deeply complicit in reinforcing the racist stereotypes. They presented endless news pieces and features on black crime and violence. The black family was routinely typecast by many sociologists as a "tangle of pathology." Black men were portrayed as irresponsible, self-indulgent, and derelict; black women were welfare cheats and sexually loose. Terms like *subculture of violence, subculture of poverty, cultural deprivation,* and *IQ deficiencies* were routinely tossed around by the media and academics to explain alleged black failures and intellectual incompetence. All this reinforced suspicions that blacks were not only different than whites but inferior to them. The signs that racist thinking had spread its tentacles even deeper into American society grew.

The Anti-Defamation League found in a 1993 poll that 31 percent of whites age eighteen to thirty thought that blacks were lazy and crime-prone. In 1994, for the first time in the seven years that the Times-Mirror Company polled racial feelings, a majority of whites told interviewers that the push for equal rights had gone too far. Cynical politicians and much of the white public anxiously geared up to annihilate affirmative-action programs while they busily created the fiction that America had become a "color-blind society."[15]

None of this was particularly new. Racism in America has always had a chameleon-like capacity to camouflage itself in variant shades. A century ago, William Sumner Jenkins, in his proslavery apology *Pro-Slavery Thought in the Old South,* noted that "slavery had defenders whenever defenders were needed; the exact nature of the defense was determined to a great extent by the degree to which and by the way in which the welfare of slavery was endangered." Substitute the word *racism* for *slavery,* and Sumner could easily have described the attitudes of many whites in the 1990s.[16]

During their heyday in the 1920s, Klan leaders hid their white sheets, hoods, burning crosses, bullwhips, guns, and dynamite in the closet when they faced the general public and press. They waved the flag and proclaimed themselves the guardians of the Constitution and American values. They swore that they were not antiblack and would uphold the laws. Their ruse worked.

The Klan had thousands of members and millions of sympathizers nationally and internationally. The organization was bankrolled by businesses and endorsed by dozens of state and local officials. Republican presidents Harding, Hoover, and Coolidge refused to denounce the Klan and made only halfhearted speeches condemning mob violence. They enjoyed widespread public approval and knew that there would be no political consequences for the White House.

The pattern has repeated itself. The modern militia and patriot groups are not composed of isolated crackpots. Like the old Klan, they have the ears of dozens of local, state, and national officials and probably the quiet support of many others. Their publications are widely circulated, and they have thousands of paid subscribers. They use cyberspace and the Internet to relay messages and communiqués to each other, recruit new members, and solicit funds.[17]

In the wake of the Oklahoma City bombing, Clinton and Reno sternly lectured the media and the public about hate speech and promised to crack down on hate terror. The tough talk was reminiscent of what Presidents Roosevelt, Truman, Eisenhower, Kennedy, Johnson, Carter, Reagan, and Bush employed during times of domestic or racial conflict. But taking action was another matter.

There was little evidence that the federal government would shift gears, broaden its enforcement net, and arrest and prosecute the leaders of terrorist groups. If anything, Clinton and Congress went in reverse. They cautioned the public against overreacting, and promised to bend over backward to avoid violating the civil liberties of these groups and risking confrontations with them.[18]

Clinton's counterterrorist proposals misfired and only reinforced the federal government's head-in-the-sand denial about the roots of domestic terrorism. They would also abusively expand FBI authority and power, erode civil liberties, and give federal agencies permanent legal license to witch-hunt immigrants and Arab-Americans. The proposals would not have stopped the Oklahoma bombers or checked the spread of racist hate groups. The double standard in the enforcement of federal law remained glaring.[19]

During the 1950s, the FBI and the Justice Department indicted the leaders of the Communist Party, ruthlessly harassed liberal and leftist writers, artists, and politicians, and stifled public dissent. During the 1960s, Hoover, with the tacit consent of Nixon and Attorney General John Mitchell, directed supersecret and illegal counterintelligence operations that included the use of hundreds of informants, police agents, provocateurs, poison-pen letters, mail covers, and wiretaps to harass, intimidate, arrest, and prosecute Black Panthers, SNCC and CORE activists, black nationalists, and student radicals.

If the federal government could move in perfect legal and political harmony when confronted with what it perceived as the threat of black violence, then why couldn't it do the same when confronted by the real threat of white violence? It could. But the remedy to racially motivated violence was not more police, prisons, prosecutors, costly and ineffectual repressive laws, an expanded death penalty, or constitutionally corrosive crime bills and counterterrorist proposals. The federal government needed only to enforce the laws that were already on the books.

Since Reconstruction, the government has had sufficient laws to arrest and prosecute white supremacists on charges of illegal weapons violations and on the basis of the conspiracy statutes. If the government had consistently made arrests and brought prosecutions in strategic, nonpolitically selected cases, it would have sent a message that lawlessness would not be tolerated.

Attorney General Ramsey Clark recognized that federal prosecution of racially motivated violence was both legally possible and morally and politically correct. He knew that, based on past history, the chance of southern whites convicting police officers for killing blacks was virtually nonexistent. He still brought federal charges against the South Carolina state troopers that gunned down three black students at Orangeburg State College in 1968. He gambled that a doomed prosecution attempt was better than nothing and that it would put law enforcement on notice that the federal government would take action against racially motivated violence and hate crimes when local officials would not. "From a law enforcement standpoint I would say that it would have a stabilizing effect on law enforcement."[20]

Clark was right. But he did not fully understand the power of racism to immobilize federal law when black lives were at stake. A half century ago, Swedish sociologist Gunnar Myrdal, in his monumental *American Dilemma*, simply and accurately explained why this was the case: "Slavery had disappeared, but caste remained." In other words, America had removed the physical chains from blacks but not the destructive legacy of slavery and segregation from society.[21]

Blacks still did not enjoy the equal protection of the law. It took a militant political campaign led by the NAACP for nearly a half century and an energized civil rights movement to force the White House to prosecute more racially motivated crimes and for Congress to strengthen the criminal civil rights statutes.

But the victory has been incomplete. The judgment of history during the past century on the federal government's handling of racial violence remains unchanged. In criminal civil rights cases, the White House has regarded federal law as an expedient measure used mainly to buy racial peace rather than promote justice or guarantee equal protection to blacks. The gains have been fleeting and momentary. And they can easily be lost in the destructive fury over a Rodney King or Arthur McDuffie or in the blood-drenched rubble of an Oklahoma City.

Notes

---•◆•---

The following abbreviations are used throughout the notes:

CD	*Chicago Defender*
CR	*Congressional Record*
CRC	Commission on Civil Rights
CSM	*Christian Science Monitor*
CT	*Chicago Tribune*
FBI	Federal Bureau of Investigation
LAPD	Los Angeles Police Department
LAT	*Los Angeles Times*
LAT Mag.	*Los Angeles Times Magazine*
MH	*Miami Herald*
NAACP	National Association for the Advancement of Colored People
NOTP	*New Orleans Times-Picayune*
NYT	*New York Times*
NYT Mag.	*New York Times Magazine*
PP of P	Public Papers of the Presidents of the United States
SAC	Special Agent in Charge
WP	*Washington Post*

Introduction

1. LAT, April 30, 1992, 1.

2. Robert K. Carr, *Federal Protection of Civil Rights: Quest for a Sword* (Ithaca: Cornell University Press, 1947), 56–77, 163–176; John T. Ellif, "Aspects of Federal Civil Rights Enforcement: The Justice Department and the FBI, 1939–1964," *Perspectives in American History* 5 (1971), 605–673.

3. Arthur Selwyn, *The Roles of the Attorney General of the United States* (Washington, D.C.: American Enterprise Institute, 1968), 44–49; Clayton Cornell, *The Politics of Justice* (London: M. E. Sharpe, 1992), 48–83.

4. LAT, May 2, 1992, 2.

5. Harvard Sitkoff, *A New Deal for Blacks* (New York: Oxford University Press, 1978), 267–298.

6. Mark Twain, *The Adventures of Huckleberry Finn* (New York: W. W. Norton, 1977), 174–175.

7. John Hope Franklin, *From Slavery to Freedom* (New York: Random House, 1969), 267–268.

8. Eric Foner, *Reconstruction* (New York: Harper & Row, 1988).

9. Richard Kluger, *Simple Justice* (New York: Alfred A. Knopf, 1976), 80.

10. Rayford W. Logan, "The Negro as Portrayed in Representative Northern Magazines and Newspapers," in Barry N. Schwartz and Robert Disch, eds., *White Racism* (New York: Dell, 1970), 392–398; George M. Frederickson, *The Black Image in the White Mind* (New York: Harper & Row, 1971).

11. Lionel McPherson, "News Media, Racism and the Drug War," *Extra!* (April-May 1992), 5.

12. W.E.B. Du Bois, *The Souls of Black Folks* (1903; reprint, New York: Avon, 1990); Robert E. Conot, *Rivers of Blood: Years of Darkness* (New York: Bantam Books, 1967); National Advisory Commission on Civil Disorders, *Report of the National Advisory Commission on Civil Disorders* (New York: Bantam Books, 1968).

Chapter 1

1. NAACP Special Correspondence Papers, "Report of the Field Secretary: Interview with Warren G. Harding," August 8, 1920.

2. CR, 66th Cong., 2nd sess., HR 14097, 7188.

3. Robert Zangrando, *The NAACP Crusade Against Lynching, 1909–1950* (Philadelphia: Temple University Press, 1980), 236.

4. NAACP Special Correspondence Papers, Harding to Shillady, February 20, 1920; Kirk H. Porter and Donald Bruce Johnson, *National Party Platforms, 1840–1968* (Urbana: University of Illinois Press, 1970), 236.

5. U.S. Bureau of the Census, *Negroes in the United States, 1920–1932* (Washington, D.C.: GPO, 1935), 55; *Crisis* 20 (September 1920), 230.

6. NAACP Special Correspondence Papers, "Report of the Field Secretary," August 8, 1920. For background on Harding, see Andrew Sinclair, *The Available Man: The Life Behind the Masks of Warren Gamaliel Harding* (Chicago: Quadrangle Books, 1969).

7. NAACP Special Correspondence Papers, Warren G. Harding to James Weldon Johnson, February 14, 1921, George B. Christian Jr. to James Weldon Johnson, March 30, 1921; *Crisis* 22 (July 2, 1921), 68.

8. NYT, April 13, 1921, 2.

9. "Negro Migration in 1923," *Monthly Labor Review* 18 (April 1924), 176; *Crisis* 19 (January 1920), 105; *Congressional Directory, 67th Cong., 2nd sess.* (Washington, D.C.: GPO, 1922), 129, 131.

10. NAACP Special Correspondence Papers, Warren G. Harding to James Weldon Johnson, June 18, 1921, and "Resolutions," June 26, 1921; *Crisis* 22 (September 1921), 213, and 23 (December 1921), 71; NYT, October 21, 1921, 10.

11. William B. Hixson, "Moorfield Storey and the Defense of the Dyer Anti-Lynching Bill," *New England Quarterly* 42 (March 1969), 71–72.

12. *Congressional Quarterly Guide to the Congress of the United States: Origins, History and Procedure* (Washington, D.C.: GPO, 1971), 81–83.

13. NAACP Papers, James Weldon Johnson to Harding, September 15, 1921; NYT, September 16, 1921, 12.

14. NYT, September 21, 1921, 19; Ralph McGill, *The South and the Southerner,* excerpted in NYT, March 27, 1965, 11.

15. NYT, October 18, 1921, 6; House Committee on Rules, *Ku Klux Klan: Hearings Before the Committee on Rules,* 67th Cong., 1st sess., October 31, 1921.

16. Janet Powell and Steven Anzozin, eds., *Speeches of the American Presidents* (New York: H. H. Wilson, 1988), 422; Frances Russell, *The Shadow of Blooming Grove: Warren G. Harding in His Times* (New York: McGraw-Hill, 1968), 472; quote is from *Crisis* 23 (December 1921), 56, and also see 23 (January 1922), 129–132.

17. NAACP Special Correspondence Papers, George B. Christian Jr. to James Weldon Johnson, December 1, 1921.

18. CR, 67th Cong., 2nd sess., 62, pt. 1: 1698–1745; NYT, January 26, 1922, 6, and January 27, 1922, 17; quotes are from Zangrando, *The NAACP Anti-Lynching Crusade*, 64.

19. *Crisis* 23 (April 1922), 262.

20. *Crisis* 23 (June 1922), 69–72, 24 (July 1922), 80–82, 24 (August 1922), 122–124, and 24 (September 1922), 215–216.

21. James Weldon Johnson, *Along This Way* (New York: Viking, 1937), 369; *Crisis* 23 (May 1922), 25, and 24 (October 1922), 261.

22. NAACP Special Correspondence Papers, George B. Christian, Jr. to James Weldon Johnson, June 23, 1922, and George B. Christian Jr. to James Weldon Johnson, September 8, 1922.

23. *Crisis* 24 (October 1922), 264; NYT, August 15, 1922, 10; *Crisis* 25 (January 1923), 119.

24. Quote is from NYT, November 21, 1922, 1, and also see November 27, 1922, 1, November 28, 1922, 23, and December 5, 1922, 3.

25. NAACP Special Correspondence Papers, George B. Christian Jr. to James Weldon Johnson, November 22, 1922; Arthur M. Schlesinger Jr., *The State of the Union Messages of the Presidents, 1790–1966*, vol. 3 (New York: Chelsea House, 1966), 2628–2640.

26. Quote is from NYT, November 29, 1922, 1, and also see November 30, 1922, 4.

27. CR, 67th Cong., 3rd sess., 63, pt. 1: 394–405, 417–418, 442–445, 450.

28. *Crisis* 25 (January 1923), 133; quote is from NYT, December 1, 1922, 2.

29. NYT, December 2, 1922, 2.

30. NAACP Special Correspondence Papers, George B. Christian Jr. to James Weldon Johnson, December 5, 1922, and James Weldon Johnson to George B. Christian Jr., December 8, 1922; *Crisis* 25 (January 1923), 170–171.

31. Johnson, *Along This Way*, 372; *Crisis* 25 (January 1923), 133, and 25 (February 1923), 171.

32. Richard B. Sherman, "The Harding Administration and the Negro: An Opportunity Lost," *Journal of Negro History* 33 (July 1964), 152, 151–168; Johnson, *Along This Way*, 366–373.

33. Zangrando, *The NAACP Crusade Against Lynching*, 71 and 5 (NAACP table).

34. Pete Daniels, *Peonage in the South, 1901–1969* (Urbana: University of Illinois Press, 1972). Fortunately, Williams didn't get off. Local officials, probably embarrassed by the national attention, charged Williams with murder. Williams had the distinction of being the only white man convicted in the Deep South of first-degree murder of blacks in a half century. See Zangrando, *The NAACP Crusade Against Lynching*, 5 (NAACP table).

35. For a brief sketch of Coolidge's life, see John A. Garraty, *The American Nation* (New York: Harper & Row, 1966), 712.

36. FBI—NAACP Files, SAC Report, Negro Radical Activities, August 22, 1923.

37. NYT, December 7, 1923, 1. Coolidge ignored the National Equal Rights League's request, made a month before his speech, to endorse the Dyer bill. NYT, October 7, 1923, 2; Arthur M. Schlesinger Jr. and F. L. Israel, *History of American Presidential Elections*, vol. 3 (New York: McGraw, 1971), 2515; NAACP Papers, "First Annual Message," December 6, 1923, and Coolidge to White, August 18, 1923.

38. *Crisis* 26 (September 1923), 218, and 28 (May 1924), 22; NAACP Papers, C. B. Slemp to James Weldon Johnson, March 21, 1924.

39. NYT, May 26, 1924, 10.

40. NAACP Special Correspondence Papers, Calvin Coolidge to Walter White, June 20, 1924.

41. NYT, October 21, 1924, 6.

42. John L. Blair, "A Time for Parting: The Negro During the Coolidge Years," *Journal of American Studies* 3 (December 1969), 177–196; NAACP Papers, Johnson to Coolidge, March 14, 1925.

43. NYT, October 9, 1926, 1, and October 10, 1926, 28; Zangrando, *The NAACP Crusade Against Lynching,* 5 (NAACP table).

44. NAACP Anti-Lynching Papers, "Affidavit," Lucy Mooney, November 2, 1926, and "Affidavit," Charles Lee, November 2, 1926; Walter White, "The Shambles of South Carolina," *Crisis* 28 (December 1926), 55–67; *New York World,* November 22, 1926, 1, and November 23, 1926, 1; NAACP Anti-Lynching Papers, White to McLeod, October 26, 1926.

45. NYT, August 27, 1915, 11, November 10, 1926, 2, November 11, 1926, 13, November 14, 1926, 27, and November 18, 1926, 2; *Baltimore Afro-American,* November 5, 1926, 1; quote is from *New York World,* November 18, 1926, 1.

46. *Crisis* 33 (January 1927), 142–143; NYT, November 25, 1926, 8; *New York World,* December 9, 1926, 1.

47. NYT, December 8, 1926, 26; full text of Coolidge's speech in the NAACP Special Correspondence Papers, "Presidential Message 1926," December 7, 1926; Zangrando, *The NAACP Crusade Against Lynching,* 5 (NAACP table).

48. NAACP Anti-Lynching Papers, James Quimby to Walter White, December 21, 1926, December 19, 1926, December 24, 1926, December 27, 1926, December 31, 1926, and "Press Release," January 3, 1927, which is the source of quote.

49. NYT, February 15, 1927, 12, and February 14, 1927, 10.

50. NAACP Special Correspondence Papers, Calvin Coolidge to James Weldon Johnson, June 8, 1927, and May 31, 1928; Donald Lee Grant, *The Anti-Lynching Movement, 1883–1932* (San Francisco: R and E Associates, 1975), 163; Zangrando, *The NAACP Crusade Against Lynching,* 5 (NAACP table).

51. See David Burner, *Herbert Hoover: A Public Life* (New York: Alfred A. Knopf, 1979); Schlesinger, *The State of the Union Messages of the President,* 2647, speech, 2688. Although the 1928 Republican Party platform mentioned no timetable or specifics on antilynching legislation, it did call on Congress to enact a federal antilynching law "at the earliest possible date."

52. *Official Report of the Proceedings of the Nineteenth Republican National Convention, 1928* (New York: Tenny Press, 1928), 131.

53. NYT, January 26, 1929, 10, January 29, 1929, 1, and March 27, 1929, 1, 26.

54. FBI—NAACP Files, T. F. Baughman to Hoover, April 19, 1930.

55. PP of P, Herbert Hoover, January 1–December 31, 1930 (Washington, D.C.: GPO, 1976), 376.

56. Grant, *The Anti-Lynching Movement, 1883–1932,* 162, 163; NYT, November 26, 1930, 2.

57. NYT, December 1, 1931, 5.

58. Herbert Hoover Papers, Presidential Subject File, "Colored Question Lynching," Walter White to Herbert Hoover, August 15, 1930, Walter White to Herbert Hoover, October 3, 1930, Walter White to Herbert Hoover, October 20, 1930, George A. Kerson to Walter White, October 21, 1930, and Walter White to Herbert Hoover, November 13, 1930; Donald J. Lislio, *Hoover, Blacks and Lily Whites* (Chapel Hill: University of North Carolina Press, 1985), 256–257; Herbert Hoover Papers, William G. Mitchell to Herbert Hoover, January 6, 1932.

59. NAACP Papers, Herbert Hoover to James Weldon Johnson, May 18, 1932; Lislio, *Hoover, Blacks and Lily Whites,* 349; *Official Report of the Proceedings of the Twentieth Republican National Convention, 1932* (New York: Tenny Press, 1932).

60. Richard B. Sherman, *The Republican Party and Black America* (Charlottesville: University Press of Virginia, 1973), 237–238, 256 (vote total); Svend Petersen, *A Statistical History of the American Presidential Elections* (New York: Ungar, 1963), 91; Zangrando, *The NAACP Crusade Against Lynching,* 5 (NAACP table).

61. Charles S. Mangum Jr., *The Legal Status of the Negro* (Chapel Hill: University of North Carolina Press, 1940), 290; James H. Chadbourn, *Lynching and the Law* (Chapel Hill: University of North Carolina Press, 1933), 13.

Chapter 2

1. Geoffrey C. Ward, *Before the Trumpet: Young Roosevelt* (New York: Harper & Row, 1985), 215–216, and *A First Class Temperament: The Emergence of Franklin Delano Roosevelt* (New York: Harper & Row, 1989), 173, 329.

2. For general background on the Roosevelt years, see Joseph P. Lash, *Franklin Delano Roosevelt: An Intimate History* (Garden City, N.Y.: Doubleday, 1983), and Frank Friedel, *Franklin Delano Roosevelt: Launching the New Deal* (Boston: Little, Brown, 1973).

3. Robert Zangrando, *The NAACP Crusade Against Lynching, 1909–1950* (Philadelphia: Temple University Press, 1980), 102–103.

4. NYT, January 10, 1934, 1; *Crisis* 41 (September 1934), 276.

5. *Crisis* 42 (January 1935), 6–7, 10–11, 14, 22; CR, 73rd Cong., 2nd sess., February 2, 1934, 1820–1828.

6. Blacks began making a major shift toward the Democrats in most northern cities even before they began to marginally benefit from Roosevelt's New Deal reforms; see Henry Lee Moon, *The Balance of Power* (Garden City, N.Y.: Doubleday, 1948), and Harold F. Gosnell, *Negro Politicians* (Chicago: University of Chicago Press, 1967).

7. Mark Naison, *Communists in Harlem During the Depression* (New York: Grove Press, 1983), 31–89; *Party Organizer* 4 (March 1931), 19–20; *Daily Worker,* March 31, 1932, 1; Hugh T. Murray Jr., "The NAACP Versus the Communist Party: The Scottsboro Rape Case, 1931–1932," *Phylon* 28 (1967), 276–287; Charles H. Martin, "The International Labor Defense and Black America," *Labor History* 26 (Spring 1985), 164–196.

8. *Daily Worker,* August 3, 1933, 1, and August 14, 1933, 1, which is source of quote; NYT, August 2, 1933, 1, and August 14, 1933, 3.

9. Genna Rae McNeil, *Charles Houston and the Struggle for Civil Rights* (Philadelphia: University of Pennsylvania Press, 1983), 88.

10. NYT, August 15, 1933, 3, August 16, 1933, 4, and August 17, 1993, 36; NAACP Anti-Lynching Papers, NAACP Press Service, August 12, 1933, which is source of quote, and August 18, 1933.

11. NAACP Anti-Lynching Papers, Walter White to Governor B. M. Miller, August 30, 1933, and Charles H. Houston to Cummings, October 13, 1933; quote is from CD, September 2, 1933, 1.

12. CD, September 9, 1933, 1; NAACP Anti-Lynching Papers, Houston to Cummings, October 13, 1933, and Wilkins to Cummings, December 8, 1933; NAACP Press Service, December 8, 1933; NAACP Anti-Lynching Papers, William Stanley to Roy Wilkins, December 21, 1933; McNeil, *Charles Houston,* 90–91.

13. CD, February 9, 1933, 1.

14. Quote is from NYT, December 7, 1933, 1, and also see December 8, 1933, 27, 48; CD, December 16, 1933, 1.

15. CD, January 6, 1934, 1; Schlesinger, *The State of the Union Messages of the Presidents, 1790–1966,* vol. 3 (New York: Chelsea House, 1966), 2810.

16. Senate Subcommittee on the Judiciary, *Hearings Before the Subcommittee on the Judiciary* (s. 1978), February 20, 21, 1934, 9–20, 62–67, 93–102.

17. CR, 74th Cong., 1st sess., April 16, 1935, 5749, 6366–6367, and April 25, 1935, 6534–6535; Zangrando, *The NAACP Crusade Against Lynching,* 128.

18. John B. Kirby, *Black Americans in the Roosevelt Era* (Knoxville: University of Tennessee Press, 1980), 182–183; quote is from Eleanor Roosevelt Papers, White to Eleanor Roosevelt, April 30, 1934; NAACP Special Correspondence Papers, Louis McHowe to White, June 20, 1934.

19. Joseph P. Lash, *Eleanor and Franklin* (New York: New American Library, 1971), 668–678; Eleanor Roosevelt Papers, E. Roosevelt to White, May 2, 1934, White to Eleanor Roosevelt, May 6, 1934, and White to Eleanor Roosevelt, May 14, 1934.

20. Walter White, *A Man Called White* (New York: Viking Press, 1948), 168–170; *Crisis* 42 (January 1935), 11.

21. NAACP Anti-Lynching Papers, White to Franklin D. Roosevelt, May 29, 1934; Roosevelt Presidential Press Conferences, May 25, 1934, vol. 3, 375.

22. NAACP Special Correspondence Papers, Franklin D. Roosevelt to White, June 22, 1934.

23. NAACP Anti-Lynching Papers, "Memorial" to Franklin D. Roosevelt, August 28, 1934, White to Franklin D. Roosevelt, July 17, 1934, and White to Franklin D. Roosevelt, August 14, 1934; William E. Leuchtenberg, *Franklin D. Roosevelt and the New Deal: 1932–1940* (New York: Harper Torchbooks, 1963), chapter 7; Frank Friedel, *F.D.R. and the South* (Baton Rouge: Louisiana State University Press, 1965).

24. NYT, July 22, 1934, 19.

25. For background on the Lindbergh legal issues, see Jim Fisher, *The Lindbergh Case* (New Brunswick, N.J.: Rutgers University Press, 1987); Homer Cummings and Carl McFarland, *Federal Justice* (New York: Macmillan, 1937), 478–479.

26. White kept trying. Four months later when Ab Young, a young black, was lynched in Mississippi, White collected evidence that showed the mob had abducted Young from a jail in Tennessee. He demanded that Cummings prosecute the sheriff and mob members under the Lindbergh statute. Cummings again refused. NAACP Press Service news release, March 12, 1935.

27. NAACP Anti-Lynching Papers, White to Franklin D. Roosevelt, November 20, 1934, NAACP Press Service news release, November 2, 1934, and November 23, 1934; *Crisis* 41 (September 1934), 268; Eleanor Roosevelt Papers, White to Eleanor Roosevelt, November 8, 1934.

28. *Crisis* 42 (October 1935), 309–310.

29. Cummings and McFarland, *Federal Justice,* 479–484; *Annual Report of the Attorney General, 1933* (Washington, D.C.: GPO, 1933), 1; *Annual Report of the Attorney General, 1934* (Washington, D.C.: GPO, 1934), 61–75, 124–132; *Annual Report of the Attorney General, 1935* (Washington, D.C.: GPO, 1935), 56–69.

30. Eleanor Roosevelt Papers, White to Franklin D. Roosevelt, November 20, 1934.

31. NYT, December 8, 1933, 48; *Crisis* 42 (October 1935), 300; Roy Wilkins, *Standing Fast* (New York: Viking Press, 1982), 132–135; Richard Gid Powers, *Secrecy and Power: The Life of J. Edgar Hoover* (New York: Free Press, 1987), 195; *Crisis* 41 (December 12, 1934), 365; Eleanor Roosevelt Papers, White to Franklin D. Roosevelt, November 8, 1934, White to Eleanor Roosevelt, December 3, 1934; *Proceedings of the Attorney General's Conference on Crime, December 10–13, 1934* (Washington, D.C.: GPO, 1934), 19.

32. Eleanor Roosevelt Papers, White to Eleanor Roosevelt, November 20, 1934, Eleanor Roosevelt to White, November 23, 1934, and White to Eleanor Roosevelt, December 28, 1934.

33. NAACP Special Correspondence Papers, Marvin McIntyre to White, December 26, 1934; NYT, December 30, 1934, 4; Roosevelt Presidential Press Conferences, April 24, 1935, vol. 5, 243; *Crisis* 42 (June 6, 1935), 177.

34. NAACP Anti-Lynching Papers, Wilkins to Franklin D. Roosevelt, August 6, 1935, and NAACP Press Service, news release, September 20, 1935.

35. *Crisis* 43 (June 6, 1936), 180; quote is from NAACP Tuskeegee Institute Archives, March 29, 1979; Zangrando, *The NAACP Crusade Against Lynching,* 4–6.

36. *Crisis* 43 (December 1936), 369, and 44 (January 1937), 15.

37. During the 1930s, racism was so deep even among white liberals that Will Alexander, prominent southern liberal and social activist, titled a piece "The Negro as a Human Person," *The Missionary Review of the World* 59 (June 1926), 36–37; also see Mark Naison, *Communists in Harlem During the Depression* (Urbana: University of Illinois Press, 1983);

Harold Cruse, *The Crisis of the Negro Intellectual* (New York: William Morrow, 1967); David Shannon, *The Socialist Party of America* (New York: Macmillan, 1955).

38. *Crisis* 44 (March 1937), 84; George Gallup, *The Gallup Poll: 1935–71,* vol. 1 (New York: Random House, 1972), 75.

39. *Crisis* 44 (January 1937), 15, and 44 (March 1937), 76, 81 (press, etc.); NAACP Anti-Lynching Papers, White to Truman, December 30, 1936, and Truman to White, January 3, 1937; *Crisis* 44 (January 1937), 6.

40. *Crisis* 44 (May 1937), 143.

41. CR, 75th Cong., 1st sess., HR 1507; Harvard Sitkoff, *A New Deal for Blacks* (New York: Oxford University Press, 1978), 294; *Crisis* 45 (February 1938), 39; NYT, August 28, 1937, 1, January 14, 1938, 8, and January 29, 1938, 3.

42. *Time,* January 24, 1938, 9, 10.

43. Roosevelt Presidential Press Conferences, January 14, 1938, 11, 87–88; CR, 75th Cong., 3rd sess., February 21, 1938, 2201–2210; the Senate passed Rule 22 (cloture) in 1917, *Congressional Quarterly Guide to the Congress of the United States: Origins, History and Procedure* (Washington, D.C.: GPO, 1971), 85, 92–93, 117. The Senate invoked cloture for the first time on civil rights legislation when it passed the Civil Rights Act in 1964.

44. Murphy quote is from Henry A. Schweinhaut, "The Civil Liberties Section of the Department of Justice," *Bill of Rights Review* 1 (Spring 1941), 206–216; Frank Coleman, "Freedom from Fear on the Home Front," *Iowa Law Review* 29 (March 1944), 412–429; Eugene Gressman, "The Unhappy History of Civil Rights Legislation," *Michigan Law Review* 50 (1952), 1344.

45. Sitkoff, *A New Deal for Blacks,* 294; *Crisis* 45 (January 1938), 12, and 46 (January 1939), 9.

46. Zangrando, *The NAACP Crusade Against Lynching,* 161; quote is from NYT, January 21, 1939, 1; CR, 76th Cong., 3rd sess., January 10, 1940, 253.

47. Franklin Delano Roosevelt Papers, White to Edwin M. Watson, January 24, 1940, Watson to Franklin D. Roosevelt, January 26, 1940, Watson to White, January 27, 1940; Senate Judiciary Committee Subcommittee, 76th Cong., 3rd sess., March 5, 12, 13, 1940; CR, 76th Cong., 3rd sess., October 8, 1940, 13353–13355. A freshman congressman from Texas, Lyndon B. Johnson, voted against the antilynching bill. In his later memoirs, Johnson carefully avoided any mention of this or his early votes against civil rights legislation. See CR, 76th Cong., 3rd sess., 54.

48. Roosevelt quotes are from Roosevelt Presidential Press Conferences, June 5, 1940, 15, 475–476; *Crisis* 47 (February 2, 1940), 54, and 47 (November 1940), 343, 358, which is source of quote on Roosevelt.

49. Dominic J. Capechi Jr., "The Lynching of Cleo Wright: Federal Protection of Constitutional Rights During World War II," *Journal of American History* 72 (March 1986), 838; Victor Rothem, "The Federal Civil Right Not to Be Lynched," *Washington Law Quarterly* 28 (February 1943), 57–73, 58; NAACP Anti-Lynching Papers, White to Franklin D. Roosevelt, January 26, 1942.

50. NAACP Anti-Lynching Papers, Wendell Berge (Assistant Attorney General) to Marshall, February 13, 1942; FBI—Hoover, Official & Confidential Files, J. Edgar Hoover, Civil Rights and Domestic Violence, March 15, 1947; NYT, August 26, 1941, 1.

51. NAACP Anti-Lynching Papers, Memo, "Federal Protection in Lynching Cases," March 24, 1942. For background on Hoover's rabid antiblack views during this period, see Kenneth O'Reilly, *Racial Matters: The FBI's Secret File on Black America, 1960–1972* (New York: Free Press, 1989), 9–47.

52. NAACP Anti-Lynching Papers, Marshall to Berge, March 9, 1942, and Internal Memo, July 31, 1942; *New York Herald Tribune,* July 31, 1942, 1; quote is from Capechi, "The Lynching of Cleo Wright," 877.

53. Robert K. Carr, *Federal Protection of Civil Rights: Quest for a Sword* (Ithaca: Cornell University Press, 1947), 164; Coleman, "Freedom from Fear on the Home Front," 426; Jessie Parkhurst Guzman, ed., *Negro Year Book: A Review of Events Affecting Negro Life, 1941–1946* (Tuskeegee: n.p., 1947), 305.

54. CD, March 6, 1943, 6; Frances Biddle, *In Brief Authority* (Garden City, N.Y.: Doubleday, 1962), 157; Robert K. Carr, "The Georgia Police Brutality Case," *Cornell Law Quarterly* 31 (September 1945), 54.

55. "Notes, The *Screws* Case," *Yale Law Journal* 55 (April 1946), 576; CD, April 17, 1943, 1, and May 29, 1943, 5; *Crisis* 50 (November 1943), 237.

56. NYT, May 8, 1945, 34.

57. Screws vs. US, NAACP Legal Defense and Education Fund, Cases and Materials, vol. 1 (New York, 1968), 227–232. For background on William O. Douglas's legendary views on civil liberties, see William O. Douglas, *The Court Years, Nineteen Thirty-Nine to Nineteen Seventy-Five: The Autobiography of William O. Douglas* (New York: Random House, 1980), 52–53; Biddle, *In Brief Authority,* 158–159. In 1950, Truman's attorney general, Tom Clark, complained to the House Judiciary Committee that the *Screws* decision "placed great obstacles" in front of federal prosecutors. In 1951, federal prosecutors saw their case against a Miami policeman who murdered a black man collapse when the judge instructed the jury that it could not convict unless the prosecution proved "specific intent." See Carr, "The Georgia Police Brutality Case," 542–543.

58. CD, June 19, 1943, 20; LAT, June 13, 1943, 2.

59. NYT, June 22, 1943, 1; NAACP Anti-Lynching Papers, White to Franklin D. Roosevelt, June 21, 1943, and White to Franklin D. Roosevelt, June 21, 1943, which is source of quote.

60. NYT, July 29, 1943, 29.

61. *Crisis* 50 (August 1943), 231–232.

62. Dominic J. Capechi, *The Harlem Riot of 1943* (Philadelphia: Temple University Press, 1977), 117; quote is from NAACP Anti-Lynching Papers, La Guardia to White, July 16, 1943.

63. NYT, July 3, 1943, 16; *Crisis* 50 (August 1943), 249; NAACP Anti-Lynching Papers, White to La Guardia, June 29, 1943.

64. NYT, August 12, 1943, 21; Robert Shogan and Tom Craig, *The Detroit Race Riot* (New York: Chilton Books, 1964), 100, 103.

65. NYT, June 24, 1943, 1. Dies was also an unabashed white supremacist. During congressional hearings in 1914 on a House bill to segregate black employees in federal civil service, Dies had this exchange with prominent black attorney Archibald Grimke:

Dies: The point I make is that one of the races must be the ruling race. Both cannot rule, and the Negro race as rulers is unthinkable.

Grimke: That cannot be in this country.

Dies: I am only giving you my views.

Rayford W. Logan, "The Negro as Portrayed in Representative Northern Magazines and Newspapers," in Barry N. Schwartz and Robert Disch, eds., *White Racism* (New York: Dell, 1970), 365; House Committee on Reform in Civil Service, *Hearings on Segregation of Clerks and Employees*, 63rd Cong., 2nd sess., March 6, 1914.

66. NYT, June 24, 1943, 1, and July 12, 1943, 13.

67. Shogan and Craig, *The Detroit Race Riot*, 114; FBI, "Survey of Racial Conditions in the United States," quoted in Patrick S. Washburn, *A Question of Sedition* (New York: Oxford University Press, 1986), 179.

68. FBI—Hoover, Official & Confidential Files, J. Edgar Hoover, Biddle to Hoover, May 29, 1942; NYT, July 21, 1943, 1, and November 4, 1943, 25.

69. Carr, *Federal Protection*, 164–165, 169. Victor Rothem spelled out the legal argument for Biddle in "The Federal Civil Right Not to Be Lynched," 60–73.

70. FBI—NAACP Files, White to Hoover, May 22, 1944, and Report, Detroit, January 15,

1944; FBI—Detroit Race Riots File, Welch to Ladd, June 21, 1943, and Welch to Ladd, June 25, 1943.

71. Zangrando, *The NAACP Crusade Against Lynching*, 5 (NAACP table).

Chapter 3

1. Robert H. Ferrell, ed., *Letters to Bess* (New York: W. W. Norton, 1983), 341, 385, 421–422.

2. William C. Berman, *The Politics of Civil Rights in the Truman Administration* (Columbus: Ohio State University Press, 1970), 9–10; Merle Miller, *Plain Speaking, An Oral Biography of Harry S. Truman* (New York: Berkeley Publishing, 1973), 127–128; Gunnar Myrdal, *An American Dilemma* (New York: Harper & Row, 1944), 488; NAACP Anti-Lynching Papers, Truman to White, January 3, 1937; David McCullough, *Truman* (New York: Simon and Schuster, 1992), 164–165.

3. Berman, *The Politics of Civil Rights in the Truman Administration*, 24; *Crisis* 52 (May 1945), 129.

4. Henry Lee Moon, *The Balance of Power* (Garden City, N.Y.: Doubleday, 1948), 35; Robert Zangrando, *The NAACP Campaign Against Lynching, 1909–1950* (Philadelphia: Temple University Press, 1980), 170.

5. Harry S. Truman, *Memoirs*, vol. 2 (Garden City, N.Y.: Doubleday, 1956), 183; Robert Cushman, NYT Mag., January 11, 1948, 12; *To Secure These Rights: The Report of the President's Committee on Civil Rights* (New York: Simon and Schuster, 1947), 146.

6. Civil Rights Commission, *We Charge Genocide* (New York: CRC, 1951), 58–66.

7. Harry S. Truman Papers, Walter White to Harry S. Truman, November 23, 1945, Walter White to Harry S. Truman, May 13, 1946, and Harry S. Truman to Walter White, June 11, 1946.

8. Zangrando, *The NAACP Crusade Against Lynching*, 171.

9. PP of P, Harry S. Truman, August 1, 1946, and January 1, 1946–December 31, 1946 (Washington, D.C.: GPO, 1946), 186; NYT, August 2, 1946, 10.

10. *Chicago Tribune*, July 27, 1946, 1; NYT, July 27, 1946, 1.

11. NAACP Anti-Lynching Papers, "Press Release," July 26, 1946.

12. NAACP Anti-Lynching Papers, White to Clark, July 26, 1946, White to Clark, July 29, 1946, and "Press Release," July 29, 1946.

13. NYT, July 28, 1946, 1, and September 1, 1946, pt. 4, 4.

14. Even the Klan disclaimed any responsibility for the massacre. Klan leaders claimed they didn't have a chapter in the county. In this case, they were probably telling the truth. From Harrison's scant testimony, it appeared the massacre was a well-planned, coordinated, military-style operation that was almost certainly conducted with the knowledge, if not consent, of some local officials. See NYT, July 28, 1946, 1.

15. NYT, August 1, 1946, 14.

16. NAACP Anti-Lynching Papers, "Press Release," August 1, 1946, and "Press Release," August 8, 1946.

17. NYT, August 1, 1946, 14.

18. FBI—Civil Rights & Domestic Violence File, March 15, 1947.

19. PP of P, Harry S. Truman, August 9, 1946 (Washington, D.C.: GPO, 1947),409; NYT, August 10, 1947, 28.

20. FBI—Civil Rights & Domestic Violence File, March 15, 1947; FBI—Roosevelt-Biddle File, Memo, Hoover to Biddle, May 29, 1942.

21. FBI—NAACP Files, White to Hoover, August 21, 1946, and Edward A. Tamm to Hoover, September 26, 1946; Kenneth O'Reilly, *Black Americans: The FBI Files* (New York: Carroll & Graff, 1994), 19, 20. In 1961, Robert F. Kennedy also pressed Hoover to hire more black agents. He had no more success than White had had. Kenneth O'Reilly, *Racial*

Matters: The FBI's Secret File on Black America, 1960–1972 (New York: Free Press, 1989), 97–100; FBI–NAACP Files, Hoover to White, September 12, 1946.

22. *Crisis* 53 (September 1946), 265; NYT, September 20, 1946, 27; NAACP Papers, Leslie S. Perry, "Memorandum on the Conference with the President," September 19, 1946.

23. *Crisis* 53 (November 11, 1946), 340; Walter White, *A Man Called White* (New York: Viking Press, 1948), 330–331.

24. NYT, September 23, 1946, 16, and September 24, 1946, 16; CD, September 28, 1946, 1; *Baltimore Afro-American,* October 5, 1946, 1.

25. Harry S. Truman Papers, Paul Robeson to David K. Niles, September 19, 1946, and Paul Robeson to Harry S. Truman, September 13, 1946; Martin Duberman, *Paul Robeson* (New York: Alfred A. Knopf, 1988), 306–307.

26. FBI—Paul Robeson File, Informant to J. Edgar Hoover, September 25, 1946, and Hoover to Informant, October 29, 1946.

27. NYT, September 28, 1946, 14; Tom Clark, "A Federal Prosecutor Looks at the Civil Rights Statutes," *Columbia Law Review* 47 (March 1947), 184–190; *Pittsburgh Courier,* August 24, 1946, 1.

28. NYT, November 14, 1946, 33.

29. FBI—Civil Rights & Domestic Violence File, March 15, 1947.

30. NYT, December 29, 1946, 25, and January 5, 1947, 54.

31. FBI—Civil Rights & Domestic Violence File, March 15, 1947.

32. Ibid.; CD, August 10, 1946, 1, and August 31, 1946, 3.

33. NYT, December 21, 1946, 18.

34. NAACP Papers, Marshall to Hoover, May 10, 1946, and Hoover to Marshall, May 14, 1946; FBI—NAACP Files, Marshall to Clark, December 27, 1946, and Hoover to Clark, December 29, 1946.

35. FBI—Civil Rights & Domestic Violence File, Clark to Marshall, January 13, 1947.

36. FBI—Civil Rights & Domestic Violence File, March 15, 1947; J. Edgar Hoover, "Protecting Our Freedom," undated document in FBI files.

37. FBI—NAACP Files, Hoover to White, January 13, 1947; NAACP Anti-Lynching Papers, White to Marshall, January 20, 1947, Marshall to White, January 23, 1947, White to Hoover, January 24, 1947, and Hoover to White, January 28, 1947; Carl T. Rowan, *Dream Makers, Dream Breakers* (Boston: Little, Brown, 1993), 116–117; FBI—NAACP Files, White to Hoover, February 3, 1947.

38. *Federal Register* 11 (December 7, 1946), 14153; NYT, December 8, 1946, 1.

39. FBI—Civil Rights & Domestic Violence File, Carr to Hoover, March 21, 1947, Hoover to Tolson, March 22, 1947, and D. M. Ladd to Hoover, n.d.

40. Harry S. Truman Papers, Wilkins to Truman, May 22, 1947; Zangrando, *The NAACP Crusade Against Lynching,* 183, 185.

41. *Crisis* 54 (July 7, 1947), 200; NYT, June 30, 1947, 1, 3; McCullough, *Truman,* 570.

42. *To Secure These Rights,* 158; Eugene Gressman, "The Unhappy History of Civil Rights Legislation," *Michigan Law Review* 50 (1952), 1344; Henry J. Putzel, "Federal Civil Rights Enforcement: A Current Appraisal," *University of Pennsylvania Law Review* 99 (1951), 439, 441, 446.

43. NYT, October 30, 1947, 1; *To Secure These Rights,* 156–157; Zangrando, *The NAACP Crusade Against Lynching,* 185; PP of P, Harry S. Truman, November 6, 1947 (Washington, D.C.: GPO, 1947), 482.

44. George Gallup, *The Gallup Poll, 1935–71,* vol. 1 (New York: Random House, 1972), 658.

45. NAACP Papers, "Memorandum for a Press Release," January 21, 1948; Zangrando, *The NAACP Crusade Against Lynching,* 192.

46. *Addresses and Messages by President Harry S. Truman* (Washington, D.C.: Public Affairs Press, 1948–1949), 15.

47. Harold F. Gosnell, *Truman's Crises* (Westport, Conn.: Greenwood Press, 1980), 391–412; David Caute, in *The Great Fear* (New York: Simon and Schuster, 1978), tells the story of America's anti-Communist hysteria during the Truman years.

48. PP of P, Harry S. Truman, 179; *The Gallup Poll*, vol. 2, *1948* (Washington, D.C.: GPO, 1948), 747, 783; NAACP Papers, "Press Release on the Anti-lynching Bill," June 15, 1948.

49. NAACP, "Declaration of Negro Voters to the Democratic National Platform Committee," July 8, 1948; NYT, July 27, 1948, 1.

50. *Crisis* 46 (May 1949), 42–45; Berman, *The Politics of Civil Rights*, 129.

51. CR, 81st Cong., 1st sess., 5211, April 28, 1949, 6301, and May 16, 1949, 1842.

52. NYT, March 17, 1947, 1, June 17, 1949, 4, June 18, 1949, 6, and June 22, 1949, 22.

53. *Crisis* 56 (June 1949), 169.

54. NAACP Anti-Lynching Files, "Tuskeegee Report," July 31, 1952; FBI—NAACP Files, Rosen to Ladd, June 25, 1951.

55. NYT, December 27, 1951, 1.

56. NYT, December 28, 1952, 13.

57. NYT, January 3, 1952, 17; *Crisis* 59 (January 1952), 24.

58. NYT, January 9, 1952, 60, and January 19, 1952, 10; FBI—Hoover, Official & Confidential Files, Tolson to Nichols, January 18, 1952.

59. FBI—NAACP Files, Edward Scheidt to Hoover, January 25, 1952, Tolson to Nichols, March 15, 1952, White to Tolson, March 25, 1952, Hoover to White, April 1, 1952, and Memo, "NAACP—Philadelphia Branch," May 1, 1952.

60. NYT, June 29, 1952, 34; FBI—NAACP Files, Nichols to White, July 16, 1952.

61. NYT, October 5, 1952, 51, October 8, 1952, 64, October 21, 1952, 76, and December 10, 1952, 42.

62. Walter White, *How Far the Promised Land* (New York: Viking Press, 1955), 230; *Crisis* 60 (February 1953), 103.

Chapter 4

1. Dwight D. Eisenhower, *The White House Years*, vol. 1, *Mandate for Change, 1953–1956* (Garden City, N.Y.: Doubleday, 1963), 55; Stephen E. Ambrose, *Eisenhower*, vol. 1, *1890–1952* (New York: Simon and Schuster, 1983), 476–477; quotes from Robert Frederick Burk, *The Eisenhower Administration and Black Civil Rights* (Knoxville: University of Tennessee Press, 1984), 28.

2. NYT, June 6, 1952, 1; Sherman L. Adams, *First Hand Report: The Story of the Eisenhower Administration* (New York: Harper & Brothers, 1961), 332; NYT, August 5, 1952, 1. Quote from NYT, September 9, 1952, 16.

3. *Charleston News and Courier*, October 1, 1951, 1.

4. NYT, October 26, 1952, 78, and October 30, 1952, 26; *Amsterdam News*, November 1, 1952, 1; NYT, October 21, 1952, 78.

5. *Crisis* 57 (December 1952), 616–617; Michael Barone, *Our Country* (New York: Free Press, 1990), 275. As early as 1946, the NAACP called on the Republican National Committee to end the "coalition" with southern Democrats. See NYT, April 11, 1946, 16.

6. NYT, November 22, 1952, 1, 22, and November 23, 1952, 76; FBI—Hoover, Official & Confidential Files, Hoover Personal Memo, December 1, 1952; John T. Ellif, "Aspects of Federal Civil Rights Enforcement: The Justice Department and the FBI, 1939–1964," *Perspectives in American History* 5 (1971), 635.

7. Elliff, "Aspects of Civil Rights Enforcement," 636; Kenneth O'Reilly, *Racial Matters: The FBI's Secret File on Black America, 1960–1972* (New York: Free Press, 1989), 34; FBI—Hoover, Official & Confidential Files, James P. McGranery, "Memo to All Officials of the DOJ," December 30, 1952.

8. Ellif, "Aspects of Federal Civil Rights Enforcement," 635; Don Whitehead, *The FBI Story* (New York: Random House, 1956), 260–261.

9. House Committee on the Judiciary, *Hearings Before the Special Subcommittee to Investigate the Department of Justice,* 83rd Cong., 1st sess., 1953, 5, 104–105, 191–192, 239; see *Attorney General's Annual Report, 1952* (Washington, D.C.: GPO, 1952); NYT, February 17, 1953, 1, February 18, 1953, 1, and March 1, 1953, 1.

10. *Annual Report of the Attorney General of the United States (1955)* (Washington, D.C.: GPO, 1955), 131–132.

11. PP of P, Dwight D. Eisenhower, March 10, 1954 (Washington, D.C.: GPO, 1954), 30; NYT, February 3, 1953, 15; Ike's statement to Warren is found in Earl Warren, *The Memoirs of Earl Warren* (Garden City, N.Y.: Doubleday, 1977), 291–292. Although some historians debate what Ike really thought about the Brown decision, Arthur Larson claimed that Ike said directly, "I personally think that the (Brown) decision was wrong." Given Ike's political philosophy and personal beliefs, there's little reason to believe that he thought otherwise. See Larson, *Eisenhower: The President Nobody Knew* (New York: Harper & Row, 1968), 124.

Brownell, who generally defended Ike's civil rights record in his memoirs, still admitted that Ike distanced himself from the Brown case with the excuse that "the federal government was not a party to the action." See Herbert Brownell, *Advising Ike* (Lawrence: University Press of Kansas, 1992), 190, 10.

12. PP of P, Dwight D. Eisenhower, January 7, 1954 (Washington, D.C.: GPO, 1955), 310–311.

13. Neil R. McMillen, *The Citizens Council: Organized Resistance to the Second Reconstruction* (Urbana: University of Illinois Press, 1971).

14. CD, May 21, 1955, 1, May 28, 1955, 1, and August 13, 1955, 5.

15. NYT, May 22, 1955, 61.

16. CD, June 4, 1955, 2.

17. *Crisis* 62 (August–September, 1955), 393–394; NYT, July 8, 1955, 10.

18. CD, September 10, 1955, 1; NYT, September 2, 1955, 10.

19. For background on the Till lynching, see Stephen J. Whitfield, *A Death in the Delta* (New York: Free Press, 1988); NYT, September 1, 1955, 1, and September 2, 1955, 1; CD, September 3, 1955, 1, and September 10, 1955, 1.

20. CD, September 3, 1955, 1, September 10, 1955, 1, and September 17, 1955, 1; *Crisis* 62 (October 1955), 429.

21. NYT, September 7, 1955, 30, September 26, 1955, 10, and September 30, 1955, 10; *Crisis* 62 (November 1955), 547.

22. FBI—NAACP Files, October 4, 1955, SAC, Buffalo, to J. Edgar Hoover, January 16, 1956, January 11, 1956, and J. Edgar Hoover to Assistant Chief of Staff, Army Intelligence, January 26, 1956; FBI—COMIN File—Negro Question, "Memo," September 26, 1955, and "Memo," September 27, 1955.

23. Dwight David Eisenhower Papers, Morrow Files, Morrow to Rabb, November 29, 1955, and Douglas to Rabb, December 22, 1955; E. Frederick Morrow, *Black Man in the White House* (New York: Coward-McCann, 1963), 46.

24. *Crisis* 62 (December 1955), 623; NYT, December 17, 1955, 14.

25. NYT, December 18, 1955, 67, and December 7, 1955, 3; Richard Gid Powers, *Secrecy and Power: The Life of J. Edgar Hoover* (New York: Free Press, 1987), 328; Joseph Bruce Gorman, *Kefauver: A Political Biography* (New York: Oxford University Press, 1971), 249–252.

26. Brownell, *Advising Ike,* 204.

27. *Crisis* 62 (December 1955), 555, 62 (May 1956), 363, 296, and 63 (November 1955), 555; Whitfield, *A Death in the Delta,* 74; NYT, December 31, 1955, 6.

28. Morrow, *Black Man in the White House,* 46.

29. Burk, *The Eisenhower Administration,* 208–209; J. W. Anderson, *Eisenhower, Brownell and the Congress* (University: University of Alabama Press, 1964), 15–17; PP of President, Dwight David Eisenhower, January 5, 1956, 24–25.

30. Ambrose, *Eisenhower*, 444–445; Adams, *First Hand Report*, 336; Burk, *The Eisenhower Administration*, 210; Anderson, *Eisenhower*, 18, 20.

31. Church Committee, Hoover to Executive Assistant of the Attorney General, March 9, 1956, Book 2, 250–251; Kenneth O'Reilly, *Racial Matters: The FBI's Secret File on Black America, 1960–1972* (New York: Free Press, 1989), 34.

32. Anderson, *Eisenhower*, 19–20; Ellif, "Aspects of Federal Civil Rights Enforcement," 621; Adams, *First Hand Report*, 336; Burk, *The Eisenhower Administration*, 210; Brownell, *Advising Ike*, 217.

33. Attorney General to the Vice President, April 9, 1956; House Committee on the Judiciary, *Hearings on Civil Rights Proposals*, 84th Cong., 2nd sess., 1956, 64–68; NYT, April 6, 1956, 20.

34. NYT, March 25, 1956, 28.

35. NYT, June 10, 1956, 5.

36. Dwight David Eisenhower Papers, Republican National Committee Files, 1932–1965, "Background Material—Election Issues of 1956," September 1956.

37. Richard Kluger, *Simple Justice* (New York: Alfred A. Knopf, 1976), 753–754; Ike is quoted from NYT, September 6, 1956, 1.

38. NYT, October 30, 1956, 1.

39. Moses Rischin, *"Our Own Kind": Voting by Race, Creed or National Origin* (Santa Barbara, Calif.: Center for Democratic Society, 1960), 13–22.

40. NYT, January 12, 1957, 38.

41. PP of P, Dwight David Eisenhower, January 10, 1957 (Washington, D.C.: GPO, 1968), 24; NYT, February 2, 1957, 1.

42. Dwight David Eisenhower Papers, Byrnes to Ike, September 20, 1957, and Ike to Byrnes, September 23, 1957.

43. Dwight David Eisenhower Papers, Morrow File, Morrow to Sherman Adams, July 12, 1957, and Washington to Ike, July 18, 1957.

44. Brownell, *Advising Ike*, 224, 226; Dwight David Eisenhower Papers, Morrow File, Washington to Lyndon Baines Johnson, August 6, 1957; Taylor Branch, *Parting the Waters: America in the King Years, 1954–1963* (New York: Simon and Schuster, 1988), 221–222.

45. PP of P, Dwight David Eisenhower, July 17, 1957 (Washington, D.C.: GPO, 1958), 546.

46. Dwight David Eisenhower Papers, Faubus to Ike, September 4, 1957; PP of P, Dwight David Eisenhower, September 14, 1957 (Washington, D.C.: GPO, 1958), 674.

47. Warren Olney, "Little Rock," *California Law Review* 45 (1957), 520–521.

48. O'Reilly, *Racial Matters*, 373; Adams, *First Hand Report*, 346–347.

49. PP of P, Dwight David Eisenhower, September 24, 1957 (Washington, D.C.: GPO, 1958), 694.

50. Dwight David Eisenhower Papers, Mann to Ike, September 23, 1957, and Mann to Ike, September 24, 1957; Dwight D. Eisenhower, *The White House Years*, vol. 2, *Waging Peace, 1956–1961* (Garden City, N.Y.: Doubleday, 1963), 170; Dwight David Eisenhower Papers, Morrow File, "Personal Notes of Presidential Advisor E. F. Morrow on the Little Rock Crisis," September 23, 1957, and September 24, 1957; Adams, *First Hand Report*, 355.

51. Dwight David Eisenhower Papers, King to Ike, September 25, 1957, Ike to King, October 7, 1957, Marshall to Rabb, October 17, 1957, and Ike to Marshall, October 23, 1957.

52. NYT, May 13, 1958, 53.

53. Roy Wilkins, *Standing Fast* (New York: Viking Press, 1982), 253, 258; NYT, June 24, 1959, 1; Wilkins and Ike are quoted from Congress of Racial Equality Papers, "Memo," June 23, 1958.

54. *Crisis* 65 (June 7, 1958), 358.

55. Ellif, "Aspects of Federal Civil Rights Enforcement," 657.

56. U.S. Commission on Civil Rights, *Report, Justice*, Book 5 (Washington, D.C.: GPO, 1961), 59–60.

57. NYT, June 11, 1958, 18, June 15, 1958, 68, August 10, 1958, 78, and June 17, 1958, 22 (Rogers background); Burk, *The Eisenhower Administration*, 190–191.

58. NYT, April 28, 1959, 1, and April 29, 1959, 1.

59. NYT, May 19, 1959, 18, and May 31, 1959, 42; PP of P, Dwight David Eisenhower, April 28, 1959 (Washington, D.C.: GPO, 1960), 343–344; Howard Smead, *Blood Justice: The Lynching of Mack Charles Parker* (New York: Oxford University Press, 1986), 166.

60. NYT, May 6, 1959, 1; PP of P, Dwight David Eisenhower, May 5, 1959 (Washington, D.C.: GPO, 1960), 364; Wilkins's speech was reported in NYT, May 7, 1959, 22.

61. NYT, May 23, 1957, 27, and May 26, 1959, 42; Smead, *Blood Justice*, 206–207.

62. NYT, June 4, 1959, 14, November 18, 1959, 1, and December 7, 1959, 21.

63. Smead, *Blood Justice*, 187.

64. NYT, April 2, 1960, 2; Smead, *Blood Justice*, 199.

65. Southern Regional Council, *Intimidation, Reprisal and Violence in the South's Racial Crisis* (Atlanta: Southern Regional Council, 1959), 15; NYT, June 24, 1959, 18.

66. CR, 86th Cong., 2nd sess., January 26, 1960, 1313; CR, March 16, 1960, 5726.

67. NYT, November 8, 1959, 28; quote is from Smead, *Blood Justice*, 180.

68. NYT, April 8, 1960, 30, and February 16, 1960, 18.

69. NYT, March 10, 1960, 25, and March 31, 1960, 14; PP of P, Dwight David Eisenhower, January 7, 1960 (Washington, D.C.: GPO, 1961), 17.

70. PP of P, Dwight David Eisenhower, January 17, 1961 (Washington, D.C.: GPO, 1960–1961), 11; CR, Senate, 86th Cong., 2nd sess., March 16, 1960, 5866–5867; CR, House, 86th Cong., 2nd sess., April 19, 1960, 8497–8508; *Civil Rights Act of 1960*, Titles I and II, Public Law 86–449, 74 Stat. 86.

71. Department of Justice, Civil Rights Division, *Report, Statistical Data Under Section 242, February 10, 1960*; Administrative Office of the U.S. Courts, *Report, Convictions and Sentences Under Section 242, March 1960* (Washington, D.C.: GPO).

72. NYT, December 15, 1960, 30; *Ebony*, April 1962, 47–50.

73. Theodore S. White, *The Making of the President, 1960* (New York: Atheneum, 1961), 315.

74. NYT, October 27, 1960, 22, and October 28, 1960, 1.

75. Richard M. Nixon, *Six Crises* (New York: Simon and Schuster, 1990), 362–363; White, *The Making of the President*, 315; Carl M. Brauer, *John F. Kennedy and the Second Reconstruction* (New York: Columbia University Press, 1977), 48–50, 58–59. For Nixon's views on the 1960 campaign, see Nixon, *Six Crises*.

Chapter 5

1. *Crisis* 68 (January 1960), 5; NYT, July 11, 1960, 18; LAT, July 11, 1960, 5.

2. *Los Angeles Sentinel*, June 16, 1960, 1.

3. CR, 88th Cong., 2nd sess., August 8, 1964, 18657–18658.

4. For general background on the Kennedy years, see Theodore C. Sorensen, *Kennedy* (New York: Harper & Row, 1965). Schlesinger quote is from Arthur M. Schlesinger Jr., *A Thousand Days: John F. Kennedy in the White House* (New York: Houghton Mifflin, 1965), 966. For Kennedy's views on Reconstruction, see John F. Kennedy, *Profiles in Courage* (New York: Harper & Row, 1961), 35.

5. Eric Foner, *Reconstruction* (New York: Harper & Row, 1988), xix–xxvii.

6. Michal R. Belknap, *Federal Law and Southern Order: Racial Violence and Constitutional Conflict in the Post-Brown South* (Athens: University of Georgia Press, 1987), 57–58.

7. Carl M. Brauer, *John F. Kennedy and the Second Reconstruction* (New York: Columbia University Press, 1977), 25–26.

8. CR, Senate, 86th Cong., 2nd sess., April 19, 1960, 8501; CR, 86th Cong., 2nd sess., March 16, 1960, 57329.

9. NYT, June 25, 1960, 13.

10. NYT, July 10, 1960, 48, and July 11, 1960, 20; *National Party Conventions, 1831–1984* (Washington, D.C.: Congressional Quarterly, 1987), 106.

11. Congress of Racial Equality Papers, Charles Oldham to John F. Kennedy, November 16, 1960; *Crisis* 68 (January 1961), 13.

12. Harold E. Gosnell and Robert E. Martin, "The Negro As Voter and Officeholder," *Journal of Negro Education* 32 (Fall 1963), 419; *Crisis* 67 (December 1960), 658.

13. PP of P, John F. Kennedy, March 16, 1961 (Washington, D.C.: GPO, 1961), 157.

14. Grant McConnell, *Steel and the Presidency, 1963* (New York: Norton, 1963); *Crisis* 68 (March 1961), 161; Sorensen, *Kennedy,* 475–476.

15. For background on Robert F. Kennedy, see Ralph de Toledano, *Robert F. Kennedy: The Man Who Would Be President* (New York: G. P. Putnam's Sons, 1967).

16. Senate Judiciary Committee, *Hearings on the Nomination of Robert F. Kennedy,* 87th Cong., 1st sess., January 14–15; NYT, January 14, 1961, 8, 37–38.

17. Senate Judiciary Committee, *Hearings on the Nomination of Burke Marshall,* 87th Cong., 1st sess., 1961, 2–9; NYT, December 29, 1961, 21.

18. NYT, March 3, 1961, 14.

19. NYT, March 16, 1961, 16; Marshall is quoted in Michal R. Belknap, "The Vindication of Burke Marshall: The Southern Legal System and the Anti–Civil Rights Violence of the 1960s," *Emory Law Journal* 33 (Winter 1984), 93–95.

20. "Robert Kennedy Speaks Out," *Look* 25 (March 28, 1961), 24; NYT, June 8, 1961, 28.

21. David J. Garrow, *Bearing the Cross: Martin Luther King, Jr., and the Southern Christian Leadership Conference* (New York: William Morrow, 1986), 127–172, 217; Brauer, *John F. Kennedy,* 104–105.

22. Congress of Racial Equality Papers, James Farmer to Robert F. Kennedy, April 20, 1961, and August 25, 1961.

23. Interview with Charles Jones, in Emily Stoper, *The Student Nonviolent Coordinating Committee* (New York: Carlson Publishing, 1989), 40.

24. Burke Marshall Papers, "Memo—Demonstrations in Jackson, Mississippi," March 29, 1961, Burke Marshall to Phillip Hart, March 22, 1961, Burke Marshall to Joseph Clark, April 1, 1961, Burke Marshall to Aaron Henry, March 31, 1961, and Burke Marshall to Frank D. Reeves, March 31, 1961; interview with Burke Marshall, August 31, 1994.

25. Kenneth O'Reilly, *Racial Matters: The FBI's Secret File on Black America, 1960–1972* (New York: Free Press, 1989).

26. Burke Marshall Papers, Burke Marshall to Byron White, July 14, 1961.

27. Taylor Branch, *Parting the Waters: America in the King Years, 1954–1963* (New York: Simon and Schuster, 1988), 509–512 (Lee murder); NYT, October 11, 1961, 28, and October 12, 1961, 32.

28. U.S. Commission on Civil Rights, *Justice in Mississippi* (Washington, D.C.: GPO, 1961), 45–55; Foster Rhea Dulles, *The Civil Rights Commission, 1957–1965* (Lansing: Michigan State University Press, 1968), 148–150 (Hoover); Burke Marshall Papers, Burke Marshall to Byron White, December 12, 1961; Harris Wofford, *Of Kennedys and Kings: Making Sense of the Sixties* (New York: Farrar, Straus and Giroux, 1980), 162 (Hoover); interview with Burke Marshall, August 31, 1994.

29. John T. Ellif, "Aspects of Federal Civil Rights Enforcement: The Justice Department and the FBI, 1939–1964," *Perspectives in American History* 5 (1971), 659.

30. Congress of Racial Equality Papers, James Farmer to Burke Marshall, August 25, 1961; Burke Marshall Papers, James Farmer to Robert F. Kennedy, August 25, 1961; Congress of Racial Equality Papers, Gordon R. Carey to Burke Marshall, March 15, 1962,

Nathan Horowitz to JFK, January 12, 1962, August 15, 1962, and Burke Marshall to James Farmer, January 18, 1962.

31. Burke Marshall, *Federalism and Civil Rights* (New York: Columbia University Press, 1964), 81, 95–96; Belknap, *Federal Law,* 96; U.S. Commission on Civil Rights, *Law Enforcement: A Report on Equal Protection in the South* (Washington, D.C.: GPO, 1965); interview with Burke Marshall, August 31, 1994.

32. U.S. Commission on Civil Rights, *Law Enforcement,* 106; Richard A. Wasserstrom, "Burke Marshall and Federalism: A Review," *University of Chicago Law Review* 37 (Winter 1966), 406–413. A quarter century later, Marshall seemed to have developed a different view on the power of the attorney general. When Clinton was trying to pick an attorney general, Marshall wrote that he or she "can influence the direction of the civil rights division in controversial matters." He specifically cited the example of civil rights law enforcement. See LAT, February 14, 1993, 1; interview with Burke Marshall, August 31, 1994.

33. Interview with Burke Marshall, August 31, 1994.

34. Wofford, *Of Kennedys and Kings,* 162; O'Reilly, *Racial Matters,* 96–97; "The FBI and Civil Rights—J. Edgar Hoover Speaks Out," *U.S. News & World Report,* November 30, 1964, 57–58.

35. U.S. Commission on Civil Rights, *Law Enforcement,* 160–161.

36. Ovid Demaris, *The Director* (New York: Harper & Row, 1975), 212–213; FBI—Hoover, Official & Confidential Files, Hoover Internal Memo, n.d.

37. O'Reilly, *Racial Matters,* 61, 89; Kenneth O'Reilly, *Black Americans: The FBI Files* (New York: Carroll & Graff, 1994), 126–127; FBI—King-Levinson File, "SCLC Field Report," June 17, 1963.

38. Ellif, "Aspects of Federal Civil Rights Enforcement," 637, 639, 656–657, 659; U.S. Commission on Civil Rights, *Justice in Mississippi,* 212–221; Richard Gid Powers, *Secrecy and Power: The Life of J. Edgar Hoover* (New York: Free Press, 1987), 412–415.

39. Kennedy quoted in Edwin O. Guthman and Jeffrey Shulman, eds., *In His Own Words* (New York: Bantam Books, 1988), 138; Church Committee, Testimony of Nicholas B. Katzenbach, November 12, 1975, Book 3, 213.

40. NYT, March 14, 1962, 29, March 18, 1962, 83, and March 20, 1962, 27.

41. NYT, March 22, 1962, 23; interview with Burke Marshall, August 31, 1994.

42. Burke Marshall Papers, Burke Marshall to Robert F. Kennedy, March 27, 1962.

43. Congress of Racial Equality Papers, Press Release, March 16, 1962, Marvin Rich to Eleanor Roosevelt, May 24, 1962, Associated Press, Press Release, June 30, 1962, and Marshall to Farmer, May 10, 1962.

44. Howard Zinn, *Albany—A Study* (Atlanta: Southern Regional Council, 1962), 31; NYT, November 19, 1962, 21; Adam Fairclough, *To Redeem the Soul of America* (Athens: University of Georgia Press, 1987), 86–109, 105; Southern Christian Leadership Conference Papers, Wyatt Tee Walker speech, "The American Dilemma in Miniature: Albany Georgia," March 26, 1963; Garrow, *Bearing the Cross,* 216–217.

45. NYT, July 27, 1962, 1; Burke Marshall Papers, Doar, "Monday Report to Robert F. Kennedy," August 7, 1962.

46. NYT, September 10, 1962, 1, September 11, 1962, 20, and September 14, 1962, 1, 20; CD, September 6, 1962, 3.

47. Interview with Harris, in Stoper, *The Student Nonviolent Coordinating Committee,* 147.

48. CD, September 11, 1962, 3, and September 12, 1962, 3.

49. PP of P, John F. Kennedy, September 13, 1962 (Washington, D.C.: GPO, 1962), 676.

50. Harris, quoted in Stoper, *The Student Nonviolating Coordinating Committee,* 157; CD, September 13, 1962, 8, and September 14, 1962, 2.

51. NYT, September 15, 1962, 12, and September 18, 1962, 1.

52. CD, September 5, 1962, 3; NYT, August 30, 1962, 17, and September 18, 1962, 1, 26;

CD, September 19, 1962, 3; NYT, September 21, 1962, 13; Victor Navasky, *Kennedy Justice* (New York: Atheneum, 1971), 119–120.

53. NYT, September 26, 1962, 23.

54. Branch, *Parting the Waters*, 633–672; NYT, August 30, 1962, 17; Burke Marshall Papers, Burke Marshall to James Farmer, January 22, 1963.

55. Wofford, *Of Kennedys and Kings*, 163; Burke Marshall Papers, Hannah to Robert F. Kennedy, January 2, 1963, and Robert F. Kennedy to Hannah, March 26, 1963; Mississippi Advisory Committee to the U.S. Commission on Civil Rights, *Administration of Justice in Mississippi*, 1963; Belknap, *Federal Law*, 118–119; Burke Marshall Papers, Burke Marshall, "Memo to the President," re: CRC Resolution, April 8, 1963.

56. Branch, *Parting the Waters*, 768–770; PP of P, John F. Kennedy, May 8, 1963 (Washington, D.C.: GPO, 1963), 372; Guthman and Shulman, *In His Own Words*, 173.

57. Burke Marshall Papers, Memo, General B. E. Powell, May 22, 1963; JFK quoted in Branch, *Parting the Waters*, 800.

58. Seth Cagin and Phillip Dray, *We Are Not Afraid: The Story of Goodman, Schwerner and Chaney* (New York: Macmillan, 1988), 314; PP of P, John F. Kennedy, June 11, 1963 (Washington, D.C.: GPO, 1964), 468–470; PP of P, John F. Kennedy, June 19, 1963 (Washington, D.C.: GPO, 1964), 483–494.

59. Kastenmeier, CR, July 23, 1963, HR 7702; CR, Senate, June 19, 1964, HR 7152, October 2, 1964.

60. *NAACP Annual Report, 1961* (New York: NAACP, 1962), 37; NYT, October 16, 1963, 1, October 17, 1963, 1, October 18, 1963, 1; House Judiciary Committee, *Hearings*, 88th Cong., 1st sess., 2652–2662; interview with Burke Marshall, August 31, 1994.

61. Burke Marshall Papers, Burke Marshall to Gilbert Harrison, October 30, 1962.

62. *Attorney General's Annual Report, 1963* (Washington, D.C.: GPO, 1964), 192; interview with Burke Marshall, August 31, 1994.

Chapter 6

1. Lyndon Baines Johnson Papers, Speeches of Lyndon Baines Johnson, May 22, 1948, vol. 1, 9–10; Statements of Lyndon Baines Johnson, vols. 1 and 2.

2. Robert A. Caro, *Means of Ascent* (New York: Random House, 1990), 196; CR, 88th Cong., 2nd sess., August 8, 1964, 18657–18658; Monroe Billington, "Lyndon B. Johnson and Blacks: The Early Years," *Journal of Negro History* 52 (January 1977), 19–34; Lyndon Baines Johnson Papers, Senate Congressional File, Lyndon Baines Johnson to John Stennis, October 25, 1948.

3. Seth Cagin and Phillip Dray detailed the story of the three murdered civil rights workers in *We Are Not Afraid: The Story of Goodman, Schwerner and Chaney* (New York: Macmillan, 1988).

4. Reported in *Chicago Sun Times*, June 29, 1964, 26.

5. PP of P, Lyndon Baines Johnson, June 23, 1964, and August 8, 1964 (Washington, D.C.: GPO, 1965), 808, 938.

6. Burke Marshall Papers, Marshall to Alice Lake, July 14, 1964; Michal R. Belknap, *Federal Law and Southern Order: Racial Violence and Constitutional Conflict in the Post-Brown South* (Athens: University of Georgia Press, 1987), 128–158.

7. NYT, July 1, 1964, 23; "See Here, General Kennedy," *Time*, July 10, 1964, 45.

8. CR, 88th Cong., 2nd sess., May 30, 1964, 15645–15646, and August 8, 1964, 18661–18662.

9. *Attorney General's Report for Fiscal Year 1965* (Washington, D.C.: GPO, 1965), 185–186.

10. NYT, July 14, 1964, 13–14, July 15, 1964, 17, and July 16, 1964, 13.

11. Don Whitehead, *Attack on Terror* (New York: Funk & Wagnalls, 1970), 98–100.

12. Burke Marshall Papers, Burke Marshall to N. Katzenbach, June 5, 1964; interview with Burke Marshall, August 31, 1994.

13. Victor Navasky, *Kennedy Justice* (New York: Atheneum, 1971), 105–106.

14. "The FBI and Civil Rights—J. Edgar Hoover Speaks Out," *U.S. News & World Report*, November 30, 1964, 57–58.

15. NYT, July 10, 1964, 1, July 11, 1964, 1, and July 12, 1964 , 55.

16. Church Committee, Memo, J. H. Gale to Tolson, July 30, 1964, Book 3, 18–19, and Katzenbach testimony, December 3, 1975, Book 3; *1965 FBI Manual*, Sec. 122, 1–2; Robert Wall, "Why I Got Out of It," in Pat Watters, Reese Cleghorn, and Stephen Gillers, eds., *Investigating the FBI* (Garden City, N.Y.: Doubleday, 1973), 381.

17. Church Committee, Memo, FBI Headquarters to Atlanta Field Office, September 2, 1964, Book 3, 1; NYT, November 19, 1964, 1; Kenneth O'Reilly, *Racial Matters: The FBI's Secret File on Black America, 1960–1972* (New York: Free Press, 1989), 195–227.

18. Church Committee, FBI Memo from Moore to Sullivan, October 11, 1967, Book 2, 252, Memo from FBI Headquarters to All SACs, October 17, 1967, and Memo to Church Committee, August 20, 1974; U.S. Government Accounting Office, *Report to the House Committee on the Judiciary, FBI Domestic Intelligence Operations—Their Purpose and Scope: Issues That Need to Be Resolved*, 95th Cong., 2nd sess., February 24, 1976, 84–85, 137.

19. NYT, September 15, 1962, 1, and September 19, 1962, 21; House Select Committee on Assassinations, *Hearings on the Investigation of the Assassination of Martin Luther King, Jr.*, 95th Cong., 2nd sess., vol. 6, 93–94.

20. Anthony Summers, in *Official & Confidential: The Secret Life of J. Edgar Hoover* (New York: G. P. Putnam's Sons, 1993), 357–358, claimed that Hoover hated King because he was a "sexual degenerate." David J. Garrow, in *The FBI and Martin Luther King, Jr: From "Solo" to Memphis* (New York: W. W. Norton, 1981), debunked the myths about the Hoover-King conflict. He also suggested that Hoover hated King more because he violated Hoover's pristine standard of morality rather than because he criticized the FBI.

21. Church Committee, Memo, Catha DeLoach to John Mohr, December 2, 1964, Book 3, 165, and Andrew Young Testimony, February 2, 1973, Book 3, 166.

22. Burke Marshall Papers, Burke Marshall to Harry Levine, October 2, 1964, Burke Marshall to John W. Nason, October 5, 1964, Burke Marshall to Katzenbach, September 28, 1964, and Burke Marshall to Lee C. White, November 18, 1964.

23. NYT, November 19, 1964, 1; Church Committee, DeLoach to Mohr, Martin Luther King Exhibit F-438E, December 2, 1964, House Select Committee on Assassinations, *Hearings on the Investigation of the Assassination of Martin Luther King, Jr.*, 169.

24. NYT, January 1, 1965, 10, January 31, 1966, 42, and January 4, 1965, 18.

25. Church Committee, Andrew Young Testimony, February 1973, Book 3, 167.

26. NYT, March 27, 1965, 1. See Gary Rowe, *My Undercover Years with the Ku Klux Klan* (New York: Bantam Books, 1976); O'Reilly, *Racial Matters*, 197; NYT, March 28, 1965, 1 (King); PP of P, Lyndon Baines Johnson, March 26, 1965, vol. 1 (Washington, D.C.: GPO, 1966), 134–135; NYT, October 27, 1978, 34.

27. NYT, February 19, 1965, 1, February 20, 1965, 1, March 4, 1965, 23, March 11, 1965, 1, March 12, 1965, 1, March 15, 1965, 22. King's eulogy quoted in NYT, March 17, 1965, 29.

28. See Robert E. Conot, *Rivers of Blood: Years of Darkness* (New York: Bantam Books, 1967). LAPD violence attracted federal attention following the "zoot suit" riot attacks on blacks and Latinos by off-duty servicemen in 1943. Many eyewitnesses said the attackers were egged on and in some cases joined by LAPD officers. LAT, June 13, 1943, pt. 2, 2.

29. O'Reilly, *Racial Matters*, 99.

30. Joseph A. Califano, *The Triumph and Tragedy of Lyndon Baines Johnson: The White House Years* (New York: Simon and Schuster, 1991), 60–64; FBI—Summer Riots File, 1964, in FBI—Hoover, Official & Confidential Files, and Hoover to Tolson, September 9, 1964; PP of P, Lyndon Baines Johnson, September 9, 1964, vol. 2 (Washington, D.C.: GPO, 1965), 1055; U.S. Governent Accounting Office, *FBI Domestic Intelligence Operations*, 87.

31. NYT, August 15, 1965, 1, August 26, 1965, 21, and August 27, 1965, 1. Johnson quote is from PP of P, Lyndon Baines Johnson, August 15, 1965 (Washington, D.C.: GPO, 1966), 14.

32. NYT, December 17, 1965, 25, and December 18, 1965, 17; *Report of the National Advisory Commission on Civil Disorders* (New York: Bantam Books, 1968), 302; George Gallup, *The Gallup Poll 1935–71,* vol. 3 (New York: Random House, 1972), 1935; Church Committee, Hoover to SACs, New York, October 12 and 19, 1961, Book 3, 18.

33. NYT, November 14, 1965, 30.

34. Johnson quote from PP of P, Lyndon Baines Johnson, January 12, 1966, vol. 1 (Washington, D.C.: GPO, 1967), 5; NYT, January 13, 1966, 1.

35. History of the Department of Justice Papers, William L. Taylor to Wilfred Rommel, April 21, 1966, and Louis Claiborne to Ramsey Clark, July 18, 1966.

36. NYT, March 29, 1966, 1.

37. Lauren B. Frantz, "Federal Power to Protect Civil Rights: The Price and Guest Cases," *Law in Transition Quarterly* 4 (March 1967), 63–73. As part of a deal, Johnson would appoint Clark's son, Ramsey, as attorney general. In exchange, Clark would give up his seat to Marshall. See Califano, *The Triumph and Tragedy,* 208.

38. White House Conference, *To Fulfill These Rights* (Washington, D.C.: GPO, 1966), 141–142, 148–149.

39. Sam Ervin, *Preserving the Constitution: The Autobiography of Sam Ervin* (Charlottesville, Va.: Mitchell, 1984), 165.

40. Erwin quoted in NYT, June 6, 1966, 23; NYT, June 8, 1966, 26.

41. CR, 89th Cong., 2nd sess., 18455–18474, and 18739–18740; PP of P, Lyndon Baines Johnson, August 10, 1966, vol. 2 (Washington, D.C.: GPO, 1967), 814.

42. "Backlash Jitters," *New Republic* (October 22, 1966), 5–6; *Revolution in Civil Rights* (Washington, D.C.: Congressional Quarterly Press, 1967), 62; *Congress and the Nation, 1965–1968* (Washington, D.C.: Congressional Quarterly Press, 1969), 5.

43. Hoover quote from J. Edgar Hoover, "The Resurgent Klan," *American Bar Association Journal* 52 (July 1966), 617–620; *Attorney General's Report, 1966* (Washington, D.C.: GPO, 1966), 191.

44. Steven Lawson, *In Pursuit of Power: Southern Blacks and Electoral Power, 1965–1972* (New York: Columbia University Press, 1985), 6; PP of P, Lyndon Baines Johnson, September 21, 1966, vol. 2 (Washington, D.C.: GPO, 1967), 1049.

45. History of the Department of Justice Papers, Pollack to Doar, January 20, 1967, John Doar to Ramsey Clark, January 26, 1967, and William Taylor to James M. Frey, February 13, 1967.

46. History of the Department of Justice Papers, John Doar, Memo, "Effect of Title V on Law Enforcement," n.d.; interview with Ramsey Clark, September 5, 1994.

47. History of the Department of Justice Papers, "Memo," August 15, 1967, and August 16, 1967; CR, 90th Cong., 1st sess., August 15, 1967, 22076–22077, 22680; NYT, October 11, 1967, 3.

48. Belknap, *Federal Law,* 222.

49. *Report of the National Advisory Commission on Civil Disorders,* 6–7; FBI—King-Levinson File, Memo to Levinson, July 24, 1967.

50. *Report of the National Advisory Commission on Civil Disorders,* 537, 539.

51. PP of P, Lyndon Baines Johnson, June 19, 1968, Johnson to Phillip Hart, January 19, 1968, January 24, 1968, vol. 1 (Washington, D.C.: GPO, 1969), 1, 243, 58–59. It would take $2.5 million, a small army of FBI agents, DOJ attorneys, and federal prosecutors, and a number of appeals and delays to convict seven of the nineteen men two and a half years after their indictment. The *New York Times* hailed the verdict as a decisive blow against racial terror. The *Times,* however, failed to say that this was the first time since Reconstruction that the federal government convicted white men for the murder of a black man. Some would add that they were convicted only because two other white men died

with him. NYT, October 22, 1967, 1; Stoper, *The Student Nonviolent Coordinating Committee,* 40.

52. History of the Department of Justice Papers, Stephen Pollack to Clark, January 25, 1968, Pollack to Grady Norus, January 26, 1968, and Pollack to Clark, February 13, 1968; NYT, February 8, 1968, 1.

53. Hugh Davis Graham, "On Riots and Riot Commissions: Civil Disorders in the 1960s," *Public Historian* 2 (Summer 1980), 18–19; Hugh Davis Graham, "The Ambiguous Legacy of American Presidential Commissions," *Public Historian* 7 (Spring 1985), 7–9; NYT, March 1, 1968, 1, March 2, 1968, 2, and March 3, 1968, 1; Califano, *The Triumph and Tragedy,* 261–262.

54. NYT, March 23, 1968, 1, 15; Lyndon Baines Johnson, *Vantage Point: Perspectives of the Presidency, 1963–1969* (New York: Holt, Rinehart and Winston, 1971), 173; NYT, October 18, 1968, 13. A year later, virtually none of the commission's recommendations for urban reform had been implemented; see *One Year Later: An Assessment of the Nation's Response to the Crisis Described by the National Advisory Commission on Civil Disorders* (New York: Urban America, 1968). On the twenty-fifth anniversary of the Kerner Commission report, the Eisenhower Foundation warned that the plight of the ghetto poor remained unchanged. See LAT, February 28, 1993, 1.

55. Kenneth O'Reilly, "The FBI and the Politics of the 1960's Riots," *Journal of American History* 75 (June 1988), 108.

56. NYT, March 2, 1968, 1; Jerome H. Skolnick, *The Politics of Protest: A Staff Report to the National Commission on the Causes and Prevention of Violence* (Washington, D.C.: GPO, 1969), 203–217; interview with Ramsey Clark, September 5, 1994.

57. NYT, March 6, 1968, 1; CR, 90th Cong., 2nd sess., March 6, 1968, 5546–5550.

58. NYT, April 6, 1968, 1, April 7, 1968, 1, May 10, 1968, 46, and April 11, 1968, 18.

59. 18 U.S.C. *245 (1976); Michal Belknap, "The Legal Legacy of Lemuel Penn," *Howard Law Journal* 25 (1982), 503–505; interview with Ramsey Clark, September 5, 1994; Robert F. Kennedy quoted in CR, 90th Cong., 2nd sess., March 6, 1968, 5540–5541.

60. For a brief summary of Clark's views on crime and justice in America, see Ramsey Clark, *Crime in America* (New York: Simon and Schuster, 1970); Califano, *The Triumph and Tragedy,* 221–222.

61. Jack Nelson and Jack Bass, *The Orangeburg Massacre* (New York: World Publishing, 1970), 164; Pat Watters and Weldon Rougeau, *The Events at Orangeburg* (Atlanta: Southern Regional Council, 1968), 18–20; NYT, February 9, 1968, 1, and February 11, 1968, 37.

62. De Ford quoted in Nelson and Bass, *The Orangeburg Massacre,* 172–173; Watters, Cleghorn, and Gillers, eds., *Investigating the FBI,* 182–183.

63. Nelson and Bass, *The Orangeburg Massacre,* 171–178, 183; NYT, December 21, 1968, 16.

64. Clark quoted in Nelson and Bass, *The Orangeburg Massacre,* 223; NYT, May 28, 1969, 1; interview with Ramsey Clark, September 5, 1994.

65. Hoover quoted in *Annual Report of the Attorney General, 1968* (Washington, D.C.: GPO, 1969), 105; Richard O. Wright, *Whose FBI?* (LaSalle, Ill.: Open Court, 1974), 386.

66. Jerris Leonard to the author, April 28, 1994.

Chapter 7

1. *Houston Post,* September 6, 1968, 1; Nixon quoted in NYT, September 7, 1968, 1.

2. NYT, September 18, 1968, 1; Reg Murphy and Hal Gulliver, *The Southern Strategy* (New York: Charles Scribner's Sons, 1970), 258–263; Stephen E. Ambrose, *Nixon: The Triumph of a Politician, 1962–1972* (New York: Simon and Schuster, 1989), 125–126, 144–145, 162–163, 186–187, 261.

3. PP of P, Richard M. Nixon, January 23, 1970, March 25, 1970, June 11, 1970, and June

25, 1970 (Washington, D.C.: GPO, 1971), 341–343, 321–323, 494–496, 525. *Final Report of the National Commission on the Causes and Prevention of Violence* (New York: Signet, 1969), 147–148.

4. Tony Platt, "U.S. Criminal Justice in the Reagan Era: An Assessment," *Crime and Social Justice* 29 (1987), 59.

5. Edward Jay Epstein, "The Panthers and the Police," *New Yorker*, February 13, 1971, 45–77; Airtel to SAC, Albany, August 25, 1967, re: Counterintelligence Program Black Nationalist-Hate Groups, in Baxter Smith, *The FBI Plot Against the Black Movement* (New York: Pathfinder Press, 1974), 18; Ward Churchill and Jim Vanderwall, *Agents of Repression: The FBI's Secret War Against the Black Panther Party and the American Indian Movement* (Boston: South End Press, 1988), 64.

6. Kenneth O'Reilly, *Racial Matters: The FBI's Secret File on Block America, 1960–1972* (New York: Free Press, 1989), 310–311.

7. Counterintelligence and Special Operations, Letter to SAC, San Francisco, in Smith, *The FBI Plot Against the Black Movement*, 22–23; NYT, January 22, 1969, 28, July 28, 1969, 29, and January 14, 1970, 14.

8. O'Reilly, *Racial Matters*, 311–312; Churchill and Vanderwall, *Agents of Repression*, 75.

9. CT, December 11, 1969, 1, December 12, 1969, 1, December 20, 1969, 1; *Black Panther Party Paper*, December 27, 1969, 7.

10. *Search and Destroy: A Report of the Commission of Inquiry into the Chicago Raid on the Black Panthers Headquarters, December 4, 1969* (New York: Metropolitan Applied Research Center, 1973), 220; NYT, May 16, 1971, 14, and January 18, 1970, 20.

11. O'Reilly, *Racial Matters*, 314; NYT, February 6, 1970, 20, and February 9, 1970, 30.

12. NYT, January 22, 1970, 1; Churchill and Vanderwall, *Agents of Repression*, 75, 404(fn); CT, March 22, 1974; O'Reilly, *Racial Matters*, 314 (fn); NYT, May 9, 1970, 1, 15.

13. NYT, May 16, 1970, 1, 14; *Search and Destroy*, 222; Jerris Leonard to the author, April 28, 1994.

14. O'Reilly, *Racial Matters*, 312.

15. House Committee on the Judiciary, Subcommittee 5, *Hearings on S. 30*, 91st Cong., 2nd sess., 1970, 121; O'Reilly, *Racial Matters*, 252–254.

16. NYT, May 23, 1970, 12, June 17, 1970, 14, July 5, 1970, 1, August 25, 1971, 1.

17. NYT, October 26, 1982, 18, and November 14, 1982, 82; LAT, October 24, 1982, 1.

18. PP of P, Richard M. Nixon, May 19, 1970 (Washington, D.C.: GPO, 1971), 440; NYT, May 19, 1970, 61, 38.

19. Tim Spofford, *Lynch Street: The May 1970 Slayings at Jackson State University* (Kent, Ohio: Kent State University Press, 1988), 39, 193; LAT, May 21, 1970, 1, and June 1, 1970, 1; Nixon quoted in WP, May 21, 1970, 1.

20. PP of P, Richard M. Nixon, June 13, 1970 (Washington, D.C.: GPO, 1971), 498.

21. Church Committee, Memo from Jackson Field Office to FBI Headquarters, November 27, 1968, Book 3, 46; O'Reilly, *Racial Matters*, 331, 337.

22. Jerris Leonard to the author, April 28, 1994; Spofford, *Lynch Street*, 132; *Jackson Clarion Ledger*, May 16, 1970, 1, May 17, 1970, 1, May 16, 1970, 1, May 17, 1970, 61, and May 19, 1970, 1.

23. Spofford, *Lynch Street*, 132–133.

24. Bayh quoted in NYT, May 20, 1970, 1; May 21, 1970, 25.

25. Spofford, *Lynch Street*, 132–133; NYT, May 20, 1970, 1, and May 22, 1970, 20.

26. John T. Ellif, *Crime, Dissent and the Attorney General: The Justice Department in the 1960s* (Beverly Hills, Calif.: Sage Publications, 1971), 132; Jerris Leonard to the author, April 28, 1994.

27. Spofford, *Lynch Street*, 130–131.

28. For a brief background on Cox's racial bias, see Michal R. Belknap, *Federal Law and*

Southern Order, Racial Violence and Constitutional Conflict in the Post-Brown South (Athens: University of Georgia Press, 1987), 169; NYT, May 25, 1970, 28; Jerris Leonard to the author, April 28, 1994.

29. NYT, June 20, 1970, 1, and October 2, 1970, 1; U.S. President's Commisson on Campus Unrest, *The Report of the President's Commission on Campus Unrest* (Washington, D.C.: GPO, 1970), 452–459, 462; NYT, October 2, 1970, 18.

30. Spofford, *Lynch Street,* 172–174; NYT, March 26, 1972, 32; Spofford, *Lynch Street,* 174; Jerris Leonard to the author, April 28, 1994.

31. Paul Takagi, "Abuse of Authority Is a Very Explosive Situation," *U.S. News & World Report,* August 27, 1979, 29; Kenneth Clark, *Race and Police Killings: A Summary of Findings,* in House Judiciary Committee, *Hearings,* 97th Cong., 1st sess., March 4, 1981, June 3, 1981, and November 12, 1981, 14–18; Floyd R. Finch Jr., "Deadly Force to Arrest: Triggering Constitutional Review," *Harvard Civil Rights–Civil Liberties Law Review* 11 (1976), 360–385; Catherine H. Mitchell, *Police Use of Deadly Force, Police Foundation* (Washington, D.C.: Police Foundation, 1977), 22–23.

32. Richard Reeves, *Old Faces of 1976* (New York: Harper & Row, 1976), 30, 24–33; PP of P, Gerald Ford, vol. 2, June 19, 1975 (Washington, D.C.: GPO, 1976), 849; PP of P, Gerald Ford, vol. 3, September 23, 1976 (Washington, D.C.: GPO, 1977), 2346; *Annual Report of the Attorney General, 1976,* 107–108.

Chapter 8

1. James Wooten, *Dasher: The Roots and the Rise of Jimmy Carter* (New York: Summit Books, 1978), 165–166, 235–236.

2. Betty Glad, *Jimmy Carter: In Search of the Great White House* (New York: W. W. Norton, 1980), 328; Jimmy Carter, *Keeping Faith: Memoirs of a President* (New York: Bantam Books, 1982), 66–73.

3. PP of P, Jimmy Carter, February 24, 1977, vol. 1 (Washington, D.C.: GPO, 1977), 233–234.

4. NYT, January 26, 1977, 15, and February 27, 1977, pt. 6, 41.

5. U.S. Commission on Civil Rights, *Who Is Guarding the Guardians? A Report on Police Practices* (Washington, D.C.: GPO, 1981), 116.

6. Gilbert Pompa, "Police Use of Excessive Force: A Community Relations Concern," NAACP Region Conference III, March 17, 1978, cited in U.S. Commission on Civil Rights, *Who Is Guarding the Guardians?* 2; NYT, July 15, 1978, 7.

7. PP of P, Jimmy Carter, June 26, 1978, vol. 2 (Washington, D.C.: GPO, 1978), 1181; NYT, October 12, 1977, 1; WP, May 18, 1978, A8; *Houston Post,* May 10, 1978, 24A; Houston Civil Rights Commission Hearings, cited in *Guardians,* 113–114, 118; U.S. Commission on Civil Rights, *Who Is Guarding the Guardians?* 106.

8. U.S. Commission on Civil Rights, *The State of Civil Rights* (Washington, D.C.: GPO, 1978), 27–28; U.S. Commission on Civil Rights, *Who Is Guarding the Guardians?* vii, 43, 46.

9. Charter of the City of Houston, Art. V, Sec. II (1961), and Art. VI, Sec. 17a (1961), in Hearing Before the U.S. Commission on Civil Rights, Houston, Texas, September 11, 1979, Houston Hearings, U.S. Commission on Civil Rights, cited in *Who Is Guarding the Guardians?* 162.

10. Days is quoted in U.S. Commission on Civil Rights, cited in *Who Is Guarding the Guardians?* 116; John T. Ellif, "Aspects of Federal Civil Rights Enforcement: The Justice Department and the FBI, 1939–1964," *Perspectives in American History* 5 (1971), 655.

11. Houston Civil Rights Commission Hearings, in U.S. Commission on Civil Rights, *Who Is Guarding the Guardians?* 139–140.

12. NYT, July 15, 1978, 7, July 22, 1978, 22, November 25, 1978, 10, and July 20, 1979, 1; interview with Benjamin Civiletti, August 28, 1994.

13. PP of P, Jimmy Carter, May 4, 1978, vol. 1 (Washington, D.C.: GPO, 1978), 838.

14. NYT, April 14, 1970, 16.

15. Joseph P. Daughen and Peter Binzen, *The Cop Who Would Be King* (Boston: Little, Brown, 1977), 117–121. For general background on Rizzo, see Fred Hamilton, *Rizzo* (New York: Viking Press, 1973); NYT, April 15, 1979, 16.

16. NYT, April 22, 1979, 14; *Philadelphia Inquirer*, April 24, 1977, 1, 12A, April 25, 1977, 1, April 26, 1977, 1, April 27, 1977, 1, and May 15, 1977, 1 (the source of the detective's remark); *Time*, August 27, 1979, 20.

17. NYT, June 24, 1978, September 22, 1978, 14, November 23, 1978, 11, December 22, 1978, 14, and January 17, 1979, 1; U.S. Commission on Civil Rights, *Who Is Guarding the Guardians*, 79.

18. *The FBI Manual of Investigations and Operations Guidelines* is partially described in the U.S. Commission on Civil Rights, *Hearings: Police Practices and Civil Rights, Philadelphia, April 8, 1979*, vol. 1, also see pp. 74–75.

19. NYT, April 17, 1979, pt. 2, 10, April 18, 1979, pt. 2, 7, and August 19, 1979, 35; U.S. Commission on Civil Rights, *Hearings: Police Practices and Civil Rights, Philadelphia, April 17, 1979*, vol. 1, 247.

20. U.S. Commission on Civil Rights, *Who Is Guarding the Guardians?* 39; NYT, August 31, 1979, 13.

21. U.S. Commission on Civil Rights, *Who Is Guarding the Guardians?* 38, 41–42. A year later, in April 1980, the department finally got around to clarifying its rules on deadly force. The new rules specified that an officer must know that the person fleeing possesses a deadly weapon or has committed or attempted a "forcible felony." The list of forcible felonies did not include auto theft (see U.S. Commission on Civil Rights, *Who Is Guarding the Guardians?* 37–40, 44–45); 18 Pa. Cons. Stat. Ann., Sec. 508 (Purdon 1973); PILCOP, "A Study of the Use of Firearms by Philadelphia Policemen from 1970–1974," April 1, 1975, 23.

22. "The Authority of the Attorney General to Institute Police Brutality Suits—United States v. City of Philadelphia," *American Criminal Law Review* 17 (1979), 255; NYT, August 13, 1979, 1, August 14, 1979, pt. 4, 15, and August 16, 1979, 21.

23. LAT, August 14, 1979, 7; CSM, August 21, 1979, 12; LAT, August 13, 1979, A4.

24. "The Authority of the Attorney General," 255; LAT, October 31, 1979, 4, CSM, November 1, 1979, 2.

25. "The Authority of the Attorney General," 265; J. David Hoeveler Jr., "Reconstruction and the Federal Courts," *Historian* 31 (August 1969), 615–616.

26. "The Authority of the Attorney General," 266.

27. NYT, November 2, 1979, 31, and November 10, 1979, 9; Rizzo was quoted in LAT, October 31, 1979, A4.

28. NYT, February 26, 1980, 12, and February 30, 1980, 8; interview with Benjamin Civiletti, August 28, 1994.

29. PP of P, Jimmy Carter, September 3, 1980, vol. 2 (Washington, D.C.: GPO, 1980), 1640; *Annual Report of the Attorney General, 1976*, 107–108; *Attorney General Report, 1977*, 153–154; *Attorney General Report, 1978*, 135–136; *Attorney General Report, 1979*, 111; *Attorney General Report, 1980*, 126–127.

30. Michael Barone, *Our Country* (New York: Free Press, 1990), 581–586. For an insider's view of the Carter presidency, see Hamilton Jordan, *Crisis: The Last Year of the Carter Presidency* (New York: G.P. Putnam's Sons, 1982).

31. NYT, January 5, 1980, 8; Wright is quoted in MH, December 12, 1979, 1.

32. Florida Advisory Committee to the U.S. Commission on Civil Rights, *Policed by the*

White Male Minority (Washington, D.C.: GPO, 1976); MH, May 22, 1980, 20; NYT, May 21, 1980, 22.

33. *Time,* June 2, 1980, 14; *Newsweek,* June 2, 1980, 39; *Time,* January 21, 1980, 32; NYT, December 29, 1979, 12, and January 26, 1980, 8.

34. NYT, January 5, 1980, 8; MH, December 29, 1979, 1, and January 4, 1980, 1B, 12; Marvin Dunn and Kirk Porter, *The Miami Riot of 1980: Crossing the Bounds* (New York: Lexington Books, 1980), 166.

35. NYT, January 14, 1980, 10. Hooks had a good case. In 1981, after San Jose police chief Joseph McNamara initiated a restrictive firearms policy and a review process, the number of police shootings and citizens' complaints dropped sharply. Police officials noted that the city's crime rate also dipped sharply. In Chicago, which did not implement a comprehensive firearms discharge policy, the number of complaints of police abuse continued to soar; NYT, November 13, 1983, 30.

36. CSM, May 23, 1980, 7; MH, May 18, 1980, 1 (the issue from which Reno is quoted); May 19, 1980, 1, and May 20, 1980, 1.

37. NYT, May 20, 1980, 1, and May 21, 1980, 22 (from which Carter is quoted); MH, May 21, 1980, 15 (from which Civiletti is quoted).

38. MH, May 24, 1980, 23, and May 23, 1980, pt. 2, 4.

39. LAT, June 1, 1980, pt. 7, 3, and May 30, 1980, pt. 4, 11; MH, December 26, 1980, 23.

40. Collins referred to the volcanic explosion at Mount Saint Helen's, Washington, a week earlier. This was a jibe at Carter's rush to visit Mount Saint Helen's and declare it a disaster area; NYT, June 10, 1980, 10.

41. MH, June 10, 1980, 1, 12; LAT, June 10, 1980, 10; MH, June 11, 1980, 21.

42. PP of P, Jimmy Carter, June 10, 1979, vol. 2 (Washington, D.C.: GPO, 1982), 1074, 1076–1077, 1980–1981.

43. NYT, July 10, 1980, 13; LAT, July 10, 1980, 4.

44. MH, July 28, 1980, 1; NYT, July 27, 1980, 21; Veverka is quoted in MH, July 29, 1980, 1.

45. *Time,* August 11, 1980, 58; PP of P, Jimmy Carter, August 6, 1980, vol. 2 (Washington, D.C.: GPO, 1982), 1501.

46. NYT, July 30, 1980, 12, December 10, 1980, 14, and December 16, 1980, 20.

47. NYT, December 13, 1980, 54.

48. Ibid., study by the International Association of Chiefs of Police, in NYT, November 13, 1983, 30; *Annual Report of the Attorney General, 1980,* 126–127; MH, May 22, 1980, 20.

Chapter 9

1. NYT, August 4, 1980, 11; LAT, August 4, 1980, 1; Reagan was quoted in *Neshoba Democrat,* August 7, 1980, 1; Caroly Bennett Patterson, "Mississippi Grand Reunion," *National Geographic* 157 (June 1980), 854–866. Reagan had not won the presidency yet. He still had to present at least the appearance of not tilting too far to the political right. To balance things politically, Reagan immediately flew to New York to address the National Urban League convention.

2. Memorandum V, Richard Wirthlin to Ronald Reagan, October 9, 1980, in Elizabeth Drew, *Portrait of an Election* (New York: Simon and Schuster, 1981), 384–385. Although Republican strategists never spoke of it publicly, Reagan, like Nixon, had a "southern strategy"; see William H. Greider, "Republicans," in Richard Harewood, ed., *The Pursuit of the Presidency* (New York: G. P. Putnam's Sons, 1980), 159–178; Laurence I. Barrett, *Gambling with History* (New York: Penguin, 1984), 1–20; Ronnie Dugger, *On Reagan* (New York: McGraw-Hill, 1983), 195–219.

3. *Time,* February 25, 1985, 19; *Newsweek,* October 6, 1986, 27; Victoria Sackett, "Ignoring the People," *Policy Review* (Spring 1980), 17; PP of P, Ronald Reagan, 1981

(Washington, D.C.: GPO, 1982), 58.

4. NYT, May 13, 1981, 18, June 8, 1981, B10, and August 21, 16; LAT, August 21, 1981, 13.

5. NYT, July 16, 1981, 1; Rochelle L. Stanfield, "Reagan Courting Women, Minorities, But It May Be Too Late to Win Them," *National Journal* (May 28, 1983), 1119.

6. NYT, September 29, 1981, 14; *Time*, May 13, 1985, 58.

7. NYT, February 24, 1982, B20.

8. Time, February 25, 1985, 19–20; U.S. Bureau of the Census, *Statistical Abstract of the United States, 1982–1983* (Washington, D.C.: GPO, 1982), 183.

9. NYT, January 8, 1983, 11.

10. NOTP, November 11, 1980, 17.

11. NOTP, November 12, 1980, 16, November 13, 1980, 13, and November 15, 1980, 28.

12. NOTP, November 23, 1980, 1, and November 14, 1980, 1; *Black Enterprise* 13 (March 1983), 23.

13. NOTP, November 15, 1980, 28, November 16, 1980, 11, November 18, 1980, 1, November 19, 1980, 1, and November 25, 1980, 1.

14. NYT, April 21, 1981, 12, and May 17, 1981, 25.

15. NYT, July 10, 1981, 1, and September 11, 1981, 16; NOTP, June 19, 1982, 1.

16. NYT, October 14, 1982, 16; Reynolds was quoted in *Jet*, November 12, 1982, 25; NYT, December 17, 1982, 16; Charles Fried, *Order and Law* (New York: Simon and Schuster, 1991), 105–106, 107–108; NYT, January 12, 1983, 19. Robert R. Detlefson made a vigorous if tortured defense of Reagan's stance on affirmative action in *Civil Rights Under Reagan* (San Francisco: Institute of Contemporary Studies, 1991), 59–103.

17. NYT, January 8, 1983, 11, January 16, 1983, 1, and January 17, 1983, 1. On juror race bias, see Richard Seltzer, Mark A. Venuti, and Grace M. Lopes, "Juror Honesty During the Voir Dire," *Journal of Criminal Justice* 19 (1991), 451–462; Charles R. Lawrence III, "The Id, The Ego, and Equal Protection: Reckoning with Unconscious Racism," *Stanford Law Review* 39 (1987), 317–325.

18. NOTP, March 9, 1983, 1, and March 29, 1983, 1; NYT, March 9, 1983, 17, March 21, 1983, 8, March 29, 1983, 14, and September 6, 1983, 18. In April 1986, the city of New Orleans shelled out more than $2.8 million to settle lawsuits brought by the victims of the police beatings and killings; NYT, April 3, 1986, 16.

19. NOTP, March 30, 1983, 1.

20. NYT, April 16, 1983, 16, and April 22, 1983, 31.

21. NYT, June 7, 1983, 18.

22. James Miller Nathan, "Ronald Reagan and the Techniques of Deception," *Atlantic Monthly* 253 (February 1984), 62–68; Norman C. Amaker, *Civil Rights and the Reagan Administration* (Washington, D.C.: Urban Institute Press, 1988), 146–147.

23. PP of P, Ronald Reagan, vol. 1 (Washington, D.C.: GPO, 1985), 904; House Judiciary Committee, *Hearings Before the Subcommittee on Constitutional Rights*, 99th Cong., 2nd sess., April 17, 1986, 16–17; CSM, April 4, 1985, 6; NYT, June 3, 1985, 14; *Time*, May 13, 1985, 58.

24. NYT, May 14, 1985, and May 15, 1985, 1; LAT, May 21, 1985, pt. 2, 5, and August 10, 1985, 2.

25. CSM, November 8, 1985, 6; NYT, December 8, 1985, 1; CSM, November 11, 1985, 2 (FBI–DOJ probe); NYT, May 18, 1985, 6. Eastland and Meese were silent a year later when the commission that Goode appointed to investigate the bombing condemned Goode, the police, and other city officials as "reckless" and called the bombing "ill-conceived"; see NYT, May 11, 1986, 40, May 9, 1986, 1, March 3, 1986, 1, and March 1, 1986, 1.

26. CSM, September 9, 1985, 23; NYT, February 27, 1984, 21, and March 1, 1984, 1.

27. NYT, February 7, 1987, 1, and February 13, 1987, 18; PP of P, Ronald Reagan, vol. 1 (Washington, D.C.: GPO, 1989), 95.

28. House Judiciary Committee, *Hearings Before the Subcommittee on Criminal Justice,* May 11, 1988, July 12, 1988; "Racially Motivated Violence," 3, 11; House Judiciary Committee, *Hearings Before the Subcommittee on Civil and Constitutional Rights,* 100th Cong., 1st sess., 1989, 177.

29. For background on Bush's political rise, see Fitzhugh Green, *George Bush: An Intimate Portrait* (New York: Hippocrene Books, 1989); Peter Goldman and Tom Matthews, *The Quest for the Presidency* (New York: Simon and Schuster, 1989), 305–307.

30. NYT, July 26, 1988, 1; PP of P, George Bush, September 18, 1989, vol. 1 (Washington, D.C.: GPO, 1990), 1219; NYT, December 26, 1989, 20.

31. NYT, December 18, 1989, 1, January 4, 1990, 1, January 7, 1990, 18, April 13, 1990, 14, and June 29, 1991, 1.

32. PP of P, George Bush, April 23, 1990, vol. 1 (Washington, D.C.: GPO, 1991), 547. FBI officials claimed that the bureau would permanently count hate crimes in its annual *Uniform Crime Report;* see Michael Lieberman, "Preventing Hate Crimes: New Tools, New Expectations for Law Enforcement," *Police Chief* 59 (June 1992), 36; "Hate Violence and White Supremacy," The Klan Watch Project of the Southern Poverty Law Center, December 1989, 17; Lieberman, "Preventing Hate Crimes," 27.

33. *FBI Law Enforcement Bulletin,* January 1991, 17.

34. *Attorney General's Annual Report, 1989,* 22; *Attorney General's Report, 1990,* 19–20.

35. Linda K. Davis to the author, May 13, 1994.

36. NYT, April 28, 1992, 17.

37. LAT, March 17, 1991, B1.

38. NYT, July 12, 1988, and July 13, 1988, 14; Reagan and Thornburgh quoted in Mary A. Fischer, "The Witch Hunt," *Gentlemen's Quarterly* (December 1993), 245–246.

39. Gates was quoted in LAT, September 17, 1988, 20; WP, March 22, 1991, 3; see Daryl Gates, *Chief: My Life in the LAPD* (New York: Bantam Books, 1992), in which Fitzwater was quoted.

40. PP of P, George Bush, vol. 1 (Washington, D.C.: GPO, 1992), 218–222; WP, March 12, 1991, 4; PP of P, George Bush, March 21, 1991, vol. 1 (Washington, D.C.: GPO, 1992), 295–296; *National Law Journal* (March 8, 1993), 1.

41. WP, March 13, 1991, 2; *Time,* March 25, 1991, 17; LAT, March 13, 1991, 22.

42. *Federal Response to Police Misconduct: Hearings Before the Subcommittee on Civil and Constitutional Rights,* 102nd Cong., 2nd sess., May 5, 1992, 104; Rosenthal was quoted in WP, March 19, 1991, 1; *Hearings Before the House Subcommittee on Civil and Constitutional Rights,* 101st Cong., 1st sess., February 27, 1990, 284; *Hearings Before the House Subcommittee on Civil and Constitutional Rights,* 101st Cong., 2nd sess., March 22, 1991, 269.

43. WP, March 23, 1991, 3; LAT, March 15, 1991, 1, and March 21, 1991, 24; Linda K. Davis to the author, May 13, 1994; LAT, March 27, 1991, B1.

44. LAT, March 25, 1991, B1, and March 26, 1991, 1.

45. *Federal Response to Police Misconduct,* 10.

46. NYT, October 10, 1991, B16; Dan Fagin, "In Winning His Battle for Rights Commission, Did Reagan Lose the War?" *National Journal* (December 17, 1983), 2622–2624; Robert J. Thompson, "The Commission on Civil Rights," in Tinsley Yarbrough, ed., *The Reagan Administration and Human Rights* (New York: Praeger, 1985), 192–195.

Chapter 10

1. Garrett is quoted in WP, May 1, 1992, 1; LAT, May 14, 1992, 10, and May 2, 1991, 1.

2. LAT, May 30, 1992, 1, and October 17, 1991, 18; WP, November 12, 1991, 2.

3. *Los Angeles Daily Journal,* May 5, 1992, 11; Barr's *Face the Nation* comment quoted in LAT Mag., June 27, 1993, 10, 13.

4. LAT Mag., June 27, 1993, 12; LAT, May 7, 1992, 3, and July 31, 1992, 1.

5. NYT, March 5, 1993, B16.

6. LAT, May 2, 1992, 1; *American Lawyer* 14 (September 1992), 62–69; *The National Law Journal* (March 8, 1993), 30, and (April 26, 1993), 13–14.

7. NYT, August 7, 1992, A26, February 19, 1993, B7, and March 28, 1993, A26; LAT, August 28, 1992, B1.

8. DePasqualie quoted in LAT, August 5, 1992, A1; Braun quoted in LAT, August 7, 1992, A1; interview with Harland Braun, May 10, 1994.

9. LAT, July 24, 1992, B7.

10. LAT, October 20, 1992, B1, and October 6, 1992, B1.

11. LAT, November 13, 1992, A1, and August 28, 1992, B1.

12. LAT, November 13, 1992, 1, May 23, 1992, B1, and March 26, 1993, 1; Stacey Koon, *Presumed Guilty* (Washington, D.C.: Regenery Gateway, 1992), 87–90; LAT, October 15, 1992, B3.

13. NYT, November 20, 1992, A15, and November 21, 1992, 7; Lowell quoted in LAT, November 20, 1992, A1; interview with Harland Braun, May 10, 1994.

14. *Newsweek,* November 30, 1992, 44. The section never solved the case; Bakewell quoted in LAT, November 22, 1992, B1; Linda K. Davis to the author, May 13, 1994.

15. LAT, January 10, 1993, B1; Linda K. Davis to the author, May 13, 1994; *Newsweek,* February 8, 1993, 68.

16. LAT, February 18, 1993, B1; Davies quoted in LAT, January 27, 1993, B1; jurors quoted in LAT, March 16, 1993, A1, and April 23, 1993, A1.

17. Interview with Harland Braun, May 10, 1994; Rinzel quoted in LAT, February 24, 1993, A1.

18. *Los Angeles Daily Journal,* April 8, 1993, 16.'

19. LAT, April 18, 1993, 1, 20.

20. LAT, April 19, 1993, 3, 21, April 23, 1993, 1, and June 3, 1993, B4; interview with Harland Braun, May 10, 1994.

21. LAT, April 28, 1993, B8.

22. *Los Angeles City Council, Summary Report of the Independent Commission on the LAPD* (Los Angeles, Calif: Los Angeles City Council, 1991), 3–4.

23. LAT, October 6, 1992, B6, August 15, 1993, pt. 6, 6, and July 7, 1991, 12.

24. Duke quoted in LAT, April 23, 1993, 28; *Los Angeles Wave,* August 11, 1993, 1.

25. LAT, August 1, 1993, 1.

26. Davis quoted in *Los Angeles Wave,* August 3, 1993, 3; LAT, August 6, 1993, 1.

27. Linda K. Davis to the author, May 13, 1994; *U.S. News & World Report,* August 16, 1993, 18; LAT, August 8, 1993, 1, and August 20, 1994. For the complete testimony of the "missing" eyewitnesses on King's actions before the beating, see Garry Howard, "The Three Trials of Rodney King: The System and Its Implications," 1994, manuscript, copy in the author's possession.

Conclusion

1. Linda K. Davis to the author, May 13, 1994.

2. NYT, January 23, 1993, 1.

3. LAT, March 10, 1993, 1.

4. LAT, February 13, 1993, 8.

5. Linda K. Davis to the author, May 13, 1994.

6. LAT, April 22, 1995, 1.

7. PP of P, Lyndon Baines Johnson, March 26, 1965, vol. 1 (Washington, D.C.: GPO, 1966), 134–135.

8. Richard O. Wright, *Whose FBI,* 386.

9. *Annual Report of the Attorney General, 1968,* 105.

10. NYT, December 26, 1989, 20.

11. *Time,* May 8, 1995, 20–30.

12. LAT, November 10, 1994, 1.

13. LAT, April 27, 1995, 1.

14. Thomas Pettigrew, "New Patterns of Racism," *Rutgers Law Review* 37 (Summer 1985), 687–691.

15. *Jet,* July 5, 1993, 26–28.

16. Quoted in Barry N. Schwartz and Robert Disch, eds., *White Racism* (New York: Dell, 1970), 139.

17. LAT, April 25, 1995, 1.

18. LAT, April 28, 1995, 1, 21, 26.

19. *Los Angeles Village,* April 28–May 4, 1995, 6.

20. Interview with Ramsey Clark, September 5, 1994.

21. Gunnar Myrdal, *An American Dilemma* (New York: Harper & Row, 1944), 205.

Bibliography

---◆---

Books and Pamphlets

Adams, Sherman L. *First Hand Report: The Story of the Eisenhower Administration.* New York: Harper & Brothers, 1961.

Amaker, Norman C. *Civil Rights and the Reagan Administration.* Washington, D.C.: Urban Institute Press, 1988.

Ambrose, Stephen E. *Nixon: The Triumph of a Politician, 1962–1972.* New York: Simon and Schuster, 1989.

Barone, Michael. *Our Country.* New York: Free Press, 1990.

Belknap, Michal R. *Federal Law and Southern Order: Racial Violence and Constitutional Conflict in the Post-Brown South.* Athens: University of Georgia Press, 1987.

Berman, William C. *The Politics of Civil Rights in the Truman Administration.* Columbus: Ohio State University Press, 1970.

Biddle, Frances. *In Brief Authority.* Garden City, N.Y.: Doubleday, 1962.

Branch, Taylor. *Parting the Waters: America in the King Years, 1954–1963.* New York: Simon and Schuster, 1988.

Brauer, Carl M. *John F. Kennedy and the Second Reconstruction.* New York: Columbia University Press, 1977.

Brownell, Herbert. *Advising Ike.* Lawrence: University Press of Kansas, 1993.

Burk, Robert Frederick. *The Eisenhower Administration and Black Civil Rights.* Knoxville: University of Tennessee Press, 1984.

Cagin, Seth, and Phillip Dray. *We Are Not Afraid: The Story of Goodman, Schwerner and Chaney.* New York: Macmillan, 1988.

Califano, Joseph A. *The Triumph and Tragedy of Lyndon Baines Johnson: The White House Years.* New York: Simon and Schuster, 1991.

Capechi, Dominic J. *The Harlem Riot of 1943.* Philadelphia: Temple University Press, 1977.

Caro, Robert A. *Means of Ascent.* New York: Random House, 1990.

Carr, Robert K. *Federal Protection of Civil Rights: Quest for a Sword.* Ithaca: Cornell University Press, 1947.

Carter, Jimmy. *Keeping Faith: Memoirs of a President.* New York: Bantam Books, 1982.

Caute, David. *The Great Fear.* New York: Simon and Schuster, 1978.

Churchill, Ward, and Jim Vanderwall. *Agents of Repression: The FBI's Secret War Against the Black Panther Party and the American Indian Movement.* Boston: South End Press, 1988.

Clark, Ramsey. *Crime in America.* New York: Simon and Schuster, 1970.

Cummings, Homer, and Carl McFarland. *Federal Justice.* New York: Macmillan, 1937.

Daughen, Joseph P., and Peter Binzen. *The Cop Who Would Be King.* Boston: Little, Brown, 1977.

de Toledano, Ralph. *Robert F. Kennedy: The Man Who Would Be President.* New York: G. P. Putnam's, 1967.

Drew, Elizabeth. *Portrait of an Election.* New York: Simon and Schuster, 1981.

Dugger, Ronnie. *On Reagan.* New York: McGraw-Hill, 1983.

Dulles, Foster Rhea. *The Civil Rights Commission, 1957–1965.* Lansing: Michigan State University Press, 1968.

Dunn, Marvin, and Kirk Porter. *The Miami Riot of 1980: Crossing the Bounds.* New York: Lexington Books, 1980.

Eisenhower, Dwight D. *The White House Years.* Vol. 1, *Mandate for Change.* Garden City, N.Y.: Doubleday, 1963.

Ellif, John T. *Crime, Dissent and the Attorney General: The Justice Department in the 1960s.* Beverly Hills, Calif.: Sage Publications, 1971.

Ervin, Sam. *Preserving the Constitution: The Autobiography of Sam Ervin.* Charlottsville, Va.: Mitchell, 1984.

Fairclough, Adam. *To Redeem the Soul of America.* Athens: University of Georgia Press, 1987.

Ferrell, Robert H., ed. *Letters to Bess.* New York: W. W. Norton, 1983.

Foner, Eric. *Reconstruction.* New York: Harper & Row, 1988.

Friedel, Frank. *Franklin Delano Roosevelt: Launching the New Deal.* Boston: Little, Brown, 1973.

Fried, Charles. *Order and Law.* New York: Simon and Schuster, 1991.

Gallup, George. *The Gallup Poll: 1935–71.* 3 vols. New York: Random House, 1972.

Garrow, David J. *The FBI and Martin Luther King, Jr.: From "Solo" to Memphis.* New York: W. W. Norton, 1981.

_____. *Bearing the Cross: Martin Luther King, Jr., and the Southern Christian Leadership Conference.* New York: William Morrow, 1986.

Gates, Daryl. *Chief: My Life in the LAPD.* New York: Bantam Books, 1992.

Guthman, Edwin O., and Jeffrey Shulman, eds. *In His Own Words.* New York: Bantam Books, 1988.

Johnson, Lyndon Baines. *Vantage Point: Perspectives of the Presidency, 1963–1969.* New York: Holt, Rinehart and Winston, 1971.

Kirby, John B. *Black Americans in the Roosevelt Era.* Knoxville: University of Tennessee Press, 1980.

Koon, Stacey. *Presumed Guilty.* Washington, D.C.: Regenery Gateway, 1992.

Lawson, Steven. *In Pursuit of Power: Southern Blacks and Electoral Power, 1965–1972.* New York: Columbia University Press, 1985.

Lislio, Donald J. *Hoover, Blacks and Lily Whites.* Chapel Hill: University of North Carolina Press, 1985.

Marshall, Burke. *Federalism and Civil Rights.* New York: Columbia University Press, 1964.

McCullough, David. *Truman.* New York: Simon and Schuster, 1992.

McGovern, James R. *Anatomy of a Lynching: The Killing of Claude Neal.* Baton Rouge: Louisiana State University Press, 1982.

Morrow, E. Frederick. *Black Man in the White House.* New York: Coward-McCann, 1963.

Navasky, Victor. *Kennedy Justice.* New York: Atheneum, 1971.

Nelson, Jack, and Jack Bass. *The Orangeburg Massacre.* New York: World Publishing, 1970.

O'Reilly, Kenneth. *Racial Matters: The FBI's Secret File on Black America, 1960–1972.* New York: Free Press, 1989.

_____. *Black Americans: The FBI Files.* New York: Carroll & Graff, 1994.

Powers, Richard Gid. *Secrecy and Power: The Life of J. Edgar Hoover.* New York: Free Press, 1987.

Reeves, Richard. *Old Faces of 1976.* Harper & Row, 1976.

Rowan, Carl T. *Dream Makers, Dream Breakers.* Boston: Little, Brown, 1993.

Russell, Frances. *The Shadow of Blooming Grove: Warren G. Harding in His Times.* New York: McGraw-Hill, 1968.

Schlesinger, Arthur M. Jr. *A Thousand Days: John F. Kennedy in the White House.* New York: Houghton-Mifflin, 1965.

_____. *The State of the Union Messages of the Presidents, 1790–1966,* vol. 3. New York: Chelsea House, 1966.

Search and Destroy: A Report of the Commission of Inquiry into the Chicago Raid on the Black Panthers Headquarters, December 4, 1969. New York: Metropolitan Applied Research Center, 1973.

Selwyn, Arthur. *The Roles of the Attorney General of the United States.* Washington, D.C.: American Enterprise Institute, 1968.

Shogan, Robert, and Tom Craig. *The Detroit Race Riot.* New York: Chilton Books, 1964.

Sitkoff, Harvard. *A New Deal for Blacks.* New York: Oxford University Press, 1978.

Skolnick, Jerome H. *The Politics of Protest: A Staff Report to the National Commission on the Causes and Prevention of Violence.* Washington, D.C.: GPO, 1969.

Smead, Howard. *Blood Justice: The Lynching of Mack Charles Parker.* New York: Oxford University Press, 1986.

Smith, Baxter. *The FBI Plot Against the Black Movement.* New York: Pathfinder Press, 1974.

Sorensen, Theodore C. *Kennedy.* New York: Harper & Row, 1965.

Southern Regional Council. *Intimidation, Reprisal and Violence in the South's Racial Crisis.* Atlanta: Southern Regional Council, 1959.

Spofford, Tim. *Lynch Street: The May 1970 Slayings at Jackson State University.* Kent, Ohio: Kent State University Press, 1988.

Stoper, Emily. *The Student Nonviolent Coordinating Committee.* New York: Carlson Publishing, 1989.

Summers, Anthony. *Official & Confidential: The Secret Life of J. Edgar Hoover.* New York: G. P. Putnam's Sons, 1993.

Ward, Geoffrey C. *Before the Trumpet: Young Roosevelt.* New York: Harper & Row, 1985.

_____. *A First Class Temperament: The Emergence of Franklin Delano Roosevelt.* New York: Harper & Row, 1989.

Warren, Earl. *The Memoirs of Earl Warren.* Garden City, N.Y.: Doubleday, 1977.

Watters, Pat, Reese Cleghorn, and Stephen Gillers, eds. *Investigating the FBI.* Garden City, N.Y.: Doubleday, 1973.

White, Walter. *A Man Called White.* New York: Viking Press, 1948.

Whitehead, Don. *Attack on Terror.* New York: Funk & Wagnalls, 1970.

Whitfield, Stephen J. *A Death in the Delta.* New York: Free Press, 1988.

Wilkins, Roy. *Standing Fast.* New York: Viking Press, 1982.

Wofford, Harris. *Of Kennedys and Kings: Making Sense of the Sixties.* New York: Farrar, Straus and Giroux, 1980.

Wooten, James. *Dasher: The Roots and the Rise of Jimmy Carter.* New York: Summit Books, 1978.

Zangrando, Robert. *The NAACP Crusade Against Lynching, 1909–1950.* Philadelphia: Temple University Press, 1980.

Articles

"The Authority of the Attorney General to Institute Police Brutality Suits—U.S. v. City of Philadeiphia." *American Criminal Law Review* 17 (1979), 253–270.

Barron, John. "The FBI's Secret War Against the Ku Klux Klan," *Reader's Digest* (January 1966), 87–92.

Belknap, Michal R. "The Vindication of Burke Marshall: The Southern Legal System and the Anti–Civil Rights Violence of the 1960s," *Emory Law Journal* 33 (Winter 1984), 93–133.

Billington, Monroe. "Lyndon B. Johnson and Blacks: The Early Years," *Journal of Negro History* 52 (January 1977), 19–34.

Blair, John L. "A Time for Parting: The Negro During the Coolidge Years," *Journal of American Studies* 3 (December 1969), 177–196.

Capechi, Dominic J., Jr. "The Lynching of Cleo Wright: Federal Protection of Constitutional Rights During World War II," *Journal of American History* 72 (March 1986), 859–887.

Carr, Robert K. "The Georgia Police Brutality Case," *Cornell Law Quarterly* 31 (September 1945), 45–55.

Clark, Tom. "A Federal Prosecutor Looks at the Civil Rights Statutes," *Columbia Law Review* 47 (March 1947), 184–190.

Coleman, Frank. "Freedom from Fear on the Home Front," *Iowa Law Review* 29 (March 1944), 412–429.

Ellif, John T. "Aspects of Federal Civil Rights Enforcement: The Justice Department and the FBI, 1939–1964." *Perspectives in American History* 5 (1971), 605–673.

"The FBI and Civil Rights—J. Edgar Hoover Speaks Out." *U.S. News & World Report,* November 30, 1964, 56–58.

Finch, Floyd R., Jr. "Deadly Force to Arrest: Triggering Constitutional Review," *Harvard Civil Rights–Civil Liberties Law Review* 11 (1976), 360–385.

Graham, Hugh Davis. "On Riots and Riot Commissions: Civil Disorders in the 1960s," *Public Historian* 2 (Summer 1980), 18–25.

Hixson, William B. "Moorfield Storey and the Defense of the Dyer Anti-Lynching Bill," *New England Quarterly* 42 (March 1969), 65–75.

Hoover, J. Edgar. "The Resurgent Klan," *American Bar Association Journal* 52 (July 1966), 617–620.

Martin, Charles H. "The International Labor Defense and Black America," *Labor History* 26 (Spring 1986), 164–196.

Nathan, James Miller. "Ronald Reagan and the Techniques of Deception," *Atlantic Monthly* 253 (February 1984), 60–70.

O'Reilly, Kenneth. "The FBI and the Politics of the 1960's Riots," *Journal of American History* 75 (June 1988), 91–114.

Platt, Tony. "U.S. Criminal Justice in the Reagan Era: An Assessment," *Crime and Social Justice* 29 (1987), 55–65.

Sherman, Richard B. "The Harding Administration and the Negro: An Opportunity Lost," *Journal of Negro History* 33 (July 1964), 151–168.

Wasserstrom, Richard A. "Burke Marshall and Federalism: A Review," *University of Chicago Law Review* 37 (Winter 1966), 406–413.

FBI Files and Other Government Documents

Attorney General's Annual Reports, 1955–1992. Washington, D.C.: GPO, various years.

FBI—COMIN File—Negro Question.

FBI—Civil Rights & Domestic Violence File.

FBI—Detroit Race Riots File.

FBI—Hoover, Official & Confidential Files.

FBI—King-Levinson File.

FBI—NAACP Files.

FBI—Paul Robeson File.

FBI—Roosevelt-Biddle File.

FBI—Summer Riots File.

Final Report of the National Commission on the Causes and Prevention of Violence. New York: Signet, 1969.

Proceedings of the Attorney General's Conference on Crime, December 10–13, 1934. Washington, D.C.: GPO, 1934.

U.S. Bureau of the Census. *Statistical Abstract of the United States, 1982–1983.* Washington, D.C.: GPO, 1982.

U.S. Commission on Civil Rights. *Justice in Mississippi.* Washington, D.C.: GPO, 1961.

_____. *Report, Justice,* Book 5. Washington, D.C.: GPO, 1961.

_____. *Law Enforcement: A Report on Equal Protection in the South.* Washington, D.C.: GPO, 1965.

_____. *The State of Civil Rights.* Washington, D.C.: GPO, 1978.

_____. *Hearings: Police Practices and Civil Rights,* vols. 1 and 2. Philadelphia, April 8, 16, 17, 1979.

_____. *Who Is Guarding the Guardians? A Report on Police Practices.* Washington, D.C.: GPO, 1981.

U.S. Congress. House. Committee on Rules. *Ku Klux Klan: Hearings Before the Committee on Rules.* 67th Cong., 1st sess., 1921, October 31, 1921.

_____. Committee on the Judiciary. *Hearings on Civil Rights Proposals.* 84th Cong., 2nd sess., 1956.

_____. Select Committee on Assassinations. *Hearings on the Investigation of the Assassination of Martin Luther King, Jr.,* vols. 6–7. 95th Cong., 2nd sess., 1978.

_____. Subcommittee on Civil and Constitutional Rights. *Hearings Before the Subcommittee on Civil and Constitutional Rights.* 101st Cong., 1st sess., 1991.

_____. Subcommittee on Civil and Constitutional Rights. *Hearings Before the Subcommittee on Civil and Constitutional Rights.* 102nd Cong., 2nd sess., 1991.

_____. Subcommittee on Civil and Constitutional Rights. *Federal Response to Police Misconduct: Hearings Before the Subcommittee on Civil and Constitutional Rights.* 102nd Cong., 2nd sess., May 5, 1992.

U.S. Congress. Senate. Judiciary Committee. *Hearings on Civil Rights Proposals.* 84th Cong., 2nd sess., 1956.

_____. Judiciary Committee. *Hearings on the Nomination of Burke Marshall.* 87th Cong., 1st sess., 1961.

_____. Judiciary Committee. *Hearings on the Nomination of Robert F. Kennedy, Attorney General.* 87th Cong., 1st sess., 1961.

_____. Select Committee to Study Governmental Operations with Respect to Intelligence Activities. *Final Report,* Book 3, *Intelligence Activities and the Rights of Americans.* 94th Cong., 2nd sess., 1976.

_____. Select Committee to Study Government Operations with Respect to Intelligence Activities. *Final Report,* Book 3, *Supplementary Detailed Staff Reports on Intelligence Activities and the Rights of Americans.* 94th Cong., 2nd sess., 1976.

U.S. Government Accounting Office. *Report to the House Committee on the Judiciary, FBI Domestic Intelligence Operations—Their Purpose and Scope: Issues That Need to Be Resolved.* 95th Cong., 2nd sess., 1976.

U.S. President's Commission on Campus Unrest. *The Report of the President's Commission on Campus Unrest.* Washington, D.C.: GPO, 1970.

U.S. President's Committee on Civil Rights. *To Secure These Rights.* New York: Simon and Schuster, 1947.

White House Conference, *To Fulfill These Rights.* Washington, D.C.: GPO, 1966.

Manuscripts

Howard, Garry. "The Three Trials of Rodney King: The System and Its Implications." 1994. Copy in author's possession.

Private Papers and Public Papers of the Presidents

Burke Marshall Papers, Kennedy Library, Boston University, Boston, Massachusetts.
Congress of Racial Equality Papers, Library of Congress, Washington, D.C.
Dwight David Eisenhower Papers, Eisenhower Library, Abilene, Kansas.
Eleanor Roosevelt Papers, Roosevelt Library, Hyde Park, New York.
Franklin Delano Roosevelt Papers, Roosevelt Library, Hyde Park, New York.
Harry S. Truman Papers, Truman Library, Independence, Missouri.
Herbert Hoover Papers, Hoover Institute, Stanford University, Palo Alto, California.
History of the Department of Justice Papers, Library of Congress, Washington, D.C.
Lyndon Baines Johnson Papers, University of Texas, Austin.
NAACP Anti-Lynching Papers, Library of Congress, Washington, D.C.
NAACP Papers, Library of Congress, Washington, D.C.
NAACP Special Correspondence Papers, Library of Congress, Washington, D.C.
Public Papers of the Presidents of the United States: Dwight D. Eisenhower.
Public Papers of the Presidents of the United States: Franklin Delano Roosevelt.
Public Papers of the Presidents of the United States: George H. Bush.
Public Papers of the Presidents of the United States: Gerald Ford.
Public Papers of the Presidents of the United States: Harry S. Truman.
Public Papers of the Presidents of the United States: Herbert Hoover.
Public Papers of the Presidents of the United States: Jimmy Carter.
Public Papers of the Presidents of the United States: John F. Kennedy.
Public Papers of the Presidents of the United States: Lyndon Baines Johnson.
Public Papers of the Presidents of the United States: Richard M. Nixon.
Public Papers of the Presidents of the United States: Ronald Reagan.
Southern Christian Leadership Conference Papers, King Center, Atlanta, Georgia.

Interviews and Correspondence

Interview with Burke Marshall, August 31, 1994.
Interview with Ramsey Clark, September 5, 1994.
Interview with Benjamin Civiletti, August 28, 1994.
Interview with Harland Braun, May 10, 1994.
Correspondence with Jerris Leonard, April 28, 1994.
Correspondence with Linda K. Davis, May 13, 1994.

About the Book and Author

———— •◆• ————

In this timely and eye-opening book, noted political analyst and media commentator Dr. Earl Ofari Hutchinson traces the root cause of the White House's failure to protect the rights of African Americans. Drawing extensively from public and private presidential papers, private correspondence, personal interviews, and national archive documents, Hutchinson gives a rich historical account of the racial philosophy, policies, and practices of successive presidents from Warren G. Harding to Bill Clinton.

Franklin D. Roosevelt is one example. The popular view is that Roosevelt was a friend to blacks because of his enactment of New Deal programs. But he was also a prisoner of the biased racial thinking of his times. He refused to actively support antilynching legislation and repeatedly curried political favor with racist southern Democrats.

Lyndon B. Johnson is yet another example. He is known as a champion of civil rights, but Hutchinson details two crucial moments when Johnson shrank from using the full force of executive power to push Congress to enact new and tougher federal criminal civil rights statutes to punish racist violence.

In this book, Hutchinson reveals that no American president has ever signed into law a federal antilynching bill despite a 50-year campaign by the NAACP for presidential and congressional action. He documents how Nixon, Reagan, and Bush rolled back civil rights and affirmative action, failed to fully enforce equal protection provisions of the Fourteenth Amendment against police abuse and racial violence, encouraged conservative legal obstructionism, and fueled the rise of a repressive domestic security state. These actions in turn have reinforced institutionalized racism and continued the historical pattern of devaluing black lives in law and public policy.

Finally, Hutchinson warns that the century-old failure by the White House to enforce federal law to protect black lives still has dangerous consequences for American society.

———— •◆• ————

Dr. Earl Ofari Hutchinson is a noted political analyst and media commentator. His writings have appeared in the *Los Angeles Times, Ebony, Black World, Black Scholar, Newsday,* the *Nation, Emerge,* the *Chicago Tribune,* and the *Progressive.* He is the author most recently of *Beyond O.J.: Race, Sex, and Class Lessons for America* as well as of *The Myth of Black Capitalism, The Mugging of Black America, The Assassination of the Black Male Image,* and *Blacks and Reds.*

Index